My dearest Alan—

May your house
be plentiful with
happiness, good health
and love—

all our love,

Lisa, Jeff + Lisa

Hope this book will be
helpful for you
as it has been for
us.

The New York Times
Complete Manual of Home Repair

The New York Times
Complete Manual of Home Repair

by Bernard Gladstone

Times
BOOKS

Published by TIMES BOOKS a division
of Quadrangle/The New York Times Book Co., Inc.
Three Park Avenue, New York, N.Y. 10016

Published simultaneously in Canada by
Fitzhenry & Whiteside, Ltd., Toronto.

Library of Congress Cataloging in Publication Data

Gladstone, Bernard.
　　The New York times complete manual of home repair.

　　Edition for 1976 published under title:　The New
York times new complete guide to home repair.
　　Includes index.
　　1. Dwellings—Maintenance and repair—Amateurs'
manuals. I. New York times. II. Title. III. Title:
Complete manual of home repair.
TH4817.3.G55 1978　　　　643'.7　　　78–17943
ISBN: 0-517-350009

Manufactured in the United States of America

CONTENTS

IV   *Painting and Papering*   245

V   *Plumbing and Heating*   318

VI   *Electrical Repairs*   367

Introduction

THE WORD "handyman" was once used to describe someone who could be hired in any community to perform all kinds of odd jobs around the house. Regardless of whether he was needed for cutting the grass, painting the shutters or cleaning out a clogged drain, he could be employed at a reasonable hourly rate to handle any chores which the homeowner was unable—or unwilling—to tackle himself.

However, just as our living and working habits have been drastically altered by the coming of the age of specialization, so too has our conception of what a handyman is. Now when we refer to a "handyman" we are no longer discussing an "odd-jobs" man who is for hire at a modest wage. Instead we are speaking of a man who owns or rents his own house or apartment and is handy with tools.

Two factors account for this change: a shortage of labor in almost every field and the increasingly high cost of all home repair services. The all-purpose artisan, as such, has disappeared. In his place there now stands a wide variety of high-priced specialists—plumbers, electricians, painters, gardeners and carpenters, to name just a few. Even when cost is not a major factor, the howeowner is all too often faced with the problem of trying to hire someone for the small "nuisance" jobs which many professional mechanics are reluctant to tackle.

This combination of factors, coupled with a widespread reawakening in the pride of individual accomplishment, has created an increasing demand for information about home repair and home maintenance. To supply this information *The New York Times* has been publishing all sorts of "how-to" articles in the "Home Improvement" columns of each Sunday edition. Since 1956, when these columns first appeared, readers have been writing in to request reprints of past articles—or to ask that a particular "how-to" item be repeated.

This book was written to answer these many demands—as well as to furnish in one volume a complete guide to all types of home repair and home maintenance. Although it is based on the "Home Improvement" columns of the Sunday *Times,* this is essentially an original book rather than a mere collection of the columns. From a practical background in maintenance and repair, it has been written in language as simple and nontechnical as possible. The many photographs and drawings which illustrate the various subjects have been chosen carefully to make the directions still more lucid. The book is divided into seven sections, each with its own subsections arranged in alphabetical order for ready reference. The complete index at the back of the book provides further cross-referencing to aid the reader.

Though this book is primarily for the do-it-yourselfer, it will also prove valuable to those who may have no intention of undertaking repair jobs themselves. By knowing exactly what should be done, the reader will be able to save considerable money and avoid unnecessary delay and aggravation. He will not be gullible when confronted with high-pressure sales talk by an unethical operator and he will often be able to anticipate trouble before it becomes serious and expensive.

I

Tools and Materials

THIS SECTION is devoted to the tools and materials normally required for most home repair and home maintenance projects. Just as there is a right and a wrong way to perform almost any task, so too there is a right and wrong way to drive a screw, handle a file or a plane, sharpen a chisel and even to store your tools. These basic techniques—along with an explanation of how all the various tools should be used—are described in the pages which follow.

The neophyte handyman can advance to the "experienced" stage much more rapidly by first taking time out to read this section through from beginning to end—before he buys his first tools or sets out to tackle his first home repair project. The knowledge gained will not only help him in selecting the tools and equipment that will best suit his immediate needs, it will also acquaint him with some of the more specialized tools which are available. These can be added to his collection as the need for each arises.

Though no two "experts" will ever agree as to just which tools should be considered essential for every home, the tools illustrated are those which, in this writer's experience, are most often required for simple home repairs, as well as for minor improvements such as hanging pictures or installing shelves and curtain rods.

Intended merely as a starting point for the home handyman who now has little or nothing in the way of tools, this list is in no way indicative of what a well-stocked workshop should have. It is designed only to equip the homeowner with those tools which he is most likely to need in order to keep his house in smooth-running condition. Though the idea of buying tools only when and if they are actually needed is generally a good one to follow, if carried to extremes the homeowner would always be getting stuck on weekends or evenings when an emergency repair may be required—and when stores in the neighborhood are usually closed.

A leaky faucet, a clogged drain or a sagging door can often be repaired in minutes—provided the right tools and materials are available. Just as no sensible automobile owner would think of waiting for a flat tire before he went out to buy a jack, so too should the homeowner be prepared for normal emergencies by having at least a basic assortment of tools on hand, as shown in the illustration.

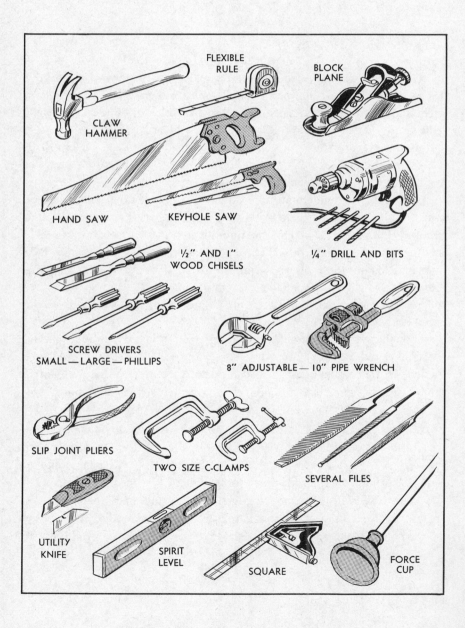

Among those which he will most likely want as soon as he outgrows this basic assortment are: a hacksaw for cutting metal, an oilstone for keeping tools sharp, a wood rasp or serrated wood-forming tool, a soldering iron, a larger assortment of wrenches and pliers, a nailset and a center punch.

Though not usually thought of as a tool, a vise is also highly desirable for many repair jobs. This can be a permanent type which is bolted down to a workbench or table in the garage or basement, or it can be one of

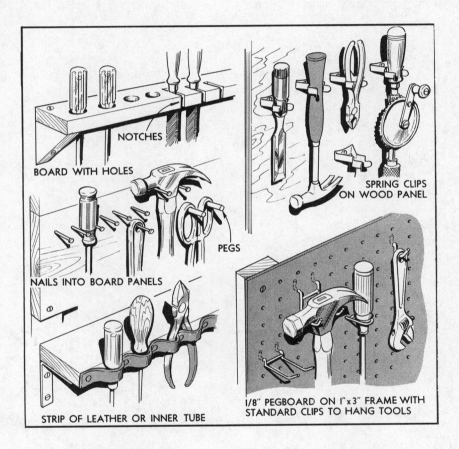

NOTCHES

BOARD WITH HOLES

NAILS INTO BOARD PANELS

PEGS

SPRING CLIPS ON WOOD PANEL

STRIP OF LEATHER OR INNER TUBE

1/8" PEGBOARD ON 1"x3" FRAME WITH STANDARD CLIPS TO HANG TOOLS

the many clamp-on varieties which are available.

Tools should always be kept sharp, clean and in good repair. A dull chisel or knife is more likely to slip and cause accidents than is a sharp one, and a loose or greasy handle on any tool is always a hazard.

All tools should be stored neatly in racks or holders and they should always be returned to the same spot when the job is done. If no space is available, a portable tool carrier similar to the one illustrated can be built instead.

Regardless of the size of his tool collection, the homeowner should always avoid buying low quality "bargain" tools. Good tools will last for many years, and they make every job simpler and quicker to perform. Poorly made tools not only fail to perform as expected, but also increase the possibility of accidental injury because of slippage or breakage that can occur when pressure is applied.

Adhesives, Selection and Use

Though modern glues and adhesives can be used to bond almost anything, failures sometimes occur because the wrong type of glue or adhesive was used or because it was improperly applied. To insure satisfactory results on every job, the user must familiarize himself with the important characteristics of the various types, and he should know something about the advantages and limitations of each.

To avoid confusion, remember that the terms "glue" and "adhesive" are now used almost interchangeably. At one time the word glue referred only to products which were derived from an organic material,

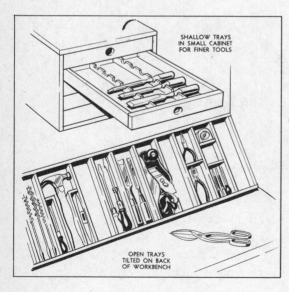

SHALLOW TRAYS IN SMALL CABINET FOR FINER TOOLS

OPEN TRAYS TILTED ON BACK OF WORKBENCH

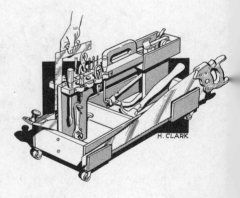

H. CLARK

such as hide or animal hooves, and glue was used only on wood, paper and similar porous materials. The word adhesive was used only to describe products derived from a synthetic material. However, nowadays most glues also are made with synthetic plastic or resin bases, and many can be used for other jobs in addition to their primary function of gluing wood and similar materials.

The wood glues most widely sold in local hardware stores generally fall into one of five categories: liquid animal (hide or fish), white polyvinyl, casein, plastic resin and resorcinol.

The liquid animal glues are actually a ready-mixed version of the old-fashioned hide glues which cabinetmakers once boiled or cooked in a pot. They are good for most general woodworking repairs where strong

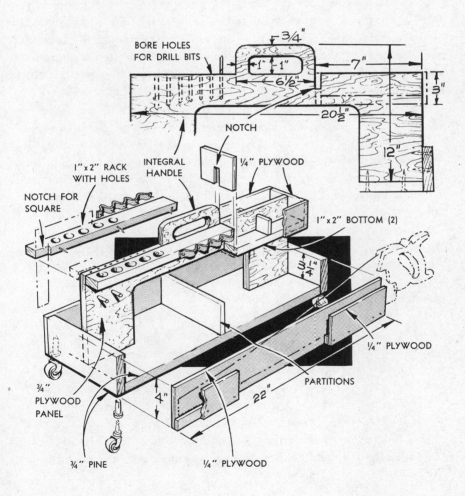

joints are needed, but where little or no dampness will be encountered. They do not stand up well where a great deal of heat is present, and some types will stain on light-colored woods. Because of these drawbacks, and because of the introduction of newer types in recent years, animal and fish glues are not as widely used as they once were.

For most interior woodworking jobs around the home where a waterproof joint is not required, the white polyvinyl acetate glues are by far the most popular. Usually packaged in plastic squeeze bottles, these inexpensive, milky white glues dry clear and are fast-setting. Ready for use as they come from the bottle, these glues are widely used for bonding paper, fabric, cardboard, cork and leather, as well as wood. They can withstand a moderate amount of strain but are not really designed for conditions where high stress will be encountered.

Since these white glues dry clear, they are nonstaining and completely safe for use on all types of wood and other materials. To insure a good bond, the joint should be clamped with a moderate amount of pressure while drying, and the materials should be as near room temperature as practical. The glue sets up in 20 to 30 minutes, though full strength is not really attained for about 24 hours.

Most of these white glues are not very resistant to moisture, so they should not be used where water or a very damp atmosphere is likely to be encountered. Various brands differ in this respect, as well as in the strength of the bond that results (some are recommended only for light duty work or for use on paper and cardboard). The newer aliphatic types, which are generally a little darker in color (they actually vary from a pale yellow to a light tan in shade, though they all dry almost clear), are stronger and have more "tack" or "grab." This makes them easier to work with, especially when assembling sizable projects where their added strength is also an advantage. Like the other white glues described above, however, they also require moderate clamping pressure to insure a good bond.

For stronger joints, and for all woodworking assemblies where a high degree of water resistance is required, a plastic resin glue should be used. This is a powdered glue which must be mixed with water before use. It forms a very strong and highly moisture-resistant joint which will actually be stronger than the wood itself. The joint must be firmly clamped for at least five or six hours, and surfaces must be clean and snug-fitting if a good bond is to be insured. When mixed to proper consistency, this glue is thin, so it will not fill in voids on loose-fitting joints. In addition, this type of glue should not be used when temperatures fall much below 70 degrees.

When maximum strength and complete resistance to moisture are required, a two-component, waterproof resorcinol glue should be used. Consisting of a liquid resin and a powdered catalyst which must be mixed together before use, this wood glue is ideal for use on exterior construction, including outdoor furniture, boats and other projects where an exceptionally strong, waterproof bond is required.

These two-part waterproof glues cost more than the other wood glues, but the added expense will be more than repaid when exceptional durability is required. They can be used on plastics and crockery, as well as on wood, and they are ideal for assemblies where extremes of heat or cold may be encountered. Parts must be firmly clamped together for at least 8 to 10 hours, and the glue should be used only when temperatures are at least 70 degrees.

Regardless of the type of glue being used, successful wood-gluing calls for attention to details. Here are five simple rules that should be followed, if strong, neat-looking wood joints are to result:

(1) Be sure to mix and use the glue exactly according to the manufacturer's directions. When specific temperature limits are given, do not work in unheated basements or garages where temperatures may be lower than the minimums listed. Also remember that when cold pieces of lumber are dragged in from outside, some hours may be required before the material warms up to the room temperature inside.

(2) Be sure all joints are clean and dry before any glue is applied. To insure a good bond, scrape off all paint or old glue before assembling, so that the glue can penetrate into the porous face of the wood. This is particularly important on furniture repairs where old joints are being reglued.

(3) Apply the glue evenly in a smooth layer over all points of contact. To insure uniform coverage, apply on both surfaces wherever possible. A small brush or wooden spatula works well on most jobs. For larger surfaces a piece of hacksaw blade or an old windshield wiper blade makes an excellent spreader.

(4) Always make joints as snug-fitting as possible. While it is true that some glues do have a limited capacity for filling in small voids and openings, all glues hold better (and joints look neater) if the pieces are a snug fit.

(5) Make certain you can clamp the work firmly in position while the glue is drying. Many different types of clamps are available for just this purpose (see CLAMPS, WOODWORKING). Use protective blocks

of scrap wood under these clamps to prevent damage to the surface and to help spread the pressure evenly over the entire joint. Use enough pressure to close the joint snugly, but avoid the common mistake of applying too much pressure. This not only warps or twists the pieces out of alignment, but may also squeeze out so much of the glue that the joint will be almost dry.

When a clamp of the right size or shape is not available, pressure can often be applied with a rope tourniquet. Wrap a length of rope loosely around the outside, then apply pressure as needed by using a short length of wood to twist the rope in the center. To keep the rope from damaging the corners, protect the surface by inserting folded pads of cardboard or heavy paper at all pressure points.

On rough work or on projects where one side will not show, permanent metal fasteners such as wood screws, corrugated fasteners or threaded nails can be used to hold the work tightly together while the

Rope tourniquet holds drawer together

glue sets. These can then be left permanently in place since they will add extra strength to the assembled joint.

Because it grips instantly—on contact—and without need for clamps, nails or weights, a contact-type cement is ideal for many awkward gluing jobs around the house. Available in all sizes, from small squeeze tubes to gallon cans, this adhesive is most widely used for applying plastic laminates to counter tops and furniture. It can also be used for bonding leather, rubber and similar materials to wood or metal, as well as for replacing loose wall tiles, installation of stair treads, application of weatherstripping around doors and windows and repairing of plastic raincoats. Contact cement is also widely used to apply plywood and hardboard panels to walls and studding.

There are two different varieties available: a highly flammable, solvent-thinned cement, and a newer, water-thinned type. The water-thinned contact cement is nonflammable and quick-drying, and it gives off no toxic odors (a problem with many of the solvent-thinned varieties). These water-base types are generally higher in price, though they do cover slightly more area than most of the solvent-base cements.

Regardless of type, all contact cements are used in basically the same manner. A liberal coat of the adhesive is spread on over each of the two surfaces to be bonded. This is then allowed to dry thoroughly— anywhere from 5 to 40 minutes depending on the manufacturer's recommendations for that particular brand. To test for complete dryness, a piece of ordinary brown wrapping paper can be pressed lightly against the surface and then lifted off. If any of the cement comes off on the paper, the adhesive is not yet dry enough for a good bond. If in doubt, it is always best to wait a little longer, rather than to bring the surfaces together too soon.

On porous surfaces a second coat may be required after the first coat is completely dry. One way to check on whether or not this is needed is to examine the dried film to see whether the surface is uniformly glossy. Dull spots are an indication that a second coat is needed. Remember that you will seldom have to worry about applying too much cement—but that you can easily run into trouble if too little cement is used. Difficulties may also arise if the surfaces are not completely clean and dry, and if old paint or other finishes have not been removed first.

After the cement is dry, the bond is completed by pressing the two surfaces together. Since you won't be able to shift the pieces once they come into contact, it is important that they be positioned accurately before allowing them to touch. Pressure is then applied to every square inch by tapping with a hammer and a wood block, or by using a heavy roller.

When applying large sheets of plastic laminate to a table top or counter top, it is sometimes difficult to line the sheet up accurately before allowing it to touch. The best way to do this is to use a paper "slip sheet" to help position the laminate before making the bond. To do this, wait till the cement coating on the laminate and on the table top is thoroughly dry, then lay a sheet of wrapping paper over the top of the table. You can now slide the laminate around on top of the paper. This will keep the two cement-coated surfaces from coming in contact, since the paper will not stick to either surface. With the paper in place, one corner of the plastic is lifted up and the paper folded back. The laminate is now pressed down to make contact, after which the paper can be slowly withdrawn from the other end while pressure is applied to the laminate behind it. After the entire sheet of paper has been removed, the bond is completed by tapping over the entire surface with a hammer and block of wood.

Epoxy adhesives are undoubtedly the strongest of all glues or adhesives. Available in clear, white or metallic finish, all true epoxies come in two separate parts—a resin and a hardener or catalyst. These must be mixed together (in definite proportions) before the adhesive is used. Once mixed, the material will set up permanently in a specified length of time—even under water or while still in the container. This time can vary from a few minutes to as much as 24 hours, depending on the manufacturer's formulation and on the room temperature. The bond formed is completely waterproof and permanent, and it will withstand

Epoxy is ideal for patching leaking water pipe

Clear epoxy will mend glass utensils

attack by practically all common solvents when final curing is complete (from one to seven days in most cases).

Because epoxy adhesives harden into a solid mass when mixed, they can also be used as a patching or filling material for many difficult repair jobs around the home. For example, epoxies can be used to make permanent repairs on cracked pipes or radiators, as well as on rotted wooden or metal gutters. They can even be used for installing soap dishes and other fixtures on ceramic tile walls and for permanent bonding of china, marble, glass and masonry.

To insure a good bond, surfaces must be absolutely clean before the epoxy is applied. Though no clamping pressure is required, arrangements should be made to support the parts in proper alignment while the epoxy is hardening. Drying time in most cases will vary from 2 to 4 hours, though full strength is seldom achieved for at least 24 hours. Since temperature has a definite effect on setting time, most manufacturers recommend that their epoxy compounds be used at room temperature. Cold greatly slows up the hardening action and may interfere with final curing. To speed up the drying time, an infrared lamp or other mild source of heat can be applied to the joint.

Anchors, Hollow Wall. SEE FASTENERS, HOLLOW WALL.

Anchors, for Masonry Walls. SEE FASTENERS, MASONRY.

Chisels, Wood

Though chisels are made in a wide range of sizes and styles, the most widely used models are those which have a beveled blade similar to the one illustrated. The handle may be attached to the blade in one of two ways: there may be a hollow, tapered shank on the blade into which the handle fits, or the blade may have a pointed tang that fits into a hole in the end of the handle.

The standard length chisel (about 6 inches) is commonly referred to as a firmer chisel. Chisels with shorter blades (about 3 inches long) are available for working in tight corners where a longer blade might be awkward. These are commonly called butt chisels. Both styles come with blades which vary from ⅛ to 2 inches in width, though the handyman will find that four sizes will serve for practically all normal requirements: ¼-, ½-, ¾- and 1-inch blades.

To get maximum efficiency when using a wood chisel and to maintain the razor-sharp cutting edge as long as possible, remember that chisels are basically designed as finishing tools and must be used with care. Wherever practical, a saw should be used to remove large amounts of wood first, after which the chisel is used to do the final trimming.

For most light finishing cuts, the chisel is held in both hands—the right hand grasping the handle and applying the needed pressure, while the left hand holds the blade firmly to guide it over the work. A mallet is used only when rough cuts are being made, or when a great deal of wood must be removed. Mallets are sometimes required also for cutting across the grain or when working with hardwoods.

When driving a chisel with a mallet, always hammer with a series of light taps rather than with heavy strokes. This makes the blade easier to control and lessens the chance of splitting the wood or gouging too deeply. Incidentally, a wood mallet or a rubber or plastic-faced hammer is the only tool that should be used for this job. Using a conventional hammer may cause splitting or "mushrooming" of the handle and will shorten its life considerably, unless a special steel-headed chisel is used.

To insure maximum control and smoothness of cut, a chisel should always be moved so that its blade is at an angle to the direction of cut. This causes the tool to cut with a paring action which is much easier to control and which gives a much neater finish than does a straight thrust. The work should be securely supported or held in a vise to minimize slipping, and cuts should always be made with the grain wherever possible. To provide maximum control, the left hand should grasp the blade as close to the cutting edge as practical, but at no time should the fingers be allowed to get in front of the cutting edge.

Skilled cabinetmakers will always make the first cut in the waste part of the wood, rather than starting right on the line. Thus, if the wood splits—or if the chisel slips—damage will occur in the part that will be

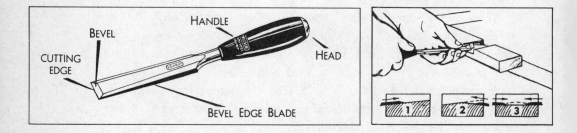

removed anyway. Progressive cuts are then made, working back toward the finished line. This technique of removing only a little at a time— even when a comparatively large amount must be chiseled off—is always safer than trying to hack off large amounts in a single operation.

For roughing cuts—as when deep slots or dadoes are being cut— the chisel is held with the bevel side down. This makes it easier to keep the blade from biting too deeply into the work and permits the user to make progressively shallower cuts as he works his way down toward the finished line. For the final finishing cut, and for delicate paring cuts when wood must be trimmed to an exact dimension, the chisel is held with the bevel side up. The flat side of the blade is then pressed against the surface so that the beveled blade will gradually shave off the wood in thin layers.

When cutting across the grain on the edge of a board or across the face of a narrow board, always cut halfway in from each edge first, removing the center part last. By the same token, when trimming end grain, always work from each edge in toward the center. Allowing a chisel to run off the end will almost certainly result in splintering or chipping the corners.

To cut recesses, such as those which may be required when setting hinge leaves into the edge of a door, always use the chisel vertically first. Make shallow cuts (tap with a mallet for this) at each end of the recessed pocket. Then, make additional cuts across the grain at several points along the length of this recess so that when the wood is chipped out afterward individual chips will be short and less likely to split across into other parts of the work.

After these crosscuts have been made, the wood is removed by chiseling across the grain with the chisel held with the beveled side down. After most of the wood has been removed, the chisel is turned over (bevel side up) for final paring cuts which will shave the recess to the exact depth required.

Clamps, Woodworking

To make certain that a glued joint will hold properly and that maximum strength will be achieved, adequate pressure must be applied to the individual parts while the glue is setting. To apply this pressure, some type of wood clamp will be required, or some form of clamping arrangement must be devised.

While wood clamps are made in hundreds of different sizes and styles, many of these are highly specialized models, designed for industrial use only. The ordinary home handyman will find that most of his needs can be met with only a few inexpensive clamps which are available in all hardware stores. These are used not only for gluing, but for holding pieces temporarily in position while assembling joints with nails, screws or bolts—or while drilling holes through adjoining members which must be held in accurate alignment.

Probably the most frequently used of all clamps is the common C-clamp. It can be used for a wide variety of jobs around the house, and it comes in all sizes. Two or three, with maximum jaw openings of from

1: *Hand Screw*
2: *Bar Clamp*
3: *Spring Clamp*
4: *C-clamp*
5: *Extension Bar Clamp*

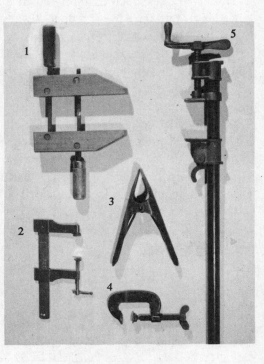

3 to 6 inches, will generally be sufficient for the home handyman's toolbox. They will have either a wing-shaped handle or a sliding T-bar handle. Use these principally where surfaces are parallel (or nearly so), and never try to get added pressure by using a wrench or bar on the handle to increase leverage. This will only warp the frame or bend the screw, and it may ruin the clamp.

The best all-round clamping tools for woodworking projects are the hand screws. Made of hard maple, these clamps have two screws and handles to provide parallel gripping pressure throughout the entire length of their jaws. To open or close them quickly, grasp one screw handle in each hand. Both are then turned simultaneously by rotating the entire clamp between your hands so that the jaws revolve around the spindles. Rotating in one direction opens the jaws, while rotating in the other direction closes them.

After rotating till the approximate opening is obtained, place the clamp over the work with the middle spindle or screw as close to the work as possible. Adjust both screws so that the clamp grips the work lightly with the ends of the jaws not quite touching the surface. Apply final pressure by tightening the outside screws only, making certain to double check that pressure is being applied along the full length of the jaws—not just at the ends or along the edge.

Most hand screws are adjustable; that is, the jaws can be pivoted to clamp on surfaces that are not parallel. The work can also be gripped with one jaw advanced farther than the other where irregular projections are required. Nonadjustable types are also available, but these are more limited in use since the jaws remain always parallel. They cannot be used on irregularly shaped objects or where work surfaces are not parallel.

For clamping wide objects which are beyond the scope of ordinary C-clamps or hand screws, bar clamps are the tools to use. Steel units which have one fixed head and one movable head can be purchased in lengths from 18 to 72 inches. The fixed head at one end has an adjustable jaw mounted at the end of a steel screw with a crank handle for tightening. The nonadjustable jaw at the other end of the bar can be slid to the approximate opening desired. It is held in place by a friction clutch which grips the bar automatically wherever it is set.

Home handymen can easily fashion their own bar clamps in any length by buying special clamping fixtures which fit over ½-inch or ¾-inch black iron pipe. These clamping fixtures are similar to the type used on regular bar clamps. The fixed jaw is threaded to screw onto one end of the pipe, while the movable jaw slides over the other end. One advantage of this type of bar clamp is that its length can be extended at any time simply by adding on another length of threaded pipe.

Short bar clamps (from 4 to 30 inches in length) with the sliding head containing the screw handle for tightening have become increasingly popular with home craftsmen in recent years. They can be used wherever C-clamps can be used, but they have greater capacity and are quicker to adjust.

Steel spring clamps which resemble oversized clothespins are also handy for many light-duty clamping jobs around the home or workshop. They are fast and easy to apply since the jaws are opened by simply squeezing the handles together. A built-in spring applies mild pressure when the handles are released. They are handy for those jobs where only one hand can be used while the other hand positions the parts or applies the glue. They are also handy where an extra pair of hands is needed to hold pieces temporarily in position while assembling.

When suitable clamps are not available, a rope tourniquet can often be fashioned to apply the needed pressure. Simply wrap rope around the pieces that must be held together (or around the entire outside circumference of the piece of furniture if necessary), and then apply pressure by twisting the cords, tourniquet style, using a short stick or length of dowel as a winch. This type of "Spanish windlass" can be used to apply a great deal of pressure over odd-shaped pieces, but corners should be protected with wads of folded cardboard to prevent denting.

Another clamping arrangement that can be used to apply pressure over a large horizontal area is to pile on heavy weights, such as bricks, blocks or pails of water and sand. A protective sheet of plywood should be laid over the work first to prevent marring.

In all clamping operations be careful to avoid squeezing the joint too tightly. Too much pressure will squeeze much of the glue out and may weaken the joint severely. In addition, excessive pressure may damage the very piece you are trying to repair by buckling, warping or crushing it. Before tightening clamps permanently, always check carefully to make certain that pressure is being applied in the proper direction and that clamp jaws are evenly seated on the work surfaces.

Drills, Electric

A portable electric drill is undoubtedly the first power tool that most do-it-yourselfers will acquire—and rightly so. It is one of the most-used, and with suitable accessories, one of the most versatile power tools in any workshop or tool kit.

Although most people start out by first shopping for a ¼-inch drill (the size refers to the size of the drill's chuck—that is, the largest bit it will hold), in most cases the ⅜-inch size is a better choice. It has more power, costs only slightly more, and its larger capacity will come in handy for many jobs.

When shopping for a drill it might also pay to look for one with extra features such as double-insulation so that you need only a two-prong plug and extension cord and don't have to worry about working in damp locations. Also, if the extra cost is not a serious deterrent, a variable-speed model is better for many chores since it enables you to control the speed by simply varying your pressure on the trigger. This is handy when starting a hole in hard materials or on smooth surfaces —you can start very slowly to keep the bit from skipping around, then speed up to normal cutting speed when the bit starts to "dig in."

Drill bits come in a hardened steel version that will drill hard metals, as well as wood and other materials, or in less expensive carbon steel types that are only good for wood or soft metals. For drilling holes larger than the maximum capacity of the chuck, you can buy drill bits with smaller shanks—for example, a ½-inch bit that will fit

Electric drills have many uses

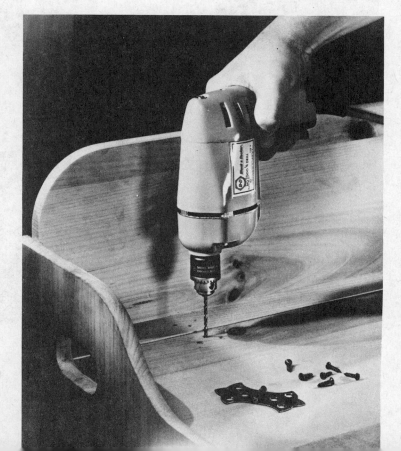

into a ¼-inch chuck. However, care is required to avoid overloading the drill motor.

There are also spade bits which will bore holes up to one inch in diameter in wood, and an assortment of different types of hole saws for making larger holes in wood and metal. Some can be used with the smaller ¼-inch drills, but others are designed only for use with heavy duty ⅜-inch or ½-inch drills.

In addition to its basic function of drilling holes, a good quality electric drill can also be equipped with a myriad assortment of accessories which will enable it to be used for sanding, polishing, routing, shaping, grinding, cutting and power-driving of bolts and screws. However, it must be remembered that because an electric drill is mainly designed for drilling holes, it is engineered primarily to take end thrust —that is, to take pressure lengthwise along its shaft. It is not really designed to take much side pressure or angular pressure, so when the drill is used for sanding or with similar accessories that require that you do press sideways or at a considerable angle to the length of the

Drill stands enable drills to be used for buffing or grinding

Buff attachment in use

shaft, it is best to handle the tool carefully and not exert too much pressure. This is generally less of a problem with the heavier duty ⅜-inch or ½-inch models than it is with the light duty ¼-inch drills, but moderation is still advisable when using the drill for these "extra" jobs.

Incidentally, it is when a drill is to be used with many of these non-drilling accessories, that the variable-speed feature is particularly useful—slower speeds are safer and easier to handle with some large-diameter hole saws, spade bits and sanding disks. The variable-speed feature also enables the drill to be used for driving or removing screws —when it has a screwdriver bit inserted instead of a drill bit.

The sanding disk is probably the most popular of all electric drill accessories. Usually consisting of a partially flexible backing pad or disk that has an arbor which fits into the drill chuck, these come in various sizes and are usually designed so that the sandpaper or abrasive disk is fastened in place with a recessed nut and cup-shaped washer in the center. Some are held in place with an adhesive backing that eliminates the need for the washer in the center, and some are secured with a snap-like attachment in the center.

To make these sanding disks even more useful, and to enable the drill to be used with a grinding wheel in the chuck so that the drill serves as bench grinder for sharpening and grinding, there are also compact stands you can buy which will hold the drill firmly in a horizontal position. The stands can be bolted or screwed to a table or bench top, and the drill can be quickly released or clamped into position when different uses for it arise. Locked in place on one of these stands, the drill serves as a sanding disk against which work can be held, or as a bench grinder. In this position it can also be equipped with a wire wheel brush or buffing wheel for polishing and cleaning metal and other materials.

Most sanding disks can also be fitted with lambswool-type polishing pads for buffing, waxing and polishing of automobiles, furniture, boats and other objects.

For trimming, shaping and smoothing of wood, plastic and similar materials, there is also a wide variety of rotary rasps and files that can be purchased—usually with ¼-inch shanks so they will fit all electric drills. There are large drum-shaped rasps that will remove wood and plastic quickly and so can be used to speed up many shaping and trimming jobs, as well as smaller rasps for reaching into tight places. Smaller, hardened steel rotary files are available for use on metal. Both the files and the rasps come in an assortment of different sizes and shapes.

Rotary files and rasps

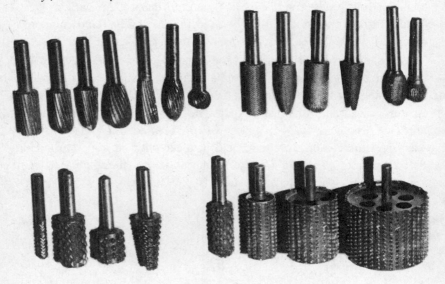

Fasteners, Hollow Wall

Sooner or later everyone runs across the problem of fastening something to a wall inside the house. Though the first impulse may be simply to drive a nail into the wall, this seldom proves a satisfactory solution. Since interior walls are usually hollow, the nail merely breaks through into empty space—leaving you with little more than some cracked plaster and a useless hole for your trouble.

To provide a more satisfactory solution to this problem, there are many special wall fasteners that can be used. Regardless of the size or weight of the fixture being hung, chances are there is a fastener available which will do the job. The load that can be supported is limited only by the strength of the wall material itself.

For light-duty jobs, such as hanging small pictures and decorative plates, there are hangers available which can be cemented in place against the wall. Some of these come with a separate liquid adhesive, while others are adhesive-backed. Since this type of device sticks to the surface only, it is limited by the strength of the surface coating (paint or wallpaper) which is already in place on the wall.

When greater strength is needed to support pictures, small mirrors or decorative shelves, picture hooks which hold nails at an angle are often used. These are simply driven into the wall with a hammer, and they come in various sizes to support objects up to 35 pounds. The hooks are designed so that they hold the nail at the proper angle to provide the greatest holding strength in either plaster or gypsum board. To keep from cracking the plaster while hammering these fasteners in place, stick a wide strip of tape over the spot where the nail will enter.

For maximum holding strength in all types of hollow walls, expansion-type toggle bolts or anchors should be used. These fit into holes which must be drilled in the wall beforehand. They have expanding wings or ribs which open up behind the wall when a bolt or screw in the center of the unit is tightened. Three types are widely available: toggle bolts, which have spring-operated folding wings; expansion-type screw anchors, which have metal sleeves that spread out behind the wall when the bolt is tightened; and anchors or plugs, which may be made of lead, fiber or plastic. The last type takes standard wood screws or threaded nails. The plastic anchors are designed so that they split when a screw is inserted, thus spreading out to grip firmly behind the wall, as well as inside the hole.

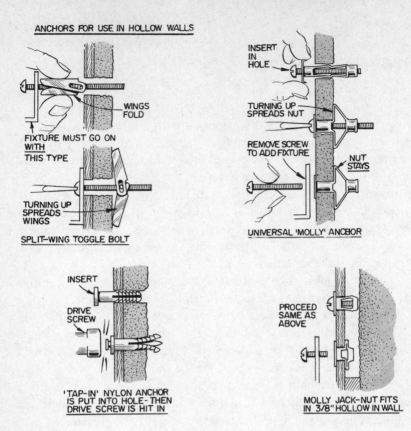

ANCHORS FOR USE IN HOLLOW WALLS

WINGS FOLD

FIXTURE MUST GO ON WITH THIS TYPE

TURNING UP SPREADS WINGS

SPLIT-WING TOGGLE BOLT

INSERT IN HOLE

TURNING UP SPREADS NUT

REMOVE SCREW TO ADD FIXTURE

NUT STAYS

UNIVERSAL 'MOLLY' ANCHOR

INSERT

DRIVE SCREW

'TAP-IN' NYLON ANCHOR IS PUT INTO HOLE- THEN DRIVE SCREW IS HIT IN

PROCEED SAME AS ABOVE

MOLLY JACK-NUT FITS IN 3/8" HOLLOW IN WALL

To hang fixtures with a toggle bolt, you must first drill a hole slightly larger than the diameter of the unit with wings folded. The exact hole size required will be specified in the literature which accompanies the toggle bolt. The wing part is next unscrewed so that the bolt can be pushed through the fixture which is being fastened to the wall. The wing, which has a threaded nut in the center, is now screwed back onto the end of the bolt, folded, and then pushed through the hole in the wall. When the wings have been shoved all the way through into the space behind, they will spring open on the inside. Tightening the bolt draws the wings flat against the back side of the wall to lock the fixture firmly in place. Once the toggle bolt is in position, it cannot be removed without losing the wings inside the wall.

Expansion-type screw anchors work in much the same manner as toggle bolts. However, they do not need as large a hole as a toggle bolt, and they have the added advantage in that the bolt can be removed whenever necessary while the anchor remains locked in its original position in the wall. This not only simplifies installation, it also enables you to take down fixtures whenever necessary (by simply unscrewing the bolt) and to replace them with the same anchor.

To install one of these patented screw anchors, a hole must be drilled to accept the metal tube or sleeve which forms the body of the fastener. The assembled fastener is then pushed through this hole until the small flange under the bolt contacts the face of the wall. Tightening up on the bolt causes the sleeve to split open and expand in back of the wall until it is gradually drawn up tight against the back of the plaster. This locks it firmly and permanently in position, even after the bolt is withdrawn. The bolt can now be removed, passed through the fixture being hung, then reinserted in the threaded hole in the fastener to complete the mounting job. These anchors come in various lengths to accommodate walls of various thicknesses. Very short models are also available for such jobs as hanging mirrors or other appliances on hollow-core flush doors, as well as for fastening to thin plywood and composition board.

Anchors or plugs which are designed for use with wood screws actually consist of a hollow sleeve which is inserted in a hole drilled in the wall. The hole in the center of this plug is tapered so that it is narrower at the tip than it is at the surface. Thus, when a screw is inserted, it splits the back end open to wedge it tightly inside its hole. These plugs or anchors come in various lengths and diameters to accept various size wood screws and to handle varying loads.

Fasteners, Masonry

When a handyman is faced with the problem of trying to fasten shelves, cabinets or other fixtures to solid masonry walls (in basements or on the outside of the house), there are a number of different fasten-

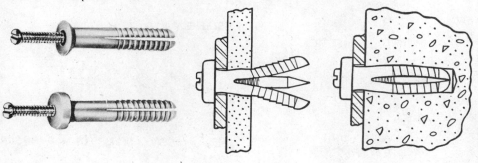

Combination plastic anchor can be used in hollow or solid wall construction

ing devices that he can use. Suitable for masonry floors as well as walls, these fasteners can also be used when appliances, railings or fixtures must be bolted down on a cellar or garage floor or on an outside terrace.

When furring strips or 2x4's must be fastened against a masonry surface, the quickest and simplest way to do the job is to use hardened steel nails which are made especially for this purpose. These are much tougher than ordinary nails and can be driven into concrete with a hammer without predrilling pilot holes. They should be driven through the wood first, since the thickness of the wood is needed to keep them from bending while they are being hammered in. Care must be taken to drive them in with powerful, straight blows. If not struck squarely on the head, the nails tend to break rather than bend. These nails are not recommmended for supporting shelves or other fixtures since they do not offer adequate resistance to pulling out.

ANCHORS FOR SOLID WALLS AND MASONRY

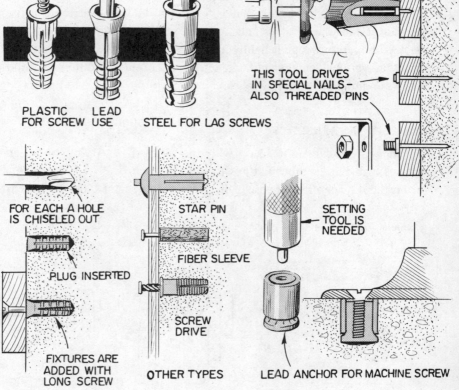

PLASTIC LEAD
FOR SCREW USE   STEEL FOR LAG SCREWS

THIS TOOL DRIVES
IN SPECIAL NAILS –
ALSO THREADED PINS

FOR EACH A HOLE
IS CHISELED OUT

PLUG INSERTED

FIXTURES ARE
ADDED WITH
LONG SCREW

STAR PIN

FIBER SLEEVE

SCREW
DRIVE

OTHER TYPES

SETTING
TOOL IS
NEEDED

LEAD ANCHOR FOR MACHINE SCREW

When a stronger and more permanent fastener is needed, expansion-type anchors or expansion shields are usually used. The anchors are less expensive and they come in smaller sizes than the shields. Usually made of lead or a special heavy-duty fiber, the anchors start at about ⅛ inch in diameter and are designed to take standard bolts or machine screws. Expansion shields, on the other hand, require a deeper hole and the smallest size takes a ¼-inch machine screw or bolt.

Basically speaking, both work on the same general principle. A hole of the proper size to accept the anchor or shield being used is first drilled in the masonry wall. Then, when the proper screw or bolt is inserted, the shield or anchor expands inside its hole to lock itself firmly—and permanently—in place. To hold their positions in the holes before the bolts are inserted, most expansion anchors must be "set" by rapping sharply with a hammer and a special punch. This step is not usually required with shields, since these can be slipped into their holes by tapping lightly.

To drill the required holes in a masonry wall, you can use either a star drill or a carbide-tipped masonry drill bit. Star drills are hammered in much like a cold chisel. Instead of a single cutting edge (like a chisel), the star drill has two crossed cutting edges which form a sort of star-shaped pattern. To drive one of these, a heavy hammer should be used. The drill is struck repeatedly with steady blows, rotating it slightly after each stroke.

A carbide-tipped bit is used with an ordinary electric drill. Bits up to ½ inch in diameter can be purchased with ¼-inch shanks so that they can be used in standard ¼-inch drills. To keep bits from wearing rapidly, bear down hard with steady pressure so that the bit cannot slip inside its hole. Releasing pressure while the bit is turning will permit it to slip—and will cause it to dull rapidly.

For light-duty jobs where the stress is parallel to the surface (rather than straight out), smaller fiber or plastic anchors can be used. These come in smaller sizes than the lead anchors and are designed to accept conventional wood screws rather than bolts. Anchors of this kind are particularly suitable for use in brick walls, and they are widely used for such jobs as hanging fireplace tools on a mantel, hanging pictures or mirrors and fastening shutters on brick or stucco.

For jobs where a great many fasteners are required, there are special tools which can be used. These enable the handyman to anchor wood or metal to concrete almost as easily as ordinary lumber can be nailed up. The tools drive in threaded studs or nail-like fasteners which are made of specially tempered steel. They will hold permanently in concrete, cinder block or brick, and they eliminate the need for boring holes beforehand.

Called stud drivers, these tools generally fall into one of two categories. The commercial or industrial models are powder-actuated. That is, they use gunpowder in special cartridges which are similar to those used in ordinary firearms. Instead of a metal bullet or slug, the driver "fires" a steel stud or nail into the concrete.

Powder-actuated stud drivers are actuated by pulling on a trigger or by tapping lightly with a hammer on an exposed firing pin at the top. The better quality models have built-in safety features which prevent accidental discharge when the base is not in contact with the concrete. However, caution and careful attention to handling instructions are still required when handling them. Most are large, heavy-duty models which are quite expensive, though they can be rented from tool rental agencies in many communities.

Far more popular with do-it-yourselfers, and much lower in price, is the newer, hammer-in type of stud driver. These are hand-actuated. That is, power is delivered by striking with a hammer on an anvil or head at the top. Using the same principle as the powder-actuated models, these hammer-in tools hold the nail or stud in a tight-fitting tube or sleeve. An anvil in the other end of this sleeve projects at the top so that it can be struck with a hammer to force the nail or stud into the masonry when the base of the driver is held snug against the surface. Nail-type fasteners or drive pins up to 3 inches in length can be used, or they will accept threaded studs up to 2 inches in length. The threaded studs have a nail-like point which is driven into the surface so that the threaded end is left projecting. Nuts can then be screwed on over the threaded end to hold angle brackets or similar fixtures in place. For best results, a heavy hammer weighing at least 2½ pounds should be used. Lighter hammers set up excessive vibration, making it difficult to deliver the necessary power with accuracy.

When strips of lumber are to be nailed against the wall, the nail-type fasteners are usually used. These can be driven directly through the lumber into the concrete. However, it is important that the lumber be held tight against the surface while nailing, and washers which are specially designed to fit onto the nailhead should be used. These washers serve two functions: they help guide the fastener while it is being driven home, and they help create a better grip after the piece has been nailed into place.

Files, Selection and Use

Files are inexpensive, handy tools which can be used for dozens of different jobs around the home and in the workshop. They are indispensable for many shaping and smoothing jobs on metal, wood and plastics, and they are often required for sharpening tools and garden implements. Though files are made in dozens of different sizes and styles, the home handyman need only concern himself with a few basic types. These vary according to size (length), shape (cross section) and coarseness of cut (the kind of teeth it has).

The teeth on most files are cut at an angle across the face. Files which have a single row of parallel teeth are called single-cut. Those which have a second row of teeth crisscrossing the first are known as double-cut. Single-cut files give the smoothest finish. Double-cut files will cut faster, but they do not leave as smooth a surface.

Both the single-cut and the double-cut files vary as to coarseness. The most widely sold models are the grades referred to as bastard-cut. For use on wood, leather, lead and other soft materials, rasp-cut files (usually called wood rasps) are also available. They have individually shaped

Wood rasp is used for smoothing panel edges

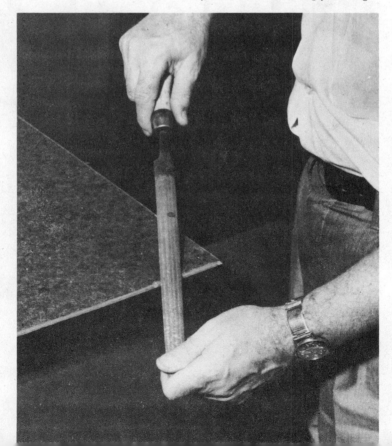

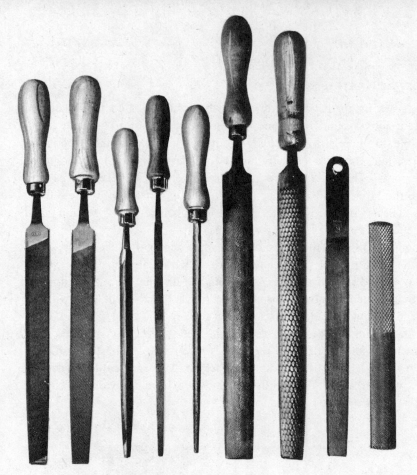

Useful files of various types described in the text

teeth and give a rough cut which removes stock rapidly. Home handymen will find them useful for shaping and smoothing lumber, as well as for trimming joints to a snug fit. Like the metal files, these wood rasps also come in various degrees of coarseness.

In addition to the type of cut, files vary in cross section and shape. The most frequently used shapes are rectangular (flat files or mill files), square, round or triangular. Each comes in various lengths, and as the files increase in length, they also become larger in cross section. They may be either tapered (narrower at one end) or blunt (uniform in thickness from end to end).

The home handyman will find that two rectangular (flat) files will handle most of his metal-smoothing and sharpening jobs: an 8- or 10-inch mill file (these are single-cut) and a flat bastard file (these are double-cut) of about the same length. The mill file will be used for sharpening tools and for final smoothing of hard metals, while the double-cut bastard file will be used for all-around heavy work when large amounts of metal must be removed.

Other files which come in handy are illustrated in the accompanying photo. The triangular file is useful for sharpening saw blades, filing notches, straightening damaged screw threads and similar jobs. Round files are most often used for reaming out or enlarging holes and for inside filing of tight curves on wrought iron pieces and metal moldings. The half-round file simplifies the job of smoothing concave surfaces, while the all-purpose file illustrated is handy for use on rotary lawn mower blades and similar jobs. It is double-cut on one side and single-cut on the other. The combination shoe rasp is also half-round. It has two grades of rasp teeth, as well as single- and double-cut teeth on both sides.

In addition to the standard files and wood rasps mentioned above, there is another type of shaping tool which can be roughly classified as a file. Available in models which can be used as either a file or a plane (according to the type of handle or grip with which it comes equipped), these tools have serrated steel blades with hundreds of separate little teeth along the face. They work with a cutting action which is somewhere between that of a rasp (or coarse file) and an old-fashioned potato grater. They are fast-acting and easy to use, and they speed up many difficult jobs, such as the trimming of plywood edges and the "planing" of aluminum doors. They can be used on all kinds of hard or soft woods, and they work equally well on composition board, plastics, asphalt tile, brass, copper and other soft metals. In addition to a standard flat style, there are also curved blades.

When using a file, the handyman should bear down on the forward stroke only. On the return stroke the file should be lifted clear of the surface to avoid dulling the teeth. The one exception to this is when working on very soft metals. In this case allow the teeth to drag slightly on the back stroke. This helps to clear out chips and filings from between the teeth.

The amount of pressure required will, of course, vary with the type of metal being filed. In general, it is best to bear down only hard enough to keep the file cutting at all times. Too little pressure allows the teeth to slide over the surface, causing them to dull rapidly. Too much pressure, and the teeth are likely to chip or clog.

As a general rule, it is best to move the file in straight lines across

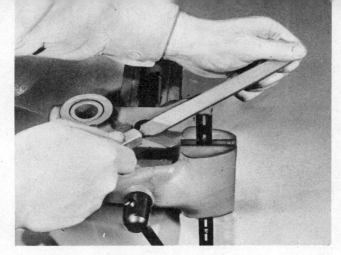

For most jobs, file should be held as shown

the surface. Where practical, it is best to grip the work in a vise so the file can be held with both hands. The handle is grasped in one hand, while the point of the file is held between the thumb and the first two fingers of the other hand.

To protect the hands, files should always be equipped with handles. Some come with plastic handles already fitted, but most require that wooden handles be purchased separately for a few cents. They are installed by simply inserting the pointed tang of the file in the handle hole, then rapping sharply on a solid surface to seat it firmly. To keep files sharp and in good cutting condition, store them in hanging racks which will keep them from banging against each other. If necessary to store in a toolbox or drawer, each file should be wrapped separately in cloth or plastic.

Glues, Wood. SEE ADHESIVES, SELECTION AND USE.

Hardboard Panels, Working Techniques

Hardboard panels can be used in many different ways around the home. Made of natural wood fibers which have been compressed into smooth, grainless sheets, the most widely used panels are those which are either ⅛ or ¼ inch in thickness and which measure 4 by 8 feet in size. Larger sheets are available on special order, and most local lumberyards will cut panels to size when smaller pieces are needed.

In its most common form, hardboard is smooth on one side, with a rougher, waffle-like texture on the other. Panels which are smooth on both sides are also available and, for a more decorative finish, there are panels which are grooved, channeled or embossed with different designs. In addition to these three-dimensional textures, there are also plastic-coated panels in various colors and in a number of different patterns. Among the more popular finishes are the simulated wood-grain patterns which look almost exactly like real hardwood when installed.

Hardboard comes in two grades: standard and tempered. The standard panels are the ones most commonly used for normal indoor applications. The tempered panels have a harder surface and are specially treated to withstand moisture. They should be used for all outdoor projects and in all areas which are subject to exceptionally high humidity.

Because hardboard has no grain to rise or check, it has equal strength in all directions and is ideal for all installations where a hard, smooth surface is desirable. For example, when used to form drawer bottoms, the panels assure a splinter-free surface which will not snag garments and which will be easy to wipe clean. These same characteristics also make hardboard ideal for covering benches, tables and counter tops, as well as for building closet and cabinet shelving.

Since these hard-surfaced panels have no knots or other imperfections, they are also frequently used for modernizing old paneled doors by converting them to flush doors. The panels are simply nailed or glued to the face of the old door and the hardware remounted on the outside. Quarter-inch-thick panels are also frequently used as lightweight sliding doors in cabinets of all kinds.

Hardboard panels also come in the popular perforated style with holes spaced at regular intervals. Standard wire fixtures can be used with this to create storage on any wall. In addition to a wide range of differently shaped hooks and brackets, there are special shelf brackets, plastic drawer units, hatracks, shoe racks and other accessories available. These can be used to create on-the-wall storage for almost any item—and in almost any room in the house. The perforated panels are made in both the ⅛-inch and the ¼-inch thicknesses. The thicker material should be used where heavier objects will be supported or where additional rigidity is required.

Generally speaking, hardboard can be worked with all ordinary woodworking tools. It should be handled like any other natural wood material. Sheets can be fastened to framing members with nails, screws or glue— or by a combination of any of these. Though ordinary nails can be used, ring-grooved or screw-type nails are recommended to minimize the possibility of nails popping loose later on. For maximum holding power wood screws should be used.

In the construction of cabinets or chests of hardboard, a supporting framework is required. Panels cannot be edge-nailed or joined together at right angles unless there is some form of blocking or framing in all the corners. To construct lightweight hollow panels of hardboard, use ¾-inch-square wood strips as a framework. Be sure to apply the same thickness panels to both sides of the framework; otherwise warping or buckling can occur. When large panels are required, build the framework of wider lumber and fasten the hardboard facing to the wood with nails or screws combined with glue. Construct the framework so that crosspieces are no more than 12 inches apart. Nails should never be driven any closer than ¼ inch from the edge, and they should be spaced no more than 4 inches apart along the edges and 8 inches apart in the center.

When nailing panels to a framework, or to a solid backing of any kind, always start driving nails in the center of the panel and work out toward the edges to make certain that the panel will lie flat. Never butt panels tightly together at the edges. Instead, place them loosely against each other or, better yet, leave a very slight space between panels to provide room for expansion. When building a cabinet, closet, bookcase or similar project of hardboard, make certain each panel has a backing or continuous support around all the edges.

Hardboard panels can be painted with ordinary flat paints, semigloss paints or enamels. However, the surface should be sealed first by applying a prime coat of shellac, enamel undercoater or alkyd-based primer and sealer. For the top coats, either a latex (water-thinned) or alkyd-based flat or enamel can be used. If a clear or natural finish is desired, varnish, lacquer or shellac can be used. To assure a smooth surface, nailheads and screwheads can be countersunk, and the resulting holes filled with wood putty before finish coats are applied.

Hoses, Garden, Repair and Maintenance

Modern garden hoses will last for many years if given a reasonable amount of care. However, if abused, even the best quality of garden hose will have its life shortened so that complete replacement soon becomes necessary. To keep a hose from cracking prematurely, never kink or bend it sharply when in use or when storing it. Attach a swivel-type connector or angle fitting to the hose spigot if you frequently pull the hose off at a sharp angle from the faucet. This will minimize the danger of creating a permanent crease just below the fitting where the hose screws on the spigot.

Always store your hose by coiling it neatly around a wide bracket or regular hose reel, never by hanging it on a sharp nail or hook. Never leave it coiled loosely in a tangled mass on the ground where people may step on it or where cars and other wheeled vehicles will be continually rolling over it. Keep the threaded ends free of dirt and other foreign material which will make it difficult to insure a watertight connection.

When winter comes, drain all water from your hose and store it indoors in neat coils. Use a small brush to clean out the threads on the fittings at each end. Replace the rubber washers at the beginning of each season so that you won't have trouble tightening the fittings when the hose goes back into use again.

When small leaks develop, they can usually be repaired quite easily. On a rubber hose, apply a layer of plastic rubber compound, allow to dry, then rub lightly with fine sandpaper. Apply a second coat covering a slightly larger area to insure a lasting patch.

Small leaks in a plastic hose can also be cemented over, using a plastic adhesive, but the cement should be reinforced by wrapping with plastic tape, or by application of a plastic patch. Dab the cement on and wait till it gets sticky, then wrap with the tape or press the patch into place. After this has dried hard, apply a second layer of cement on top of the patch, taking care to smooth off the edges.

Sizable leaks and badly split sections of hoses are best mended by cutting out the defective section entirely, then using a hose-mending coupling to join the two sound parts. The most common type of coupling is a mending tube that slips inside the two hose parts and has cleats that must be bent down around the outside of the hose to hold the coupling firmly in place. While this type can be used with either plastic or rubber hoses, compression-type fittings that have threaded collars will work better on plastic hoses since there is less likelihood of their cutting through the outside skin.

When the threaded fittings at either end of the hose are damaged, these can also be replaced by cutting off a few inches of the hose near the end. Special replacement fittings that lock on in the same way as the mending couplings can then be installed to make the hose as good as new again. Since any of these menders or replacement fittings require that a serrated or tapered tube be pushed into the inside of the hose, you'll find that a plastic hose will be easier to handle if the cut end is dipped into hot water first. This will make it more malleable and will simplify the job of forcing the fitting into place inside the hose.

Ladders, Care and Use

Since a good quality ladder (metal or wood) will last for a great many years in normal use, it is foolish economy to buy one which is poorly constructed, no matter how much of a "bargain" it may seem. Better quality ladders have a wider spread between legs, heavier side rails, sturdier rungs or steps and heavy-duty, rustproof hardware. They are also firmly braced against swaying.

Generally speaking, two kinds of ladders are required around the home: a 5- or 6-foot stepladder for interior use and for work around the lower part of the house on the outside; and a tall extension ladder for use around the upper part of the house on the outside. The size of the extension ladder required will, of course, depend on the height of the house. It should be tall enough to permit reaching the highest part (usually the chimney) when emergency repairs become necessary.

As its name implies, an extension ladder actually consists of two straight sections which fit together so that one part can be raised or extended to the height desired. The size of the ladder is determined by the combined length of the two individual sections. Actually this total length (or height) can never be fully utilized, since there must always be at least a 2-foot overlap in the center to insure adequate strength when the ladder is extended.

To permit hoisting the upper half—the narrower section—to the height desired, all extension ladders come equipped with a rope which is tied to the bottom end of the movable (narrower) section of the ladder. This rope goes up between the two sections, through a pulley on the top rung of the bottom half (the wider one), then comes down on the outside to ground level. Pulling down on the free end of this rope hoists the upper half of the ladder to the height desired. When working alone, you can do this quite easily by supporting the ladder vertically with one hand while bracing the bottom end with one foot. Your other hand can then be used to pull down on the end of the rope till you have raised the ladder to the height required.

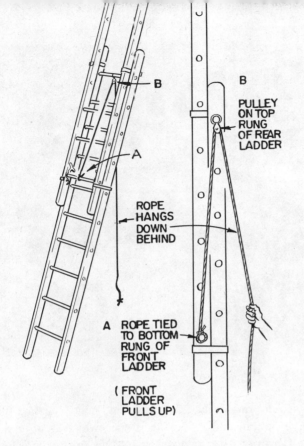

B

B

PULLEY
ON TOP
RUNG
OF REAR
LADDER

A

ROPE
HANGS
DOWN
BEHIND

A ROPE TIED
TO BOTTOM
RUNG OF
FRONT
LADDER

(FRONT
LADDER
PULLS UP)

To keep the upper half in place after it has been raised, spring-actuated hooks or locks are attached to the top section. These hook on-to one of the rungs of the bottom section when tension on the rope is released. When the ladder is to be lowered, a pull on this same rope (enough to raise the ladder about half a step) will release these locks so that a metal pivot closes them temporarily. This permits the upper half to slide down without difficulty. When lowering the ladder, feed the rope upward, hand-over-hand, rather than allowing it to slide through the fingers.

To stand one of these tall ladders up when working alone, start by placing the ladder flat on the ground with its bottom end pressed against the base of the wall, and with the rest of the ladder extending out at right angles from the wall. Grasp the ladder by its top rung (the end farthest from the house) and raise this approximately shoulder high. Move the hands from rung to rung while walking toward the house, thus raising the upper end of the ladder. When the ladder is fully raised and flat against the house wall in its vertical position, extend it to the height desired by pulling on the rope as previously described.

Ladder is raised by "walking" it up

When the ladder is fully raised, lean the upper end gently against the house, then move the bottom end out to a distance which is approximately equal to one-fourth of its extended height. This forms the safest possible working angle for any tall ladder. Remember to allow at least a 2-foot overlap in the center (2 feet on each section) to insure adequate strength and to minimize the possibility of dangerous swaying.

To move an extension ladder a short distance to one side, the simplest method is to ease the ladder along by first moving the top and then the bottom—no more than a foot or two at a time. If the ladder has to be moved a considerable distance, this type of gradual zigzagging may be impractical. In that event, the safest procedure is to lower the extension, lay the ladder down and carry it horizontally to its new location. To lower the ladder before laying it down, simply reverse the procedure used in erecting it. Pull down on the rope till the metal locks are disengaged, then release the rope slowly and steadily. When the top half is all the way down, butt the bottom end of the ladder firmly against the base of the house, then "walk" the ladder down, hand-over-hand, by walking backwards away from the wall.

Though stepladders reach only a few feet above the ground, carelessness here can still lead to a bad fall. Before climbing, always make certain that the metal braces on each side are all the way down and firmly

locked in the open position. Never climb a stepladder which is only
partly open (braces not all the way down), since in this position it
could fold up or collapse quite easily—especially when on a slippery
floor or soft ground. In addition, never go higher than the second step
from the top, and never use the top platform as a step. Always place
your ladder so that you can do all necessary work while facing toward
it, rather than away from it.

The folding platform which drops down at the back of most ordinary
stepladders is for pails or tools—it is not designed to take the weight of
a person standing on it. Some heavy-duty industrial ladders are made
with rungs up the back as well as with steps up the front, and these are
the only ones which are safe to climb from either side.

When necessary to place a stepladder in or near a doorway, care
should be taken to secure the door in either the open or shut position
so that no one can accidentally swing it into the ladder while you are
standing on it. When working indoors on highly polished floors, you can

To move sideways, tilt upper end first

Carry ladder horizontally while balancing it on shoulder

avoid scratches by nailing pieces of an old rubber heel to the bottom of each leg. This not only prevents scratching, it helps keep the ladder from sliding while in use.

All wooden ladders, regardless of whether they are stepladders or extension ladders, will last longer if the wood is treated with two coats of clear penetrating sealer or clear varnish. Never use paint or other opaque coating on a wood ladder since it tends to hide cracks or other defects. To keep the hinges and other hardware working freely, oil moving parts at least once a year, and coat the metal with clear varnish to prevent rusting. Aluminum ladders need no protective coating, though they too will benefit from lubrication of all moving parts at periodic intervals.

To prevent accidents when working with any ladder—large or small— follow these important safety rules:

(1) Always inspect the ladder—especially if it is borrowed or rented —before you climb it. Check for loose steps and rungs, cracks or faulty hardware.

(2) Always face toward a ladder when ascending or descending. Never try to come down while facing away from it, or while leaning to one side.

(3) Never place a ladder in front of any door which opens toward it unless that door is either locked shut or tied open.

(4) Before climbing any ladder, make certain the soles of your shoes are not wet, muddy or greasy. See to it that the ladder rungs are also clean.

(5) Do not use a tall ladder outdoors during a strong wind, except in extreme emergencies. If absolutely necessary to climb a ladder on a windy day, make arrangements to tie or lash the ladder in position against the house, as near the top as possible.

(6) Before climbing any ladder, always make certain that both its legs are standing firm on level ground. If the earth is soft, place a flat board under the legs to insure a solid footing, then jump lightly on the bottom step to test it before climbing all the way up.

(7) When climbing an extension ladder, always hold on with both hands. If bulky tools or other materials must be carried up, leave these items on the ground, then haul them up afterwards with a lightweight rope.

(8) When standing on a ladder, always hold on with at least one hand. If the work requires that both hands be used for a while, hook one leg through a rung of the ladder to keep yourself from falling.

(9) Never try to reach out to one side more than a comfortable arm's length away. Keep both feet on the rungs to avoid tipping sideways.

(10) When using a metal ladder, make certain it is equipped with rubber-covered safety feet to prevent slipping—especially if the ladder is standing on a paved surface.

Nails, Selection and Use

Nails are probably the oldest of all wood fasteners, having been used since ancient times for assembling wood structures of all kinds. Though

Wide board keeps legs from sinking

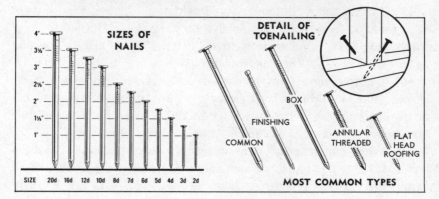

there are now dozens of different types available, many are specialized designs with limited industrial use. The most widely sold varieties are the common nail, the box nail, the finishing nail, the large-headed roofing nail and the annular-threaded nail (also referred to as screw nails).

All of these come in different lengths and in different gauges or sizes (body diameter). The common nail is used for rough framing and general construction work. It has a comparatively large flat head and a diamond-shaped point, and the shank usually has grooves under the head to help increase holding power. Box nails are similar to common nails, except that they are thinner in gauge and not quite as strong. They are useful for light construction projects where a heavy nail might tend to split the wood, and they are available with either smooth or barbed shanks in various sizes.

When the appearance of nailheads on a finished project would prove unsightly, finishing nails are generally used. These have small heads which can be easily punched down below the surface of the wood with a nailset. The holes which remain can then be filled with putty. Finishing nails are generally used for putting up moldings and trim, as well as for assembling cabinets and similar projects. Professional carpenters usually use special casing nails on wood trim, rather than finishing nails. Though they look almost the same, casing nails have slightly heavier shanks to provide increased holding power.

Small finishing nails which measure anywhere from ½ to 1½ inches in length are usually referred to as brads, rather than nails. They are graded by length and wire gauge number, and are useful for fine work where little or no stress is involved. When this same type of thin-gauge, light-duty nail is made with a flat head, it is referred to as a wire nail, rather than as a common or box nail.

Large-headed roofing nails are usually galvanized to resist rusting. As the name implies, these nails are used for nailing down roof shingles and asphalt-type roll roofing. Lengths vary from 1 to 2 inches, with head diameters varying accordingly. Since they have a rather heavy shank (in proportion to length), they are seldom used for nailing in thin lumber because they will very likely cause splitting.

A comparatively recent addition to the modern family of nails is the annular-threaded, or screw nail. Though it is driven in with a hammer—just like any other nail—it has holding power similar to that of a wood screw. Available in aluminum or steel and in various sizes, this nail also lessens the danger of splitting in any type of wood. Though the cost per pound may be more than twice that of the same size common nail, threaded nails may actually cost less on a per-nail basis. There are usually more nails per pound (the grooved shank on each nail weighs less than the smooth, solid equivalent of a common nail) and, since the nails have much greater holding power, less nails are required—or a smaller size can be used—on any given job.

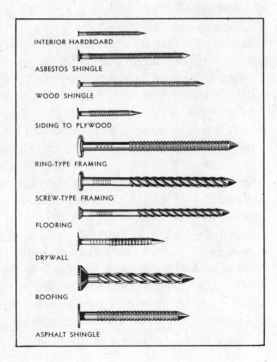

INTERIOR HARDBOARD

ASBESTOS SHINGLE

WOOD SHINGLE

SIDING TO PLYWOOD

RING-TYPE FRAMING

SCREW-TYPE FRAMING

FLOORING

DRYWALL

ROOFING

ASPHALT SHINGLE

Threaded nails are made in three basic forms. The first and most common style is the one made with helical (spiral) threads. These have a long lead angle—that is, they spiral downward toward the tip at a steep angle rather than as a tightly wound thread. Since these tend to turn while they are being driven, they form a spiral groove in the wood. The wood fibers wrap themselves around the shank, causing them to resist any upward pull which might be created later on. This type of threaded nail is most effective when driven into or through hardwood, and it is often used for fastening down hardwood flooring.

The second type of threaded nail is the annular-threaded or ringed nail which has a series of closely spaced grooves or rings around its shank. Since this "thread" does not spiral or twist, the nail does not turn as it is being driven. Instead, the wood fibers tend to wedge themselves inside the deep grooves on the shank. This creates a tight grip which offers great resistance to any tendency of the nail to work loose. Annular-threaded nails provide maximum holding power when used in soft or medium woods. They are most popular for installation of subflooring and for assembling wooden frames.

The third type of threaded nail combines the characteristics of both the annular-thread and spiral-thread nails. It has a closely spaced spiral thread which twists downward at a tight, closely spaced angle (similar to that of a conventional wood screw) so that it twists while being hammered in. Offering the advantages of the helical-thread nail, it also has deep grooves which grip like that of the annular, or ring-type, nail.

Since all of these ringed and threaded nails are quite difficult to remove once they have been driven in, they should be used only on permanent types of construction. They would be a poor choice for temporary braces or framing, and they should not be used in assembling any structure which may have to be knocked apart later on.

Regardless of the type of nail selected, always remember that larger nails have greater holding power than the smaller nails, but that they are more likely to split the wood. Therefore, always select the largest nail feasible, but avoid using nails which are so large that splitting becomes a problem. If the wood is very dry, or if hardwood is being used, it may be advisable to drill small pilot holes first. Another trick which will minimize the danger of splitting is to blunt the point first by hammering on it (while holding the nail upside down) or by filing it lightly. Blunt-pointed nails actually have increased holding power, and they are less likely to split the wood, particularly when driven in near the edge.

When several nails must be driven in at close intervals, avoid driving them along the same streak of grain. Nails should be staggered instead of being positioned in a straight line. Another way to increase holding power—particularly when driving into end grain—is to drive nails in so that they angle toward each other, rather than going in straight and parallel.

When it is impractical to drive nails in through one end (as when nailing vertical studs to floors or ceilings), toenailing techniques are usually used. This consists of driving nails in at an angle from either side of the stud or beam. It actually gives increased holding power, particularly when nails are driven in from opposite sides.

Planes, Selection and Use

Though hand planes are made in many different sizes and styles, all work on the same general principle. A sharp, chisel-like blade is held at an angle so that it shaves off a thin layer of wood when pushed forward over the surface. The edge of the blade projects down through a slot in the base of the tool. The distance it projects can be regulated by turning an adjustment screw, and this determines the thickness of the shaving produced.

Planes normally used by home handymen are of two different types: block planes and bench planes. Block planes are smaller tools which are held with one hand. They were originally introduced for trimming end grain, but they are also useful for those jobs where the work must be held steady with one hand. Because of their small size, they are also handy for working in tight corners and for trimming around curves and along edges. However, they are not really suitable for accurate trimming of long, straight pieces.

Bench planes are larger, two-handed tools which have a longer sole, or base. They are more suitable for general-purpose work such as

Block plane can be used with one hand

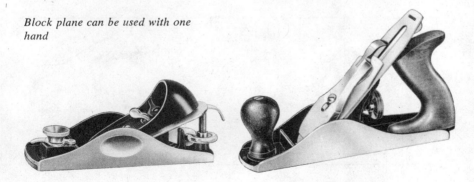

smoothing rough lumber, trimming boards to size and fitting of doors, screens and storm sash. Depending on size, bench planes are usually classified as smoothing planes, jack planes, fore planes and jointer planes.

The smoothing planes and the jack planes are the most popular models. These range from 7 inches in length to about 11½ inches in length for the longest jack planes. Fore and jointer planes vary from 18 to 24 inches in length. The principal advantage of the longer plane is the ease with which it can be used to smooth down long, straight boards. The long base tends to bridge low spots while removing the high spots.

To use a bench plane properly, grasp the large handle in one hand, and wrap the other hand around the knob at the front end. When planing the surface of a board, the plane should always be moved with the grain, rather than against it. If the wood fibers tend to tear and snag on the first stroke, the handyman should try reversing the work to achieve a smoother cut. For maximum cutting ease, and for the smoothest possible finish, always push the plane forward with straight, parallel strokes —but with the plane held at a slight angle to the direction of movement. This enables the sharp edge of the blade to "slice" through the wood neatly without tearing or snagging.

Care must also be exercised to avoid "rocking" the plane so that more material is removed at each end of the board than at the middle.

To do this properly, and to make certain the base of the plane is kept horizontal at the start of the stroke as well as at the end, you should bear down harder on the front knob as the stroke is begun. Then, as the plane passes over the far end of the board, press down harder on the rear handle. This will keep the front of the plane from dipping as it rides off the far end of the board.

The rules which apply to proper handling of bench planes also apply to block planes in most cases. However, since the blade on this tool is set at a much lower angle than that of a bench plane, it does a much smoother job of cutting end grain and edges. The tool is held in one hand, with the forefinger resting on a finger rest at the front.

To keep a plane working properly, its blade must be sharpened frequently by whetting on an oilstone. Care must be exercised to maintain the original bevel on the edge (approximately 25 to 30 degrees) by holding the blade with its beveled edge flat against the face of the stone while moving it back and forth with straight, parallel strokes. Grinding should be resorted to only when the cutting edge has been nicked or when the bevel has been badly worn.

To assure a smooth cut with uniform shavings that will curl neatly out of the way, the blade should be reassembled with the edge of the plane iron cap no more than 1/16 inch away from the cutting edge of the blade. This cap is the piece of heavy metal which clamps down on top of the plane iron blade to hold it in place against its frame.

POORLY FITTED   PROPERLY FITTED

Plywood, Working Techniques

When sawing panels to size, handle sheets so that splintering occurs on the back face only. With a handsaw this is accomplished by working with the good face up. When cutting on a circular bench or table saw the good face should also be up. However, with a portable circular saw or

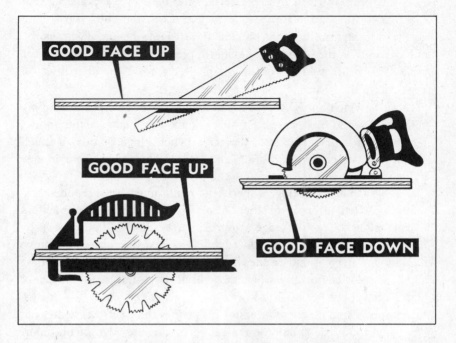

with an overhead radial arm saw the good face should always be down since the teeth cut from the opposite direction.

When it is important to get a clean cut on the back side as well as on the face, splintering can be minimized by first scoring deeply along the line of cut, using a sharp knife or a chisel. Another way to minimize splintering is to back up the sheet along the line of cut by clamping or temporarily nailing on a scrap piece of plywood or other lumber. Then cut through both at once. Splintering will occur on the scrap lumber instead of on the back side of the plywood panel.

Regardless of the type of saw being used (hand or power), a sharp blade having teeth with as little set as possible should be used. For hand sawing select a crosscut saw with fine teeth and hold it at a low angle to the surface. Power saw blades should be of the combination type, while hollow-ground blades will give the smoothest cut of all. For best results, adjust the depth of a circular saw blade so that it just protrudes through the thickness of the plywood.

To minimize splitting when boring holes, back up plywood panels with scrap pieces of lumber wherever possible. This scrap should be clamped or nailed tightly to the back side of the panel. It permits the cutting bit to pull clear through the plywood without splintering on the back. Any splintering that occurs will take place on the scrap lumber instead.

To minimize chipping when edges must be planed, always work from both ends in toward the middle. Never allow the plane blade to run off at either end. A tool which works even better than a plane for trimming plywood edges is one which has a multibladed face that is stamped out of a single sheet of flat steel—much like an old-fashioned potato grater. These tools are made in several sizes and shapes and are currently available in most hardware stores.

To minimize the problem of finishing or otherwise treating plywood edges, units should be designed so that edges are concealed wherever possible. Mitered joints or rabbeted joints will do the trick, but both these methods require power tools and careful fitting. An easier method consists of making a simple butt joint (glue should be used along with the nails or screws), then covering the exposed edge with a thin wood veneer. This can be purchased in flexible tape form, and it can be simply glued onto the edge of the plywood with contact cement or other adhesive.

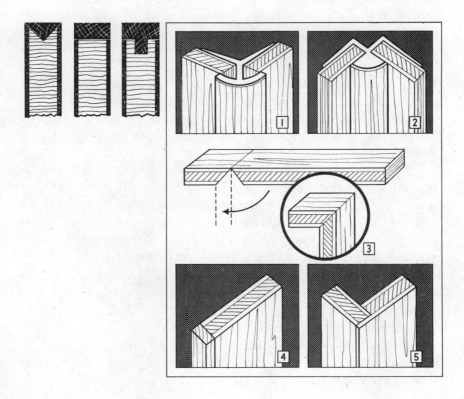

Another simple way to conceal edges when paint will be used for a final finish is to fill the exposed end grain with putty or spackling compound. These are available in both ready-mixed and powder form. Smear them on liberally and let dry, then sand smooth with fine sandpaper.

Edges can also be concealed effectively with moldings or solid wood strips which are nailed and glued into place. Even simpler to use are the special veneer-faced aluminum moldings which permit joining of panels either at right angles or end-to-end without edges being visible. Principally designed for use with hardwood paneling, these moldings are nailed directly to the supporting studs or framework. They hold panels firmly by locking onto the edges. They eliminate practically all need for nailing through the edges, and thus save on the job of countersinking and puttying.

Safety in the Workshop

To avoid unpleasant accidents when working with tools, every handyman should be familiar with a number of safety rules. The rules are a combination of ordinary common sense, coupled with a knowledge of how each tool should be handled. Here is a list of important safety precautions which should be observed when working with tools.

(1) Keep tools sharp and in good repair. Remember that a sharp cutting tool is much safer to use than a dull one. A sharp tool is less likely to slip and requires less force or pressure to get the job done. By the same token, a sharp saw or drill is less likely to cause accidents or damage to the work. Loose handles on hammers and other tools invite accidents, so replace or repair these promptly as soon as they are noticed.

(2) Wear the proper clothing for the job at hand. Snug-fitting clothing with sleeves that are short, or rolled all the way up, is best for most jobs. This is particularly true when working around power tools. Loose cuffs or dangling neckties can easily be caught or snagged, and gloves should not be worn when working with power tools. Hard-soled shoes are safer than sneakers or slippers in the workshop since they help protect the feet against nails and falling objects.

(3) When grinding, sanding or drilling in metal, stone or other hard materials, wear safety goggles to protect the eyes. Inexpensive plastic goggles with elastic headbands are available in most hardware stores for just this purpose. Goggles should also be worn when using paint remover or other caustic materials and whenever a job calls for working directly overhead.

(4) Make certain that drill bits, cutter blades and saw blades are properly installed in all power tools before starting to work. A frequent cause of accidents is a looseness or wobble which is caused by an improperly installed cutter or blade—or by a blade which flies free when full operating speed is attained.

(5) To eliminate the possibility of a serious shock (should an internal short develop), make certain that power tools are properly grounded with a three-wire cord and grounding receptacle—particularly when working outdoors or in damp locations. Some of the newer tools are available with double insulation built in to eliminate this need for grounding, but with most other tools a ground connection should definitely be provided.

(6) Keep tool handles and work areas clean. A greasy screwdriver handle or an oily power tool handle is another frequent cause of unnecessary accidents. Bench tops, shop floors and other areas where work is being done should be swept up frequently to minimize fire hazards and to eliminate accidental tripping or stumbling.

(7) Store tools properly so as to avoid nicking edges on cutting tools and to minimize the possibility of cutting your fingers when reaching into a jumbled drawer or box full of tools. Sharp tools should be neatly hung on racks or—if this is impractical—the cutting edges should be wrapped with strips of adhesive-backed tape before storing.

(8) Never lay a power tool down until all motion or rotation has ceased. On the other hand, never press the starter switch on any power

Goggles should be worn when grinder is in use

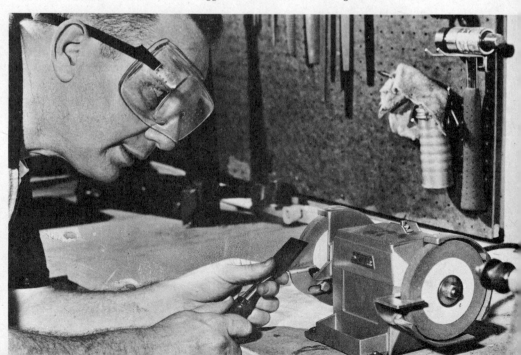

tool until you are certain you have a firm grip on it, with no likelihood of its slipping or shifting.

(9) Use the built-in guards provided on all good quality power tools. Most power saws, grinding wheels and similar tools come equipped with protective shields or guards to prevent accidental contact with moving parts. To avoid injury, make certain these guards are always in place and functioning properly before the tool is switched on. Stationary power tools should have belts shielded with protective covers of some kind wherever they are exposed.

(10) When changing blades or bits on power tools, always disconnect the power source (pull the plug out of its outlet) before making the necessary adjustments. Simply turning off the switch is not enough. All too often a tool will start accidentally when least expected—either because of a short or because the switch was inadvertently pressed.

(11) Make certain the work is held securely before using any power tool on it. Use clamps to grip small pieces, and make certain all boards are firmly supported before sawing or drilling through them. When sawing, make certain the scrap piece (the part that will be cut off) is also supported to prevent binding on the blade.

(12) Always provide adequate ventilation to permit toxic odors to escape and to help clear the air of sawdust or irritating fumes. Before using an electric tool, make certain there are no gasoline, naphtha or similar inflammable vapors present, since motors can throw sparks which might cause an explosion.

Sanding Machines, Portable

Electric sanders vary greatly in price. Light-duty, vibrator-driven models may sell for as little as $10, while a heavy-duty belt sander may cost anywhere from $50 to $100. For those home handymen who do not use these machines often enough to warrant purchasing one, there are hardware stores and tool rental agencies which rent these machines by the day or the week. Rates usually average from $1 to $5 per day, depending on size and style. Weekly rentals run from three to five times the daily rate in most cases.

Though all manufacturers do not necessarily agree on nomenclature, all portable electric sanders fall into one of three main categories: belt sanders, finishing sanders and disc sanders. Each type has definite advantages and limitations, and each is available in a wide assortment of sizes and price ranges.

Two of the most widely used types of sanding machines, the orbital sander (left)
and the belt sander (right)

The belt sander is the most powerful and the fastest-working machine
of all, and it is the one that is most frequently used by professional wood-
workers and cabinetmakers. It is ideal for smoothing down large flat
surfaces and for fast removal of heavy coats of paint or varnish. As its
name implies, the belt sander has a continuous abrasive belt which runs
over cylinders located at each end of the tool. On the bottom of the
machine there is a flat metal plate beneath which the belt runs. This
provides the necessary backing to keep the abrasive in even contact with
the work.

A belt sander is rated by the width of the abrasive belt which it uses.
Machines made for use by home handymen take belts from 2 to 4 inches
in width, with the 3-inch size being the most popular for general home
use. Special polishing belts are available for smoothing down to a final
finish and for polishing plastics, metals and similar materials.

Finishing sanders use flat sheets of sandpaper which are clamped to a
flat metal sole plate at the bottom of the machine. This plate usually has
a rubber facing to provide a cushion back for the sandpaper. It is driven
in either a straight-line (back-and-forth) or an orbital motion. Generally
speaking, finishing sanders fall into one of two classes: motor-driven

(usually called orbital or oscillating sanders) and vibrator-driven machines.

The vibrator type has a magnetic power unit rather than a conventional motor. It is intended only for light-duty polishing and fine finishing work, and moves the sandpaper with a straight-line action. It does a smooth job of fine sanding and polishing—but don't expect a vibrator unit to perform heavy-duty sanding or removing operations satisfactorily.

The motor-driven orbital or oscillating type of finishing sander is a heavier-duty machine which moves the sandpaper in a flat, oval path. It works faster than the vibrator but still retains its fine finishing characteristics. These motor-driven orbital sanders cost more than vibrator-driven machines, but they are well worth the difference. They can handle bigger jobs, and they are definitely more of an all-purpose machine than the vibrator models. Some motor-driven models give a choice of either straight-line or orbital action by operating a key at the back.

Belt sander with dust catcher

Because all finishing sanders have flat rectangular pads for holding the abrasive paper, they permit moving flush into corners and can often be used in places where a belt sander could not. They also offer savings in the cost of abrasive sheets, since all models are designed so that standard sheets of sandpaper can be cut down to the size needed. Some require that a standard sheet of sandpaper be cut into thirds, while others use a quarter- or a half-size sheet. The paper is held in place by clamps at each end of the pad.

Since all orbital sanders have a slower cutting action than the belt sanders, they are safer to use on thin veneers and wherever a high quality finish is needed. However, they are hardly practical for rough jobs, such as removing paint or finishing of rough lumber. Like the belt sander, the finishing sander can also be used for final polishing of plastics, metals and finished surfaces. Special polishing pads are substituted for the usual abrasive sheet.

The rotary disc type of sander has a round flat pad which is partially flexible. It takes circular discs of sandpaper which vary from 4 to 6 inches in diameter. The abrasive disc is usually attached with a screw which fits into a recess in the center so that it does not interfere with the sanding action.

In their most widely used form, disc sanders usually consist of spindle-mounted accessories which are clamped into the chuck of an ordinary electric drill. However, for maximum efficiency and for rugged steady use, a regular disc sanding machine which has been designed specifically for that purpose should be purchased or rented. Frequent or continuous sanding with a disc clamped in an electric drill will overload the drill bearings and may eventually burn out the drill motor.

Disc sanders are primarily intended for fast removal of stock as well as for removing accumulated coats of paint or varnish. They are not intended for use in fine finishing operations, but are ideal for polishing when a lambswool bonnet or pad is substituted for the abrasive disc.

When disc sanders are used for smoothing down rough stock or removing old finishes, they must be held so that the disc contacts the surface at an angle with only the outer half of the abrasive sheet doing the work. Amateurs will often find that it takes some experience to prevent the disc from "digging in" and making unsightly swirl marks or deep scratches in the surface. The easiest way to avoid this is to keep the disc moving continuously. Sweep it back and forth with a gliding motion and take care never to allow the edge of the disc to dig deeply in at any point. To do this it is imperative that only moderate pressure be applied, with no effort being made to press hard against the surface.

Regardless of the type of sander being used (belt, disc or finishing), the home handyman should remember to avoid bearing down excessively. Extra pressure only slows down the action of the machine and makes it cut slower—rather than faster. In addition, undue wear is caused on the abrasive paper, as well as on the motor and bearings. Always start with the coarsest grit, then work progressively down to finer grits when necessary. Wherever practical, sand with the grain only, especially on the final finish.

Never start or stop a machine while the abrasive is in contact with the work, and remember always to keep the machine moving steadily without allowing it to stand in one spot for any length of time. This is particularly important with belt sanders because they cut so rapidly. All sanders should be prevented from rocking over the edges to keep corners from being rounded off.

Sandpaper, Selection and Use

Basically speaking, there are five general types of sandpaper widely available in most paint and hardware stores. These are: flint paper, garnet paper, emery cloth, aluminum oxide paper and silicon carbide paper. Of these, the first three are natural minerals or abrasives, while the last two are synthetic materials which are tougher and longer-wearing than the natural abrasives.

Aluminum oxide is a synthetic abrasive which is exceptionally hard and long-wearing. Generally brownish in color, aluminum oxide papers cost more per sheet than the flint papers or the garnet papers, but they will last many times longer on most jobs. Because it is truly an all-purpose abrasive which can be used on wood, metal or painted surfaces, aluminum oxide is fast becoming the most widely used of all sandpapers. It is also the best type to use with all kinds of sanding machines, regardless of whether the machine is used for rough sanding or fine finishing (obviously, different grits would be used in each case).

Silicon-carbide is also a synthetic abrasive and it is even harder than aluminum oxide. However, it is very brittle, so points break off and it tends to dull rapidly. However, it is still the abrasive most frequently used on heavy-duty floor-sanding machines, as well as for sanding of ceramics, glass and hard plastics. Most of the fine-grit, wet-or-dry waterproof papers (used for final finishing) are also coated with silicon carbide.

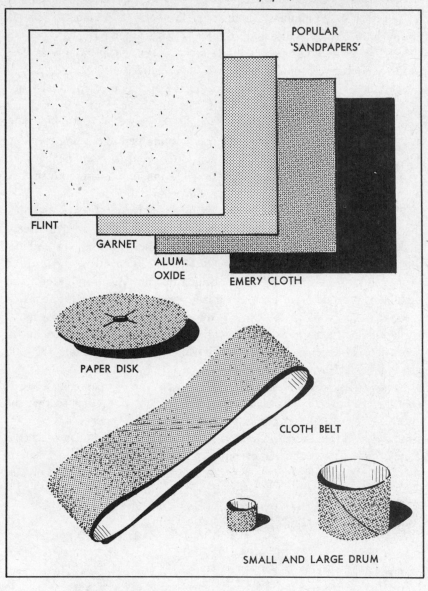

POPULAR 'SANDPAPERS'

FLINT

GARNET

ALUM. OXIDE

EMERY CLOTH

PAPER DISK

CLOTH BELT

SMALL AND LARGE DRUM

For heavy sanding on extremely rough surfaces and for removing heavy coats of paint or varnish, the very coarse (VC) grit (30) aluminum oxide paper is usually used. To remove deep grooves and other imperfections in wood or metal and for average stock removal, the coarse (C) grit (50) should be used. The medium (M) grit (80) paper is used for most preliminary sanding on raw wood, as well as to remove normal imperfections and small scratches. This grit is also used for removing light amounts of stock when creating snug-fitting joints, as well as for removing rust and other blemishes on metal.

The fine (F) grit (120) aluminum oxide paper is used for final sanding on bare wood surfaces just before the first coat of primer or sealer is applied. This grit is also used on metal surfaces for removing light coatings of rust, as well as for final conditioning before starting to paint. The very fine (VF) grit (220) is most often used for sanding between coats of paint or varnish, as well as for achieving an extra-smooth surface on hardwood which is to be given a clear or natural finish.

Wet-or-dry sandpapers have a flexible, waterproof backing so that they can be dipped into water or light lubricating oil when a lubricant is desired for finer cutting action. Usually coated with silicon carbide, this sandpaper comes in various grits (from 220 to 600) and is used principally for fine finishing and polishing operations on both wood and metal. Light crude oil or rubbing oil is generally used as the lubricant on wood surfaces, while soapy water is the most popular lubricant for metal surfaces. The finer grits (400) may be used with a suitable lubricant to rub out dust specks or air bubbles, while for final polishing the 600 grit is used—also with a lubricant.

Most sandpapers come in two styles: closed coat or open coat. Closed-coat papers have the abrasive grains packed tightly together so that the entire surface of the paper is covered. Open-coat papers have grains spread out so that there are spaces between them. As a rule, closed-coat papers cut faster because they have more abrasive particles per square inch—but they are also more likely to become clogged when used on soft

70%
COATED

OPEN COAT PAPER

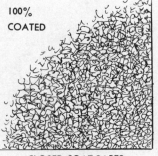

100%
COATED

CLOSED COAT PAPER

materials. An open-coat paper, therefore, will work better on softwoods, painted surfaces and similar materials since it is less likely to clog or "load up." This rule can be ignored when you are removing old paint by hand sanding. In this case a fast-cutting, closed-coat flint paper (coarse) is usually used. It will clog quickly, but its low cost makes it feasible to throw sheets away as soon as they become loaded.

Saws, Hand

The first handsaw which should be acquired by every home handyman is the ordinary crosscut saw. This is used for straight cuts in all types of wood and wood composition panels. As it name implies, the crosscut saw is designed principally for cutting across the grain rather than with it. It comes in various lengths from 16 to 26 inches, though the most popular size for all-purpose work is a 24- or 26-inch model. A shorter

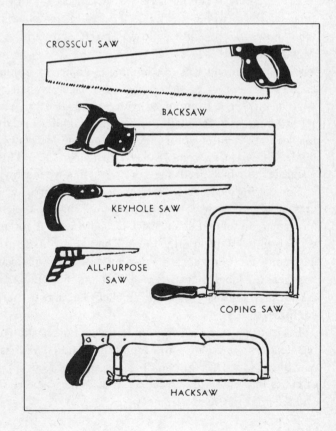

CROSSCUT SAW

BACKSAW

KEYHOLE SAW

ALL-PURPOSE SAW

COPING SAW

HACKSAW

blade may be preferred if only light work is contemplated or if the tool must be stored in a small toolbox.

In addition to different lengths, crosscut saws also vary as to the number of teeth per inch. Models are available with from 6 to 11 teeth (points) per inch. However, the most practical selection for the average home handyman is an 8-point blade. This will not leave as fine an edge as a 10- or 11-point saw, but it will cut faster and with less effort, and it can be used for ripping (cutting with the grain), as well as for cross-cutting.

Though a crosscut saw will work reasonably well when cutting with the grain (ripping) on occasional jobs, a ripsaw will do the job better and with much less effort. Resembling a crosscut saw in general appearance, the ripsaw has about the same length blade, but it has only about 5½ or 6 teeth to the inch. The teeth are also shaped differently. The cutting edges are more nearly square, so that each tooth actually resembles a small chisel. The bevels, or angles, of the teeth are also different, creating a cutting action in which each tooth actually chips out small pieces of wood, much like a series of tiny chisels (as compared to the action of a crosscut saw in which the teeth tend to slice, or cut their way through).

For fine, straight cuts in trimming moldings or in making wood joints, a special type of crosscut saw, called a backsaw, can be used. The back edge of this blade is equipped with a rigid steel brace, and the handle is set at an angle to facilitate horizontal cuts. Often used with a miter box for accurate right-angle or miter cutting, the backsaw has a fine-toothed blade which varies from 18 to 32 teeth per inch. This gives a smooth, accurate cut which needs little or no sanding when complete.

For cutting holes in the center of a panel, or in walls, floors or ceilings, a keyhole saw or compass saw is a handy tool to have. This saw has a narrow, tapered blade which can be used for inside cuts after a starting hole has been drilled first. The narrow blade also facilitates making many kinds of curved cuts; models also are available with interchangeable blades that vary in size, shape and number of teeth per inch. As a rule, keyhole saws are smaller and more sharply pointed than compass saws.

For cutting intricate curves in thin wood or plastic (up to about 1 inch in thickness), a coping saw is the tool to use. This has a very fine, narrow blade which permits sharp turns and tight curves, though the depth of cut is limited by the throat clearance (the distance between the blade and the back of the saw frame).

Coping saws have blades with pins or loops at each end for insertion in holders in each side of the frame. The blades can be turned so that the saw can be used to cut sideways as well as straight ahead, and special metal-cutting blades are available for cutting soft metals or hard plastics.

Every home tool kit should include at least one metal-cutting hacksaw in addition to the wood-cutting saws previously mentioned. This tool consists of a steel frame which takes replaceable blades that vary from 14 to 32 teeth to the inch, depending on the hardness and thickness of the metal being cut. While some hacksaw frames take only a single length blade, the most popular models are adjustable. They usually take either 10- or 12-inch blades.

Generally speaking, the coarser blades (14 or 18 teeth to the inch) should be used for thicker metals, while the finer blades (24 teeth to the inch) work best on thinner materials up to ½ inch in thickness. For thin sheet metal and thin-walled tubing (⅛ inch or less) the 32-tooth blade works best.

Combining the features of a small keyhole saw with those of a hacksaw, the all-purpose saw is a useful little tool which will cut metal as well as wood—and curves as well as straight lines. Consisting of a fine-toothed, tapered blade, which is handy for making cuts in tight corners, this saw is often used for cutting off nails behind moldings or trim, as well as for cutting hard plastics. It is also handy for cutting small openings in plaster or gypsum board.

Seldom more than 6 to 8 inches in length, these little saws are a handy "extra" to be carried in the toolbox at all times. They will handle many unexpected emergency cuts that might otherwise call for the use of a coping saw, hacksaw or keyhole saw.

Saws, Power, Portable

Portable electric saws will cut all types of material with a minimum of effort and in a fraction of the time required for hand-sawing. Though there are many variations on the market, two types are most popular for home mechanics: portable circular saws and portable jigsaws, or sabre saws.

As its name indicates, a circular saw uses a circular blade which rotates in a counterclockwise direction while the saw is passed over the top of the work. Jigsaws or sabre saws have a straight blade, and they cut with a reciprocating, up-and-down motion. They will cut curves or straight lines, but for straight cutting of heavy lumber or large boards

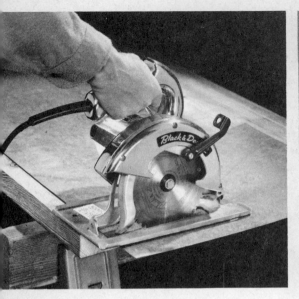

Circular saw has depth-of-cut adjustment

Sabre saw is handy for cutting panels

the circular saw is faster and more accurate. However, when curved cuts are required, or when working with thin panels of plywood or hardboard, a sabre saw or jigsaw is the tool to use.

Circular saws will make bevel cuts or angle cuts with equal ease, and they are ideal for cutting up 2x4's, large panels and structural lumber of all kinds. They are rated according to the diameter of the blade, and range in size from a little over 5 inches to as much as 12 inches in diameter. For home handymen the most popular sizes are those with blades of from 6 to 8 inches in diameter. The 6-inch models will easily rip or crosscut a 2x4, even at a 45-degree angle. For heavier timbers, an 8-inch saw would probably be a better selection. Most saws come equipped with a general-purpose combination blade which can be used for either ripping or crosscutting. If a great deal of ripping is required, a special rip blade should be purchased for faster cutting action and longer life. Crosscut blades also are available and give a smoother cut on those jobs where only crosscutting is required.

For a really smooth cut that will require little or no sanding—particularly on plywood panels—a hollow-ground combination blade should be used. This cuts more slowly than the other blades, but it is intended mainly for use in cabinetwork for cutting moldings, prefinished panels or fine hardwoods.

Base plate tilts saw for bevel cutting

There are also special fine-tooth blades available for cutting soft wall-board and thin plastics, as well as carbide-tipped blades for cutting hard materials, such as asbestos-cement boards or plastic laminates. Abrasive cut-off wheels also can be purchased for sawing through metals and masonry.

All properly designed circular saws have a spring-actuated blade guard which keeps the lower half of the saw blade covered when it is not in use. As the saw is fed into the work, the guard swings back out of the way until the cut is completed. Then it automatically swings back over the blade to cover it again. Some models also have kick-proof clutches. These eliminate the dangers of burning out the motor and of the work kicking back toward you should the blade bind or jam in the middle of the cut.

In use, the portable circular saw is basically a right-handed tool which is used much like a handsaw. The biggest difference is that the blade cuts from the bottom up—so the work should always be placed with the good face down. In this way, any ragged edges will be left on the top, or back side, of the board, rather than on the face. Always be careful to cut on the waste side of the line so that the width of the saw cut will not affect the final measurement of the board. For safe and accurate sawing, the work should always be rigidly supported, preferably with two or more

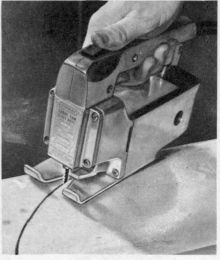

*Depth of cut when properly
adjusted*

The sabre saw follows curved line easily

sawhorses. One of them should be close enough to the line of cut to prevent vibration or binding, and a third support should be provided if the waste piece is too heavy to support with one hand.

All of these saws have a depth adjustment which permits raising or lowering the base plate to control the depth to which the saw blade will project. Generally speaking, it is best to adjust this so that the blade just cuts through the work at the bottom. This provides for maximum safety combined with the smoothest possible cut. However, it does require more power, so for hardwoods or other hard-to-cut materials, the blade will have to be set deeper. The depth adjustment also can be used for sawing rabbets, dadoes and other cuts which involve sawing only part way through the work.

Since portable sabre saws or jigsaws can cut curves as well as straight lines, they have become increasingly popular with home workshop enthusiasts since their introduction some years ago. These versatile cutting tools are light in weight and surprisingly powerful, and they can do almost everything that a stationary or table model jigsaw can do. However, they are more convenient in that they can be brought to the work, rather than having the work brought to them. This is obviously a great advantage when materials which are already fastened in place must be cut or when large sheets of plywood or plastic laminate must be handled.

Made in various sizes and styles, and by many different manufacturers, models are available which will cut lumber up to 2 inches in thickness.

Most have built-in blowers to keep the cutting line free of dust and chips while the saw is in action, and blades are available for wood, metal, plastics, rubber, leather, floor tiles and other materials. As a rule, fine-tooth blades should be used on metals and other hard materials, while coarser blades are used for ordinary lumber and generally thicker materials.

One of the neatest tricks these electric handsaws can do is to cut their own starting hole when inside "pocket" cuts or plunge cuts must be made. The motor is started while the saw is tilted all the way forward on its nose with its front edge resting on the work. With the blade in motion, the saw is gradually tilted backward to lower the blade into the wood. If done slowly, the blade will actually cut its way through until the base is flat against the work, with the blade projecting through. The cut can then proceed in the usual manner. This trick is particularly handy when openings must be cut in the centers of larger panels or when cutouts are required in walls or floors.

When cutting with one of these saws, be sure the work is firmly supported or braced in order to minimize the danger of excessive vibration. Large pieces can be placed across several sawhorses, while smaller pieces can be held with clamps or gripped in a vise. When straight cuts must

Sabre saw needs no starting hole when opening must be cut

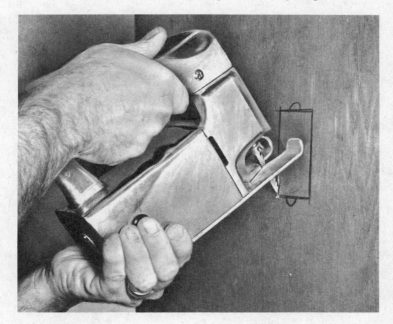

be made, accuracy can be assured by clamping a straightedge of some kind on top of the work to serve as a guide.

Saws, Power, Stationary

For really accurate cutting, and for mitering and grooving in all types of lumber and paneling, a stationary type of circular saw is undoubtedly the most widely accepted—and most widely used—power tool. Probably the most popular of all machine tools for home workshops, circular saws generally fall into one of two categories: table saws and radial arm saws. Table saws are built so that the saw blade projects up through a slot in the center of the table, while on radial arm saws the blade is mounted directly on a motor which is suspended overhead on a radial arm track. When cuts are made on a table saw, the blade remains in one place and the work is pushed forward into it to make the cut. On a radial saw, the work remains stationary and the saw blade is pulled forward over the top to complete the cut.

When accuracy is the most important consideration, a table saw is undoubtedly the number one choice. To permit cutting bevels (cuts made with the blade at other than a 90-degree angle to the surface), circular saws are designed so that either the blade or the table can be tilted. Tilting table models are less expensive than those which have tilting blades; but the tilting blade models (usually referred to as a tilting arbor saw) are much easier to use. The work always lies flat on a permanently horizontal table so that there is less danger of the lumber sliding or shifting when a bevel cut is being made—as would be the case on a tilting table saw.

An important safety feature on all table saws is the ability to raise or lower the blade so that it projects up only high enough to cut through

With radial arm saw, lumber remains stationary

Work is held tight against miter gage while pressing forward

the work. On tilting table models, it is the table which raises or lowers. On tilting arbor models the blade is raised or lowered while the table remains stationary. This ability to adjust the height of the blade is particularly valuable in operations where the saw is to cut only part way through the work, and in many grooving and sanding operations (where the saw blade is replaced by a series of special grooving cutters or by an abrasive-faced disc).

Circular saws are usually rated according to the size blade they will accommodate. Thus an 8-inch saw is one which takes an 8-inch-diameter blade—while a 10-inch saw takes a 10-inch blade. The most popular sizes for the home workshop are the 8- and 10-inch models.

For safety's sake, most table saws are equipped with a combination splitter and saw guard. The guard may be made of metal or plastic, and it is designed to slide down over the top of the blade to cover the exposed teeth while the cut is being made. The splitter consists of a vertical metal plate which is directly in line with the saw blade. As the lumber slides past, the saw kerf, or slot, is held open so that the wood will not bind or "grab" on the saw's teeth.

Crosscutting and ripping (sawing with the grain) are the two most common operations for which a circular saw is used. To facilitate accurate crosscutting at any angle, a crosscut guide, which includes a miter gauge, is provided. This slides in a groove in the saw table to feed the work into the blade. The work is held snugly against this gauge and pushed steadily forward. Most tables have a groove on each side of the blade so that cuts can be made from either side. If cuts are to be made at other than a 90-degree angle the gauge can be pivoted to the angle desired.

For ripping cuts, the miter gauge is removed and a rip guide installed in its place. This is a long metal fence which runs the length of the table.

Saw guard covers blade while cutting

It can be moved back and forth at various distances from the saw blade and is designed to remain parallel to the saw blade once initial adjustments have been made. The work is fed through the saw blade while one edge is kept in firm contact with the rip fence.

When crosscutting, press the work firmly against the gauge with one hand. To minimize shifting or wobbling of long pieces, an auxiliary wood fence can be fastened to the face of the gauge to provide additional support for the work as it is pushed forward. Care must be exercised to grip the work firmly, and the handyman should never attempt to hold on to or touch the cut-off piece until the saw blade has stopped rotating.

When ripping long boards to a narrow width, the fingers would normally have to come quite close to the saw blade—if the hand alone were being used to push the work past the blade. To prevent this, the work should be pushed forward until the end of the board is a few inches away from the saw blade. At this point, a push stick should be used instead of the fingers to push the board the rest of the way through. This push stick is simply a scrap length of wood with a notch cut at one end as shown.

When operating a power saw of any kind, the handyman should make certain that the blade is adjusted so that it projects no more than ¼ inch above the work for maximum safety. The splitter guide should be used for all ripping operations, and no ties or other loose garments should ever be worn. Sleeves should be buttoned at the wrist or rolled all the way up, and jewelry should be removed from hands and wrists. In addition, the handyman should stand slightly to one side when cutting (not directly behind the saw blade) so that if the work is suddenly thrown backward by the blade there will be no danger of his being hit by flying pieces.

Push stick is used when narrow boards are cut

Motor and saw tilts for making bevel cuts

As mentioned previously, radial saws differ from ordinary table saws in that the blade cuts from on top of the work rather than from below. The saw blade is attached directly to the motor shaft, and the motor is in turn mounted on a yoke which permits it to be swiveled or turned in any direction. This yoke hangs from a horizontal overhead arm and is mounted on a track so that the entire unit can be slid back and forth without difficulty. For crosscut work, the overhead arm and the tilting mechanism are both locked in the 90-degree position so that the saw can simply be pulled forward across the board to complete the cut. For miter-cutting the overhead arm can be swung to one side to guide the motor-and-saw unit in the required direction. In addition to swinging the arm to either side, the user can also raise or lower it by means of a crank so that the height of the saw blade above the table can be adjusted for grooving, plowing or dadoing.

When bevel cuts are to be made, the motor and saw blade are tilted inside the yoke to the angle desired. Here again, locking controls are provided to lock the blade at any angle—with positive stops usually provided at the 45- and 90-degree positions. This combination of movements permits making all types of compound miter cuts, since the saw can be drawn across the board in any direction while the blade is tilted at any angle from 90 degrees down.

Overhead arm swings for sawing at angle

All of these operations are carried out while the work lies stationary on the table, since the saw blade is drawn back and forth across the top to cut it. The one exception is when a long board is being ripped (cut lengthwise). In this case the saw blade is turned at right angles to its normal position so that it is parallel to the rip fence or guide fence at the back. Then it is locked firmly in position and the board is fed lengthwise through the blade.

To permit ripping long boards in this manner, and to facilitate handling of large panels when necessary, these power saws are usually mounted against the wall with about 6 or 7 feet of unobstructed space on either side (at table height). The saw can be placed on top of any cabinet or workbench, or it may be purchased with special metal stands which are made for the purpose. Since the radial arm saw permits cutting at almost any angle—or combination of angles—there is seldom an occasion when time-consuming or awkward jigs will be necessary to hold the work in place.

The ease with which the motor can be tilted to any position, combined with its power and speed (usually from 1½ to 2 horsepower at 3,450 rpm), makes this type of power saw ideal for other workshop operations, such as grinding, sanding, shaping and planing. For these operations the saw blade is removed from the motor spindle and replaced with the appropriate tool or accessory.

For cutting a dado (groove), a dado head is substituted for the saw blade. With the motor set in a vertical 90-degree position (so the spindle points straight down), the dado head can be used for rabbeting or for cutting tenons. By substituting a shaper head (also called a molding head) for the dado attachment, the tool instantly becomes a versatile shaper, which will cut all types of molding and will do edge jointing.

This vertical position of the motor shaft can also be used with a rotary planer attachment for surfacing boards or for cutting them down in thickness. With the motor in its normal horizontal position, sanding discs, grinding wheels and buffing wheels can be used for all types of shaping and polishing operations. In addition, an adapter chuck can be fastened in place to convert the tool to a horizontal drill press which will bore holes at any angle.

Screwdrivers, Selection and Use

Probably the most frequently used—and misused—tool around the home is the ordinary screwdriver. All too often used as a scraper, chisel, prying tool or can opener, a screwdriver blade can be easily damaged so that it no longer works satisfactorily when used on the only job for which it was designed—that of driving or loosening screws.

Whenever possible, the screwdriver selected should have a blade that just fits the slot in the screwhead, both in thickness and width. If the blade is too narrow, there will be a loss of leverage and the tip will tend to slip out of the slot. If, on the other hand, the blade is too wide, it will project beyond the screw slot on either side and will gouge out the surface of the work when the screwhead is flush against the surface.

If the screwdriver blade is too thin, it will fit loosely inside the screw slot and will be difficult to turn. In addition, a great deal of extra downward pressure will be required to keep the blade from sliding out of the slot. An excessively narrow blade will also twist or bend under heavy pressure and will wear rapidly at the corners, making it almost impossible to get a firm grip inside the screwhead.

A properly shaped screwdriver blade should be ground so that the tip is straight and square. The flat sides of the blade should gradually taper out to meet the shank, but the taper should be so gradual that the sides are nearly parallel to each other at the very end. This is necessary to assure that the driving torque is transmitted to the sides of the screw slot uniformly on both sides. A sharp edge (like a chisel blade) would keep the tip of the blade from resting solidly against the bottom of the slot.

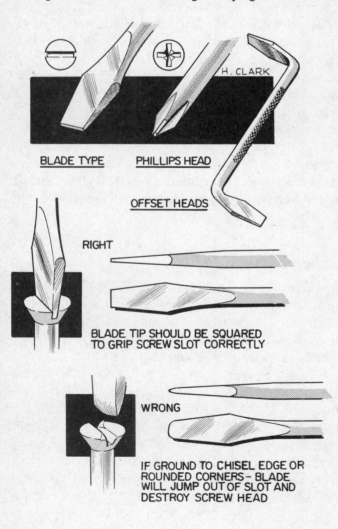

BLADE TYPE   PHILLIPS HEAD

H. CLARK

OFFSET HEADS

RIGHT

BLADE TIP SHOULD BE SQUARED
TO GRIP SCREW SLOT CORRECTLY

WRONG

IF GROUND TO CHISEL EDGE OR
ROUNDED CORNERS – BLADE
WILL JUMP OUT OF SLOT AND
DESTROY SCREW HEAD

Screwdrivers are generally sized according to the total length of blade and shaft combined. Homeowners will find that two or three sizes from 3 to 6 inches in length will handle all common jobs around the house. The standard screwdriver (commonly referred to as a Phillips head driver) will also prove useful for those screws which have this type of head. For really heavy-duty work, screwdrivers with special square shanks are also available. These resist a much greater turning force and permit the user to apply a wrench to the shank when additional leverage is required.

Though a wrench can be safely used on a square-shank screwdriver of this kind, the practice of using pliers or other tools to grip the flat blade of an ordinary screwdriver (so that increased torque can be applied) is not to be recommended. Since these screwdrivers were not designed to resist a heavy turning force of this kind, the blade could be easily bent or twisted out of shape.

For working in cramped quarters or tight corners where an ordinary screwdriver will not fit, there are special "stubby" screwdrivers which can be used. These have very short blades and squat handles, and they are made in both light- and heavy-duty models. Offset screwdrivers are also available for jobs of this kind. They have the blade end bent at right angles, and often have a blade at each end. They enable you to reach into very tight corners, while at the same time they permit applying a great deal more leverage than would be possible with a straight screwdriver.

Home mechanics who do a great deal of work involving the use of a screwdriver can save both time and effort by purchasing a spiral-type, ratchet-drive screwdriver. With this tool you merely push down on the handle to turn the blade in either direction—depending on how the ratchet control is set beforehand. The blade can also be locked rigidly in position for use as a standard screwdriver, or the "push-pull" mechanism can be locked so that the screwdriver has a simple ratchet handle without the spiral-drive mechanism.

Another screwdriving tool which can save both time and effort—particularly on large screws where additional leverage is required—is a screwdriver bit that can be chucked into an ordinary carpenter's brace just like a regular auger. Screwdriving bits of this kind come in various sizes, and with either a standard or cross-slot blade. They can be very handy for jobs where a great many large screws must be driven—particularly in hardwood.

To simplify the job of starting a screw in close quarters—and to enable you to start screws easily when only one hand is available—home mechanics can purchase special screw-holding drivers. These have little claws that hold the screwhead against the tip of the blade while the screw is being started. After the screw is in place, the claws can be easily released by a little extra pressure or by a twisting action on the handle.

When a screwdriver tip becomes worn, bent or chipped, it should be reshaped by grinding or filing. Care should be exercised to retain the original taper and to keep the sides of the blade almost parallel near the end. Never file the tip to a knifelike edge. Instead, the tip should have a square, blunt point which will seat snugly against the bottom of the screw slot when pressed into place.

Screws, Wood, Selection and Use

Wood screws enable the home carpenter to assemble quickly all kinds of woodworking projects. When properly used, they form strong, permanent joints, which will not work loose even under repeated vibration and heavy stress.

All wood screws consist of three different parts: a head, which is slotted so that the screw can be driven into the wood with a driver; an unthreaded body or shank section immediately below the head; and a threaded portion which tapers to a point at the tip. Though screws may vary in many ways, they are most often classified according to the shape

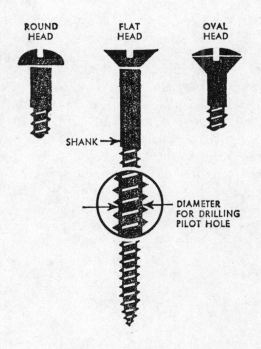

of the head. The three most popular styles are: round head, oval head and flat head. Very large screws also are available with a special hexagon or square-shaped head so they can be driven with a wrench instead of a screwdriver. These are used only in heavy-duty structural work and are seldom required for home woodworking projects.

Though most of the screws sold have an ordinary straight slot in the head, all three styles also are available with special cross-slotted heads, which are designed for use with a Phillips-type screwdriver, rather than the usual straight blade. These simplify the job of keeping the blade centered on the screwhead and permit truer driving. At the same time they enable the user to apply a greater amount of pressure with less chance of the blade slipping.

Flat head screws are usually installed so that the head sits flush with the wood surface on top. To do so, the hole for the screw must be countersunk with a special countersink bit. These bits can be used in an ordinary hand drill, electric drill or carpenter's brace. They carve out a cone-shaped depression so the head can be neatly recessed.

Oval head screws are also recessed by countersinking, but they have an oval top which projects above the surface. Because they are intended to be more decorative, these screws are most often available in brass or chrome. Round head screws do not require countersinking at all, since they are designed for installation with the heads protruding from the surface and fully exposed.

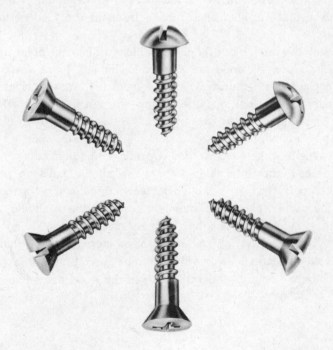

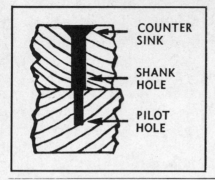

COUNTER SINK

SHANK HOLE

PILOT HOLE

Pilot Hole—Shank hole in first piece of wood is larger than the pilot hole in the second piece of wood

When two pieces of wood are joined together with screws, pilot holes must first be bored, especially in hardwood. These pilot holes not only allow the screws to be driven easily, but minimize the possibility of splitting the wood or of causing damage to the screw.

On most installations the wood screw goes through one piece of wood and the threaded portion locks into a second piece of wood behind it. The pilot hole in the second piece of wood should be smaller—about equal to the diameter of the solid center of the threaded portion of the screw. This pilot hole in the second piece of wood should be drilled deep enough so that it is about half the length of the threaded portion of the screw.

To simplify the job of drilling two different diameter holes into a joint when the pieces of wood are already assembled, home carpenters can buy special two-stage drills which automatically bore the right size pilot and shank hole in one operation. They also cut a recess in the surface at the same time for countersinking flat head screws or for counterboring any type of screw.

The length of the screw needed depends on the thickness of the pieces being joined. Ideally speaking, the screw should have an unthreaded shank or body just long enough to reach through the top board. The threaded portion can be as long as necessary—but it should always be at least ⅛ inch less than the thickness of the bottom board. Thicker (larger diameter) screws naturally have more strength than thinner ones, so the selection of size will have to be based on the strength needed in the joint, as well as on the thickness of the wood being joined.

Wood screws are made from many different metals (steel, brass, aluminum, etc.). They come with either a plain finish or a chrome, cadmium or nickel-plated finish. Steel screws generally are stronger than brass or aluminum, but unless they are specially plated to resist rust, the brass and aluminum screws are better for use outdoors where rust may be a problem. Wood-screw sizes are usually specified by two dimensions: length and diameter. Lengths are described in inches, but the diameter is designated by a gauge number. The smallest common size (#0) is about $\frac{1}{16}$ of an inch in diameter, while the largest commonly used size (#24) is a little under $\frac{3}{8}$ of an inch in diameter.

To simplify the task of selecting the right diameter drill for boring pilot holes for each size screw, most dealers have special charts which give this information for all sizes of screws. In most cases, a slightly larger hole is recommended in hardwoods, while a smaller pilot hole is adequate for softwoods.

For driving screws, a screwdriver should be used with a blade that just fits in the screwhead slot. Using too small a screwdriver not only makes the job more difficult, but increases the chances of slipping and often results in the screwhead being so chewed up that it becomes difficult to drive the screw completely in. Always keep the blade centered in the slot and apply pressure straight along the shaft of the screw to avoid any tendency toward wobbling or off-center driving. To ease installation, screw threads can be rubbed lightly over a cake of soap to lubricate them.

Soldering Guns

A moderately priced "power tool" which can be exceptionally handy is a trigger-action electric soldering gun. In addition to its basic function as an easy-to-use soldering iron which heats up almost immediately—and which greatly simplifies small soldering and electrical repair jobs—this versatile tool can be used for dozens of other jobs around the house.

Soldering guns differ from ordinary soldering irons in that they have a pistol-shaped grip and a trigger which is pressed when heat is desired. The tip heats up quickly so that working temperatures are reached within a few seconds, thus speeding up all soldering operations. When the trigger is released, the gun is automatically turned off so that current consumption is reduced to a minimum. In addition, since the tip cools quickly, the gun can be stored or laid down safely with less danger of causing accidental burn marks or scorches.

Because of the smallness of the tip, and because of the almost instant heating action of these soldering guns, they have long been the standard tool for use in electric and electronic repair work and for the soldering of all types of intricate or hard-to-reach assemblies. Tips can be changed to suit the work at hand; these range from small, needle-like points (for use in assembling hi-fi kits and similar work) to large flat tips which can be used for sweat-soldering metal assemblies.

Guns vary in capacity, from small-size units which are rated at less than 100 watts to large heavy-duty models which are rated at 300 watts or more. Since practically all of these guns are designed to accept a variety of different-shaped tips, they can be used for many other jobs besides soldering. A special smoothing tip is available for use in sealing plastic film when foods must be wrapped (supermarkets have been using these guns for just this purpose for many years), and this same smoothing tip can be used for repairing plastic toys, shower curtains, raincoats and other items made of thermoplastic material. The flat tip is allowed to reach full heat, then pressed gently over the crack or tear. The heat will literally "weld" the plastic by melting it so that it fuses back together again.

In addition to the smoothing tip, there is a knife-edged cutting tip which can be used for quickly cutting plastic floor tiles or wall tiles. For a smooth job, keep the heated cutting edge moving at a uniform pace and maintain a steady, light pressure at all times. This same knife-edged tip is also the answer to the problem of removing hardened putty from an old window frame when a broken pane of glass must be replaced. Simply

Soldering gun is ideal for electrical repairs

Knife-edged tip is used to cut plastic tile

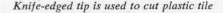

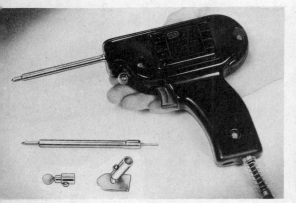
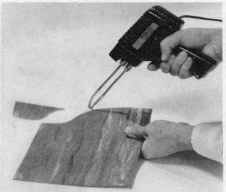

run the cutting tip slowly along the joint where the putty meets the wood. The heat will soften up the putty, while the sharp edge of the tip will peel the putty away neatly. Because of the high heat they attain, these cutting tips can also be used for burning monograms, names or other designs into wood plaques or signs.

To change tips on any of these soldering guns, you need only loosen one or two screws. Most of the better models have a built-in lamp above the tip to cast needed illumination over the work area while the gun is in use. The lamp lights up whenever the trigger is pressed.

Soldering Techniques

Soldering is a fairly simple technique which can be used for permanently joining many different kinds of metals together. It is particularly useful in electrical repairs (it makes permanent, vibration-free connections), as well as for joining sheet metal or tubing together in many applications where copper, zinc, brass, iron and steel are being used.

Ordinary "soft" solder consists of a mixture of lead and tin in varying proportions—depending on the uses to which the solder will be put. When this alloy is heated to its melting point (usually from 400 to 500 degrees), it flows into and around the preheated joint to bond the metal surfaces together as it cools. This type of solder is commonly sold in three forms: bar, solid wire, and hollow-cored wire with a soldering flux on the inside.

In addition to the soft solders, there are the so-called hard solders or silver solders. These consist of various alloys of silver or brass, and they have much higher melting points than the soft solders. Because of the higher temperatures required, some sort of blowtorch is required—rather than a heated soldering iron. Hard solders give a much stronger joint than do the soft solders, so they are frequently used for assembling jewelry and for other projects where high strength or heat resistance is required. Small propane torches seldom furnish enough heat for soldering of this kind, so small acetylene torches are usually used.

Until recently, soldering of aluminum was considered virtually impossible in the home shop. However, in recent years, new aluminum solders, combined with special fluxes, have made aluminum-soldering entirely practical for the home handyman. The technique calls for use of a torch to supply the heat required. The joint is covered with the flux to prevent oxides from interfering with the process and is kept completely covered until all the solder has melted. If the bare metal is exposed to the air without a protective coating of flux, a good bond will be virtually impossible to achieve.

Soldering flux is an essential ingredient on any soldering job, as well as when soldering aluminum (though different fluxes are used in each case). The flux helps perform three important functions: it removes tarnish and oxides from the surface; it prevents additional oxides from forming under the heat of the soldering iron or torch and it helps to "wet" the liquefied solder so that it flows more freely and rapidly into all parts of the joint.

The heat required to melt the solder and to heat the metal surfaces may be supplied by a small propane torch, a soldering gun or an electric soldering iron. Blowtorches are used for larger pieces where a great deal of heat is required, while a gun or soldering iron will do for most electrical repairs and similar jobs.

Electric soldering guns (see SOLDERING GUNS) heat up quicker than soldering irons, but the irons can handle larger jobs with greater ease. Soldering irons come in various sizes, from 100 to 350 watts in capacity, though for most light-duty work and electrical repairs a 100-watt iron will prove adequate. For general-duty work where larger pieces must be handled, a 150- or 200-watt iron will be found more useful. For sheet metal joints and for other jobs where large areas must be heated, the largest size soldering iron should be purchased.

Most soldering irons have a tip made of a hard copper alloy. This tip must be "tinned" before use to keep solder from sticking to it and to make certain it will spread the molten solder on smoothly after the joint has been properly heated. The tip should be retinned each time it becomes oxidized or pitted. To tin your iron, file each face smooth and clean down to the bare copper (this step can obviously be omitted on a new soldering iron). The iron is then plugged in and allowed to heat up until the shiny copper starts to discolor. Each face is then lightly coated with a film of rosin flux, after which solder is applied until the face is evenly covered with molten metal. In lieu of a separate flux and solder combination, a rosin-core solder (a hollow-core solder filled with rosin flux) can be used. After all sides have been evenly covered with the molten solder, the iron is unplugged and a dry rag used immediately to wipe off all excess flux or solder.

Since solder will not adhere to metal which is rusty, greasy or tarnished, the surfaces of the joint must be absolutely clean and bright before heat is applied. Cleaning can be accomplished by first wiping with benzine or naphtha, then rubbing with emery cloth, steel wool or a

Heat is applied to joint with iron till solder melts

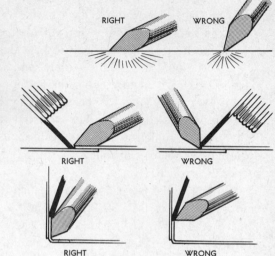

wire brush. The surface should be polished until the metal is bright and shiny, and all grit or other particles removed by wiping with a clean rag.

After the metal has been thoroughly cleaned, a light coat of flux is smeared on over the joint, unless a hollow-core solder with flux on the inside is used. An acid flux should be used for general repair work on zinc and ferrous metals, while a rosin flux should be used for soldering copper and tin, as well as for all electrical work. The work should be preheated by holding one of the flat faces of the soldering iron tip against it or by directing the flame of a torch against the heaviest part of the joint. When the flux starts to boil, the solder should be touched to the joint experimentally to see whether it melts.

Before a joint is ready for soldering, the work must be hot enough to melt the solder instantly so that it can flow freely into all crevices. When possible, the soldering iron or the flame of the torch should be held behind or under the work, while the solder is touched to the joint on the opposite side. The heat of the iron will then "draw" the liquefied solder into the joint, since the molten metal will tend to flow to the hottest part of any joint. If the solder doesn't melt instantly, more heat is needed. A large soldering iron may be required, or the work may have to be preheated with a blowtorch for a longer period of time.

When soldering two pieces together, the parts being joined should always be held firmly in position. In addition, parts should not be moved till the solder has had a chance to cool. If possible, avoid holding the work in a metal vise, since this will conduct heat rapidly away from the joint and may make it difficult to heat the work properly. Pieces to be soldered should fit together closely, and wherever possible they should be twisted or bent together so as to form a good mechanical bond as well. When the joint has been properly heated, the solder should be touched to the edge of the hot iron while the tip is moved slowly along the joint. If sufficient heat has been applied, and if the metal is clean, the molten solder will follow the tip of the iron and will spread neatly over the surface.

When two flat pieces must be fastened together (either face-to-face or overlapping), a technique known as "sweat-soldering" is used. Each piece of metal is first cleaned and fluxed where the parts will overlap, then each piece is tinned by flowing on a thin layer of solder. The pieces are then clamped firmly together with the tinned surfaces in contact with each other, after which the joint is heated from the outside. If enough heat is applied—either with a blowtorch or a large soldering iron—the solder on each of the tinned faces will remelt and flow together. This binds the two pieces firmly together in a snug-fitting joint. During the sweating process, additional solder can be fed in from the edges if necessary to add extra strength or to fill in gaps or openings where the pieces fit together.

Place beveled tip of the iron flat against the work and feed solder in as it melts

Tools, Garden, Repair and Maintenance

Garden and yard tools take a great deal of abuse, so it's only natural that they will need occasional sharpening or repair. By keeping them in good repair you will not only extend their life considerably, you will also lighten your outdoor chores.

As part of good maintenance, always clean all tools after use, before putting them away. Hoes, shovels, rakes and other metal tools are highly susceptible to rust after use in damp soil, so clean the metal parts carefully and wipe them dry each time. It's also a good idea to wipe the blades with an oily rag, or keep a pailful of oil-saturated sand handy in the garage, and work the blade of your shovel or hoe up and down in it a few times before hanging it up. The sand will scrape off dirt and polish the metal, while the oil will coat the metal parts lightly, protecting them against rusting. Each spring mix a new batch of sand with oil to replace the old lot in the pail.

Pruning shears, hedge clippers and other tools with moving parts also need occasional lubrication on pivot points and hinged sections. Oil lightly; wipe off any excess to avoid building up a sticky gum that will attract dirt.

Since splintered or rough tool handles can cause painful blisters on the hands of the user, defects of this kind should be promptly smoothed. Rub the rough spots with medium-grade sandpaper or steel wool, or wrap with waterproof plastic tape. To preserve and protect these handles, buff with fine steel wool at least once a year, then wipe on two coats of boiled linseed oil, allowing each to soak in well before wiping off the excess with a dry cloth.

A cracked or splintered handle on a shovel, spading fork, hoe or similar tool does not mean that the tool must be completely discarded. Most hardware and garden-supply dealers sell replacement handles that may be easily installed, making the tool as good as new again. Generally speaking, tool handles are designed to fit in one of two ways. Either there is a ferrule on the tool into which a tapered wooden handle fits; or there is a ferrule and hole in the end of the handle into which a metal tang, or point, on the tool fits. In either case, if you are in doubt as to the type of handle required, take the tool to the shop to make certain that you buy a properly matched handle.

To remove what is left of the old handle, you must usually remove one or more rivets or nails that fit through a hole in both handle and ferrule. Nails can be pulled out quite simply with an ordinary claw hammer, but with rivets the head must first be chiseled or filed off before removal; then the rivet can be driven out with a hammer and a punch. The stub of the handle can be pulled out by clamping it in a vise while the blade of the tool is tapped sharply.

After the old handle has been removed, the new handle is forced in until it seats securely. Even if the handle is tapered to fit inside the socket on the blade of the tool, it may still be necessary to cut it down slightly by rubbing it with coarse sandpaper or a wood rasp. Replace the rivet or nail, first drilling a hole in the right place. Flatten the head of the rivet by placing the ferrule of the tool against a solid surface, then tapping the head sharply with a hammer until it "mushrooms" or spreads out so that it cannot work loose. If necessary, a small bolt and nut can be used instead of a rivet. To keep it from working loose, the end of the bolt should be hammered down, spreading it slightly where it projects through the nut.

To make garden work easier, more efficient, blades on shovels, hoes and similiar tools should be sharpened periodically with a file. Try to maintain the original blade shape as much as possible and with light strokes work the file across the cutting edge. Scissors and clippers should be sharpened from one side only (the side that has the bevel), the file traveling from the heel to the point of the blade at each stroke. (*See also* Tools, Sharpening.)

Tools, Sharpening

As any experienced carpenter or cabinetmaker will tell you, sharp cutting tools not only are faster and easier to use, but are also much safer. Dull blades on wood chisels, planes or other cutting tools not only have to be pushed harder, they are also more likely to slip, thus increasing the possibility of an accident occurring while the tool is in use.

To sharpen most hand tools, you need only a few simple pieces of equipment: a grinding wheel (hand or power driven), an oilstone, and, in some cases, a file. The techniques involved are not particularly difficult to learn, though some practice may be required before the handyman masters the knack of maintaining a uniform angle against the sharpening stone.

Cutting edges on chisels, plane blades and similar tools consist of a bevel ground along one edge. The angle or bevel will vary with different tools, so it is important that you study the existing bevel first so that the cutting edge can be ground to its original shape when it is being sharpened. In this connection the inexperienced handyman will find it advisable to practice holding the tool against the grinding wheel at the proper angle while the wheel is standing still. He will then be able to maintain the correct grinding angle more easily when the wheel is turned on.

Wood chisels and plane blades work on much the same principle, and both are sharpened in the same manner. The edges of both blades should be ground to an angle of about 25 or 30 degrees. This angle can be measured by cutting a template out of sheet metal, or by measuring the length of the beveled face. The bevel should be slightly longer than twice the thickness of the blade.

Before sharpening a chisel or plane blade, check the cutting edge for squareness. To do this, hold the blade up to the light with the cutting edge pointing upward. Then place a small square across the top to see whether the cutting edge is perfectly square and straight. If it isn't, the edge should be ground square on the grinding wheel by holding the blade against the edge of the wheel and sliding it back and forth. Nicks in the edge should be ground out at the same time.

In grinding operations of this kind, it is important that you avoid "burning" the edge of the tool by allowing it to overheat. To prevent this, a wheel of medium to fine grit should be used, and the tool should be

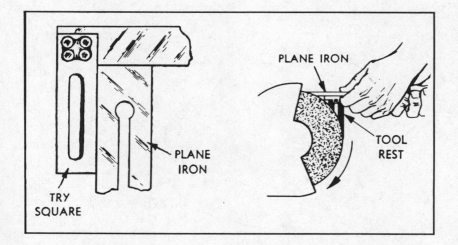

PLANE IRON

TRY SQUARE

PLANE IRON

TOOL REST

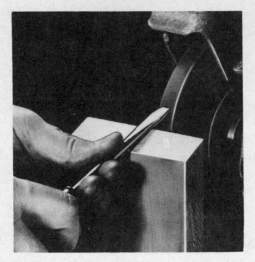

Hold blade against stone with light pressure

held against it with light pressure only. In addition, the edge should be dipped in water frequently to help keep it cool. Overheating the metal will draw its temper and the blade will no longer hold a sharp edge.

After grinding, the tool should be honed by rubbing on an oilstone. Handymen will find it most convenient to buy a combination oilstone— coarse grit on one side and fine grit on the other. The stone should be lubricated by spreading a liberal amount of lightweight oil over the surface, then allowing this to soak in. Place the beveled face of the blade flat against the stone first, then lift the handle slightly (about 5 degrees) until the edge is in full contact with the stone. Move the tool back and forth with even strokes, trying not to vary its angle of contact with the surface. Do this on the coarser side of the stone first, then repeat on the

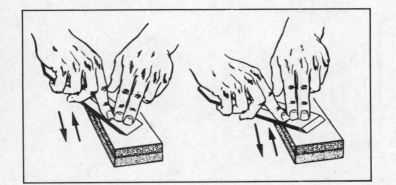

fine side. To remove the burrs or wire edges which are left, the tool should then be turned over and laid flat against the stone. It is then given a few light strokes in a sideways direction.

Though not absolutely essential, many experienced craftsmen prefer to go one step further with this sharpening process. After honing, the sharpened edge is finished off by stropping on a piece of heavy leather or by rubbing edgewise across the end grain of a block of hardwood. This gives the fine, razor-like edge preferred by most experienced craftsmen.

Unless a tool is abused—or allowed to go too long before being sharpened—grinding on a wheel is seldom required. A properly ground edge can be sharpened many times by simply honing on an oilstone, without the need for regrinding.

Pocketknives are sharpened much like a plane or chisel blade, except that there is a bevel on both sides of the blade, rather than on only one face. Drawknives, spokeshaves and similar tools are also sharpened in the same manner. Gouges (these are actually curved chisels) are sharpened like regular flat chisels, except that grinding wheels with a rounded edge and oilstones with a curved edge must be used for those gouges which have the bevel on the inside. Gouges with an outside bevel can be sharpened on an ordinary stone by simply rotating the tool while it is in contact with the surface.

Cabinet scrapers and wood scrapers have square edges (not beveled) which remove material by scraping, rather than by shaving it. To sharpen these blades, the simplest method is to clamp them in a vise, then file, drawing the file carefully across the edge at right angles. These blades also can be sharpened by touching the edges lightly against a grinding wheel and drawing them straight across while holding them at right angles to the surface of the wheel.

Torches, Propane

A propane gas torch is a versatile, inexpensive tool which can be used for dozens of different jobs around the home and workshop. Widely available in paint and hardware stores everywhere, these self-contained torches provide a dependable source of concentrated heat which is safe and convenient to handle.

Designed so that they light instantly and burn with a clean blue flame, these torches require no pumping, priming or preheating. They consist of a disposable propane fuel tank with a burner assembly which screws on top. The burner has a built-in valve which permits turning the torch on or off and regulating the size of the flame.

To light one of these torches, open the valve slightly while holding a match to the burner's nozzle. The propane fuel (in compressed liquid form) is pressure-packed inside the tank so that it comes hissing out as soon as the valve is opened. Most tanks stand about 10 inches high and contain enough fuel to last anywhere from 8 to 16 hours, depending on the size of the flame. When the tank is empty, the cylinder is simply unscrewed from the burner and discarded. Refill tanks are available at a nominal cost.

To adapt these torches for a wide range of uses, most manufacturers make an assortment of different-style burner tips and accessories. For general soldering and heating, there is the so-called utility burner or heavy-duty burner. For fine work there are narrower burners which give a pencil-like flame. To give a broad flame for burning off paint or for heating large pieces of metal, there are special flame-spreader attachments. These give a fanlike flame when screwed on over the outside of the utility burner nozzle.

In addition to the different-size burner tips, there are also special chisel-edged soldering tips, as well as pointed or beveled cutting tips. These screw on over the outside of either the utility or the pencil burner so that the flame heats them by conduction. This enables the torch assembly to be used as a high-capacity soldering iron or as a heated cutting tool for use in cutting plastic tile and similar heat-sensitive materials.

Because these compact torches provide such an easily portable source of highly concentrated heat (as high as 2,300 degrees), they are widely

Pipe joints can be soldered with torch

Tiles can be heated with flame-spreading tip

Propane torch simplifies metal bending

used for heavy-duty soldering operations—particularly for such jobs as sweat-soldering of copper tubing, or soldering of connections on metal gutters and downspouts. These soldering jobs are often done with just the standard burner tips, although the chisel-point soldering tip can also be used.

In addition to its basic function as a heat source for all types of soldering operations, the propane torch can be used for many other jobs around the house. One of its most popular uses is for burning off old paint on exterior siding, trim or furniture. For this job, a flame-spreading tip or heavy-duty burner is usually used.

A propane torch equipped with one of these flame-spreading tips is also the tool to use for such jobs as heating floor tiles to simplify cutting and laying them; defrosting frozen water pipes; antiquing wooden panels or furniture by charring the wood slightly to highlight the grain; heating lengths of metal to simplify bending to a desired shape; burning out tent caterpillars and other insect pests around the home and garden; thawing frozen downspouts and starting charcoal fires.

When equipped with a pointed or chisel-edged cutting tip, these torches can also be used for removing old putty around windows (the hot tip slices it out neatly), for mending plastic toys or other objects by "welding" cracked pieces together or for branding initials and other designs on wooden tool handles or wooden panels.

Wood, Patching Holes in

To fill holes and cracks in woodwork, cabinets or furniture, there are a number of different patching compounds that the home mechanic can use. However, for a neat-looking, long-lasting job, it is important that the right type of putty be used and that it be properly handled and applied.

Wood putty (also referred to as wood plastic or wood filler) should not be confused with the paste wood fillers which are normally used for filling pores in open-grained woods prior to finishing. These paste fillers are applied by brush over the entire surface of the board, and they are not made to fill nail holes, cracks or openings in poorly fitted joints. For patching jobs of this kind, a wood putty or wood plastic must be used.

In trying to select the best putty for each job, you can choose a ready-mixed putty or a powdered type which must be mixed with water before use. The ready-mixed putty may be either a quick-drying plastic compound or a linseed oil putty of the type normally used for sealing window glass inside the sash frame.

The quick-drying plastic compounds usually consist of an adhesive mixed with wood powder. They dry very quickly and are ready for use as soon as the can (or tube) is opened. However, their rapid drying characteristics, coupled with the comparatively coarse texture of some brands, sometimes makes them difficult to finish off smoothly—particularly in shallow depressions.

Since these wood plastics dry to a dense finish, they do not take stain readily. Therefore, when patching wood that will be finished with stain, it is best to stain the wood first. Then fill the cracks or holes with wood plastic in a color to match the final finish. Many companies manufacture a line of factory-colored patching materials for just this purpose, or you can tint your own by adding powdered pigments or universal tinting colors to the natural-colored putty.

The other kind of ready-mixed putty which is widely used for patching holes and cracks in woodwork is a prepared linseed oil putty that is normally used for glazing around windows. This compound usually contains about 10 per cent white lead, and it is very popular with professional painters because of its ease of handling and its low cost. To fill a hole with linseed oil putty, you simply press the putty into the depression with your finger or with the corner of a putty knife. It can be painted over almost immediately, and can be smoothed out easily at the surface.

However, linseed oil putty has comparatively little strength when used as an adhesive or to build up broken edges. Nevertheless, it will hold well in narrow cracks and small holes and is particularly suitable for exterior use.

Since linseed oil putty will not absorb stain, it too must be colored with the appropriate tinting colors to match the shade of the wood, after the wood has been stained. This type of putty will stick better if it is applied over a prime coat of paint or sealer, rather than directly to the raw wood.

Costing less than the ready-mixed plastic or linseed oil types, water-mixed wood putty is a good choice for those jobs where a great deal of patching and filling is required. The dry powder will keep indefinitely in its original container. When mixed with water, it hardens rapidly to a dense mass which will adhere well, even in thin layers and on edges. Unlike the ready-to-use varieties, a water-mixed putty can be smoothed out easily with a trowel or putty knife, much like ordinary plaster or spackling compound. It can be tinted when necessary by the addition of powdered colors since it also will not take stain uniformly. In addition to its use in repairing wood, a water-mixed putty can be used to repair cracks in linoleum, plaster and tile.

Professional cabinetmakers often mix their own wood putty by using fine sawdust created from the same wood and mixing this with a resin-type glue. This forms a tough, nonshrinking compound which will match the original wood in color and tone. It is ideal for those jobs where only

Sawdust and glue make good wood putty

a clear varnish or lacquer will be applied, but it is also good for doors and other surfaces that get hard wear.

When filling shallow dents, wide cracks and other sizable areas, a better mechanical bond will be achieved if the edges of the crevice are undercut first. This permits the compound to "lock" around the rim of the patch and there is less likelihood of it falling out or cracking loose. Another trick frequently used by experienced mechanics is to drive a few small tacks or brads part way into the bottom of the cavity before filling. When the compound is forced in around these tacks, the heads will serve to lock the patch securely in place as it dries. Generally speaking, it is best to fill the cavity with several thin layers, allowing each one to dry thoroughly before applying the next. The last coat should be built up slightly higher than the surrounding surface to allow for shrinkage. The excess can then be sanded off when the patch is completely dry, or the patch can be trimmed flush after the putty has partially hardened.

Workshop Safety. SEE SAFETY IN THE WORKSHOP.

Wood Joints

To insure strong, rigid joints on all types of woodworking projects, there are a number of different wood-joining techniques that can be used. Expert cabinetmakers often employ intricately formed and skillfully fitted joints which require no nails, screws or other fasteners. However, home handymen will find that the simple joints illustrated here will take care of practically all their normal requirements.

The simplest joints are those which are formed by simply butting the two pieces of wood together—end-to-end or edge-to-edge. Nails or screws can then be driven in to hold the pieces together. This type of joint may be adequate where little or no stress will be encountered, but

for greater strength and increased holding power, metal braces or fastening devices of some kind will be required.

As indicated in the drawings, these fasteners usually consist of metal
plates which are screwed to the edges or faces of the pieces so as to
reinforce the joint and keep parts from working loose. The corner braces,
mending plates, flat tees and flat corners are all held down with screws,
which should be long enough to go approximately three-quarters of the
way through the wood. The corrugated fasteners and the Skotch fasteners are simply hammered in to draw the pieces tightly together.

When a simple butt joint is assembled with screws rather than nails,
additional holding power is insured. However, when these screws are
driven into the end grain of one piece, they are much more likely to
loosen or pull free under stress. One way to provide greatly increased
holding power in this piece is to insert a dowel at right angles to the
screw as indicated. The dowel is inserted in a snug-fitting hole first, then
the screw is driven in from the side. This type of joint will withstand a
much stronger pull without working loose.

Though metal braces and other fasteners are fine on joints where the
fastening devices will not be visible, there are many projects where neat-
looking, strong joints are required—and where braces or other fasteners
would be unsightly. Strong joints can then be formed by using wood

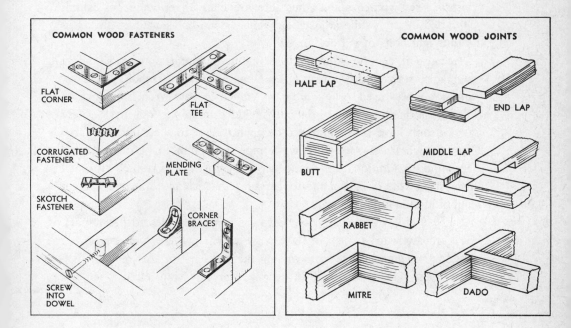

glue, and by fitting the pieces together to form one of the simple joints illustrated. Though small finishing nails or screws may be used to help reinforce each joint, the main strength is acquired from the adhesive power of the wood glue used. To insure a good bond, and to create a neat-looking joint, it is important that pieces be snugly fitted where they contact each other.

All of the joints illustrated can be most accurately cut with a table saw or circular saw. These power tools will simplify the task of cutting to a specific depth, as well as making cuts which are straight and true. However, with reasonable care, all the joints can also be formed with only a handsaw and chisel. For best results, cut pieces slightly oversize, then shave them down to fit, using a sharp chisel, wood rasp or similar tool. It is always easier to remove a little extra material (when the piece is slightly oversize) than it is to try to build up a piece after too much has been cut away.

Wood Screws. SEE SCREWS, WOOD, SELECTION AND USE.

Wrenches, Selection and Use

Broadly speaking, all wrenches can be divided into two general classes: fixed wrenches and adjustable wrenches. Fixed wrenches cannot be varied in size, while adjustable wrenches can be opened or closed to fit nuts and bolts of various sizes.

Because it can be adjusted to fit many different nuts, most home mechanics start out by buying at least one adjustable wrench. The most common model used to be a monkey wrench or auto wrench (so named because at one time it was originally included in all car-tool kits). These rugged tools have jaws which can be opened wide to accommodate large fittings, such as those found on waste pipes and plumbing fixtures around the home. In addition, the smooth parallel jaws will not scratch chromed fittings, and the design of the tool is such that it can withstand a great deal of abuse and hard wear.

Since monkey wrenches have jaws set at right angles to the handle, they are awkward to use in tight corners where there may be only a limited amount of space for swinging the handle. For this reason, they have been widely replaced in recent years by adjustable open-end

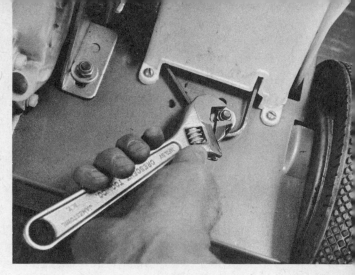

Snug fit is important when using an open-end adjustable wrench

wrenches. These have their jaws offset at the end of the handle rather than at one side. Commonly called a Crescent wrench (the name of the original manufacturer), this tool has its jaw opening placed at a slight angle to the handle to make it easier to reach into close quarters. In addition, this wrench needs only half the swing space needed for a monkey wrench, since you simply flip it over to get a new grip after swinging it to one side as far as it will go.

These adjustable wrenches come in many different sizes, ranging from

Reading from left to right: Locking Pliers, Chain Pipe Wrench, Stillson, Adjustable Open End Wrench, Monkey Wrench

4 inches to 2 feet in length. Generally speaking, the home mechanic will find he needs only two sizes to handle practically all jobs: a 10-inch wrench and a 6-inch model. Some are available with a special locking mechanism which helps the wrench keep its setting after it has been adjusted.

For grasping pipes and other round objects, pipe wrenches or Stillson wrenches are usually used. The jaws of these wrenches have teeth which bite into the metal. This, coupled with a built-in hinging action, gives them an exceptionally stubborn bite that holds stronger than a vise. Stillson wrenches also come in many sizes, but the home handyman will find that the 12- and 18-inch sizes are most useful.

Costing a few dollars more than an equivalent-sized Stillson wrench, the chain pipe wrench is an exceptionally simple tool which enables jobs to be done with greater speed and less effort. Consisting of a forged steel handle to which is attached a length of heavy sprocket chain, the tool is used by wrapping the chain around the length of pipe, then engaging the sprockets in notches on the back of the handle. Teeth on the face of the handle bite into the pipe while the chain grips it snugly to keep it from slipping. Because of its design, this wrench can be used to turn pipe in either direction, and it can be used like a ratchet wrench. That is, the handle can be loosened up, shifted and turned again without having to remove the chain from around the pipe.

Though not truly a wrench, the lever wrench or locking plier wrench is built like a pair of pliers. It has a compound lever action which enables it to be locked shut with a powerful grip. Available with either straight or curved jaws, these versatile tools come in various sizes and are adaptable for many different jobs around the home.

For really rugged service, and for a grip which will not slip, fixed wrenches are usually preferred. Of the various types available, home mechanics will find that a set of open-end wrenches will be least expensive and most useful. These are less bulky then the adjustable wrenches, hence they can be used in places where an adjustable wrench would not fit. Because the jaw openings are permanent, there is no chance of an adjustment slipping. They will usually provide a firmer grip and can withstand greater pressures. These wrenches are often sold in sets, with each end having an opening of a different size and with jaws angled at 15 degrees from the handle.

Fixed wrenches of the box-wrench type provide the toughest grip of all. They have round notched openings at either end (instead of open jaws) and they grip firmly on all kinds of nuts. They can also fit in tight

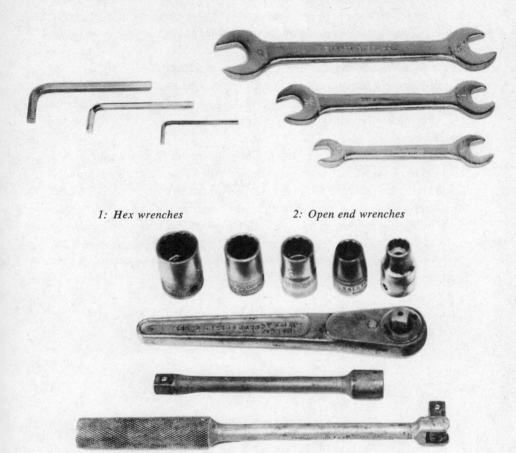

1: *Hex wrenches*   2: *Open end wrenches*

3: *Sockets*

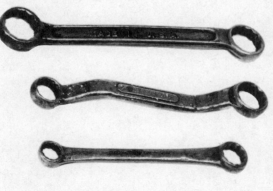

4: *Box wrenches*

places where even an open-end wrench won't. However, they are generally slower to work with and they cost more—so unless you do a great deal of work on mechanical equipment, you can probably get by without these.

Socket wrenches are another type of specialized tool which only an advanced mechanic will need. They have individual 12-point sockets which fit over a single size nut. They usually come in sets, complete with an assortment of handles which permit reaching into otherwise inaccessible corners.

One type of specialized wrench which the home handyman will find useful is the type usually referred to as an "Allen" wrench or hex wrench. These hexagonal-shaped bars of metal are designed to fit inside a hole in a recessed-head screw. Most often encountered on tiny setscrews, which hold handles and controls in place, this type of screw is being increasingly used on tools and appliances; hence a set of these inexpensive little wrenches will prove a worthwhile addition to any home handyman's tool chest.

II

Interior Repairs .

THIS SECTION describes in detail the many repairs, large and small, that are required from time to time to keep the inside of any house in good "working order." This includes repairs to walls, ceilings, doors, windows, floors and basements—to mention only a few. Each of these subjects is alphabetically listed by principal subject title, though reference to the index may be required to locate specific items in some cases.

Not included in this section are furniture repairs, electrical repairs and plumbing repairs. These are all covered in separate sections. However, remember that in many instances subjects covered in this section will be referred to when repairs are described in other sections. For example, a plumbing repair described in Section V may necessitate chopping a hole in the wall or ceiling—yet for information on how to patch that hole, you'll have to refer back to this section. In the same manner, a roof leak described in Section III will be repaired from the outside, but the resultant water damage may call for painting or papering (described in Section IV). Thus it may be seen that many repairs, both inside and outside, are interwoven, so that familiarity with all the techniques involved will be required before the job can be satisfactorily completed.

Basements, Waterproofing

A homeowner who cannot make use of his basement because of periodic dampness or occasional flooding may be wasting as much as 50 per cent of the potential living space inside his house. Ideally speaking, the best time to take the precautions necessary to insure a dry basement is while the house is still under construction. However, even if you are already living in the house, there are still a number of corrective measures that can be taken to cure almost any damp-basement condition.

Before you can effect a cure, the source of dampness must be pinpointed. In almost every case, moisture in a basement will appear in one of three forms: leakage, seepage or condensation. Leakage occurs when there is an actual flow of water that can be seen pouring in, usually through defective joints, cracks or other openings in the cellar wall. This condition is caused by an excessive amount of free water in the soil outside the foundation walls. Pressure builds up on the outside until water is forced in through the cracks or other openings. Leakage will generally be most noticeable after a spring thaw, after a heavy rain or after a long rainy spell.

Seepage may also be due to water pressure on the outside of the basement walls—or to capillary action which draws water in from the moist soil through porous spots in the masonry. It is evidenced by a general dampness in certain sections, rather than by an actual trickle or flow of water. In most cases, the dampness will be more pronounced along the bottom of the wall, or along joints where the floor and walls meet.

Condensation may also cause damp spots on a basement wall—and it will look very much like seepage. However, condensation differs from seepage in that the moisture is not coming through the wall, but from moist air on the inside. This moist air leaves condensation on the cool masonry in the same way that a pitcher of ice water "sweats" on a hot summer day. Condensation usually occurs in warm, humid weather, but it can also occur during the winter months when warm air is discharged by a clothes dryer or similar moisture-producing appliance. When this happens, the cold cellar walls cause moisture to condense out in the form of droplets, creating damp spots on the wall that can easily be mistaken for seepage from the outside.

If you are uncertain about which condition you have—condensation or seepage—there is a simple test you can make. Using a wad of chewing gum or a small dab of mastic adhesive, paste a small pocket mirror to the basement wall in the middle of one of these damp areas. Allow this to remain overnight, then examine it carefully on the following day. If the surface of the mirror is fogged over or covered with dampness, condensation is the problem. However, if the face of the mirror remains clear and dry while the wall surface around it is still damp, seepage is the problem.

If the dampness is caused by condensation, the solution lies in drying out the air inside your basement as much as possible. In most cases this can be done by simply providing adequate ventilation (keeping windows open on nice days or installing an exhaust fan); in other cases electric dehumidifiers or chemical drying agents may be needed. These will be most effective if the cellar windows are kept closed when outside humidity is high or when temperatures climb. In addition, clothes dryers should be vented to the outside, and clothes should never be hung up to dry inside the basement (see CONDENSATION PROBLEMS, HOW TO CURE).

Since seepage and leakage are both caused by excess water accumulating in the ground outside the foundation walls, it is logical to tackle this problem by first eliminating as many sources of this outside water as practical. One of the first things to check is the operating condition of your gutters and downspouts. This roof drainage system is designed to carry water safely off the roof and away from the foundation walls after a heavy rain. Each downspout should be connected to an underground dry well located at least 10 feet away from the foundation, or it should empty onto a concrete splash pan or paved area which will help carry water away. If the downspouts are clogged or gutters are defective, water will come pouring off the eaves and soak into the porous ground alongside the foundation, increasing the possibility of dampness in the basement.

Improper grading of the soil around the outside of the house can be another serious cause of improper drainage. The ground should slope

Gutters should be checked to see that water is being carried away

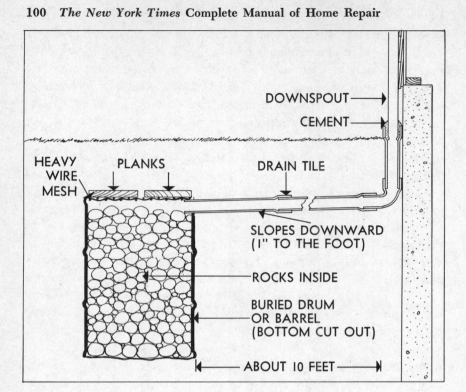

DOWNSPOUT——→

CEMENT——→

HEAVY
WIRE
MESH

PLANKS

DRAIN TILE

SLOPES DOWNWARD
(1" TO THE FOOT)

ROCKS INSIDE

BURIED DRUM
OR BARREL
(BOTTOM CUT OUT)

|←—— ABOUT 10 FEET ——→|

away from the foundation walls on all sides, so that water will be channeled away from the basement before it can seep down into the soil. A
thick sod planted over this area will also help in shedding water after a
storm.

In those cases where regrading of the entire side is impractical, or
where the house is located in exceptionally damp soil, a system of drain
tile should be installed around the outside of the foundation to carry
excess water safely away. These drain tiles are actually short lengths of
6-inch pipe made of clay or plastic. They are laid end-to-end with pieces
of tar paper placed over each joint.

To install them, the earth must be excavated down to the bottom of
the foundation. Tiles are then laid in the bottom of this trench along the
outside of the foundation footing. Discharge lines at opposite corners of
the building can then be connected to a nearby storm sewer, if practical.
If this is not possible, one or two large dry wells (deep pits filled with
stones) can be dug, and drain tiles connected to these. The drain lines
should be covered with a layer of crushed stone or gravel, at least 18

inches deep, to insure good drainage. The soil is then replaced on top of this and the ground regraded to its original slope at the surface.

A basement which is plagued by severe seepage or leakage can almost always be permanently waterproofed by applying a membrane-type waterproof covering to the outside of the foundation wall, as well as by the installation of drain tile as mentioned above. After excavating on the outside to expose the wall down to the footing, scrub the concrete clean to remove all dirt and sand. A heavy coat of asphalt or hot tar is then troweled on over the entire surface, after which a layer of heavy roofing felt is applied. This is covered with another coat of asphalt or tar, and—for best results—a second layer of felt and tar is then applied over this.

Care must be exercised when replacing the soil to shovel it in carefully to avoid damaging or breaking this membrane coating. For this reason, many experts recommend that a ½-inch-thick layer of portland cement plaster be troweled on over the tar before the soil is replaced.

Though the best way to dry out a wet basement is by eliminating the sources of outside water wherever possible, many damp basements can also be cured from the inside by applying special waterproof coatings to the inside of the cellar walls.

The most widely sold variety is the heavy-duty powdered cement which is specifically designed to hold back water on below-grade masonry walls (ordinary cement paints will not hold back seepage when applied on the inside). These powders are mixed with water to a thick, creamy

Protective cement coating should be applied liberally with wide brush

consistency, then brushed on liberally with a heavy fiber brush. In extreme cases where there are crumbling or severely porous sections, the waterproof coating can be mixed thicker than usual, then applied with a trowel instead of a brush. In any event, it is designed to bond with, and actually become part of, the masonry surface underneath.

To insure a good bond between this material and the surface underneath, the walls must be clean and porous—and preferably unpainted. If the cellar walls have previously been coated with a powdered cement paint, the surface is still reasonably porous and the waterproofing can be applied right over it, after wire brushing those sections which are loose and flaky. However, if the basement walls have previously been painted with an oil or latex paint (these seal the surface), steps will have to be taken to remove all of the old finish before this type of coating can be applied. Probably the quickest way to do this is to use a water-wash type of chemical paint remover, following the directions on the can. If the wall was painted with whitewash, it will have to be scrubbed with muriatic acid and washed clean with trisodium phosphate (sold in paint stores under the trade name of Beatsall).

If in doubt as to whether the old surface is porous enough to accept one of these cement-base waterproof finishes, you can run a simple test by splashing some water against the surface. If the water seeps in and wets the surface thoroughly, the finish is porous and the waterproof coating can probably be applied right over it. However, if the water runs

Opening should be undercut with chisel and hammer

Opening is then filled with patching cement

right off without soaking in, chances are that the old finish will have to be removed first, as described above.

Before applying these waterproof coatings, all holes and cracks should be patched with a quick-setting hydraulic cement (usually put out by the same manufacturer). These cements can be used to plug up holes or cracks even while water is still actively seeping through them. The openings should be chipped out with a cold chisel first. The area is then dampened thoroughly before forcing the mixture into the opening with a small trowel. Particular attention should be paid to the joint where the floor meets the walls, since this is the place where most basement leaks occur. Chisel out the entire joint at least ½-inch wide before filling with the hydraulic cement.

After all necessary patching has been done, the entire wall must be wet down thoroughly before the finish is applied. Though one coat will suffice in many cases, two coats are recommended where the problem is most severe. It is particularly important that a second coat be applied along the lower half of the wall and this should be allowed to lap onto the floor by at least 1 inch.

To eliminate the messy job of having to wet the wall down before painting, and to enable the homeowner to seal those walls which have already been painted with other paints, several new types of waterproofing can be used. One is a two-part epoxy resin which consists of two liquids: a resin and a reactor. The two parts are packaged separately

Spoon is handy for cementing crack where
floor meets wall

inside one can and must be mixed together immediately before use. This powerful plastic coating can be applied over any sound masonry surface —painted or unpainted—and it forms a strong bond which will resist all hydrostatic pressures normally encountered in a basement wall.

Since these epoxy waterproofers are quite expensive, and since most basement leaks occur along the joint where walls and floor meet, these coatings are usually applied only along this area. Two coats are required, with additional material applied over cracked spots and porous sections.

In addition to the epoxy-type sealers, there are several other kinds of waterproof paint available. Some of these contain special latex or plastic binders, and most come in powdered form so they have to be mixed with water before use. Some require special primers and some do not, but in any case they must be applied over a sound surface if a waterproof bond is to result. In most cases these coatings will be effective for mild seepage or occasional dampness, but they are seldom suited to curing conditions where a definite hydrostatic pressure is involved.

Before any of these waterproof coatings are applied, all cracks, holes and porous sections should be patched and filled. In addition, loose flaking paint, dirt and other foreign matter should be scrubbed off with a wire brush before the waterproof coating is applied.

Epoxy sealer can be brushed onto floor and wall

Blinds, Venetian. SEE VENETIAN BLINDS, REPAIRING.

Carpet Care

The life of any rug or carpet can be extended considerably by proper cleaning at regular intervals and by prompt removal of all stains and spills.

Most experts agree that regular carpet care should consist of a three-part program. The first part calls for a daily cleaning with either a vacuum cleaner or carpet sweeper. This cleaning should consist of at least three strokes (forward, back, forward) over each section of the carpet, and it is usually limited to open areas and sections which get heavy traffic.

The second part of the program calls for a more thorough cleaning with an electric vacuum cleaner at least once a week—and all parts of the carpet should be covered at this time. A thorough cleaning is defined as one in which each section of the carpet is covered with at least seven additional strokes. Attachments are used to clean under furniture and in corners, since the idea of this cleaning is to remove embedded dirt, as well as surface soil.

The third part of this program consists of cleaning with a shampoo or dry cleaning agent at periodic intervals. All carpet eventually becomes soiled, so that simple vacuuming is no longer effective. For best results, the rug should be taken up and sent to a rug-cleaning plant where stains can be professionally removed. With wall-to-wall carpeting, cleaning on the floor may be more convenient, but this can also be accomplished at home by professional cleaning contractors who specialize in this type of work.

Homeowners can also do a satisfactory job of cleaning their own carpets by using one of the special cleaning preparations which are sold for this purpose. To insure a thorough job and to minimize the amount of work involved, there are special rug-cleaning machines available. These can be purchased from appliance dealers, or they can be rented from a hardware store, department store or supermarket.

There are two kinds of cleaning compounds which are commonly used for carpets and rugs. One is a granular, dry cleaning compound which has been saturated with cleaning solvent or detergent. The other is a special shampoo which has a foam-type cleaning action. Both materials work well on most popular types of carpeting, and both help remove embedded dirt and soil which cannot normally be removed by simple vacuuming.

The granular absorbent powders usually consist of sawdust or similar material which has been impregnated with a cleaning solvent or detergent solution (or a combination of both). To use them, the homeowner sprinkles the moist compound over the surface of the rug, covering only a few square feet at a time. As soon as the material has been spread, a special long-handled brush is used to scrub the material well down into the nap of the carpeting. This should be done with short, rapid strokes in a crisscross pattern, and it must be done while the material is still moist.

After the entire carpet has been treated in this manner, and after the granular material has dried completely (this takes anywhere from 15 minutes to 1 hour), a vacuum cleaner is used to pick up the residue. The scrubbing action of the brush frees embedded dirt so that it will be picked up along with the dried material. Those compounds which have a great deal of fine powder in them are more difficult to vacuum; hence it is best to select a brand which is coarser and more granular in consistency.

To speed up the tedious job of scrubbing by hand and to enable the homeowner to do a more thorough job with less effort, electrically driven rug brushes or scrubbing machines are often used. These have rotating brushes (much like a floor polisher) and they will do a quick

The home shampooer is used like a vacuum cleaner

job of scrubbing the compound in to the proper depth and with uniform pressure. Many floor polishers can be converted for this purpose by simply inserting the proper type of brush. The brushes used for waxing the floor should never be used for scrubbing carpets.

Shampooing with a special detergent solution is the method preferred by most professional rug-cleaning firms. When the homeowner decides to follow this procedure himself, he should make certain he uses only a neutral detergent—never a soap or other harsh household cleaning agent. For maximum safety, it is best to purchase a detergent which is especially designed for the cleaning of rugs and carpets. These come in concentrated form and must be diluted with water according to the manufacturer's directions.

The shampoo may be applied to the carpeting in one of three ways: by rubbing with a soft cloth or sponge, by use of a push-type dispenser and scrubbing tool or with an electrically driven rug-cleaning machine which scrubs the shampoo into the fibers. Since use of a cloth or sponge involves a considerable amount of bending and "elbow grease," and since hand-scrubbing also poses the danger of excessive wetting which could damage the backing, most homeowners will find it best to do the job by machine.

These machines have a built-in dispenser which feeds the shampooing liquid onto the rug surface when a trigger or similar release is actuated. Hand-powered machines usually have a sponge-type applicator which scrubs the shampoo on over the surface. The heavier-duty electric models have rotating scrub brushes instead. These do a thorough job of scouring the surface without any effort on the user's part (except for guiding the machine).

Before wet-cleaning a carpet or rug with shampoo, the homeowner should first vacuum it thoroughly to get up as much loose dust and dirt as possible. All furniture should be moved out of the room if possible. Otherwise furniture should be moved to one side so that the cleaning operation can be done in two sections. The machine is loaded with liquid shampoo (mixed according to the manufacturer's directions), then guided over the carpet with overlapping strokes. The carpet is cleaned in sections about 4-feet square, then a good vacuum cleaner is used to pick up dirt which has been loosened by the shampoo. This can be done while the surface is still damp. The suds which are created by the machine will dry up and disappear in a short while.

After vacuuming, allow the rug to dry thoroughly before furniture is replaced. To speed drying, windows should be open if possible, and a

fan can be used to help circulate air over the surface.

To remove occasional spots and stains, the most important point to remember is that successful removal of the stain is largely dependent upon the promptness with which action is taken. If attended to before they have a chance to set, most spots can be removed without difficulty. Begin by first blotting up all liquid possible, using an absorbent cloth or sponge. Then scrape up spilled, semisolid material carefully with the back edge of a knife. Now, wipe lightly with a damp cloth, turning repeatedly to avoid smearing.

If this doesn't remove the stain, try a solution of neutral detergent. Wipe gently from the outer edge of the spot in towards the center to avoid leaving a ring, then wipe once more with a cloth dampened in clean water only. If, after drying, the spot is still visible, chances are that the stain has been caused by an oily or creamy substance of some kind. The residue that remains can then be removed with a dry cleaning fluid. Use small amounts only, and sponge carefully into the center to avoid leaving a ring and to avoid the danger of saturating—and weakening—the backing.

In all cleaning, avoid vigorous rubbing and try to hasten drying of the area by use of a fan wherever practical. Do not walk over the spot until it is completely dry, and call in a professional cleaner as soon as possible if stubborn stains persist.

Condensation Problems, How to Cure

When moisture condenses on a bathroom mirror or wall after someone has taken a hot shower, little or no damage results. However, if this same type of condensation takes place inside the hollow walls of your house or on the beams or sheathing inside an unfinished attic or basement, the problem is a much more serious one. Accumulated moisture may result in eventual rotting of the timbers, peeling of paint and staining of interior walls and ceilings.

Though water can seep in from outside to cause this same kind of hidden moisture damage, most homeowners are not aware that the trouble is more often due to condensed water vapor which originates on the *inside* of the house. This water vapor is created by the normal living habits of the family—bathing, washing, cooking and laundering. All of these, coupled with the widespread use of dishwashers, clothes dryers and similar appliances, can literally "pour" gallons of water into the air. This water is in the form of invisible moisture vapor which spreads rapidly and uniformly throughout the house.

As this moisture vapor spreads, it tends to seek out dryer air, such as that located outside the house in the wintertime. The vapor will penetrate most interior wall coverings, but in this form it does no real harm. However, when the vapor contacts a colder surface, it condenses into liquid water—in much the way that steam condenses on a bathroom mirror.

When this moisture vapor penetrates into the outside walls and comes in contact with the inner side of the cold sheathing which covers the outside wall, the moisture vapor condenses into water. This soaks into the wood siding and timbers till they become thoroughly saturated. When this happens in an attic, the excess water can actually drip down onto the ceiling below, causing water damage which is often mistaken for a roof leak. When it happens on the inner side of an exterior clapboard wall, the moisture eventually forces its way out through the siding, causing blistering and peeling of the paint as it pushes outward.

Years ago, condensation was seldom a problem because houses were larger and more spacious and not so tightly built. Without weather-stripping, storm sash and other modern improvements in home construction, there were always plenty of crevices and other openings through which moisture vapor from inside could safely escape. Modern houses are much tighter and more compact (more people crowded into a smaller area); hence moisture vapor tends to build up to a higher humidity level.

To keep vapor from penetrating into the colder outside walls, homes should be built with a vapor barrier of some sort incorporated into the construction of these walls. The usual method is to install batt-type insulation which has one side covered with a tar paper vapor barrier. An alternate method is to staple up a separate foil or plastic vapor barrier before the inside walls are plastered or enclosed.

Regardless of the method used, this vapor barrier must be continuous around the entire perimeter of the house, including attic walls and ceilings and the undersides of floors over unfinished crawl spaces. If the vapor barrier is broken or punctured in any place, its effectiveness is lost, since the vapor can seep through at these points. The function of this barrier is to keep moist air inside where it can do less harm, instead of allowing it to penetrate into the hollow spaces inside the walls.

Since a barrier of this kind must be installed during original construction (or when an extensive remodeling takes place), a house which does not have this protection built in requires extra precautions on the homeowner's part. One indication which warns the homeowner that in-

Clothes dryer is vented to the outside with stove pipe

side humidity has reached a dangerous level is condensation on the inside surfaces of windows which have no storm sash. If all windows are protected by storm sash, a test can be made by occasionally opening the inside window and watching for signs of moisture condensation on the inside of the storm sash.

The most effective cure for a condition of this kind is to provide ventilation so that moisture vapor can escape harmlessly to the outside. Kitchens should have ventilating fans built in to draw off steam created by cooking and dishwashing, and bathrooms should have windows opened immediately after bathing (unless a ventilating fan is installed). Clothes dryers should always be vented directly to the outdoors and never allowed to discharge into basements or laundry rooms.

Even in the coldest weather, living quarters can be ventilated adequately once or twice a day by opening at least two windows on opposite sides of the house for a few minutes to permit an exchange of air. The amount of heat lost will be negligible, but the amount of good accomplished in permitting moisture to escape will be sizable.

The greatest danger from lack of adequate ventilation occurs in closed-off areas of unfinished attics and crawl spaces under the floor of the house. Good building practice calls for louvers to be installed at the highest point in the attic at each end of the house. These louvers should

Attic space should be vented with louvers

Crawl spaces should also be vented with louvers

be installed above the insulation, and they should be left open at all times, though protected by screening to keep out insects and rodents.

Crawl spaces in unfinished basements should also be ventilated with open louvers which are installed underneath the floor, below the level of the insulation. In addition, if the ground in this floor space is exposed, the dirt should be covered with heavy roll roofing or with large sheets of polyethelene film (sold in all lumberyards).

As a rule, there should be at least two louvers in each crawl space—one at each end. These should have an open area of at least 2 square feet for every 25 lineal feet of foundation wall. Attic louvers should provide a minimum of 1 square foot of opening for every 300 square feet of attic floor space.

Doors, How to Hang

When a wooden door is torn off its hinges by an unexpected gust of wind—or by an overactive youngster—the labor charge for having a new one hung can often equal the cost of the door itself. To eliminate this extra expense, the home handyman who can use a plane and a chisel with reasonable skill need have no fear of tackling the job himself. Basically speaking, three steps are involved: fitting the door to its opening; installing the hinges; and installing the door lock.

To fit the new door into its opening, first trim the door to its proper height, allowing about $\frac{1}{16}$ of an inch clearance at the top, and about $\frac{3}{8}$-inch clearance at the bottom. Use a plane to trim the excess off the bottom edge. To avoid splintering the corners, always work from both edges in toward the center, and never allow the plane blade to run over the side when trimming off end grain. If more than $\frac{1}{4}$ of an inch must be removed, the door can be cut down with a sharp saw instead of a plane.

Once the height is correct, plane to the correct width where necessary, allowing about $\frac{1}{16}$ of an inch clearance on both sides. Then prop the door into its opening against the doorstop moldings in the position in which it will hang. Use thin strips of wood on the lock side to wedge the door tightly against the jamb (door frame) on the hinge side. Scrap pieces of wood or cardboard can be used along the bottom to raise the door off the floor for the required amount of clearance (about $\frac{3}{8}$ inch).

Mark the location of the hinges by jabbing the point of a knife blade crosswise into the crack between the edges of the door and the jamb. This method marks the door and jamb simultaneously and insures that both halves of the hinge (called hinge leaves) will be exactly in line when the door is ready to be hung—though each half is installed separately.

If the hinge mortise on the original door jamb is still in good condition (the wood has not been so chewed up that the hinges must be mounted elsewhere), the new hinges can be installed in the same position. In this case, simply use the old hinge mortise, or recess, as a guide and mark the door so that the other half of the hinge can be attached to the door edge in a matching position. Otherwise locate the upper hinge about 6 inches down from the top and the lower hinge about 8 inches up from the bottom.

After marking the hinge locations, take the door down and stand it on its side with the hinge edge up. Support the door by clamping it to a sawhorse or by bracing it against a workbench or large wooden box, then install each hinge in the following manner:

(1) Use the hinge leaf as a pattern to mark the outline of the mortise (recess in which the hinge leaf will sit) on the edge of the door. The long edge of the mortise should stop $\frac{1}{4}$-inch away from the inside face of the door. The thickness of the hinge leaf should be marked on the outside

Outline of hinge is marked with knife

face of the door to determine the depth to which the mortise should be cut.

(2) Remove the hinge leaf and score the outline marked by tapping lightly with a sharp chisel held vertically. Chisel out the mortise by first making a series of shallow crosscuts, then remove the excess wood by tapping the chisel in from the side, holding the blade horizontal with the bevel up. Work carefully so that you chisel out no deeper than the thickness of the hinge leaf as previously marked on the face of the door.

(3) Screw the hinge leaf in position in the mortise. Slip small pieces

Wood is chipped out by crosscutting with chisel
Complete mortise by tapping chisel in from side

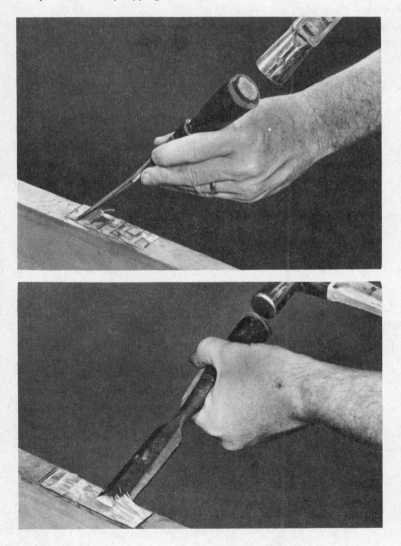

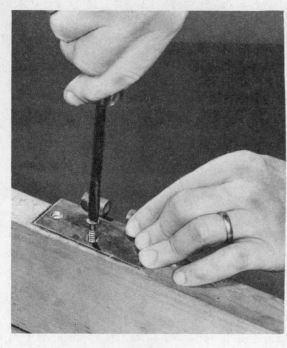

Install hinge leaf in recess with screws

*Strike should be
mortised in the jamb*

of cardboard under the leaf to shim it up slightly if the mortise has been cut too deep at some point. Properly installed, the face of the hinge should be almost flush with the edge of the door.

(4) Repeat this same process of scribing, chiseling and installing the other half of the hinge leaf on the door jamb or frame (unless the old hinge leaf mortise is being re-used). To hang the door on its hinges, place it in position inside the opening with the hinge butts interlocked so that the hinge pin can be inserted from the top.

Tubular-style door locks are easiest to install since most require that only two or three holes be drilled in the edges and face of the door. The size holes needed, and their exact location, will be clearly indicated in the instruction sheet furnished with each lock. In addition, installation is greatly simplified by a special template which is included with most brands. This cardboard template is folded around the edge of the door so that the centerpoint of each hole can easily be located by punching through it with the point of a pencil.

Locate the lock about 3 feet up from the floor, and bore holes carefully, with the drill held as level as possible so that the holes will be square to the surface. After the lock has been installed, the metal strike plate is fastened to the door jamb at the proper location. It should be mortised into the face of the jamb so that its surface is also flush.

As soon as installation is complete and the door has been tested to make sure that it works freely, both sides and all edges of the new door should be coated with a wood primer or sealer to prevent absorption of moisture and possible swelling or warping. For neatness' sake keep paint or other finishes off the new hardware by trimming carefully or by protecting with masking tape.

Doors, Repairing

When doors stick or bind around the edges, most homeowners jump to the conclusion that the trouble is caused by one of two conditions: swelling of the wood or settling action in the walls of the house. One of the first solutions that then occurs to the home mechanic is to pick up a plane and shave down the edges. However, planing is actually not required in most cases, and it should not be resorted to until all other remedial steps have failed.

In many cases the trouble is due to hinges which have worked loose or that may have been improperly mounted in the first place. Before checking for other sources of trouble, the handyman should open the door wide to expose the hinge screws, then try each of them with a large screwdriver. Tighten any that seem to be loose, bearing in mind that even a small amount of play will permit the door to sag enough to make it rub or bind in one corner. If the screws have chewed up the wood so badly that they can no longer be tightened up satisfactorily, they should be removed entirely and the holes filled with wooden plugs that have been dipped into glue and hammered into position. If preferred, the holes can be filled with a number of wooden match sticks or toothpicks, after which the original screws can be reinserted and tightened securely.

If all hinges are tight, the next step is to determine the exact place where rubbing occurs. To do this, insert a sheet of heavy paper or thin cardboard around the edges of the door while it is in the closed position. The paper should slide freely around at all points—except, of course, at the hinges and latch. Wherever the paper binds, the door is rubbing. In most cases this will be near one of the top or bottom corners along the outside edge of the door.

If the door is sticking along the bottom, near one of the outside corners, the bottom hinge is probably recessed too deeply into the door jamb (the frame). Or it may be that the upper hinge has not been set in deep enough. Either of these conditions would cause the door to be tilted slightly out of square, as indicated in the accompanying diagram, and make it rub along the bottom.

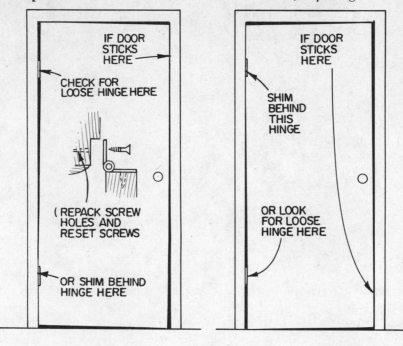

To correct a condition of this kind, the simplest procedure is to shim out the bottom hinge by inserting one or more thicknesses of cardboard behind the hinge leaf. This will tend to push the lower part of the door slightly out from the door jamb, thus raising it sufficiently to keep the bottom from rubbing. To install these cardboard shims, the hinge leaf should be unscrewed while the door is in the open position and propped up from underneath. Several magazines or a book can be slid under the open end of the door to hold it in this position. A piece of cardboard is then cut slightly smaller than the hinge leaf and slipped behind it before screwing the hinge back in place. If necessary, additional thicknesses of cardboard can be inserted when more clearance is required.

If, after shimming in this manner, the door still sticks near the bottom, it may also be necessary to trim a small amount of wood off the outside edge of the door at the point where rubbing occurs. In most cases this can most easily be done by using a small block plane, or by using a sheet of coarse sandpaper wrapped around a block of wood.

If rubbing shows up along the top of the door near the outside corner, the trouble is with the top hinge instead of the bottom one. In this case, the handyman should try shimming out the upper hinge instead of the lower one.

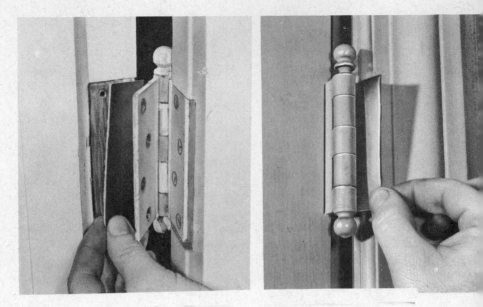

Pieces of cardboard can be used to shim out hinge leaf   *A narrow shim can be inserted behind pin*

Shimming out the hinges is also the remedy required when doors resist closing and tend to spring open if not slammed hard. To correct this condition, narrow cardboard shims about half the width of the hinge leaf should be inserted under the back half of the hinge leaf only (near the pin). This will tend to tilt the hinges more into the door opening, thus swinging the whole door around so that it can close more freely without binding. To insert these shims, simply prop the door open as previously described, loosen the hinge screws, then slip the strips of cardboard under the back edges of the hinges. Tighten the screws securely, then try the door again to see if a single thickness of cardboard will do the trick.

Sometimes a door will stick along the edge in several different places —perhaps along the middle or near the door latch. When this happens, planing or trimming is probably the only solution. If only one or two spots are involved, a hand plane can usually be used without removing the door from its hinges. However, if the door needs planing along its entire length, or if it rubs right next to the door latch, the door will have to be removed from its hinges to do the job properly.

To remove the door, drive the hinge pins upward with a hammer and screwdriver, then lift the door off carefully. Instead of planing the door along the lock side, it is easier to work along the back edge where the hinge leaves are installed. Planing on the lock side would necessitate removing the door lock, and if much planing were done, the lock would have to be reset entirely. It is therefore much easier to remove the hinge leaves and plane off the excess on this side. If necessary, the hinge mortises (the recesses in which the hinges sit) can then easily be deepened again by simply cutting out with a sharp chisel until the hinges are once more flush with the edge.

When the bottom edge of a door rubs along its entire width, the only sure cure lies in trimming off enough to provide the needed clearance. For this job also the door must be taken down. Prop it up so that it rests on its long edge, with its bottom standing perpendicular to the floor. Then use a sharp plane to trim off the bottom, working from each corner in toward the center. This means planing from the top down (while the door is resting on one edge), then turning the door over and again planing from the top down.

If a door closes easily but will not stay closed because the latch bolt does not engage the strike plate opening, close inspection will usually indicate that the opening in the strike plate (on the door jamb) is not properly lined up with the latch bolt. When this happens, the latch will not slip into the opening in the door jamb even though the door is tightly shut. This condition usually can be cured by relocating the strike plate so that it is a fraction of an inch higher or lower on the door frame. Another way to accomplish the same thing is to take the plate off and file the opening slightly larger at the top or bottom. If the strike plate is recessed too deeply into the door jamb, or if the door itself has shrunk (or

Pin is removed by driving it upward   When bottom must be trimmed, door is taken down and propped on edge

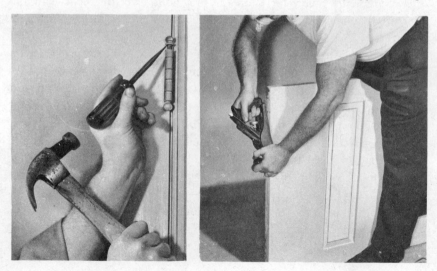

Shim is inserted to move strike plate closer to door

has been planed too much) so that the latch bolt no longer reaches into the strike plate opening, the plate can be moved closer to the door edge by shimming out behind it with one or more thicknesses of cardboard.

Floors, Sagging

When floors sag, the trouble is usually caused by weakened beams in the basement or by improperly located posts and supports. Even where original construction is not at fault, sagging can sometimes occur because of exceptionally heavy loads on the first floor level or because of improperly planned alterations which somehow weakened the original floor structure.

If neglected for long, this condition will not only get progressively worse, but will eventually result in serious structural damage. To correct it, an adjustable floor jack or steel jack post can be used. This consists of two steel tubes, one of which telescopes inside the other so that the post can be raised to various heights. The inside section has holes every few inches so that a steel pin can be used to lock the post at the desired height. It also has a top plate, a base plate and a heavy-duty adjusting screw which raises or lowers the top plate much like an oversized automobile jack. One of these posts can be placed under any sagging girder and the adjusting screw turned up a little at a time until the floor is level.

The conditions which cause a girder to sag are many and varied. If the house is old and has wooden supporting posts in the basement, it is possible that they have begun to rot, or they may have shrunk or warped excessively. It is also possible that original construction was faulty. A girder may not have had enough supports, or it may have them in the wrong places. Or it may be that the foundation or the basement floor has settled excessively, permitting posts to sink and girders to twist.

Major alterations or extensive modernizing of the upper floors are another frequent cause of sagging beams. As walls are torn down or moved, or as additional heavy equipment is installed, major changes take place in the way that the weight of the house is distributed. Additional posts may be required to handle the extra weight or to jack up those that have begun to dip.

When any of these conditions are suspected, the homeowner should watch for the following signs of trouble: windows which become exceptionally hard to operate and which stick in their frames even though many attempts have been made to free them up; doors which jam shut and are hard to open unless they are actually planed out of square; repeated cracking of the plaster, especially around stairwells and over large doorways or windows; floors that seem to slope or that don't feel solid when they are walked on.

If these defects occur repeatedly, an inspection should be made of the basement girders. Use a long straightedge and a level to accurately check those that seem to have sagged or buckled. Pay particular attention to places where beams meet, and watch for signs of cracking or rotting at the point where the beam rests on top of the existing posts. To check floors that may have sagged, use a level clamped to a long straightedge (at least 6 feet), or try letting an ordinary marble roll across the floor to see if there is a persistent slope.

Jack posts are made by many different manufacturers and they are available in all sizes up to a maximum of 8 feet, 4 inches in height. They are sold at lumberyards and hardware stores and cost anywhere from $10 to $15, depending on size and brand.

To install, first position the base plate on the floor at the point where the post is to be erected. Extend the telescoping sections until the top plate comes as close to the overhead girder as the nearest adjustment will allow, then turn the adjusting screw until the top plate just starts to bear against the girder. *Do not* apply lifting pressure at this point. Use a carpenter's level to check the post to see that it is standing plumb, then nail or bolt the top plate to the overhead beam to prevent slipping. Slowly turn up the screw until slight pressure is being applied and the post is secure, then let it set for at least 24 hours.

Jack posts must be turned up very, very slowly—no more than a half-

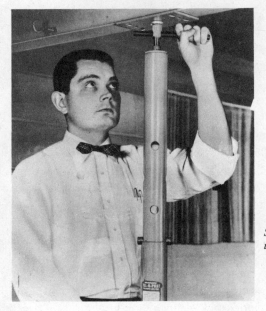

Sagging girders should be jacked up gradually

turn on the screw each week. Jacking up a sagging beam more quickly than this would be almost certain to cause additional damage to the house frame, and is a dangerous procedure. It may crack other large beams; it may cause whole sections of plaster to fall; or it may even rupture gas or plumbing lines. Jacking up slowly over a period of weeks or months permits everything to adjust gradually without danger.

If the cement floor in the basement is less than 4 inches thick, or if it is badly cracked, a footing may be required to provide a solid bearing surface for the jack post. To put in such a footing, break a hole in the floor approximately 2 feet square and at least 12 inches deep. Fill this with a concrete mixture consisting of 4 parts gravel, 2 parts coarse sand, and 1 part portland cement. Permit this to dry for about one week before installing the post on top of it.

Floors, Tile, How to Maintain

All resilient floor tiles (this includes asphalt, rubber, vinyl, linoleum and cork) should be protected by wax and washed as little as possible. Harsh cleansers and scalding water should never be used. They may fade and discolor the floors, and they will eventually make the tiles hard and brittle.

When washing is required, use only a mild, neutral soap and lukewarm water. Better yet, use one of the special cleaners which are sold for this purpose at most hardware and floor covering stores. Rinse thoroughly with plenty of clear water and mop dry. Allow it to dry thoroughly, then wax as soon as possible.

Basically speaking, all floor waxes fall into one of two general categories: polishing waxes and self-polishing waxes. The polishing waxes come in both liquid and paste form, and most have a solvent base (usually naphtha). They dry with little or no luster, since they must be buffed if a high shine is desired. Most polishing waxes will stand up longer than the self-polishing varieties, and they buff to a tougher, more water-resistant finish. Self-polishing waxes are available in liquid form only. They use water as the carrier or vehicle, since they contain no solvents, and they dry quickly to a high luster without buffing.

Before waxing any floor covering, sweep carefully with a soft brush to remove dust and grit. On vinyl, cork, linoleum and vinyl-asbestos floors, either type of wax can be used. On asphalt, and on most forms of rubber tile, only the self-polishing waxes should be used. If in doubt as to what kind of tile you have, always use a self-polishing wax.

The question of how often a floor should be waxed will depend on the amount of dirt tracked in, the size of the family and the amount of wear which that particular floor gets. As a general rule of thumb, the home-owner can assume that under average conditions a good self-polishing wax, properly applied, will last about four or five weeks. A good polishing wax should not have to be renewed for at least three or four months. Sections which get heavy wear may require touch-up applications at shorter intervals.

Regardless of which type of wax is being used, always apply in thin, even layers. Spreading the wax on too heavily will not only make it difficult to get a uniform gloss, but will actually prevent the wax from drying as hard as it should. The surface will harden, but the wax underneath will stay soft. The resultant film will catch dirt more easily and it will tend to discolor more quickly.

Many liquid waxes now on the market also act as floor cleaners when they are applied. They contain special detergents or solvents which loosen up dirt and grime so that it can be absorbed by the cloth or applicator. To avoid depositing the dirt back onto the floor, the cloth should be turned or changed frequently.

All polishing waxes have a cleansing action when applied over old wax, even if they contain no special detergents. This is because the solvent in the wax softens up the old coat underneath and permits embedded dirt to float to the surface where it can be absorbed by the applicator cloth.

When applying liquid wax of either type, always pour a pool of wax onto the floor rather than onto the applicator cloth or pad. If a polishing wax is being used, spread with a light rubbing motion to loosen the dirt. If a self-polishing wax is being used, the opposite applies. Do not rub or scrub. Instead, spread rapidly by pushing the applicator pad through the pool with light strokes.

Paste wax can be applied with a folded pad of damp cloth or with a long-handled applicator. Spread evenly in a thin coat and allow to dry for several minutes before buffing. The longer the drying time, the tougher the polishing job will be, but the more gloss it will have. For this reason, use of past wax on floors is best limited to those home-owners who own (or can rent) an electric floor-polishing machine.

If properly applied, polishing wax will never build up to the point where it will have to be removed entirely. However, this procedure sometimes becomes necessary when many layers of self-polishing wax have been applied, or when excessive accumulations of imbedded dirt have caused the floor to darken. To remove the old wax, use one of the special floor cleaners which are designed specifically for this purpose.

In addition to periodic cleaning and waxing, resilient floors also need protection against heavy furniture, which tends to dig in and permanently indent these flexible materials. To prevent this, there are oversized casters, cups and glides to fit under the legs of all kinds of furniture. These not only prevent ugly pockmarks and indentations, but also make it easier to move the furniture when necessary.

Floors, Tile, Repairing

The biggest problem in trying to patch any resilient tile floor is trying to purchase new tiles which will match the old ones in shade and color, as well as in pattern. It is in anticipation of this problem that most manufacturers and dealers recommend that extra tiles be purchased and put aside whenever a new floor is installed. The stored tiles may not match the old ones exactly (because of oxidation and natural darkening of the tiles already on the floor), but they will blend in eventually so that the replacements will soon become scarcely noticeable in the overall effect.

If leftover tiles are not available and if new ones which match reasonably well cannot be purchased, a satisfactory repair can often be made by installing tiles of a contrasting color so they form a design or pattern.

A diamond- or square-shaped effect can be formed in the center of a floor (if repairs are needed in the center), or the effect of a "runner" can be created by putting down differently colored tiles in front of a counter or table.

To attain this inlaid pattern effect, it may sometimes be necessary to remove some perfectly good tiles along with the damaged ones. For example, damage in front of a door can be repaired by putting down a long stripe of tile along one side and then laying a matching stripe at the other end of the room.

Since all floor tiles are laid with edges butted tightly against each other, care must be exercised in removing a damaged tile to avoid chipping or damaging the good tiles next to it. The method of removal varies with the type of tile. Asphalt or vinyl-asbestos tile can best be removed by first softening with a controlled source of heat.

To apply this heat, one of the best tools the homeowner can use is a special electric heating plate which measures 9x9 inches in size (the same size as most floor tiles). These heating plates are primarily a professional tool, but some dealers keep them on hand and will rent them to homeowners who do their own work. In the event that a tool of this kind is not available, heat can be applied with an ordinary electric iron. The iron should be set at its highest heat, and a wet cloth laid over the tile first, to prevent sticking or staining of the iron.

Heat can also be applied with a torch, but care must be exercised to avoid keeping the flame in one place too long. Some tiles and adhesives will catch fire if heated long enough. In lieu of these methods, a heating

Heat lamp is used to soften floor tile

HEAT LAMP

PUTTY KNIFE

lamp or infrared bulb inserted in a portable lamp or extension cord can be used as a safe, easily handled source of heat.

As heat is applied, the do-it-yourselfer should pry the tile up carefully, using a putty knife or utility knife along the seams. If necessary, the knife can carefully be used to cut away one corner of the tile so that the point can be worked underneath to permit prying the tile upward. In many cases the heat will cause the tile to curl so that little or no prying will be required to remove the damaged tile.

To pick up rubber, linoleum or vinyl tiles, a hooked linoleum knife or sharp utility knife should be used around the edges to cut away adhesive in the seams. A hammer and chisel can then be used to chip the tile away, working from the center out toward the edges. A trick that often works is to use the chisel to make three cuts in the shape of a triangle; then, holding it almost flat, chip the tile away in sections by starting from this cutout.

If the tiles are asphalt or vinyl-asbestos, chances are that the original adhesive will be tacky enough from the heat so that no additional adhesive will be required. However, if insufficient adhesive remains, or if the adhesive that is left is no longer tacky, the best bet is to scrape up as much as possible so as to leave the subfloor smooth and clean. Spread on the proper kind of adhesive for that type of tile, applying it sparingly with a trowel or brush. To minimize the possibility of excess cement

Tile can be pried up with putty knife   *New tile is laid in place of old one*

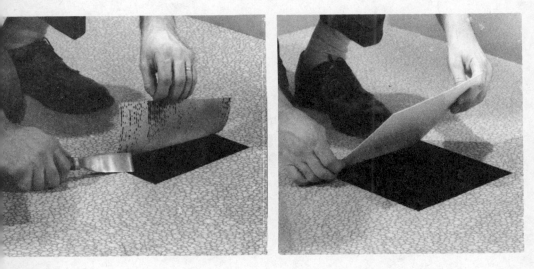

oozing up in the seams, try to keep cement a little bit away from the edges on all sides.

Fit the new tile into place, pressing firmly around the edges. Asphalt and vinyl-asbestos tiles will lie flatter if a slight amount of heat is briefly applied, while other tiles can be smoothed down by applying pressure with a small hand roller or kitchen-type rolling pin.

Floors, Wood, How to Care for

Water is the greatest single enemy of a finely finished hardwood floor. For this reason, floors should never be scrubbed with soap and water, nor should water in any form be left in contact with the surface at any time. Repeated scrubbing will not only ruin the finish and appearance of the floor, but may cause warping, cracking and buckling of the boards so that complete refinishing will eventually be required.

Regardless of the type of finish (shellac, varnish or penetrating sealer), all wood floors should be protected with wax to keep dirt from becoming embedded in the finish and to help make cleaning easier. Only a paste wax or a solvent-based liquid wax (often called a cleaning wax or polishing wax) should be used. Never use a self-polishing liquid wax on hardwood floors. These usually contain a high percentage of water, and therefore are not suitable for use on wooden floors.

To keep the floor from becoming excessively slippery, wax should be applied in thin layers and rubbed out well to an even thickness. Allow to dry thoroughly (usually from 15 to 30 minutes), then buff to the gloss desired by using an electric polishing machine.

Routine cleaning of a properly waxed hardwood floor is best accomplished by daily dusting with a dry mop or vacuum cleaner. Do not use an oily mop or rag, since the oil may attack the wax, causing clouding and softening of the finish. Soiled spots which do not come off easily can usually be removed by rubbing with a clean cloth which has been dipped into a little bit of the same wax. Rub vigorously till the spot disappears, remembering to turn the cloth frequently as it becomes dirty. Then buff with a dry cloth to restore the original luster.

For very stubborn spots (such as black heel marks, etc.), fine steel wool dipped into the wax may have to be used instead of the cloth. If this fails, the steel wool should be dipped into turpentine or denatured alcohol instead. This latter treatment is rather drastic and will probably remove at least part of the original finish, so a touch-up will probably be required before fresh wax can be applied.

Periodic overall cleaning of a hardwood floor is best accomplished by using a liquid cleaning or polishing wax which contains no water. This "dry cleaning" method actually renews the old wax and lifts up dirt while applying a fresh new finish. After vacuuming off loose dust and dirt, pour a small amount of the liquid wax onto the floor, then spread by rubbing vigorously with a soft cloth or long-handled applicator. The rubbing action will loosen up dirt and old wax so that it can be picked up by the applicator or cloth. For this reason it is best to work in sections, wiping up excess dirt and liquid with a clean cloth as you proceed. Allow the wax to dry completely, then buff thoroughly with an electric polisher. Bear in mind that the harder the wax is buffed, the brighter the polish will be and the longer its luster will last.

For maximum protection, the average hardwood floor should be thoroughly cleaned and waxed in this manner at least three or four times a year. If maintained regularly in this manner, the old wax will probably never need to be removed entirely, and the finish should last almost indefinitely.

If a floor has been so badly neglected that it is already deeply stained with ground-in dirt, it will probably require far more than just a normal cleaning or waxing. If the condition is not too bad, a prepared liquid floor cleaner which is specifically designed for wood floors can be used. This will remove all of the old wax (and part of the old finish) and may

Wax can be put on with lamb's-wool applicator

clean it sufficiently so that a simple rewaxing is all that will be required. If the floor is too far gone for even this drastic treatment, chances are that the only sure cure lies in complete refinishing.

To remove all of the old finish, and to correct floors which have buckled or warped, a floor-sanding machine is usually used. This can be rented by the day, or a professional floor finisher can be called in to sand the floors.

Floors which are not too badly worn can often be stripped down to the raw wood by means of a chemical remover—without need for sanding. These removers, which are specifically designed for use on wood floors, are scrubbed on with steel wool, then mopped up with rags or a squeegee. They will remove all of the old finish, and they also have a mild bleaching action which tends to remove stains and discolorations. Most of these removers are highly inflammable and must be used with caution in a well-ventilated room.

If this treatment leaves the floor still partially discolored, a uniform appearance can be achieved by bleaching with oxalic acid. This material is available in crystal form at most paint stores. It is mixed in the proportions of 3 ounces of acid to ½ gallon of hot water. Apply with a cloth and allow to dry, then neutralize by applying a mixture of half-and-half vinegar and warm water. Allow to dry thoroughly before proceeding with the refinishing operation. (See FLOORS, WOOD, REFINISHING.)

Floors, Wood, Refinishing

Even with the best of care, wood floors eventually become so worn and dirty that they must be sanded down and completely refinished in order to restore their original beauty.

This is a job that is well within the capabilities of the average home handyman, provided that several work-saving machines are rented from the local paint store, hardware store or tool rental agency. Two machines will be required: a drum-type floor sander and a smaller, disc-type edge sander. A rotary floor polisher can also be rented to speed the waxing job after the final finish has been applied.

Prepare the room by first removing as many furnishings as possible. The sanding operation will leave a fine film of dust over everything, so remove all furniture if possible. Don't forget pictures, draperies and venetian blinds or shades.

Examine the floor boards carefully for protruding nailheads, and countersink any you discover with a fine nailset to avoid tearing the abrasive paper on the sander. Loose, squeaky boards should be tightened by driving 3-inch finishing nails into the joint between the boards at a 45-degree angle.

Before beginning the sanding operation, open several windows and close all doors to the room. Follow the dealer's instructions on how to load the drum with sandpaper for the first cut. Three different grades of paper will be used. The first serves principally to remove all of the old finish and is usually a coarse (#4 or #3½) open-coat paper. The other two will be progressively finer grits which are used to achieve a smooth finish with a second and third sanding. With one possible exception all sanding should be done with the grain—that is, lengthwise, or parallel to the floor boards. The exception would be in the case of an unusually rough or uneven floor. This may require that the first cut be made at a 45-degree angle to the grain to knock off the worst of the high spots.

Begin sanding along one side of the room, starting near a corner and working forwards and backwards from wall to wall. Start the machine with the drum tilted back so that the paper is not in contact with the floor. Move forward slowly while lowering the drum till it touches the floor. Advance at a steady, even pace till the machine is within a few

This machine is used for scraping wood floors

Disk sander is used to sand the edges

inches of the baseboard, then raise the drum gradually from the floor before coming to a halt. Now start walking slowly backward while easing the drum down again till it contacts the floor. Pull the machine back along the full length of this first cut before moving over to the next stretch.

Continue this steady, forward-and-back motion until the entire floor has been rough-sanded. Never allow the machine to stop moving while the drum is in contact with the floor. Always start the machine while it is tilted back, so that the drum is off the floor, and wait until the drum is raised off the floor again before bringing the machine to a halt. Be sure to empty the bag when it is about one-third full.

The large drum sander will do most of the floor, but it will not reach to within the last 3 or 4 inches next to the baseboards. The smaller edging machine is used for this purpose. Load it with the same coarse-grit paper as just used on the drum sander, and sand off the small border which is left. Move the machine in a series of brisk semicircular strokes right against the edge of the quarter round molding. This will still leave small, unsanded areas in corners and behind radiator pipes, so a hand scraper will be needed for this job.

After the entire floor has been rough-sanded, a second smoothing cut is made with a medium-grit (#2½ or #2) paper. As before, sand

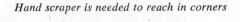

Hand scraper is needed to reach in corners

An electric buffer speeds up final waxing

with the grain, and complete all edges with the disc sander, using the same grit paper. A third and final cut is then made with the finishing grade paper (#½ or #0) on both the drum sander and the edger.

Before the finish is applied, the entire room should be cleaned of all dust with a vacuum cleaner. In addition to the floor itself, don't forget the baseboards, the tops of all door and window frames and all other woodwork. Dust left in these areas may settle on the wet finish and prevent your getting a smooth job.

Many different types of floor finishing materials are available at all paint stores. Generally speaking, these fall into one or two overall categories: the penetrating floor sealers, which do not leave a surface film but soak down into the pores of the wood, and the surface finishes, such as varnish, shellac and some specialized synthetic finishes. The choice depends on the type of finish preferred, and is best decided after consultation with your dealer.

Whatever the finishing material selected, apply it carefully according to the manufacturer's directions. Allow sufficient drying time, then spread on a thin coat of good quality paste wax. Buff this to a lustrous sheen with a rotary electric polishing machine.

Floors, Wood, Repairing

Wood floors that squeak or sag are not only a nuisance, they can also be dangerous. In many cases the condition can be cured with a few simple repairs, provided that the cause of the trouble is first accurately diagnosed.

Most wood floors actually consist of a double layer of flooring. On top are strips of oak or other finished hardwood, beneath which is a rough subfloor of wider boards. The finished flooring fits together with tongue-and-groove joints, and it is held down with nails driven in at an angle along the tongue edge. The nailheads are then covered up by the grooved edge of the adjoining board.

On most installations, the subflooring is nailed diagonally across the tops of the joists, the heavy beams which support the floor. The finished flooring is then nailed down on top of this at right angles to the joists. Between the two layers of flooring there is a layer of building paper to keep out dust and drafts.

When a floor squeaks noisily every time certain boards are stepped on, the problem is usually caused by loose boards. The trouble may be due to finished flooring which has not been nailed down properly, to subflooring which has worked loose so that boards have pulled up from

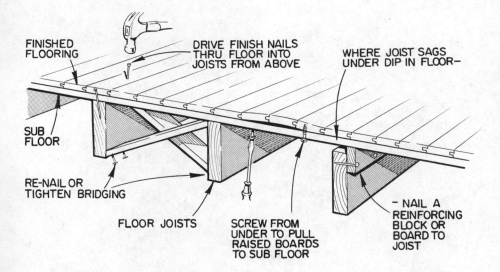

the joists or to a combination in which both finished flooring and sub-flooring has worked loose.

To silence the squeak temporarily, a dry stainless powdered lubricant can be squirted into the cracks between the offending boards. However, for a more permanent cure, the loose boards must be tightened up so that no further movement is possible. The homeowner will find it easier to do this work from below, provided that the floor is over an unfinished basement so that joists and floor boards are exposed underneath.

After locating the offending boards from below (by having someone walk around on the floor above while you listen from below), drive thin wooden wedges into the space between the bottom of the floor board and the top edge of the joist which supports it. This will support the loose boards by taking up slack.

Another way to support floor boards which have bulged upward is to nail a supporting block to the side of the joist. This block consists of a short length of 2x4 or 2x6 with its top edge forced tight against the bottoms of the floor boards.

When the loose boards occur at some point between the joists, a cure can be effected by installing a bridge or crosspiece of 2x6 between the joists and at right angles to them. Before nailing this bridge in place, hammer it upward as high as possible so that its upper edge supports the floor boards. If necessary, thin wooden wedges can also be driven

Where underside is exposed, wedges can be driven under boards to silence squeaks

in place above it to support floor boards which still bulge upward in the center.

If there are loose floor boards on a floor which has a finished ceiling below, repairs will have to be made from above. After locating the loose boards, drive two 3-inch finishing nails in at an angle so that they form a V. To avoid damaging the floor with the hammer head, drive the nails almost all the way in, then finish by using a nailset to drive the heads below the surface. Pilot holes slightly smaller than the nails should be drilled to simplify hammering and to avoid splitting the boards.

Where practical, these nails should be driven into a floor joist, rather than merely into the subflooring. To locate the joists, the surface of the flooring can be tapped with a block of wood and a hammer. There will be a dull, hollow sound when tapping between the joists. When directly over a joist, the sound will be more solid. Bear in mind that the joists usually run at right angles to the floor boards, and they are almost always spaced at 16-inch intervals. Holes which remain after the nails have been countersunk can be filled with matching colored wood plastic or wood putty.

In those cases where a floor board is badly worn or split, the only sure cure lies in cutting out the damaged board and replacing it with a new piece. To do this, holes should be drilled through the defective

Crossed nails will tighten loose flooring

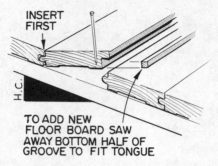

INSERT FIRST

H.C.

TO ADD NEW
FLOOR BOARD SAW
AWAY BOTTOM HALF OF
GROOVE TO FIT TONGUE

board at each end of the damaged section; drill carefully so as not to go through the subflooring below. Then, using a chisel, carefully split out the defective board without damaging the tongue or groove edge of the boards at either side.

A new length of flooring is then cut for a snug fit. The bottom half of the grooved side is trimmed off with a chisel or plane. This new piece can then be dropped neatly in place from above and nailed down securely with finishing nails.

Floors which have sagged because of weakened or warped joists or girders can usually be cured by installation of steel supporting posts which have a built-in jack at the top. For information on installing these, see FLOORS, SAGGING.

Glass, Replacing

The job of replacing a broken pane of glass in windows or storm sash is a comparatively simple home repair project which can be handled while the sash remains in place in its frame, though the job will be easier if the sash can be removed first and laid horizontally.

Where possible, the old, broken glass should be removed from the outside. Wear heavy work gloves for this job, and gently pull pieces out in as large sections as possible. If a piece is held tight by the hardened putty, rock it cautiously back and forth to break the bond, then pull straight out. Have a carton or other container handy so that broken pieces can be dropped in immediately without need for further handling. Stubborn chips which become embedded in corners can be knocked out by hammering gently with a hammer and chisel.

After the broken glass has been removed, scrape out all of the old, hardened putty with a narrow chisel or a heavy screwdriver. In most cases it will be necessary to hammer the chisel lightly in order to free up the hardened putty. Care must be exercised to keep the chisel angle low so as to avoid gouging or chipping the sash frame.

While removing the old putty, pull out all glazier's points (the triangular bits of flat metal which are used to hold the glass in place) by using a pliers or by prying them out with a corner of the chisel. On metal sash there will be special spring clips or glazing strips which will have to be removed instead. These can be pried out with a screwdriver. If the putty is so hard that difficulty is encountered in chipping it out, try heating the hardened putty with a hot soldering iron or by waving the flame of a propane torch gently over the putty. The heat will soften it sufficiently to permit it to be scraped out much more easily.

After all putty has been removed, the groove should be cleaned out thoroughly and then painted with a coat of boiled linseed oil or thinned-down exterior house paint. This preliminary priming is an important step which is often skipped, but it is necessary to insure a good bond. It keeps the wood from absorbing too much oil from the glazing compound and will help the compound to adhere better and stay pliable longer.

Measure the opening to determine the size glass needed and have

Gloves should be worn when removing broken glass

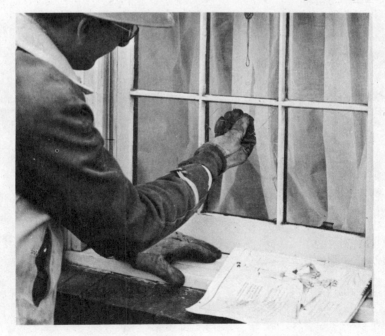

the pane cut to size by your dealer. Remember to order it approximately ⅛-inch smaller (horizontally and vertically) than the actual measurements of the opening. This will allow for about 1/16-inch clearance on all sides, making installation easier and leaving room for expansion or irregularities in the sash frame. For small, multiple-paned sash, single strength glass is adequate. For metal sash, and for larger panes, double strength glass is often recommended.

Before placing the glass inside its opening, apply a thin layer of putty or glazing compound to the groove or rabbet where the glass will fit. This "bed" of glazing material is advisable on wood sash and is absolutely essential on metal sash. It helps cushion the glass against shock or uneven stress and minimizes the danger of leakage around the edges of the pane.

Press the glass gently but firmly into its cushion of putty, then fasten it securely in position by driving glazier's points into the frame around all four sides. These can be driven in by hammering lightly with the side of a screwdriver or chisel, or they can be driven in with a hammer and a special driving tool which is included with many packages of points. For average-sized panes, use two points along each side. On large sheets, three to four points will be required on each side. Remember, it is these

Putty is placed in grooves, then glass replaced

Glazier's points are used to hold the glass firmly in place

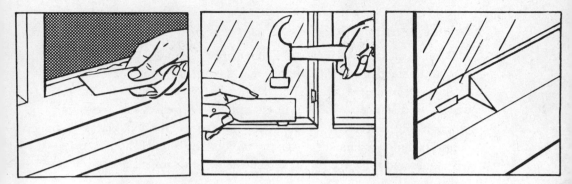

points which hold the glass in place—not the putty or glazing compound which is applied afterward.

On metal sash, the glass is held in place by special spring clips which fit into holes in the frame and which press against the edge of the glass. Some types of metal sash have glazing strips which must be pressed in place with a screwdriver instead. Regardless of style, make certain the glass is anchored firmly in place with clips, strips or points before proceeding to make it weathertight with putty or glazing compound.

As mentioned above, either a conventional linseed oil putty or a synthetic type of glazing compound can be used. The glazing compounds differ from older-style putties in that they are formulated from special nondrying oils. They remain resilient and flexible over a longer period of time, and they are also less sticky to handle. This makes them easier to spread and generally simpler to work with.

To apply the glazing compound or putty, first roll the material into long strips about the thickness of a pencil. Lay these rolled strips into the groove around the edge of the sash, and use a putty knife to press the glazing material firmly into position. Smooth it so as to form a triangular-shaped bevel between the sash edge and the glass. The glazing material should come up high enough on the glass so that it matches the level of the molding on the inside.

Excess glazing material should be "cut off" after each stroke by using a corner of the putty knife or by rolling up with the finger tips. Putty smudges on the face of the glass can be removed, after the putty has been allowed to dry for a day or two, by wiping with a rag moistened with turpentine. To prolong the life of the glazing material, it should be painted after a week or two by flowing on a liberal coat of exterior paint. Allow this paint to run slightly onto the glass (about $\frac{1}{16}$ inch) so as to assure a weathertight seal at the point where the putty contacts the glass.

Insect Controls

Because most insect pests are quite adept at keeping themselves hidden, it is much more difficult to get rid of them after they become established inside the house. For this reason, prevention is by far the wisest—and simplest—method of control. In most cases the preventive program will consist of three parts: eliminating breeding places and points of entry, eliminating sources of food by proper housekeeping techniques and using the proper insecticide when treatment does become necessary.

INSECTS AND WAYS TO CONTROL THEM		
INSECT	**CHARACTERISTICS**	**CONTROL METHODS**
House Flies	Breed in food, garbage and decaying organic matter and are frequent carriers of many human diseases.	Equip garbage cans with tight covers and do not let food stand uncovered. Keep screens on all openings and use space or aerosol spray to kill them indoors.
Mosquitoes	Breed in stagnant water during spring, summer and fall. Besides biting, some types carry disease.	Pools of water should be eliminated, covered or sprayed. Gutters should be cleaned to prevent puddles. Aerosol spray can be used indoors.
Ants	Breed in nests which may be indoors or outdoors. Usually follow same path to food supply, so can be traced carrying food back.	Seal cracks and openings through which they can enter. Apply insecticide containing baygon or diazinon. Apply as surface spray along path and near openings, and in nest if possible.
Spiders	Except for black widows most are harmless to humans in U.S. Black widows are black, about ½-inch long and have globular body.	Remove piles of loose trash from yard and knock down webs when noticed. Use liquid spray or dust containing chlordane or diazinon, if available.
Cockroaches	Vary from ½ to 2 inches in length and from yellowish brown to black. They hide in dark places and come out at night to feed on human food, garbage, starch or glue in cartons.	Periodic cleaning of all corners and crevices to eliminate dirt. Apply surface spray or dust containing diazinon, malathion or baygon. A pyrethrum spray in crevices will drive them out into the open.
Clothes Moths and Carpet Beetles	Larvae of both these insects feed on wool, mohair, fur and a wide range of clothing and furnishings. They vary in color from yellowish to brown and grow to about ½-inch.	Frequent cleaning of rugs, closets, radiator enclosures and upholstery. Use stainless protective spray containing methoxychlor or Perthane. Store clothing and woolens in airtight chest or closet and enclose napthalene flakes or balls, or paradichlorobenzene crystals.
Bed Bugs	Brown, flat bugs, ¼ to ⅜ inch long. They feed on human blood and bites cause itching. Lays eggs in crevices and around tufts in mattresses.	Apply surface spray containing lindane, malathion or pyrethrum. Mattresses should be covered, but not soaked; and spray must not contain more than 0.1 per cent lindane or 1 per cent malathion.
Silverfish	Slender wingless insects less than ½-inch long and shiny or pearl gray in appearance. Active at night, they like cool places and eat anything which is high in protein, sugar or starch. Will frequently eat paper and bookbindings.	Use surface spray or dust containing diazinon or malathion. Spray closets, baseboards and places where pipes go through walls.

Preventative spraying will keep sink cabinets free of insects

The chart lists some of the more common insect pests and briefly describes the characteristics and control techniques for each. Since good housekeeping and proper sanitation are an important part of any pest control program, thorough cleaning of all corners and crevices where spilled food or organic matter can collect is essential. This will eliminate places where the insects can hide and feed. Particular attention should be paid to corners in cupboards and closets, as well as to openings under baseboards, in floors and behind kitchen drawers. Another place that needs frequent cleaning is the space under the kitchen and bathroom sinks and around all water pipes, toilets and other plumbing fixtures.

All food should be stored in tightly closed containers, as should garbage and other waste material. Accumulation of trash or refuse against the outside of the house can provide a ready breeding ground for many insect pests and may provide a convenient means of entry into the house itself. To close up as many of these entry points as possible, calking compound should be used to seal up permanently as many openings as possible, especially where pipes or utility lines pass through foundation walls.

Insect pests may also be carried into the house in cartons or in packages of groceries and other materials. Cockroaches and silverfish, for example, may be hidden in the seams or crevices of a cardboard carton. From here they will crawl out into the house to establish colonies which will eventually infest the entire home. Moth larvae may also be hidden in dirty clothing which is brought back from a summer home or resort. Before storing, these should be thoroughly cleaned or laundered.

When—in spite of all preventive measures—insects do invade the home, insecticides of various types will be required to control or eliminate them. Generally speaking, these fall into one of two categories: surface sprays and space sprays (or aerosols).

As its name implies, a surface spray is applied to surfaces inside the home where insects tend to crawl or congregate. The liquid wets the surface and leaves a deposit which tends to kill insects that come in contact with it even after a period of weeks has elapsed. They may be applied with a hand-type spray gun or with a pressurized spray can. Many types can also be applied with an ordinary paint brush, though tests should be made first to make certain that no damage will occur on some types of floor tile and on some plastics.

Space and aerosol sprays are designed for flying insects, such as mosquitoes and houseflies. They form a fine mist which remains suspended in the air for long periods of time so that flying insects will contact them while still in flight. Since they leave little or no residue when dry, they are not suitable for use as a surface spray and have no lasting effect. Most of the widely sold brands are available in aerosol cans, though a properly designed hand spray gun can also be used with bulk liquids if extra economy is desired.

When using any spray, always cover all food, as well as cooking and eating utensils and all cooking or eating surfaces. Space sprays and aerosol sprays should be applied while windows and doors are closed, and they should be used according to the directions on the container. To prevent adverse effects, the homeowner should leave the room immediately after spraying, and it should be left closed and unoccupied for at least half an hour before re-entering.

Most household pesticides and insecticides are at least mildly toxic, so they can be injurious to humans and household pets if not properly handled. To prevent trouble when using or storing insecticides, here are a number of safety rules that should be observed:

(1) Always read the label on the package carefully, then follow all precautions and recommendations as to its use and storage. Bear in mind that products of different manufacturers may be formulated differently, so read each new package before using it.

(2) Store insecticides in their original containers where children and pets cannot reach them. Never store insecticides in medicine cabinets or in the pantry, and keep away from all food packages.

(3) Never spray on exposed food, dishes or eating surfaces; and remove aquariums and pets (and their food and water dishes) from the room before applying space sprays of any kind.

(4) Handle all oil-based sprays as you would any other flammable liquid, and keep away from open flames or furnaces. For the same reason, never smoke while handling this type of insecticide.

(5) Avoid prolonged physical contact with any insecticide, and always scrub face and hands with soap and water after using one. When using an aerosol spray, try to avoid breathing in any more than absolutely necessary.

(6) Never save or try to re-use empty containers and don't dispose of excess materials outdoors where they may contaminate water, fish or wildlife.

(7) If insecticide is accidentally swallowed, a physician should be called at once and the label contents read to him so that he can determine the chemical ingredient which may be dangerous. Antidote instructions on the label should also be followed, particularly if a physician cannot be reached immediately.

(8) If quantities of an insecticide are accidentally spilled on clothing, the clothing should be removed immediately and laundered before it is worn again.

Lightning Protection

Though city dwellers have comparatively little to fear from lightning (nearby tall buildings usually have steel frames and are well grounded), homeowners in rural and suburban areas would do well to familiarize themselves with how lightning works and with the protective measures that can be taken to prevent damage to lives and property. Nothing can be done about actually preventing lightning, but fortunately there are methods of controlling it. Foremost among these is the installation of a properly grounded system of UL (Underwriters' Laboratories) approved lightning rods.

To understand how these work, the homeowner must first understand why a lightning flash occurs. When storm clouds form, atmospheric conditions sometimes cause great quantities of electrical charges to gather—all positive or all negative. As these charges build up, they cause an equal quantity of opposite charges to build up in the earth's surface immediately below.

Since opposite electrical charges have a great attraction for each other, the ground charges tend to flow upward into the tallest structures in an effort to get closer to the clouds. Simultaneously, the myriads of air-borne charges tend to reach downward toward their earth-borne opposites. The potential between the two builds up till a point is reached when they finally leap across the barrier of air between them. This releases tremendous energy (consisting of millions of volts and thousands of amperes) in a tiny thousandth of a second and often causes nearby air molecules to actually heat up and explode—thus creating the mighty clap of thunder which accompanies most lightning strokes.

The bolt has spent its energy when the air-borne charges have found their way into the ground below. Damage to trees, buildings or other structures is caused by the resistance offered to the path of this huge spark as it seeks its way down to a damp spot on the ground.

By providing a safe, resistance-free path for lightning to follow, a properly grounded protective system permits the charges to travel harmlessly through on their way to the ground. The system begins with a series of air terminals or rods which project above the roof so that strokes will contact them before touching other parts of the house. The rods are connected to each other by heavy cables, and these in turn are connected by equally thick wires to metal plates, pipes or rods buried deep in permanently moist earth. Each rod is connected to at least two conductors so that the path of the bolt is divided on its way to the ground.

Installation of one of these protective systems is definitely not a job for do-it-yourselfers. Professional installers, using equipment approved for this purpose by the Underwriters' Laboratories, are required. For guaranteed results, the contractor should furnish a Master Label plate indicating that the materials used are satisfactory and that the installation was made with a sufficient number of conductors, grounds and rods. A Master Label also assures the owner that proper installation procedures have been followed and that only approved materials and fittings have been used.

Though installation costs are lowest if a system is put in while the house is being built, adequate protective systems can also be installed on existing homes. In many cases insurance rates will go down anywhere from 10 to 15 per cent, thus amortizing a considerable portion of the cost.

In addition to installation of grounded lightning rods, houses which stand out on open areas should have television antennas grounded and equipped with suitable lightning arresters. Water pipes, waste lines and wiring systems should also be grounded and equipped with protective devices. Tall trees near a house (especially if on an exposed hill) should be protected by installation of lightning rods connected by cables to a suitable ground. Metal fences with wooden posts should also be grounded (by driving pipes into the ground at 100-foot intervals), since these can become dangerously charged even when not struck directly.

Locks, Door, Repair and Replacement

There are four basic types of door locks in general use: (1) auxiliary rim locks or night latches which are mounted on the inside face of the door and require no mortising; (2) mortise locks which, as the name implies, are mortised or recessed into the edge of the door; (3) tubular locks which are much simpler to install, since they require only that two holes be bored in the door; (4) cylindrical locks which are also installed with two bored holes, but which are usually more rugged in construction.

The better locks afford additional security in the form of an automatic deadlocking feature. This makes it impossible for a prowler to jimmy the lock by pressing back the movable part of the latch.

When a door lock begins to stick or otherwise misbehave, it may be in need of lubrication. The movable latch bolt should be lubricated with graphite once or twice a year to assure freedom of action. Graphite is also the lubricant to be used in the tumbler mechanism. It can be blown in through the keyhole or simply spread on over the blade of the key. Slipping the key in and out of the lock a few times will then distribute the graphite inside the mechanism.

Night latch gives added security

Cylinder deadlock has a keyhole in the handle

If lubrication fails to free up a sticking lock, it will have to be removed from the door to check for further trouble. Begin by removing the inside knob and the decorative escutcheon plate or other trim. If the knob has a set screw, loosen this first. Then slide the knob off the spindle, or unscrew it if it is threaded on. On some locks the knob is permanently assembled to the round escutcheon or rose plate, so that unscrewing this decorative trim from the face of the door will also release the knob.

Many cylindrical and tubular locks (which have the keyhole in the knob) are a little trickier in their assembly, so closer inspection will be required to determine the method to be used to release the inside knob. Some have a small catch on the shank of the knob which must be pressed down before the knob and trim can be slid off. On others a small square or round hole will be visible on this shank. Insert a small

A close-up of a deadbolt

nail in this hole to depress a retainer catch which releases the knob so that it can be easily slid off. If this small retainer is not visible through the hole, try turning the knob counterclockwise about 45 degrees till the retainer is visible.

If the escutcheon plate is a separate piece, it can usually be removed by one of several methods. It may have a small wire catch on the inside edge which must be depressed. It may have a slot on the outside edge in which a small screwdriver is inserted to pry it off. Or it may simply unscrew from the lock case once the knob has been removed.

When the inside knob and trim have been removed from most tubular locks, the entire assembly will usually slip out easily from the opposite side. However, in many cases (particularly with cylindrical locks) there will be a rose plate or mounting plate on the inside which must first be unscrewed. This plate will not be visible till the inside knob and trim have been removed. It is usually held in place with two screws. When this has been taken off, the latch bolt mechanism is removed by un-screwing the two latch plate screws from the edge of the door. Since this unit is usually a snug fit, it may be necessary to pry the latch out with a screwdriver after the screws have been removed.

Mortise-type lock sets can be easily slipped out after the knobs and

Mortise lock slides out easily

spindle have been removed. Loosen the screws from the lock face in the edge of the door and simply slide out the entire mechanism.

Examine the disassembled parts of the lock for obviously broken springs or other defects. In some cases you can save the cost of a new lock by bringing the old one to a locksmith for replacement parts or repairs. Or it may be that the original grease inside the lock has become gummy and clogged with dirt.

If this seems to be the trouble, wash the entire chassis in gasoline, using an old toothbrush to scrub out accumulated sludge. Assemble the lock on the bench top, and try out the mechanism. If it works freely, spread a small amount of thin cup grease over the vital working parts and reinstall in the door. Avoid heavy greasing, as too much lubricant tends to gather dust which may clog up the lock in a short while.

In those instances where simple cleaning and oiling will not do the trick, it is best to discard the lock and replace with a new one. To simplify installation, try to purchase one which matches the holes already bored or mortised into the old door. If slight variations cannot be avoided, use a half-round file or rasp to ream out the hole if a larger opening is required. If the new lock requires a smaller hole, shim out the opening with thin strips of wood and pack the bare spaces which are left with plastic wood. In extreme cases it may be necessary to fill up the old opening by gluing in scrap blocks of wood and then boring new holes as required.

All new locks come packed complete with illustrated instruction sheets which give step-by-step installation procedures. In almost every case the manufacturer will also include a special cardboard template which is used to accurately locate the proper size holes required for installing the new lock.

The job of modernizing a door having an old-fashioned, mortise-style lock by installing one of the newer types of cylindrical or tubular locks with modern trim has been greatly simplified by the introduction of modernization or conversion kits. Since the opening left in the edge of a door when a mortise lock is removed is much larger than the small hole required for a modern lock set, some skilled carpentry was always necessary to carefully fill this in with blocks of wood before new holes could be drilled.

The kits eliminate this job. They contain two oversized trim plates (one for each side of the door) and one oversized latch plate (to fit over the large opening in the edge of the door). They also include a long brass strike plate to fit over the jamb and to provide a new opening at

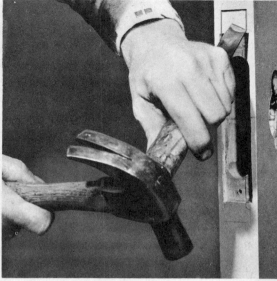

Removing old mortise lock prior to replacing

Extending mortise to accept new edge plate

the proper height. This combination completely covers up the scars left by removal of the old hardware, and plates are predrilled with the right size holes in the proper location to accept one of the newer door locks.

New latch unit covers door edge

New cover plate covers old holes

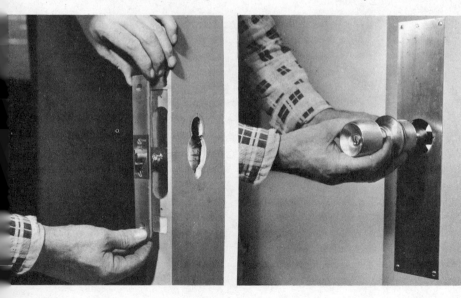

Metals, Care and Maintenance

To restore the original brilliance to tarnished metal surfaces you may choose from a wide variety of excellent metal polishes. Most of these work on the same basic principle. They contain a chemical which dissolves (or converts) the oxides which form the tarnish back into their original metal form. This chemical is usually combined with some sort of polishing agent, a mild abrasive that helps to rub off the more stubborn stains.

Plated metals should not be polished too often or the life of the plating is shortened. Frequent rubbing with even the finest of metal polishes will eventually wear through the thin coating of plate, exposing the unpolished metal underneath. On this type of surface always use a good quality, nongritty metal polish and use it sparingly; on silver plate, use only a silver polish. Rub only as hard as is necessary to clean properly and polish the surface, then rinse thoroughly with denatured alcohol (handle with caution since this is highly flammable) to remove all residue left from the polishing. Wipe dry with a clean, lintless cloth, then apply at least two coats of clear, glossy lacquer with a soft camel's-hair brush.

Copper, brass and bronze will all tarnish rapidly unless protected by clear lacquer or a similar coating. However, before this coating is applied, all dirt and tarnish should be completely removed with a metal polish designed for the purpose. When polishing is needed again, wash off old lacquer with lacquer thinner, then polish according to the directions on the can. Wipe away residue of polish with denatured alcohol, then recoat the piece with clear lacquer.

For cleaning exceptionally heavy tarnish or deeply embedded stains on copper pots, or badly pitted andirons or other objects of solid brass or bronze, a more vigorous cleaning may be required. Start by scrubbing with a kitchen cleanser, then rub the stains which remain with a rag dipped into a solution of vinegar and salt; keep dipping and rubbing vigorously until the pitted areas are clean, then rinse quickly in hot water. Finish the job by cleaning with metal polish as previously described.

Stainless steel and chromium usually require only an occasional washing with soap and water to keep them new-looking and clean. However, certain foods which contain salts or acids may pit these metals if allowed to dry on the surface for extended periods; always wipe off spilled materials promptly. If a cloudy film forms, or if metal exposed to the weather has some pitting, then a liquid metal polish should occasionally be rubbed on sparingly, and the metal well polished. For outdoor exposure, chrome-plated surfaces can be protected with a light coat of paste wax.

Aluminum requires comparatively little maintenance, but under certain atmospheric conditions it is subject to pitting. When used outdoors it will benefit greatly from periodic coatings of liquid wax. Kitchen utensils and ornamental aluminum hardware can be seriously damaged by caustic solutions containing lye or other strong alkalis; *never* use cleaning agents which contain these ingredients. Even harsh soaps may darken or discolor aluminum pots and decorative moldings; always rinse promptly after cleaning. Fine steel wool loaded with soap is one of the best ways to clean and polish objects made of this metal. Always rub in one direction only—never use a circular motion.

Nickel-plated hardware will generally need frequent polishing to keep it from darkening. The surface should be washed off with hot soap suds and rinsed thoroughly with clean hot water. Dry with a soft cloth. Shine it by rubbing with a metal polish diluted half and half and applied with a damp sponge. (*See also* Rust Prevention in Section III and Metal Surfaces, How to Paint in Section IV.)

Plaster Patching

Cracks and holes in ceiling and walls are almost inevitable in the average house. They may be caused by shrinking or settling of the framework or by alterations and repairs which necessitate chopping holes to get at utilities on the inside. In either case, the defects will have to be neatly patched and filled before a new coat of paint is applied. In most cases only a few simple tools and materials are required.

Small cracks and holes are usually filled with spackling compound or a commercial crack filler. These usually come in a dry powdered form (similar to plaster) and are mixed with water immediately before use. Unlike plaster (which dries very rapidly), most patching compounds are slow-setting and remain in a soft, workable condition for several hours. The material should be mixed to a smooth, lump-free consistency which is stiff enough to hold its shape without sagging, yet plastic enough to permit easy spreading.

To save the job of mixing, many companies also make a spackling compound in paste form. Not only does this material eliminate the need for mixing up a fresh batch each time a small amount of compound is needed, it also assures the home mechanic of a prepared compound which is of exactly the right consistency. In addition, it eliminates waste and is less likely to cause suction spots when paint is applied over it later on.

The best tool to use for all crack repairs is a flexible putty knife at least 3 inches in width. Narrower tools do not bridge a wide enough area, and they make it difficult to "feather" the edges out so that the patch will blend in smoothly with the surrounding surface.

Though small nail holes and hairline cracks can sometimes be patched satisfactorily without cutting them open, for best results the edges should always be undercut, so that the crack is wider at the bottom (the inside) than it is at the top (at the surface). This will insure a good mechanical bond when the patching compound is pressed into place. Begin by first scraping out all loose, crumbling material, using a crack cutter, a beer can opener or similar pointed tool to do the job. Then undercut the edges at each side and use a stiff brush to clean out dust and loose material.

To fill the crack, scoop up some spackling compound with your putty knife, then smear it on over the crack or hole. Make a second stroke at approximately right angles to the first one, holding the blade so that it is almost flat against the wall. Crisscross several times in this manner

Deep openings should be cut out with a pointed tool

Patching material is applied with a flexible putty knife

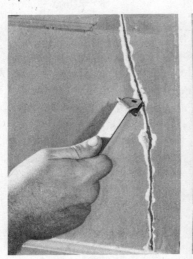

to wipe excess compound off the wall and to leave a smooth, even finish which will require very little sanding after it has dried. If necessary, a thin second coat can be spread on afterward to fill in voids or hollow spots which remain.

Cracks which are more than ¼ inch in width, and holes which are much larger than an ordinary nail hole, are best handled with several layers of patching plaster—at least up until the final smoothing coat is applied. Each layer of plaster is allowed to harden before the next layer is applied, and the final application should not quite fill the hole. After dusting the crack out to remove loose particles, wet it down with clean water before plastering.

The first application should fill the crack or hole halfway to the surface, then be allowed to dry till hard. The second application should bring it almost flush with the surrounding surface, and this too allowed to dry. A final application of spackling compound should then be used to complete the job. When hard, this can be rubbed smooth with medium-grit sandpaper if necessary. If a large patch is required to fill a hole several inches square or more, patching plaster alone should be used. Since plaster hardens quickly (about 20 minutes), it should be mixed in small quantities and only as needed. If trouble is encountered with the plaster setting up too quickly, drying time can be retarded by mixing the plaster with a solution of half-and-half vinegar and water, instead of with water alone.

To smooth the plaster onto the wall, two tools will be needed: a flexible putty knife at least 3 to 4 inches in width and a square plasterer's trowel. Though any small container could be used for mixing the plaster, you will find a small pie tin or baking pan most convenient.

When repairing a section where plaster has buckled or crumbled, or when repairing a deep crack that goes clear through to the supporting lath underneath, the first thing you'll have to do is chip out all of the old plaster which is no longer solid. For sizable sections, it may be necessary to use an old chisel and a hammer. However, in most cases the loosened sections can simply be pried off with a putty knife. Regardless of the method used, defective plaster should be chipped away till only solid material remains around the edges. The edges should then be undercut to provide a better grip for the new plaster.

In most cases this preparatory work will result in exposing the supporting lath underneath. Depending upon the age of the house, this lath may be made of wood, woven metal or gypsum board. Whatever the lath, the patch will have to be built up to the full depth of the plaster, so for best

Loose plaster should be chipped away first

results the patch should be applied in layers. A single, thick coat is liable to shrink excessively, and will often crack as it dries.

After mixing the plaster to a thick, buttery consistency, the area to be patched should be wet down thoroughly with a brush and water. The first coat of plaster is then applied with the putty knife, packing it in tightly around the edges and filling the hole about halfway to the surface.

Wet with water prior to patching

First coat of plaster is pressed into place

To insure a good bond when the second coat is applied, the surface of this first coat should be left rough—or the finish can be lightly scratched after the plaster has begun to harden.

The second coat of plaster is applied after the first coat has dried completely. The surface is first wet down again, then the new plaster is troweled on to bring the patch level with the surface. For this application, the square plasterer's trowel should be used. It bridges a larger area, and will simplify the job of troweling the surface to a smooth finish. Plaster is scooped out of the mixing pan with a putty knife first, then scraped onto the surface of the trowel. This is then slapped on over the patch, using enough pressure to pack it tightly and to make the finish as smooth as possible.

To get a smooth, glassy finish on this final coat, the plaster should be allowed to stiffen slightly. A clean brush is then used to rewet the surface of the patch, while the trowel is dragged over the surface immediately behind the brush. The trowel should be held almost flat against the plaster with its leading edge raised only slightly. For best results, the handyman should bear down hard on the rear edge of the trowel as it is rubbed over the wet surface.

To eliminate the need for building up the patch in layers, professional painters often prefer to nail in a snug-fitting piece of plasterboard as a base. The thickness of this plasterboard must be at least ⅛-inch less than the thickness of the plaster so there will be room for a layer of plaster over the surface after the board is in position. The plasterboard

*Trowel is best for final
smoothing*

Piece of plasterboard can be nailed over opening first

can be nailed directly to the lath underneath or to exposed studs around the edges.

After the board has been nailed into the depression, a layer of plaster is troweled on over the surface. Care should be taken to pack plaster in tightly where the board meets the edges of the old plaster. In most cases, a single application of patching plaster is all that will be needed to get a smooth job on patches repaired in this manner.

One of the most annoying patches to make is the so-called bottomless hole which has no backing. This occurs when a light fixture has been moved or when a hole is punched clear through both plaster and lath.

If the hole is large enough, the easiest method is to chop away enough plaster to expose one or more studs. A piece of plasterboard can then be nailed in as described above to provide a backing for the plaster. However, this is impractical where only a small patch is required, since the hole would have to be enlarged to many times its original size.

Though there are several techniques for filling holes of this kind, one

*Hole is stuffed with paper till it
stays in place*

Plaster is then troweled on over surface

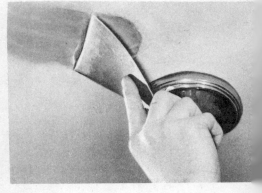

of the easiest methods is to first wad in large amounts of old newspaper.
The paper is stuffed in until it begins to grip on the back side of the
partition. This creates a backing for a first layer of plaster, which can
then be packed in around the edges. When this first application dries,
additional plaster is applied, working from the edges in toward the
center of the hole, till the surface of the paper is entirely covered. This
is then allowed to harden completely. Additional layers of plaster can
then be applied to bring the patch up level with the surrounding surface.

Shades, Window

A balky window shade which does not roll up and down smoothly
when the cord is pulled can be quite a nuisance. In most cases there
is no need to tolerate this condition, since repairs are usually quite
simple to make. To begin with, you should understand how a window
shade works. The wooden roller is hollow at one end and has a spring
on the inside. This spring is attached to the flat rotating pin which protrudes at one end. When the shade is pulled down, the spring is wound
up. Small ratchet pawls or catches on the outside drop into place to lock
the roller and to keep the spring from rolling back up after the shade
has been pulled down as far as desired.

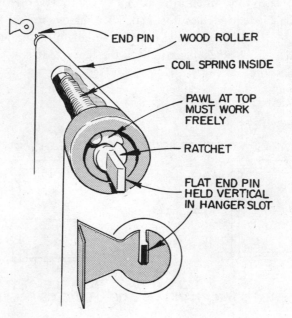

END PIN   WOOD ROLLER

COIL SPRING INSIDE

PAWL AT TOP
MUST WORK
FREELY

RATCHET

FLAT END PIN
HELD VERTICAL
IN HANGER SLOT

When the shade is to be raised, a slight downward pull causes the pawls or ratchets to flip out of their locked position, thus permitting the spring on the inside to roll the shade back up. The opposite end of the roller has a round fixed pin which acts as a pivot bearing to support the other end of the shade. The pawl-and-ratchet mechanism is usually exposed on the end of the roller, or it may be partially covered with a metal end cap.

The brackets which support the roller at either end are of two different types. One supports the fixed pin end and has a plain round hole in it. The other one supports the rotating flat pin and it has a slot in it. To install the shade between these brackets, the fixed pin is first inserted in the round bracket. Then the flat pin is dropped into the slotted bracket at the other side. Brackets are usually mounted on the inside of the window casing, but they may also be mounted on the outside of the frame against the face of the casing.

When a shade refuses to wind up properly, the trouble is often caused by a lack of tension in the spring. To wind the spring more tightly, pull the shade about two-thirds of the way down. Then remove the roller from its brackets and roll the shade up by hand. While holding it tightly rolled, replace the shade in the brackets and try it once more. If tension is still weak, repeat the process.

If spring tension is excessive, the blind will tend to snap up, out of control, each time an effort is made to raise it. To correct this condition, raise the shade as high as it will go. Then remove it from its brackets and unroll by hand about halfway down the length of the window. Replace the roller in its brackets and check the tension. If still too tight, repeat the procedure.

When a window shade refuses to catch or stop after it has been pulled

TO INCREASE ROLLER TENSION, WIND SHADE THIS WAY

PULL SHADE DOWN   REMOVE AND   REPLACE - TEST
                   HAND WIND UP   FOR GOOD RAISING

down, the trouble is usually caused by ratchets or pawls that are not working properly. Sometimes they stick and do not catch in the ratchet mechanism when pressure is released. To remedy this, take the shade down and examine the pawls (it may be necessary to remove the end cap first) to see if they are clogged with dirt or otherwise stuck. In almost every case the defect can be corrected by brushing clean and applying a little lubrication on the pivot pins. Light oil or powdered graphite should be used.

If a shade rolls up and down unevenly, or if it tends to wobble excessively, the trouble is probably due to a bent pin (the fixed pin). To repair this, straighten the pin with a pair of pliers. If the pin looks rusty or is caked with dirt, rub lightly with a small piece of sandpaper before replacing the roller in its brackets. If the uneven operation is due to a broken spring (this is usually indicated by a lack of tension or winding ability), the only sure cure is to replace the roller completely.

A window shade which tends to fall out of its brackets repeatedly is not mounted properly. The trouble is caused by the fact that the supporting brackets are too far apart. If the brackets are mounted against the outside of the window frame, the simplest cure lies in moving one of the brackets a little closer, leaving just enough clearance to permit the roller to turn freely without binding.

If the brackets are mounted on the inside of the window frame (so they face each other), the distance between them can be lessened by removing one of the brackets and shimming it out with several thicknesses of cardboard. This will bring it slightly closer to the bracket on the opposite side, thus reducing the distance between them. Another way to cure this condition is to pull out the fixed pin slightly from the end of the roller so that it projects more than normal.

In those cases where a roller tends to stick because the brackets are too close together, the handyman will have to do just the opposite—that is, increase the distance between brackets, if possible. This is simple when brackets are mounted on the outside face of the window, but impractical with inside-mounted brackets. The first technique that can be tried is to tap each bracket lightly with a hammer. This will tend to flatten them against the window frame, thus increasing the distance between brackets. If this doesn't do the trick, the metal cap with the fixed pin attached should be pried off. This will expose the solid wood of the roller. A saw or coarse sandpaper can then be used to shorten the roller slightly. The cap and pin are then replaced on the end of the roller, and the assembled unit reinserted between the brackets.

Stains, Fabric, Removing

The most important rule to observe in removing any stain from fabric is to tackle the job as promptly as possible. A stain that can be removed easily when fresh will often be difficult (or even impossible) to remove after it has dried or after the stain has been "set" by heat.

The proper treatment depends on the kind of stain involved and on the type of fabric. In some cases the stain-removing chemicals required may cause damage to the fabric or dyes, so that the material will look even worse than it did before. To avoid this possibility, always test first on a hidden corner of the same fabric. If the chemicals cause damage, the best solution lies in sending the article to a professional cleaner. He has the special equipment and knowledge required to handle some of the more difficult stains and fabrics.

Freshly spilled liquids should always be mopped up as quickly as possible. Use clean, absorbent cloths or cotton, blotting paper or a clean sponge and soak up carefully without rubbing the stain in. Avoid spreading the liquid as this will only make the stain bigger. In many cases, powdered chalk, cornstarch or talcum powder can be spread over the stain to soak it up before it dries. Remove the powder as it becomes saturated and apply fresh powder until no more liquid is absorbed. Since these powders are all white, this method is not always suitable for use on very dark fabrics. The powder may cause its own white stain if it cannot be brushed off completely.

The chart outlines methods for tackling a few of the more common stains that may occur on fabrics around the home. Generally speaking, greasy stains are removed with a grease solvent of the type usually referred to as dry cleaning fluids. These are available at grocery stores and hardware stores and they should be carefully used according to directions on the label. Some are flammable, and practically all have vapors which are dangerous if inhaled in a confined area. The flammable kind should not be used where any open flame or danger of electrical spark is present.

Nongreasy stains usually are tackled with some other type of solvent or remover: water, liquid detergent, rubbing alcohol, turpentine, acetone or amyl acetate. Many stains will actually be a combination of greasy and nongreasy ingredients; therefore successive treatments with both types of solvent will be required.

When a fabric is not washable yet the stain requires treatment with

REMOVING COMMON STAINS FROM FABRICS

TYPE STAIN	SUGGESTED TREATMENT	ADDED MEASURES
Gravy, syrup, chocolate, catsup, egg, mucus, vomit, ice cream, citrous fruits, perspiration (fresh), urine (fresh), blood.	Sponge thoroughly with cool water. If stain remains, soak for several hours, then sponge with detergent solution and rinse again. If a greasy stain still remains, sponge with dry cleaning fluid.	Some of these stains will change color of fabric. If so, try sponging with dilute ammonia. When stain persists try a bleach.
Coffee, tea, non-citrous fruits, soft drinks, beer, mustard, grass, foliage.	Sponge with cool water immediately. Rub in mild liquid detergent and soak for half hour. Rinse in clear water. If fabric permits, pour boiling water through stain from 2 or 3 feet. On non-washable articles stain can sometimes be removed by sponging with rubbing alcohol.	Some of these stains are invisible when dry but turn brown after laundering or cleaning. If stains persist bleach can be tried.
Butter, grease, oils, lipstick, cosmetics, salad dressings.	If stain is oily and fresh try sprinkling on talcum powder or corn starch (not on dark fabrics) to absorb excess. Brush off, then sponge thoroughly with dry cleaning fluid.	If stain persists and article is washable try sponging with undiluted liquid detergent.
Wax, crayon, shoe polish.	With dull knife scrape away as much as practical. Then sponge with dry cleaning fluid. If colored stain remains, sponge with alcohol.	If stain persists bleach can be tried.
Ballpoint ink.	Sponge stain repeatedly with acetone. On fabrics of acetate, Arnel or Dynel use amyl acetate instead.	If stain is old or set, bleaching may be required.

water, rubbing alcohol often can be used instead. Test the effect of the alcohol on a corner of the fabric. If the dye is not affected, the alcohol can be used safely. Alcohol can be used also on nonwashable fabrics instead of water to flush out detergent when this treatment is called for. The alcohol dries quicker and is less likely to cause shrinkage or other damage. It should be diluted with 2 parts of water when used on acetate fabrics.

To use a grease solvent effectively with least possible damage to the fabric, always work from the back side when possible. Place the stain face down on a clean pad of absorbent cloth, then apply solvent to the back with another pad of clean cloth. To avoid spreading the stain, always apply sparingly and work from the center out toward the edges with light brushing strokes. Make repeated light applications, rather than one or two large ones, to avoid spreading the stain. Spread solvent to an irregular line around the edges and feather out the strokes to minimize the possibility of forming a ring. If the fabric will not be harmed by it, a ring of absorbent powder also can be sprinkled around the stain before applying the solvent.

When acid-type stains or acid-bearing liquids cause the colors of a dye to change, the color often can be restored by treating with household ammonia. Sponge on lightly or moisten the stain with water and hold over an open container of ammonia so that the fumes can act on it. This neutralizes the acid and often restores colors which have been changed by its action.

Bleaches can be used to remove many stains which will not come out with solvents, detergents or other treatment. However, bleaches are quite strong and may react with some fabrics or dyes to cause lasting damage. Therefore always test carefully before using and follow the manufacturer's directions as to strength and application.

The three most widely available household bleaches are chlorine, sodium perborate and hydrogen peroxide. These are all sold in drugstores and grocery stores and are available under various brand names. Chlorine is usually used in dilute form (2 tablespoons of the chemical to 1 quart of water) and is not recommended for use on silk or wool. Sodium perborate is safe for use on all fabrics when mixed with lukewarm water. When mixed with hot water it should never be used on silk, wool or Dynel. Hydrogen peroxide (3 per cent) is also safe for use on all fibers, but it is slower acting than the other two.

Bleaches should be applied to small stains with a medicine dropper and to large stains by soaking. Chlorine should be allowed to soak on the fabric for no more than five or ten minutes at a time and then rinsed well with water. Several short applications are safer than one long one. Sodium perborate bleaches are usually allowed to work longer—from one-half hour up to several hours if necessary. Hydrogen peroxide bleach is more effective if the stain is covered with a cloth dampened in the solution, then covered with a second dry cloth and pressed with a hot iron. All bleaches should be rinsed out with plenty of water when the job is done.

Stair Repairs

Complete rebuilding and strengthening of an old, weakened stair frame is a job that calls for the services of a professional builder. However, the elimination of annoying squeaks, the tightening of loose handrails and the repairing of worn or cracked treads are all jobs that can almost always be performed by the average home handyman equipped with only ordinary hand tools.

Most stair squeaks are caused by a partially loosened tread which is rubbing against the top of a riser or against one of the stringers. The

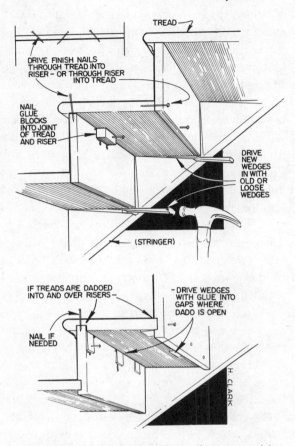

stringers are the long wide boards which support the staircase at either side. One is against the wall, and the other runs along the opposite side, underneath the balusters. A slight squeak can often be silenced temporarily by squirting powdered graphite or other dry powdered lubricant into the joints between tread and riser or between tread and stringer. However, this is only a temporary expedient which silences the squeak without eliminating the probable cause: a tread which is loose at some point, so that it shifts up and down when weight is placed upon it.

For a permanent repair the loose joints between tread and riser must be tightened up. This can most easily be done by driving nails in at an angle. Have someone stand on the offending tread so that his weight holds it down. Then drive two nails (eight penny finishing nails) into the tread at an angle to each other so that they form a wide V. Space them 2 or 3 inches apart, then countersink with a nailset and fill with matching colored putty.

When treads are made of heavy oak or other hardwood which is difficult to nail, screws can be used instead. Drive the screws downward through the tread into the top edge of the riser below. Drill pilot holes first, making them large enough to permit the body of the screw to pass through without difficulty. However, do not drill into the riser. Use soap or paraffin to help lubricate the screw threads and countersink so that the screwheads can be covered up with wood plugs or colored putty.

Fastening down with nails or screws as described above is the method usually used on stairs which have been assembled with plain butt joints. For those which have been put together with groove-and-rabbet joints, a different method can be used. Thin wooden wedges are driven upward into the loose joint immediately under the stair nosing. If the steps have a cove molding under the nosing, pry this off first to expose the joint. Then coat wedge-shaped strips of wood with glue and drive them upward into the recess until they fit snugly. After driving wedges upward till the joint is tight, trim off any surplus wood which sticks down and renail the cove molding.

To tell whether the stairs in your home are assembled with butt joints or groove-and-rabbet joints, pry off the cove molding (if there is one) and poke upward with a knife blade along the face of the riser. If solid wood is encountered on the bottom side of the tread, the stairs have butt joints. If there is a crevice which permits the knife blade to slide upward, then treads and risers are jointed with rabbeted joints.

On cellar stairs, or other stairways where the underside is exposed, wedges which have worked loose between treads and stringers can be tightened by coating with glue and hammering in until they are snug. Secure them permanently by driving finishing nails in at an angle after hammering them in as tight as possible.

An examination of the underside of an exposed staircase of this kind may disclose that the bottom edge of a riser has been pushed backward from constant kicking so that it no longer is tight against the back edge of the tread immediately below it. When a defect of this kind is discovered, hammer the joint shut from behind, then angle-nail as previously described.

When splits or cracks develop in the nosing (front edge) of a tread, glue the split pieces back in place by working glue behind the splinters with a thin toothpick. If the split is bad, reinforce by driving in a small wood screw near the underside of the tread. Countersink the screw head, then fill with putty. Allow glue and filler to dry hard, then sandpaper smooth before refinishing.

If a tread is badly split down the middle, or if it is damaged beyond repair, it should be replaced. In those cases where stairs are built with treads simply butted against the wall stringer, removal of the old tread is fairly simple. Pry off all moldings, then hammer upward against the bottom of the nosing to lift the tread upward without damaging the riser. Use this old tread as a pattern and cut (or have cut at the lumberyard) a new tread to match. Then replace in the staircase, using nails and glue to hold it securely in position.

In those cases where the tread is recessed into the wall stringer at either side so that it cannot be lifted straight up, replacement is a much more difficult job and calls for the services of an experienced carpenter. An emergency repair often can be made by temporarily nailing a sheet of ½-inch plywood over the top of the tread till a carpenter can be called in.

Loose handrails are usually caused by loosened wall brackets which support the handrail. Remove the screws that hold the bracket in place, then repack the hole with wooden toothpicks or wood slivers before reinserting and tightening the screws. If the screws do not strike studs in the wall, the bracket should be moved up or down slightly till a position is found where screws do strike solid wood. If this is impractical, use toggle bolts or expansion anchors instead of ordinary wood screws to hold the bracket in place.

When a handrail which is not fastened to the wall begins to get shaky, the trouble can usually be traced to loosening of the main support—the heavy newel post at the bottom. This can sometimes be strengthened by working glue in behind the post and then toenailing treads to it with large finishing nails. Or the post can be tightened with one or two very long screws, counterboring each one deeply so that the head is recessed an inch or two. Fill the hole which remains by hammering in a matching wood plug or a short length of dowel.

Tiles, Ceramic, Care and Repair

Though ceramic tiles often will last for the life of the house, minor repairs will sometimes become necessary. This may occur when walls must be opened to get at hidden plumbing for repairs, when individual tiles are accidentally scratched or cracked or when tiles work loose and fall out completely.

There are a number of different reasons why tiles may work loose on kitchen or bathroom walls. The most frequent cause is poor workman-

To replace tiles, spread cement on the back and press into position

Grout can be smeared into joint with finger

ship during the original installation. However, it may also be caused by settling of the foundation, by leaks within the wall which cause rotting of the backing material, by heavy vibrations nearby or by accidental damage when nearby repairs are being made.

Whatever the reason, the replacement of these loose tiles has been greatly simplified in recent years by the introduction of ready-mixed tile cements which are available at most paint and hardware stores. These eliminate the necessity for working with mortar cement, which must be mixed before each job, and they can be purchased in small cans as well as in quarts or gallons. This type of tile adhesive is applied in thin layers to the back of the tile, rather than in the thick applications usually required with conventional mortar cements.

Before resetting the loose pieces, scrape off all of the old cement from the back and edges of each tile. Butter the back of the tile with a liberal smear of adhesive and then press firmly into position on the wall. Allow to set until the adhesive is hard, then fill in the open joints around each tile with grout. Grout is the white material used to fill in the spaces between the tiles. Professional tile setters use a white portland cement mortar which they mix up on the job. However, home handymen will find it simpler to purchase ready-mixed grouting material from the hardware store or the tile dealer. This is rubbed into the open joints with your finger tip, and the excess wiped off promptly with a damp sponge or cloth.

When old tiles must be removed because they are badly damaged or because it is necessary to make an opening in the wall, start by first using the corner of a stiff putty knife to scrape away as much grout as possible around all four sides of the first tile. Next, tap at the corner of this tile, using a cold chisel and a hammer. In most cases the corners are not backed up with mortar so they can be crushed inward without damaging adjacent tiles. Chip away all four corners in this manner until the backing material is exposed. Then remove the center portion by prying with the chisel, tapping it lightly with the hammer if necessary. After the first tile has been removed, adjacent pieces will come off easily by tapping from the side with the hammer and chisel.

When grout must be applied to a large number of tiles after whole sections have been replaced, it is easier to thin the grouting material slightly with water and then spread it on over the entire area with an old paintbrush. Rub well into each joint with a soft cloth, then smooth the joints by rubbing with your finger tip. Wipe off the excess with a damp cloth or sponge till the faces of all tiles are clean.

When tiles must be cut to fit in corners or around fixtures, score the glazed surface first with a sharp glass cutter. Then lay the tile face up with the score mark directly on top of a large finishing nail or small metal rod. Step on both sides with your feet to break it cleanly along this line. Rough edges can be smoothed off by rubbing with a file or a coarse abrasive stone. For curved cuts, score with a glass cutter, then use a pair of nippers or pliers to break off the waste. Do this with a series of

Score glazed face of tile with glass cutter   *Position over nail and press down on both sides*

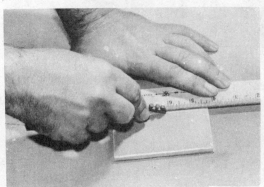
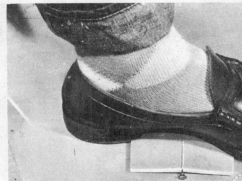

small nipping or "biting" actions, rather than by trying to break out the whole section at one time.

Joints that open up around bathtubs, sinks and shower stall floors are another frequent cause of trouble. Due to slight settling of the fixtures or to repeated heavy scrubbing, the grout in these areas sometimes loosens and falls out. Or it may become so thoroughly caked with dirt that it must be scraped out and replaced. A neat, watertight job of sealing these joints can be accomplished with special calking materials. These come in tubes which have a special applicator tip so you can squeeze them out like toothpaste.

Ceramic tiles are probably the easiest of all household surfaces to clean. Waxes, polishes, plastic finishes or other special coatings are generally not recommended. Instead, simply clean with detergent (not soap) and warm water. Rinse with clear water, then wipe with an old turkish towel. Abrasive materials will eventually scratch the finish, but scouring powder can be used to clean out exceptionally dirty joints. Scrub with a small stiff brush, such as an old toothbrush or nailbrush. Tile floors should be given a thorough cleaning at least twice a year with household scouring powder.

Although the tiles themselves are practically impervious to all types of household stains, spilled matter should be wiped up promptly, since there is always the possibility of its penetrating the joints between the tiles. Rust stains on floors or bathroom fixtures can be removed with oxalic acid crystals. Make a thin paste by dissolving the crystals in hot water and allow this to stand over the stain for 15 or 20 minutes. Wipe off and rinse with clear water, then repeat if necessary.

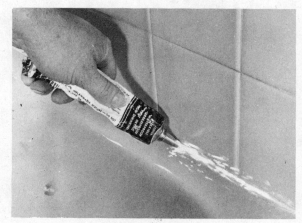

Waterproof compounds will fill these openings

Venetian Blinds, Repairing

Venetian blinds can easily be repaired at home with replacement cords and prefabricated tapes which are widely available in hardware and houseware stores.

Most troubles are caused by lift tapes or the horizonal "ladder" strips which have been torn or by cords which have become frayed or badly worn. In either case, the prescription is the same: the blind must be taken apart so that new cords and tapes can be installed. If one or more of the slats are broken, replacement slats can usually be purchased from a local blind manufacturer and installed at the same time. Since tapes and cords are both relatively inexpensive, it pays to replace them both whenever repairs are made, regardless of whether both are defective at that time.

The drawings show the basic construction of a typical venetian blind. Wood blinds differ from metal blinds in two respects: The mechanism at the top sits on a wood bar which is concealed by a removable wood facing or valance, and the tapes at the bottom are stapled to the bottom bar instead of being attached with a clamp.

Though repairs can be made while the blind is left hanging in the window, it will be simpler to take the blind down and hang it up at a convenient height in the basement or workshop, using loops of wire or string to suspend each one. The blind itself should then be studied carefully and compared with the drawings which accompany this article.

It will be noted that the lift tapes at each side consist of two vertical strips joined by a series of horizontal "ladders." It is these ladders which support the individual slats. The upper end of each tape is attached to the tilt mechanism with clamps (on metal blinds) or staples (on wood blinds). The lower ends are also attached to the bottom bar by staples or clamps, depending on whether the blind is wood or metal.

The cord which raises or lowers the blind is actually one continuous loop. Facing the blind so that this lift cord is hanging free at the right, you will note that the cord is first attached to the bottom left corner of the blind. It travels up between the tapes, across the top of the upper rail and then down through the lift cord lock on the right side. The cord then loops back up through the cord lock mechanism and comes down between the right hand tape to fasten to the bottom bar at the right hand side. A knot in each end keeps this cord from pulling through the bottom bar. A small clip or equalizer on the lift cord permits adjusting the length of the cords so that the blind will pull up evenly from both sides.

To take the blind apart, the lift cords must be removed first. Since the knots which hold it in place on the bottom bar are often concealed by the tapes, the tapes will have to be pried free at the bottom first. The knots can then be untied or cut off and the cords pulled free from the top. With the cords out of the way, the slats can be removed by simply sliding them out from between the tapes—this is the time to wash, clean or repaint them if necessary.

Remove the tapes next by freeing them from the mechanism at the top. On wood blinds they will simply be stapled to the tilt bar, but on metal blinds a loop may be required at the upper end of each tape where it fits over the clamp, as indicated in the drawing. Either way, cut the new tapes to the same length as the old ones by laying them side by side on a workbench or similar surface. To get enough material for fastening to the tilt mechanism at the top, it will probably be necessary

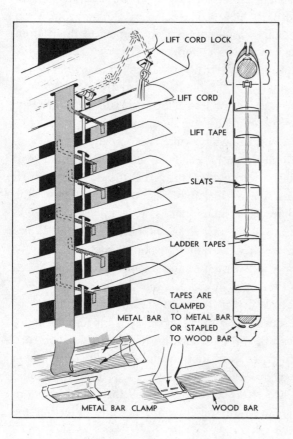

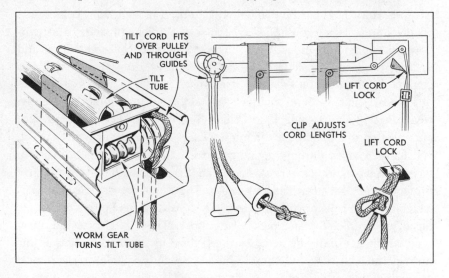

TILT CORD FITS OVER PULLEY AND THROUGH GUIDES

TILT TUBE

LIFT CORD LOCK

CLIP ADJUSTS CORD LENGTHS

LIFT CORD LOCK

WORM GEAR TURNS TILT TUBE

to cut out three or four of the ladder strips at the upper end. The new tapes can then be attached to the tilt mechanism at either side with staples or clamps as required.

To replace the slats, simply fit them between the tapes so that they rest on the ladder strips at each side. The new lift cord is then installed by starting at the bottom left and threading it up through the hole in each slat. Make certain the cord passes ladder strips on alternate sides as shown, then run the cord across the top and down through the lift cord lock. Thread it through the equalizing clip as shown, then loop it back up through this clip and the cord lock mechanism. Now thread it down through the holes on the right side. Knots are then tied in the ends of the cord at each side to secure it to the bottom bar. The lift tape ends can now be stapled or clamped to the underside of this bar to cover the knots.

Since most repair kits include cord and tassels for the tilt cord also, it pays to replace these at the same time. The old cord is simply lifted off the tilt pulley, then cut off at the bottom. The new cord is now placed over the tilt pulley and the new tassels slipped on over the ends. To hold the tassels in place, a knot is tied in each end of the cord.

Weatherstripping, Doors and Windows

Small cracks or openings which are left around loose-fitting windows and doors can permit a surprising amount of heat to leak out during cold weather, and they can be a continuing source of annoying cold drafts on the inside. When multiplied by the total number of doors and windows throughout the house, a tiny crack around each opening can add up to a total area of 2 or 3 square feet—an opening large enough to command the attention of any homeowner.

To seal cracks around windows and doors which do not fit tightly, weatherstripping of some kind is usually installed. The most efficient and most permanent type is the interlocking grooved metal variety which is usually installed during original construction. However, there is also a large variety of other types which can be installed later on to give protection against heat loss and drafts. These may be flexible materials which come in rolls or coils, or they may consist of rigid strips which are faced with resilient foam, plastic or rubber. There is also an all-metal type which is usually made of spring bronze or aluminum. This is the most permanent type you can use, and if properly installed, it is almost as good as the professionally applied grooved type. Unlike the surface-mounted types of felt, rubber or plastic, this metal stripping fits inside the frame so that it cannot be seen when the window or door is closed. It is available in precut lengths or in long rolls from which the desired strips can be cut. It consists of a ribbed, springy metal molding which has nail holes along one edge only. The metal is so shaped that when

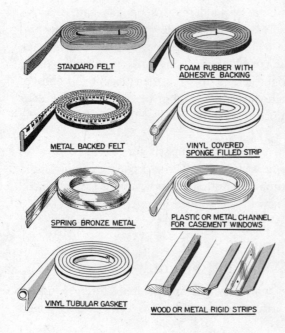

STANDARD FELT

FOAM RUBBER WITH
ADHESIVE BACKING

METAL BACKED FELT

VINYL COVERED
SPONGE FILLED STRIP

SPRING BRONZE METAL

PLASTIC OR METAL CHANNEL
FOR CASEMENT WINDOWS

VINYL TUBULAR GASKET

WOOD OR METAL RIGID STRIPS

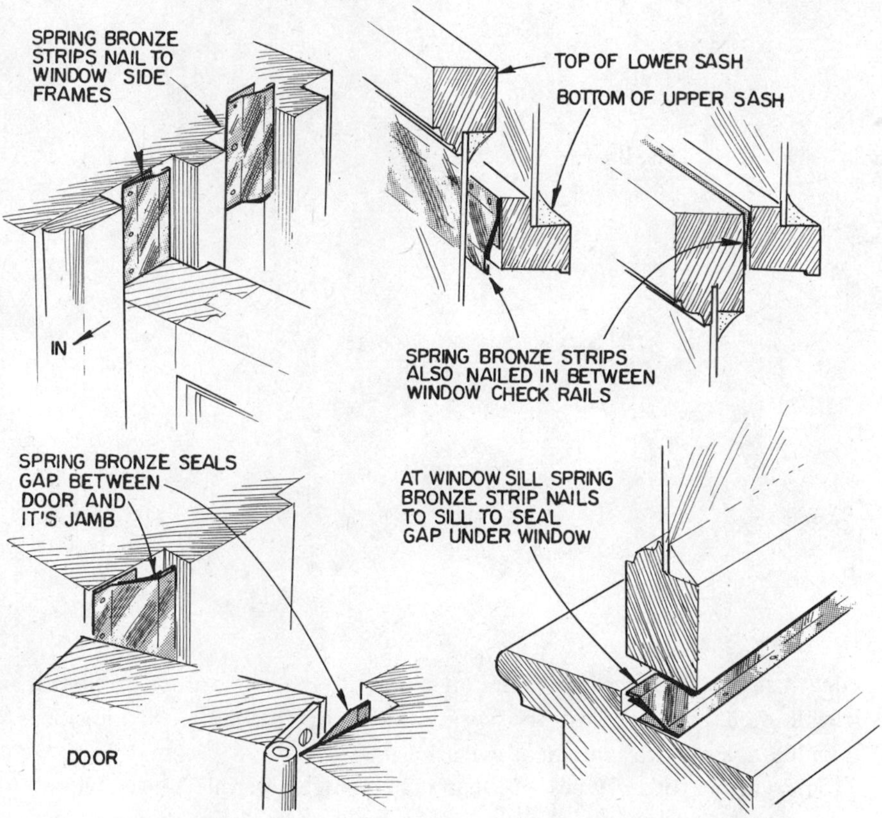

SPRING BRONZE
STRIPS NAIL TO
WINDOW SIDE
FRAMES

IN

TOP OF LOWER SASH

BOTTOM OF UPPER SASH

SPRING BRONZE STRIPS
ALSO NAILED IN BETWEEN
WINDOW CHECK RAILS

SPRING BRONZE SEALS
GAP BETWEEN
DOOR AND
IT'S JAMB

AT WINDOW SILL SPRING
BRONZE STRIP NAILS
TO SILL TO SEAL
GAP UNDER WINDOW

DOOR

this edge is nailed against the frame, the other edge will be raised away from the surface by about ¼ inch. As shown in the drawings, this free, springy edge presses out against the edge of the window sash or door to create an effective seal which will keep air from leaking in or out.

Though this spring-metal weatherstripping is installed inside the frame, the job can be accomplished without removing the sash. Strips are cut to length with ordinary tin snips, then nailed into position inside the window channels after first sliding the sash all the way up (or down) so that it is out of the way. An extra strip is then nailed to the inside of the bottom rail of the upper sash so that it will press against the outside face of the lower sash when the window is closed. This seals up cracks or spaces which are normally left between the two sashes when the window is fully closed.

To install this spring-bronze weatherstripping around a door, simply nail strips into place against the door frame so that the free (unnailed)

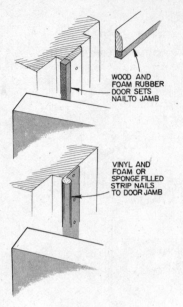

WOOD AND
FOAM RUBBER
DOOR SETS
NAIL TO JAMB

VINYL AND
FOAM OR
SPONGE FILLED
STRIP NAILS
TO DOOR JAMB

edge just barely clears the doorstop molding. When the door is closed, it will then press against the springy edge of the metal, sealing the opening against drafts or heat leaks.

The various other types of weatherstripping materials illustrated all work on the same general principle: a resilient material of some sort presses against the inside face of the window or door to seal up the opening the way the gasket around a refrigerator door seals up that opening. These gasket-like materials are all installed by nailing, stapling or cementing (some are adhesive-backed). The rigid types are installed with nails or screws.

The flexible types are easiest of all to install, since very little cutting or fitting is required. Many of them can be bent around corners in one continuous piece, then nailed or stapled in place. The oldest and least expensive type consists of a dense wool felt which has a notched, flexible metal backing. It is nailed into place so that its felt edge fits snugly against the face of the window sash or door. This is a semipermanent type which will have to be renewed periodically as the felt wears out or becomes caked with paint and dirt.

The newer types of vinyl or plastic weatherstripping will generally last longer and look better. To install them on wood frames, small tacks or rustproof nails are usually included. To install them on metal frames, either an adhesive-backed type should be purchased, or contact cement can be used to paste the stripping in place.

Regardless of the type selected, the weatherstripping is installed with the window or door in the closed position and with its resilient face pressed firmly against the movable member. However, on double-hung windows, avoid pressing the strip too tightly against the face of the sash. Otherwise opening and closing will become exceptionally difficult.

To seal off drafts at the bottom of a door, special rigid strips, called door bottoms, are usually installed. One popular type consists of a rigid, metal-backed felt strip which is screwed in place on the inside, so that its bottom edge just contacts the threshold when the door is closed. A longer-lasting type is one which has a plastic or foam-type seal rather than felt.

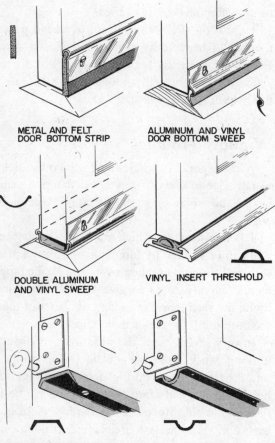

METAL AND FELT
DOOR BOTTOM STRIP

ALUMINUM AND VINYL
DOOR BOTTOM SWEEP

DOUBLE ALUMINUM
AND VINYL SWEEP

VINYL INSERT THRESHOLD

TWO RUBBER CHANNEL TYPES UNDER GARAGE DOORS

For a neater and more permanent job, a special aluminum threshold can be installed to replace the existing one. This has a flexible, vinyl bulb insert which runs down the middle of the threshold, so that the top of the bulb presses against the bottom of the door when the door is closed. Another version is one which has the vinyl bulb or strip screwed to the bottom of the door instead. This presses down against the top of the metal threshold when the door is closed.

For doors that swing inward and must clear carpets or rugs, there are also a number of automatic door bottoms available. These are designed so that they raise up automatically when the door is open, yet press down snugly when the door is closed. To raise or lower the plastic-faced strip, a projecting bumper button at one end is located so that it presses against the door jamb when the door is closed, and this forces the seal downward. A built-in spring action raises the strip back up again when the door is opened.

To seal off the bottom of an overhead garage door, there are also a number of heavy-duty rubber and plastic stripping materials available. Especially designed for overhead doors, these are generally nailed or screwed to the bottom, so that they will press down against the garage floor when the door is shut.

Window Troubles

When wooden, double-hung windows stick or bind, the trouble is usually due to one of two causes: dampness may have resulted in swelling of the wood or carelessly applied paint has hardened around the edges.

To open windows which are stuck shut because of hardened paint, the seal can be broken by forcing a stiff putty knife between the edge of the sash and the stop molding as shown. While tapping the blade in, twist the handle slightly so as to give the tool a prying action which will help break the sash free. Pry along both sides of the sash and along the sill at the bottom till the sash can be raised.

In very severe cases, the windows may have to be pried open from the bottom; work from the outside, if possible, to avoid damaging the interior trim. The ideal tool for this job is a carpenter's hatchet or ax-head. Tap it gently into the crack where the bottom of the sash meets the window sill. Move it along the full width of the window, lifting gently each time until the sash breaks free. If done carefully, neither the sill nor the sash will be marred or damaged.

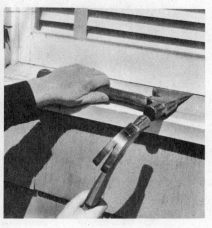

Tapping with stiff putty knife between molding will break the seal

Hatchet is used on the outside to free stuck window

Once the window has been raised, use a wood chisel to scrape accumulated paint off the outside edge of the stop molding where it contacts the inside face of the sash. Scrape carefully to avoid chipping or gouging the wood, then smooth with a piece of fine sandpaper wrapped around a small block of wood. Also check the outer edge of the window sill to see whether the bottom of the sash is rubbing at this point.

Sometimes a window sticks because the wood has swollen from the absorption of moisture, rather than because of accumulations of paint. If the condition is not severe, a cure often can be effected simply by tapping the stop molding inward, using a wooden block and a hammer. Raise the window sash all the way up, then place the block against the outside edge of the stop molding (the edge that presses against the sash when the window is closed). Smack the block sharply with the hammer, working it up and down the full length of the molding on both sides of the frame.

If this doesn't do the trick, the stop molding will have to be removed entirely by prying off with a chisel. If done carefully, the molding can be saved and renailed after the edge has been trimmed off slightly to provide additional clearance.

While the stop molding is off, try moving the window up and down a few times. If it still binds, the sash itself is probably swollen. When this happens, the entire sash will have to be lifted out by undoing the sash cord or by unscrewing the spring balance which holds it in place. The swollen edge then can be trimmed until the sash slides easily.

Windows that are merely stiff (not stuck) often can be cured by simple lubrication. Rubbing with a block of paraffin (a heavy candle

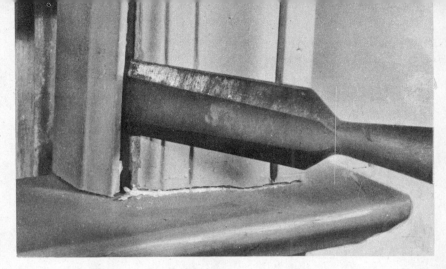

To remove molding pry off with chisel

works well) on the inside of both vertical tracks will often improve the sliding action and permit the window to be raised and lowered easily. Special grease sticks and aerosol lubricants also are available for this purpose. They work well on windows which have built-in metal weather-stripping in the channels (rubbing the metal beforehand with fine steel wool is a good idea).

On double-hung windows which have sash cords, attention also should be given to the pulleys over which these cords run. Pull down the upper sash to expose the pulley at the top of the frame on each side. Place a drop of oil on each pulley shaft on both sides of the wheel. To get the oil into the narrow space on each side of the pulley, use a small "precision" oiler, or place one or two drops on the bearing with a bent piece of wire. Graphite dust (sold for lubricating locks) also will do the trick. This is simply puffed into the opening by squeezing the flexible cartridge in which it comes.

When a window becomes difficult to open or close because the cords have broken or stretched badly, the only cure lies in replacing the cord, preferably with metal sash chain. The chain costs a little more than new rope, but it will last almost indefinitely and it will actually be easier to install. The replacement job can be done by any home handyman equipped with simple hand tools and can be accomplished from inside the house.

To replace the cords in the lower sash (these usually break first because they get the most wear), begin by first removing the stop molding on the side on which the cord is broken. This strip of wood holds the sash in place. It is nailed to the window frame on the inside so that its outer edge forms one side of the channel in which the lower sash rides.

To remove this stop molding, raise the lower sash as high as it will go, then pry the molding off with a wide chisel or putty knife (not a screwdriver). Pry gently, working from the bottom up and moving the chisel or putty knife up a few inches at a time. Where possible, do most prying from the far side (the outside edge) of the strip and try to avoid damaging the molding or the finish, so that the piece can be used again without repainting.

After the stop molding has been removed, the lower window sash can be swung inward on that side and pulled out of its track in the window frame. This exposes the cord groove and knot pocket on each side where the cord is fastened to the edges of the sash. Pull out the broken cord and release the cord on the opposite side even if it is not broken. The weight inside the pocket in the window frame will draw this cord upward out of the way, but the knot in the cord will keep it from being pulled through the pulley at the top.

Put the sash down out of the way, then remove the access panel cover to expose the sash weights on the inside. To remove this panel cover,

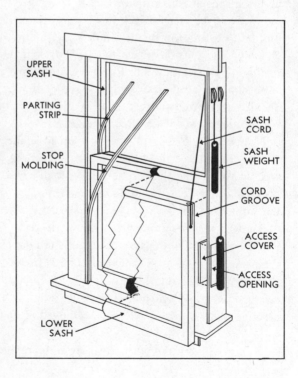

one or two screws must be taken out first. If the cover has never been removed, its outlines may be completely hidden by caked-on paint. If so, try tapping with a hammer till cracks appear around the edge to outline this cover. In some cases this cover may never have been cut completely free during original construction. If this is the case, use a keyhole saw to finish the partial cut left by the builder. There are also some types of window frames in which the parting strip must be removed first in order to expose the access panel cover (see below).

Lift out the sash weight with its broken cord attached, then take the length of sash chain needed and feed it over the pulley at the top of the window frame so that it falls down through the weight box. Its end can then be reached through the access panel opening. To determine the amount of chain needed, use the old length of broken cord as a guide, or set the sash temporarily on the sill to estimate the length of chain needed.

To keep the outside end of the chain from slipping through the pulley at the top, slip a nail or hairpin through one of the chain links on the outside. Fasten the inside end of the chain to the sash weight by looping the chain through the eye at the top of the weight, then lock it securely with the special clips provided.

Now put the weight back inside the pocket in the window frame and pull it up to the top of the window by pulling down on the end of the chain on the outside. Place the sash back in its frame with its bottom resting on the window sill. Pull the chain down as far as it will go, then slip it into the cord groove with its end resting in the knot-retaining hole. Secure this permanently in place by driving in one or two small nails and cut off any excess chain which remains.

Now raise the sash all the way up to make certain it works freely. By watching through the access panel opening, check the action of the weights to see that they do not hit bottom. Then replace the access panel cover and nail the stop molding back in place in its original position at the side of the window.

Though the directions given above describe the steps involved in replacing only one of the sash cords, it is advisable to replace both sides at the same time—even though only one is broken. Chances are that even though the other one looks all right, it is at least partially frayed and stretched and will go soon. To do the other side, the access panel cover on that side will also have to be removed after the sash has been taken out.

When cords for the upper sash are to be replaced, the lower sash must first be removed by prying off the stop molding and swinging the sash outward as described above. This permits the handyman to remove the access panel cover so that he can get at the sash weights. Bear in mind that the one panel cover on each side serves both upper and lower sash weights.

After the lower sash has been removed from its channel in the window frame and disconnected from the cords, the parting strip molding must also be removed. This narrow wooden strip is the dividing piece which separates the channels for the upper and lower sashes. It fits into a groove cut in the window frame. In some cases it can be pulled loose with the fingers, but in most cases additional prying or pulling will be required to free it from its wedged-in position and from caked-on coats of paint. Use pliers to grip it with adequate leverage, and pad the jaws with pieces of cardboard or cloth to avoid damage to the molding or its finish. Start pulling it out at the bottom, and work slowly and carefully upward, sliding the top sash down out of the way as the bottom is worked free.

After the parting strip on one side has been removed, the upper sash can be swung out in the same way as was the lower sash. The cords at each side can then be removed and replaced with chain as previously described. Replace the top sash in its position in the frame, tap the parting strip back into position, and reinstall the lower sash after its cords have been replaced.

Steel casement windows which hinge at the sides may also become difficult to open or close without forcing, or they may fail to close as tightly as they should. This condition not only permits cold drafts and wind-blown rain to enter, but can result in a considerable loss of heat in the wintertime.

The most common ailment is rust, particularly around hinges and along the edges. To prevent this, steel windows should be periodically painted with a good quality exterior trim paint or enamel. Rusty areas should be scraped clean, down to the bare metal, then touched up with a rust-resistant metal primer. Allow this to dry thoroughly before proceeding with the top coat.

Before painting a steel window, check the condition of the putty or glazing compound around the outside of the glass. Cracked or dried-out putty provides a ready means for moisture to enter, permitting rust to develop inside the channels. The old putty should be scraped out completely and the bare metal primed with a rust-resistant coating before new putty or glazing compound is applied. In a properly glazed window, the glass is bedded in putty from both sides, so make certain that putty is pressed firmly into the groove to cover the edges as well as the face of the glass.

In addition to painting and puttying, casement windows should be lubricated at least once a year to keep all parts operating smoothly. Apply a few drops of oil to each hinge, making certain that the oil penetrates into the space between the hinge leaves, as well as to the pin which joins the two halves together. To insure uniform penetration and coverage, the hinge should be oiled twice—once when slightly open, and again when opened all the way. If necessary, caked-on paint should be scraped away to permit the oil to penetrate.

Most steel casement windows are actuated from the inside by a crank or handle at the bottom. This handle contains a geared mechanism which pushes an arm out to open the sash. The end of this arm slides in a grooved track on the bottom as it swings the sash open or closed. When this fails to slide smoothly along its track, extra pressure on the handle is required each time the window is opened or closed.

When this happens, the handyman should open the window all the way and inspect the bottom of the sash frame from the outside. A wire brush should be used to scrape out rust and accumulated dirt or old grease, then a liberal application of new grease should be applied by rubbing it into the groove. An aerosol-type lubricating spray can also be used, though the track should still be cleaned before this is applied.

In some cases the gear mechanism inside the handle becomes stiff or inoperative because of a lack of lubrication on the inside. If a few drops of oil in the joint where the handle enters the case do not do the trick,

Groove underneath sash should be
cleaned out with wire brush

Track underneath sash should be smeared
with grease

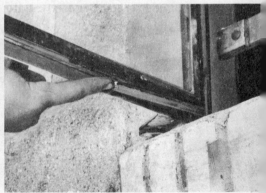

the handle mechanism should be removed by unscrewing the two bolts at each side. Wash out the old hardened lubricant with kerosene or a similar solvent, then apply fresh grease of the white or nonstaining type. If the gears are worn so badly that they no longer mesh properly, the entire handle should be replaced.

To lock the windows shut, most casements have a locking handle in the frame about halfway up. This has an eccentric hook which fits through a slot in the frame to engage the edge of the sash when fully closed. When this handle is pressed down, the hook draws the sash in tight. If the hook does not close the sash tightly enough, try bending the lip of the strike plate on the outside edge of the sash frame.

Another way to insure tighter closure is to remove the locking handle entirely and place a thin shim of fiber board, plastic or sheet metal against the frame before reinstalling the locking handle. This tends to draw the locking handle inward, thus shortening the hook on the outside and pulling the sash even more tightly closed when the handle is pressed all the way down.

Aluminum windows (casement or sliding) generally do not need painting for protection, though they may be painted for decorative purposes. However, since it is subject to pitting—particularly if your house is located near the seashore—metal parts of windows should be waxed periodically to help preserve the metal and keep it from becoming badly stained. If the metal is already pitted, rub lightly with fine steel wool before applying the wax. Don't forget to apply wax to all edges and inside the tracks as well. On sliding windows, at least once a year clean out the grooves to keep them operating smoothly. (*SEE* METALS, REPAIR

Oil should be applied to hinge once a year   *Handle assembly is removed for greasing*

AND MAINTENANCE *IN SECTION II AND* METAL SURFACES, HOW TO PAINT *IN SECTION IV.*)

A problem that often develops with hinged casement windows is failure to close tightly around the sides. This allows drafts to enter when the wind is blowing in the right direction. To check, a thin strip of cardboard can be slid around the rim while the window is closed. If the cardboard slides easily when the window is tightly shut, the casement is not closing as tightly as it should. In some cases this condition can be cured by taking the steps outlined above. However, if this fails, it may be necessary to bend the lip of the window frame outward slightly by grasping the edge with a wrench and applying leverage. Do not try to bend by hammering since this would tend to loosen the entire frame where it fits against the walls.

When bending of the metal frame is impractical, or when this fails to provide a draft-free closure, plastic or vinyl weatherstripping can be applied. Several kinds of self-adhesive stripping are available in lumberyards and hardware stores. They can be cemented in place around the inside of the opening to seal out drafts and moisture. Some brands are cemented in place with contact cement while others come with an adhesive backing so that no cement is needed.

III

Exterior Repairs

THE OLD ADAGE which says that "an ounce of prevention is worth more than a pound of cure" was never more pertinent than when used to describe the need for preventive maintenance around the outside of the house. Because leaking gutters, loose shingles, small cracks and other minor defects are scarcely noticeable when they first appear, most homeowners tend to ignore them. As a result, the condition usually gets worse and eventually a major repair job is required. Yet, in nine cases out of ten, a few minutes' work at the beginning would probably have taken care of the necessary repairs.

Since these minor defects obviously will not cry out for attention (until they finally become serious), you should get into the habit of inspecting the outside of your house at regular intervals, usually in the spring and fall. Take a slow walk around the outside, inspecting windows and doors, as well as exterior walls, siding and masonry surfaces. Use a ladder to check the condition of the roof and to see that gutters and downspouts are all in good repair. Don't forget to check for signs of wood rot where posts and columns come close to the ground, and watch for cracked boards, peeling paint or other signs which may indicate that repairs are necessary.

When trouble is discovered, refer to the pages which follow to determine what steps you will have to take to make the necessary repairs. The quicker the job is attended to, the less the total damage or loss will be.

Blacktop Driveways, Resurfacing and Repair

To protect blacktop driveways against the ravages of weather and hard wear and to resurface those which have become stained or pitted, homeowners can use special waterproofing sealers that can be put on with an ordinary pushbroom.

Designed so they can be applied right out of the can without need for heating or for adding solvents of any kind, these blacktop sealers waterproof the surface so that moisture cannot penetrate to cause frost damage during the winter. They also form a tough, elastic film which protects asphalt pavement against its chief enemies: oil, gasoline, battery acids and road salts.

Available from paint and hardware stores, and from lumber dealers in many communities, most blacktop sealers are heavy-bodied water emulsions which have a coal-tar pitch or neoprene base. Usually sold in 5-gallon cans, these sealers contain no flammable solvents and are perfectly safe to handle. A 5-gallon can will coat anywhere from 200 to 300 square feet, depending on the porosity of the surface and the thickness of the coating.

Though these sealers will fill in minor cracks and shallow pit marks, larger holes and badly worn sections may require additional preparation. If the crack or hole is small, a simple patch can be applied by mixing the sealer with sharp sand to form a thick paste. This is troweled on over the crack and allowed to dry before proceeding with the resurfacing operation.

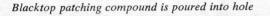

Blacktop patching compound is poured into hole

Another method for repairing surfaces which have a great many small voids is to first spread dry sand over the surface. The sand is then swept off all the smooth areas without removing it from the crevices and voids. You can now apply the blacktop sealer in the usual manner (as described below), brushing it on over the entire area, including the sand-filled voids.

When a driveway has sizable holes or badly eroded sections that need patching, a specially prepared, cold-mix asphalt patching compound should be used. Requiring no mixing or heating, this material can be purchased in various-size bags, ready for use as soon as the container is opened.

To make a patch with one of these cold-mix compounds, first dig out all loose material from the bottom of the hole. If the hole is deep, gravel and stones should be placed over the bottom and tamped firmly to provide a solid foundation for the patching material. The hole is then filled with patching compound to within 1 inch of the top. This is tamped firmly, using a length of 2x4 or 4x4 lumber.

Additional cold-mix is then poured on till the surface of the patch is about ½-inch higher than the surrounding surface. A final rolling or tamping will compress the material to the required density and bring it down level with the surrounding surface. For this final tamping operation

Car is then used to tamp material down

NEW PATCH
OF BLACK TOP

you can simply drive your car back and forth over the surface a few times. Or a water-filled garden roller can be used.

After all cracks, voids and broken areas have been patched, the final step is the application of the blacktop sealer. This is best done on a day when the weather is dry and warm, preferably while the sun is shining on the surface. With most brands there are just three steps to follow:

(1) First sweep the surface absolutely clean to remove all dust, dirt and foreign material. Greasy areas and oil slicks should be scraped up, then scrubbed thoroughly with a detergent solution.

(2) To simplify spreading and to assure a good bond, the surface of the driveway should be wet down thoroughly by sprinkling with a hose. Care should be taken to make certain the entire surface is uniformly wet, though puddles should be swept away if water collects in low spots.

(3) The blacktop sealer is next stirred thoroughly and poured on while the surface is still damp. A long-handled pushbroom or roofing brush is used to spread the coating evenly over the entire area. The sealer should be allowed to dry overnight (or longer if recommended by the manufacturer) before normal traffic is resumed.

In most cases one coat of sealer will be sufficient. However, for surfaces in poor condition a second coat may be required. This should not be applied until the first coat is completely dry.

Blacktop sealer is applied with pushbroom

Though blacktop sealer is most often used on old driveways to restore the original surface, most manufacturers recommend that a coat of sealer also be applied on new driveways as a protective measure. Some brands require that new asphalt be allowed to age for some time before the first coat of sealer can be safely applied, so for specific information consult the manufacturer's specifications.

Calking Outside Openings

Calking compound, properly applied and periodically renewed, can be one of the homeowner's most effective weapons in protecting his house against the ravages of weather. It not only serves to keep out moisture, cold drafts and insects, it also prevents heat loss in the wintertime, thus helping to lower fuel bills considerably.

Calking compound consists of a combination of pigment and oils blended into a putty-like material. It will stick tightly to wood, metal and masonry, and it remains permanently elastic, so that it can expand and contract with surrounding surfaces. It is this long-term flexibility which makes it so efficient in sealing up cracks and open joints in all types of material—and in all kinds of weather.

Calking is available in bulk form (quarts and gallons) and in dis-

Calking is forced out much like toothpaste

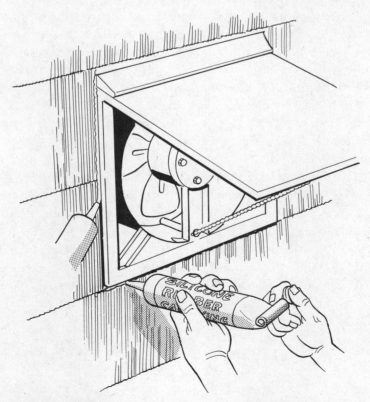

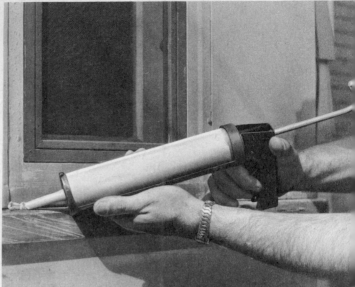

"Drop-in" type calking gun uses disposable cartridge   *Calking gun eases job of applying compound around frames*

posable cartridges for use with a calking gun. For small jobs the home-owner can also purchase squeeze tubes which work much like an over-sized toothpaste tube. These often come with a special key which simplifies the job of squeezing the compound out at a steady rate.

Though bulk calking is manufactured in a wide range of colors, most retail stores stock it only in white, gray and black. Cartridges are also available in these same colors, with white and gray being the most pop-ular. Black calking is used mainly inside gutters and around roofs, and it differs from the other compounds in that it usually contains asphalt which may be reinforced with fibered asbestos. Though the black re-mains elastic for long periods of time, it will not take paint satisfactorily since the asphalt causes bleeding and staining of any paint which is ap-plied over it.

For an efficient seal, calking is usually applied with some type of gun which forces the compound out through a narrow nozzle. Pressure is applied by a plunger which is trigger-actuated while the nozzle is moved steadily along the joint being filled. Calking guns generally come in two types: a full-barrel type, which is designed for filling from bulk con-tainers, and a half-barrel or drop-in type which is intended for use with disposable cartridges. The cartridges used in these half-barrel guns

Compound should also be applied where frames meet siding

have their own plastic nozzles. When the cartridge is empty, the entire unit is simply thrown away. This eliminates the messy job of cleaning out a calking gun each time it is used.

Though cartridges cost slightly more than bulk calking, most home-owners will find it more convenient to buy calking in this way. The cartridges are simpler and quicker to use, and they are available in white, gray or black. They are designed so that the user can change from one color to another without waiting till the first one is completely empty.

When applying compound to open joints around window frames or door frames (the most common use for calking compound), the handy-man should attempt to lay the material on in a neat bead which is convex rather than concave at the surface. A concave bead tends to stretch and crack sooner than a convex one, so it is bad practice to smooth the compound down with a finger or tool in order to form a smooth-looking bead.

To get a ribbon or bead of uniform thickness, the gun's trigger should be squeezed with a steady, uniform pressure, rather than in a series of spurts. A little practice in determining the amount of pressure to be applied, as well as in determining the rate of speed at which the tip should be moved, will soon enable the handyman to lay down a neat ribbon of uniform thickness and appearance.

Because calking compound will not adhere satisfactorily to a dirty, damp or greasy surface, it is important that the surface be properly prepared before the compound is applied. A stiff brush should be used to clean out dirt and debris, and the material should never be applied while the surface is damp. If the crack is very narrow, a sharp knife or chisel should be used to widen it out so as to form a deep V. To make certain there is no oily or greasy scum on the surface (a common problem in areas where oil burners are widely used), each joint should be wiped down with a rag moistened in paint thinner before calking is applied.

Another error frequently made when recalking old joints is to apply the fresh compound directly over the old material. For a secure bond, all dried-out calking should be scraped out first. If the crack is very deep or wide, it should be packed with oakum first. This ropelike material is available from hardware stores, marine supply stores and plumbing supply dealers. It should be packed to within 1 inch of the surface, and the calking then applied in the usual manner.

Squeeze the calking out while moving the gun along slowly at a steady pace and holding it at an angle so that the bevel on the nozzle is parallel to the surface. Do not pump the trigger spasmodically. Instead, maintain an even pressure on the trigger if you want to insure a neat-looking job. When the ratchet clicks at the end of each stroke, release your grip and

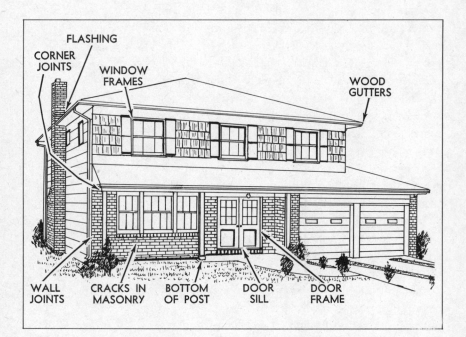

start a fresh stroke with the same steady pressure, moving the gun at the same rate.

In addition to calking around window frames and door frames, attention should also be given to all corners and to every joint where wood and masonry or metal and masonry come together. Calking compound is also the ideal material to use for filling fine cracks in stucco, as well as for sealing up cracks in siding and other exterior woodwork. Particular attention should be paid to joints where porch columns meet porch floors; joints where the vertical trim on windows meets the horizontal sill; the joint between the top or side of a stoop and the house wall itself and any other place where two boards meet, either edge-to-edge or at right angles to each other.

When purchasing calking, always buy the best grade available. Inferior compounds will dry up and crack out prematurely. Properly formulated blends will skin over within a few days, but they will remain soft underneath for years, thus providing the elasticity needed to withstand the constant expansion and contraction which is always encountered on the exterior of any house.

Concrete Patching

Though most people think of concrete as an indestructible type of building material that never needs maintenance or repair, this is only partly true. Constant exposure to alternating cycles of freeze-and-thaw weather, coupled with the settling of supporting foundations or subsurface soil, can cause cracking and crumbling in all types of masonry construction. Regardless of whether repairs must be made on a concrete walk or driveway, on steps or patio floors or on basement foundations and walls, the tools and techniques involved are practically the same.

The basic material used in all types of concrete and cement work is powdered portland cement. When mixed with sand and water (1 part cement to 3 parts sand), the mixture is referred to as cement and is used for such jobs as patching cracks in masonry walls and floors and for making small patches in stucco and concrete. To make mortar, lime is added (1 part cement, 1 part lime, 3 parts sand). To make concrete, gravel is added (1 part cement, 2 parts sand and 3 parts gravel).

Though you can mix your own materials by purchasing sand, cement and gravel separately, a great deal of time and trouble can be saved by purchasing dry, premixed concrete. This comes in different-size bags (from 10 to 80 pounds) and is sold in hardware stores and lumberyards everywhere. No measuring or proportioning of ingredients is required. All you do is add water according to the directions on the bag. Mixing can be accomplished in a wheelbarrow, on a flat piece of plywood or directly on a sidewalk or basement floor.

When purchasing these ready-mixed materials, remember that there are three different "mixes" or formulas available: sand mix, mortar mix, and gravel mix. The sand mix is used for the majority of home patching jobs where cracks and holes must be filled in or where small broken sections must be replaced. Mortar mix is used for assembling brick, stone or cement block walls, while gravel mix is used for building walks, driveways and foundation walls. When in doubt, the homeowner should consult his dealer before the purchase is made.

When mixing cement or concrete, always empty the bag completely so that the ingredients can be thoroughly dry-mixed beforehand. The easiest way to do this is to turn the pile several times with a shovel or hoe. If only part of the bag will be used, put back whatever is not needed before the water is added. Add water gradually, measuring out the right quantities as recommended on the package. Too much water will not only make a soupy mix that will be hard to handle, it will also result in a weak patch which will not stand up as it should.

To patch small cracks or broken pieces on concrete floors, walls, or walks, here is the procedure to follow:

(1) Use a cold chisel and a hammer to undercut the sides of the opening so that it is wider at its deepest part than it is at the surface.

Chisel out opening so that it is wider at bottom than at surface   *Wet down and pack tightly with cement-sand mixture*

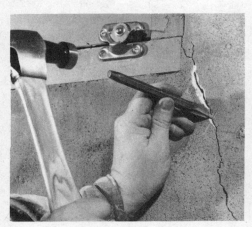

Gravel mix is shoveled into hole being patched

This is necessary to insure a good mechanical bond which will keep the new concrete from falling out as it dries.

(2) Use a stiff brush (a wire brush is best) to scrub out thoroughly all loose particles and chips and make certain the cavity is clean.

(3) Wet down the area inside and around the crack so that the old concrete will not draw water out of the new cement before it has had a chance to set properly. The surface should be thoroughly damp, but there should be no surface water visible.

(4) Pack in freshly mixed cement (sand mix), using a small triangular-shaped pointing trowel. Tamp firmly, then smooth off at the surface to make it even with the surrounding area.

(5) For maximum hardness, patches should be kept damp for several days. The easiest way to do this is to allow the cement to set till partially stiff, then cover with wet burlap or straw. Sprinkle this periodically to keep it from drying out.

When you must replace large broken sections in a concrete sidewalk or patio, the same basic procedure is followed. Gravel mix is used instead of sand mix to assure matching of the original surface in texture and strength. Undercut the edges of the old concrete and make certain that the sides of the broken section do not slope outward. This would

Large patches are smoothed with steel trowel

necessitate troweling the cement out to a feather edge, which would almost certainly result in having it crack out within a short while.

If the repair does not go all the way through the old surface, chop it out deeply enough to make certain that the new section will be at least 1-inch thick at all points. Roughen the bottom as well as the sides of the cavity before the new material is applied.

After the concrete is poured, it should be leveled off by dragging the edge of a long straight board across the top. Allow the patch to stiffen slightly, then rub with a wooden float (a trowel with a wooden face).

Triangular trowel is used for patching mortar joints

For a smoother finish the concrete can be slicked down by rubbing a second time with a steel plasterer's trowel.

To repair crumbling mortar joints in a brick wall, mortar mix is the best material to use. Scrape out the cracked or crumbling mortar to a depth of at least ½ inch, then brush clean and wet down. Pack tightly with mortar cement, then finish by scraping off excess mortar with the tip of the trowel.

To simplify the problem of applying a concrete patch where only a thin layer of cement is needed and to eliminate the need for undercutting, chipping and prewetting of the surface, there are two other types of concrete patching material which can be used. Each consists of a dry powdered cement, but one type comes with a special liquid latex which you use instead of water. The other type is mixed with water, but it has a special vinyl binder added to the cement which greatly increases its adhesive power. Both of these patching cements can be spread on in layers as thin as $\frac{1}{16}$ of an inch, and there is no need for preliminary wetting, chipping or undercutting. They also have a very strong bonding action, making them ideal for use in replacing loose bricks on stoops or terrace borders.

Latex cement can be troweled onto floor in thin layers

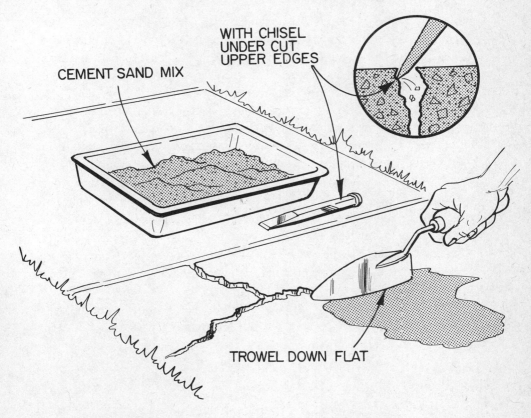

WITH CHISEL
UNDER CUT
UPPER EDGES

CEMENT SAND MIX

TROWEL DOWN FLAT

Fence Repairs

A neat-looking fence is an asset to the appearance of any home, but to keep it neat-looking periodic maintenance is required. Posts which work loose in the ground, making the entire fence wobble or sag, are one of the most frequent causes of trouble. This is particularly true if care was not taken during original construction to tamp the earth firmly around the bottom of each post when the holes were filled. Alternate freeze-and-thaw cycles during a severe winter (especially if the soil is sandy) can also cause posts to work loose. To correct a condition of this kind, several remedies are possible.

(1) Two 2-foot lengths of 2-inch angle iron can be hammered down alongside each post to reinforce it. Each length of angle iron should be held tight against the corner of the post, then hammered down to a depth of about 30 inches. To keep the hammer head from bouncing off the narrow edge of the iron while it is pressed tightly against the post, use a scrap length of iron or a large bolt as a drive punch. This works better than trying to hammer directly on the edge of the angle iron. The two lengths of iron should be driven in at opposite corners of each loose post, then fastened to the post with long wood screws inserted through holes drilled in the metal.

(2) Four-foot lengths of 2x4 can be used instead of angle irons. They can be driven into the ground on opposite sides of the loose post, and flush against it. These, too, should go down at least 30 inches, and they should be screwed to the post with 4-inch lag screws which are inserted through holes drilled in the 2x4 braces. To facilitate driving the 2x4's into the ground, the bottom ends should be shaped to a rough point beforehand. Hammer each one down by placing a wood block over the top to prevent splitting, and be sure you treat these braces by soaking in wood preservative to prevent rotting.

(3) Diagonal braces can be nailed in place with one end at the top of the wobbly post and the other end nailed to a short stake driven into the ground at some distance away. Braces of this type make a fence extremely rigid, but they may be a potential hazard to persons walking nearby. However, they can be safely used wherever they can be concealed by thick shrubbery or if they can be placed in corners where they will be out of the way.

The most permanent way to cure a wobbly fence post is to set the post in concrete. To do this when posts are already up, excavate around each

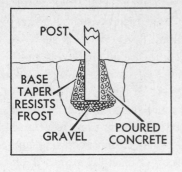

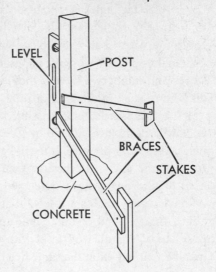

one with a narrow, round-nosed shovel, digging down to within a few inches from the bottom of the post. Make the hole at least 12 inches wide, then fill with freshly mixed concrete. Prepackaged dry materials which contain the necessary proportions of sand, gravel and cement are available at most lumberyards and building materials dealers. These need only the addition of water to be ready for use. The concrete should be poured into the hole till it is slightly higher than the level of the surrounding ground, then troweled to a slope at the top so that it will shed water away from the post.

To make certain the post is vertical before filling in around it, brace it temporarily by nailing braces from the top to stakes driven into the ground several feet away. Allow the concrete to harden for several days before removing these braces. If a small space appears next to the wood, fill this in by packing with roof cement or a similar waterproof compound.

Fences often deteriorate because the wood was not properly treated against rot before the posts and rails were assembled. The only sure cure for a condition of this kind is to replace the rotted sections completely, then protect the balance of the fence against weathering by frequent painting with a good grade exterior paint (if the fence is already painted) or a penetrating sealer (if the fence is unpainted). Be sure you coat all the exposed sides and edges of the wood, and renew the coating whenever it shows signs of wear.

Whenever you have to replace an entire section of the fence, remember to purchase one of the rot-resistant woods, such as cedar, redwood or oak. If possible, buy lumber which has been factory-treated against rot; otherwise coat each piece with a liquid preservative, such as pentachlorophenol or zinc naphthenate. These are available at paint stores and lumberyards, and they will be most effective if the posts are allowed to soak in a pailful of the liquid for several hours.

Since it is practically impossible to install fence posts so that the upper ends will all be level after they have been set in place in their respective holes, the usual practice is to make each post taller than necessary and trim off the excess afterward. One of the corner posts is trimmed off first, then a long string is stretched to the corner post at the other end. A line level (a small spirit level that hangs from the line) is then used to adjust the free end of this string up or down so that the second corner post can be trimmed off level with the first one. Intermediate posts can then be marked off at the same height by making a mark where the string crosses the outside of each post.

To keep water from soaking into the top of a post, the upper end should be beveled to facilitate runoff. An alternate method is to nail cap pieces or ornamental tops onto each post to help seal off the exposed end grain.

On any fence the gate will take particularly heavy abuse. If the hardware is rusted or badly bent, replace it with one of the new, rust-resistant varieties. All hinges should be lubricated frequently to keep them working properly. A wire brace tied diagonally from the bottom corner of the outside edge to the top corner of the hinge side can often straighten a gate which has begun to sag badly. Tie the wire to screw eyes driven into each corner, then insert a turnbuckle in the middle. Tightening up on this turnbuckle will draw the bottom edge upward till the gate is square.

Gutters, Maintenance and Repair

Gutters and downspouts cannot be ignored year after year if they are to continue doing the job for which they were designed. They need to be inspected annually and cleaned out, and they will periodically need minor repairs and adjustments. Most jobs are simple and require no special tools or equipment.

If there are any tall trees near the house, at least one cleanout per year is an absolute must—preferably in the fall right after the leaves have fallen. Cleaning is most easily accomplished with an old whisk broom or other stiff brush, and may have to be repeated several times

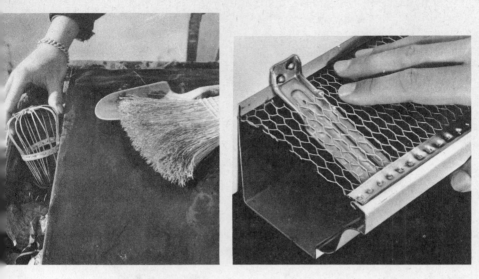

Wire cages should be installed   Mesh guard protects open roof gutters
to prevent downspouts clogging

as leaves continue to fall. Otherwise accumulated debris will clog the
downspouts or dam up the gutters, causing water to back up and overflow.

To keep downspouts from becoming clogged, the opening at the top
should be protected with a special wire strainer or cage which fits into
the upper end of the downspout. This permits water to flow through, but
stops leaves and other trash from falling into the opening. Remember that
this, too, will have to be checked at regular intervals. Heavy accumulations of wet leaves may mat against the outside of the strainer and effectively stop water from getting through.

A better method for keeping debris out of the gutters is to cover the
entire length with strips of ¼-inch mesh hardware cloth (a coarse screen
wire). One edge is pushed up under the bottom row of roof shingles
and the other edge is fastened to the outside rim of the gutter with sheet
metal screws or wood screws. This acts as a "strainer" over the entire
length of gutter to keep leaves and debris out.

To simplify installations of this kind, ready-made gutter guards, or
protectors, are available at many hardware stores. These do not require
any cutting to make them fit since they have specially designed clips
which enable you to snap them quickly into position. They come in various lengths and in long rolls which you cut to length.

Aside from cleaning when necessary, gutters should be inspected at
least once a year for signs of cracking, rotting or rusting. The life of the
gutters can be lengthened considerably by coating the insides with pro-

Paint insides of gutter with protective coating

Loose hanger straps should be renailed as shown

tective compounds. Use linseed oil on wood gutters and liquid roof coating on tin or galvanized metal. (It's a good idea to have the painter do this each time the outside of the house is done.) While copper and aluminum do not rust, they do oxidize, so they also will benefit from being coated periodically on the inside. Roof coating or spar varnish can be used.

While cleaning and recoating the gutters, make a quick inspection of all hanger straps and other fastenings. Any that have worked loose should be tightened or renailed. Those that have rotted away entirely should be replaced with new ones.

In some cases an excessive snow or ice load during the previous winter may have bent hanger straps out of shape so that the gutter sags or no longer slopes properly. This can be quickly checked by pouring a bucket of water into the trough to see that it drains properly. If it doesn't, the slope should be corrected by bending one or more of these mounting straps slightly or by adding extra ones where required. At the same time check all connecting joints and end caps for possible leaks. If any are noticed, smear a liberal dab of heavy roof cement over the joint.

Spots that have rusted through can frequently be repaired well enough to extend the life of the gutter by several years. Begin by scraping away all accumulated dirt and rust, using coarse steel wool or a wire brush. Smear on a liberal application of roof cement, then press on a strip of

Fiber-glass patching material is excellent for downspouts

heavyweight aluminum foil or canvas and cover with another layer of cement.

Plastic repair kits that contain a fiber-glass cloth which you saturate in a special mixture of resin and catalyst are even better. They are available at most hardware stores for about $1, and patches made with them will last indefinitely. They work equally well on all types of metal and wood gutters.

One thing should be kept in mind. When a badly rusted spot is noticed, there is strong likelihood that more areas are about to break through. So before wasting time on repairs, check the rest of the length to determine whether or not the gutter is worth fixing.

If water seems to drain out slowly, or if it doesn't drain at all, the downspout may be partially clogged. When this occurs, try unclogging it by tapping gently with a stick till the trapped debris falls out of the free end at the bottom. If the end is connected to an underground drainpipe, unhook this first. If tapping doesn't do the trick, try flushing it out with a strong stream from a hose. In extreme cases a wire "snake" or auger (the type used by plumbers to clean out sink drains) will be required. This is also the best tool for cleaning out stoppages in curved elbows at the top or bottom of each downspout.

To make certain the water will run off harmlessly, you should try to rearrange the position of your downspouts so that water is discharged onto a nearby patio, walk, driveway or other paved area. In many cases this can be accomplished simply by adding an extra elbow or length of pipe at the bottom end or by turning the existing elbow so that water flows off in a different direction.

If a paved area is located too far away for the existing downspout to reach it, there is another simple modification that can often be made. The downspout is cut off several feet up from the bottom, and a 45-degree elbow is installed to direct water off to one side. This elbow is then extended with additional leader pipe, so that water is discharged onto the paved area, rather than onto the ground directly below.

When downspouts empty into plant beds or lawn areas, splashboards or pans can be installed to divert the water. These may consist of slabs of stone, brick, tile or similar material, or, better yet, a concave slab of concrete can be poured in place. Splash pans should be at least 2 to 3 feet in length and should flare out at the discharge end so that water is spread over as wide an area as possible before it flows out onto the soil.

Instead of a permanent masonry splash pan, there are a number of other devices the homeowner can buy for use under the bottom of each downspout. One type consists of a factory-molded, plastic pan which comes ready for use. Another device is a flexible plastic hose which fits over the lower end of the downspout. When not in use (during dry weather), the plastic hose is rolled up in a neat coil against the building. When water starts to pour down the pipe during a rain, the hose unrolls automatically. Perforations along the top then permit the water to flow out gently with a soaking action which prevents flooding. After the storm is over, the tube is rerolled by hand.

The best solution to the problem of providing adequate drainage is to install an underground pipe, usually called drain tile, which will carry the water away for permanent disposal. This drain line can empty into a nearby storm sewer in communities where this type of installation is permissible. When no storm sewer is available, as in communities which

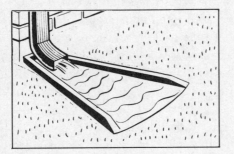

forbid this practice, drain tiles are sometimes installed so that water flows into a drainage ditch or culvert instead.

Since many suburban homes are located where there is no convenient drainage ditch or storm sewer nearby, the most common solution is to install a dry well into which drainpipes can empty. A dry well is merely a large underground hole—usually filled with rocks or gravel—which permits water to seep away harmlessly.

A hole is dug deep enough to permit sinking a 55-gallon drum into the ground with its upper end at least 12 inches below the surface. The drum is cut open at the bottom, then placed in the excavation and filled with large rocks. An opening is cut near the upper end for the drain line, then a heavy wire mesh is placed over the top. Before filling with earth, lay several heavy planks over the top and pack dirt tightly around all sides. To provide proper protection, dry wells should be installed at least 10 feet away from foundation walls.

The underground drainpipe or tile consists of a special terra-cotta or tar-impregnated fiber pipe 3 to 4 inches in diameter. It should be installed so that there is a downward pitch of at least 1 inch for each foot of underground length.

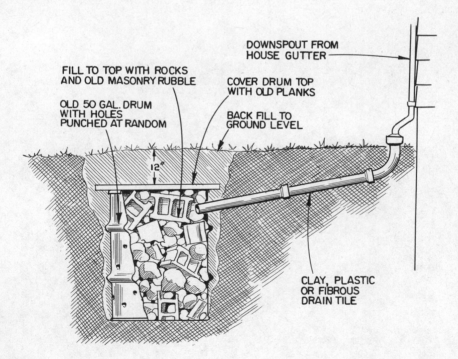

DOWNSPOUT FROM
HOUSE GUTTER

FILL TO TOP WITH ROCKS
AND OLD MASONRY RUBBLE

COVER DRUM TOP
WITH OLD PLANKS

OLD 50 GAL. DRUM
WITH HOLES
PUNCHED AT RANDOM

BACK FILL TO
GROUND LEVEL

12"

CLAY, PLASTIC
OR FIBROUS
DRAIN TILE

For a really permanent dry well, the excavation should be at least 6 feet in diameter. The dry well is then built of concrete blocks (similar to the type used in building cesspools) instead of by burying a steel drum. Since this requires a much larger excavation and a reasonable amount of skill in working with masonry block, this is a job which usually calls for the services of a professional masonry contractor.

Gutters, Replacing

To replace old gutters which have begun to rot or rust, home handymen can easily install new gutters and leaders of lightweight, easy-to-handle aluminum. Only simple hand tools are required, and in most cases the entire installation can be completed over a single weekend.

Aluminum gutters are sold at lumberyards and by roofing supply dealers in 10-foot lengths. They may be cut to size when necessary with a fine-toothed hacksaw. Individual lengths are joined together by means of special slip connectors which are also used when assembling corner sections (called miters) and downspout outlet sections. The outlet sections have a short length of metal pipe soldered into the bottom so that the leader (the vertical pipe which carries the water down to the ground)

New aluminum gutters are simple to install

Elbows are used to provide needed offset

can be slipped over it from below when the gutter has been fastened in position against the eaves.

There should be one of these downspouts or leaders for each 40 running feet of gutter—so when ordering supplies, figure accordingly. To make up the material list, first make a sketch of the roof area on a large sheet of paper. Add up the number of feet of gutter that must be installed to determine the number of 10-foot lengths that will be needed. From the plan, figure out how many miters or corner pieces (remember that there are both inside and outside miters to be considered) will be needed. Then figure up the number of downspout outlet sections that will be required. One slip connector will be required at each point where individual lengths of gutter meet or where outlet sections or miters are installed. Wherever the gutter ends, special end caps (specify right or left) will be needed.

The material list also should include the required amount of downspout or leader as well as any elbows necessary to install them. One elbow will be needed at the bottom end of each leader to throw the water away from the house. Others may be required at the top if overhanging eaves call for an offset connection to permit leaders to be mounted flush against the house. Where this type of offset is required, two 60-degree elbows are usually used. To fasten the leader in position, two decorative aluminum straps are used—one at the top, and one at the bottom. These are bent to fit around the leader and are nailed to the side of the house with rustproof nails.

To hang the gutters, long spikes and aluminum ferrules are used. One is needed for every 30 inches of gutter length. Each spike requires that a hole be drilled through the front and the back of the gutter near the top edge. The long spike is then pushed through the front hole in the gutter and fed through the tubular ferrule previously positioned behind it inside the trough. Push through till it comes out the back side of the gutter, then hammer into the fascia board or wooden cornice along the eaves. Instead of spikes and ferrules, aluminum strap hangers can be used. These are screwed in position across the top of the gutter and have long metal straps which are nailed to the roof sheathing while holding the bottom row of shingles up out of the way.

Regardless of the method used to mount them, gutters should be sloped to provide good drainage. Allow about ½ inch of slope for every 8 feet of gutter length. For exceptionally long runs (over 35 feet), it is best to keep the gutter higher in the middle and have it slope down to both ends. Also make certain that the outside edge of each gutter is below the level of the roof itself. To test for this, lay a straight board on the roof, then position the gutter so that its outside edge does not quite touch the bottom of this board at its highest point. This is necessary to protect against sliding snowdrifts during heavy storms.

Slip connectors and other fittings should be attached to individual

Gutter is hung by hammering spike through the trough

Sections are joined by pressing on slip connector

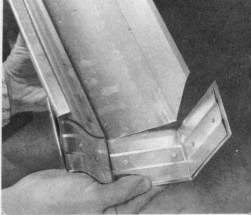

gutter lengths while still on the ground. A special aluminum calking mastic is applied to each connector before sliding it in place over the end of the trough to assure a watertight connection. When working alone, fit connectors onto only one length of gutter at a time so that long, unwieldy sections will not have to be raised into position. A single length of gutter with fittings at one end is light enough to be handled easily by one man on a ladder. To help support the far end of each section while hooking up the near end with the section already in position, drive a large spike into the fascia board to support it temporarily. A loop of cord tied to a smaller nail can also be used at the far end for temporary support.

Masonry Repairs. SEE CONCRETE PATCHING; MORTAR JOINTS; STUCCO PATCHING.

Mortar Joints

Brick, stone and cement block are probably among the most durable of all exterior building materials. However, the mortar joints which hold them together do require occasional maintenance. When these joints begin to crack and crumble and mortar starts working loose, repairs must be made promptly or serious leakage will develop. If not corrected in time, this could result in eventual weakening of the entire wall.

The job of repairing these joints (called tuck pointing) is a time-

When lengths are assembled, edge of connector is bent over with pliers   *Downspouts and corners are attached to gutter while on ground*

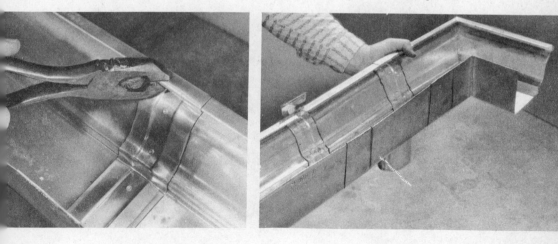

consuming one and therefore an expensive one to have done professionally. On the other hand, this is one task which any home handyman is capable of handling since it requires no special skills or expensive tools. The only equipment needed is a hammer, a narrow cold chisel, a small triangular (pointing) trowel, a stiff scrub brush or wire brush, a scrap board about 8x12 inches and the mortar mix ingredients.

Deterioration of mortar joints is almost always caused by moisture which penetrates through porous areas or tiny hairline cracks. During cold spells this water freezes and causes additional cracking and crumbling until the mortar finally works loose entirely. The only way to prevent this is to make repairs promptly when defects are noticed and to make certain that all calking and flashing is in good repair wherever the masonry walls come in contact with roof shingles, overhanging eaves or other surfaces. By stopping water leaks at these points with a liberal application of roof cement or calking compound, the danger of freeze damage will be greatly lessened. Brick chimneys are particularly vulnerable to this type of damage.

To repair a defective joint, begin by first removing all of the loose or crumbling mortar. In some cases this can easily be pried out by hand, using the point of an old screwdriver or a narrow cold chisel. In most cases the mortar will have to be chiseled out by tapping lightly with a hammer. Care must be exercised to prevent hitting so hard that the bricks or blocks themselves are loosened. Strike the chisel only hard

Chisel is used to remove defective mortar

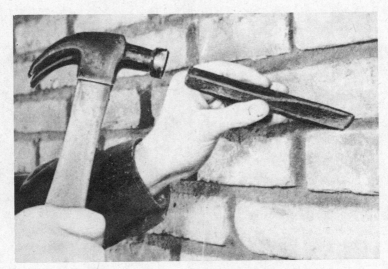

enough to remove mortar to a depth of about 1 inch, holding it at a sharp angle to the surface so that the chisel does not get wedged into the joint.

A prepared mortar mix which contains all the necessary ingredients in dry form can be purchased at most lumberyards and at many hardware stores. These need only the addition of water to give a properly formulated mix of exactly the right consistency. Mix up no more than can be used in about one hour, since the material stiffens up rather quickly. The mix should be stiff enough to hold its own shape without sagging when piled on top of a trowel or other tool.

For those who prefer to mix their own, a standard formula consists of 3 parts clean, sharp sand and 1 part special mortar cement (available from all building materials dealers). If portland cement is used, the mix should consist of 1 part hydrated lime, 1 part cement, and 6 parts sand —all measured by volume.

Regardless of whether the homeowner mixes his own or uses a prepared formulation, all ingredients should first be dry-mixed before water is added. Add water slowly till the correct consistency is reached (stiff, yet buttery) and keep mixing until the whole batch is uniform.

Before using the mortar, wet the bricks on either side of the joint thoroughly. After wetting, press the mortar firmly into place, packing it in tightly with a small triangular pointing trowel as shown. Use a scrap piece of plywood as a "hawk" to carry the mortar over to the wall. Hold

Fresh mortar is packed tightly into joint

this directly under the joint while working to catch any excess mortar which drops off.

Best results will be obtained if the material is applied with a series of small strokes so that no more is smeared over the face of brick than absolutely necessary. Make sure joints stay damp and apply additional water if necessary. It is a good idea also to wet the surface of the wooden hawk to keep the mortar moist longer. If the mortar starts to stiffen, additional water can be added, but this should be avoided since the mix will lose some of its strength every time water is added.

After the freshly filled joints have been allowed to set for a few minutes, finish off each of them to match existing joints. This process (called "striking" in the trade) consists of trimming off excess mortar by using the point of the trowel, or by drawing a bent rod or pipe along the length of each joint. This compacts the mortar and creates a slight depression which will help it to weather better. Concave joints are most popular for exterior walls and they can easily be made by using a length of narrow-diameter pipe or a piece of wooden dowel. The raked or beveled joint is made by trimming with the tip of the trowel held vertically.

When large cracks occur in the middle of a brick or block, repairs are made in almost the same way. Use a chisel to first widen the crack to about ½ inch in width, tapping gently to avoid causing additional damage. Then wet and pack with mortar as just described. If appearance is important, this "joint" can be camouflaged by touching up with a little paint the color of the brick. In extreme cases where bricks are badly cracked, the entire brick should be carefully removed, all old mortar scraped out and a new brick installed.

When several bricks in the same vertical line are cracked, or when many cracks occur through the bricks in a single area, it may be an indication that dangerous shifting of the foundation has taken place. If this is suspected, a professional building contractor should be called in as soon as possible to make the necessary repairs.

Preservatives, Wood

Wood rot is caused by a plantlike organism similar to the fungus which causes mildew and food spoilage. Like all other plants, this organism can thrive only when moisture is present. That is why it is especially important that wood which is in contact with the ground, or which is continuously exposed to dampness, be properly protected.

For years the only effective wood preservative available was creosote.

This has several disadvantages. It leaves an unpleasant, lingering odor, and it has a dark, ugly color which is practically impossible to paint over. However, in recent years new types of wood preservatives have been introduced which eliminate most of the disadvantages encountered in creosote.

Though these preservatives are sold under various brand names, most contain either pentachlorophenol or zinc naphthenate. They are sold as clear solutions and are often mixed with a water repellant to give added protection to the wood. They not only protect against rot and insect attack, they also reduce warping, checking and swelling. Some also act as a primer for the wood so that they actually improve its ability to hold paint.

Pentachlorophenol (called "penta" for short) is usually sold in the form of an oil-base solution which can be applied by brush or spray, or by soaking and dipping. Since the preservative must penetrate to give maximum protection, soaking or dipping is by far the most effective method of application. Where practical, soak the bottom ends of fence posts and similar pieces by standing them upright in a can full of the liquid, or try laying long pieces into a shallow trough built of sheet metal or wood lined with plastic sheeting.

When dipping or soaking is impractical, the preservative should be brushed or sprayed directly onto the bare dry wood. Flood the liquid on, taking special care to work it into crevices and into exposed end grain. If the piece is small, place a large tub or other container under the work to catch excess liquid which drips off. When spraying, use a coarse, low-pressure spray to apply the material. Always wear a respirator mask for this job, and spray in a well-ventilated area only.

Wood preservatives which contain zinc naphthenate in a clear solution are used in pretty much the same way as those which contain penta. Some of these are exceptionally clear and are designed to act as a wood sealer as well. They can be used under varnish when a clear natural wood finish is to be applied.

In addition to applying these wood preservatives to new lumber, the homeowner should also apply them to existing wood structures at sensitive points. For example, preservative should be brushed liberally onto the bottom and top edges of garage doors and entrance doors and into the joints of wooden porches and steps. Wooden gutters, shutters, storm sash, window frames and fence rails all will benefit from having wood preservative brushed onto exposed sections and joints when paint peels or cracks away.

To reach into tiny crevices and tight corners, such as underneath a

Preservative is applied to wood frame before painting

door sill, an ordinary pump-type garden sprayer or pressure-type oil can is usually used. Remember, wherever two pieces overlap or meet, a pocket is created where moisture is likely to collect and remain. These joints are particularly susceptible to attack by fungus, so give them an extra dose at periodic intervals.

When applied to wood which has begun to rot, the preservative will not restore the wood which is already decayed. However, it will effectively stop the rot from spreading if it is properly applied. For best results, remove the section of decayed wood entirely and replace with a new piece which has been thoroughly coated with preservative on all sides.

Besides its use on the house itself, wood preservative should be used to protect ladders, garden furniture, picnic tables and similar items. Soak the bottom ends of the legs, and try to work preservative into the joints where cross-members are fastened together or where wood crosses wood. In these joints moisture becomes trapped so that the wood remains damp for long periods of time, making conditions ideal for rot to develop.

When applying penta by spray, brush or dipping, homeowners should avoid contact with the skin since the chemicals will irritate most people.

If some does get on the hands, wash immediately with soap and warm water.

Roof Repairs

Even after a roof leak is first noticed, its exact location is often difficult to determine. If the attic is unfinished so that roof boards are exposed, inspect them from the inside during a rainstorm: trace the leak back to its source, bearing in mind that water can sometimes travel for a considerable distance along a sloping rafter or horizontal beam before it finally drips off.

If there is a finished ceiling in the attic, this obviously will prevent a visual inspection from the underside. In this case, the only solution lies in locating the wet spot by measuring from the nearest outside wall, then climbing up on the roof and checking from the top. The handyman should start his inspection of the roof shingles at a point which he estimates to be directly above the wet spot; then he continues looking right and left and higher up along the roof till the defect is located.

For safety's sake when climbing on the roof, wear shoes with soft rubber soles (tennis shoes are ideal). This not only assures a firm footing, it also minimizes the possibility of doing further damage to the shingles, such as might be caused by hard soles or heels. Avoid climbing on days which are windy or rainy, and avoid walking erect on a sloping roof whenever possible.

For steep slopes where the footing is definitely precarious, you can provide a safe "catwalk" by laying a section of straight ladder flat on the roof so that it extends from the peak down. The upper end is secured by tying a rope to the top rung, then throwing this over the peak and tying it to a tree or other firm object on the other side. To haul the ladder up into position on the roof, this same rope can be used. An assistant pulls the ladder up from the opposite side of the house while you help push it up from below.

When checking for leaks in a shingle roof, look first for shingles which have bent or curled upward or for nails which have pulled loose. Raised shingles should be pressed down and made to lie flat by applying a liberal dab of asphalt roofing cement under the raised edge. Loose nails should be tapped back into position, and nailheads covered with the same roofing compound.

When roof shingles are split, cracked or otherwise badly damaged, an effective repair can be made by sliding a sheet of aluminum, copper or

Cement holds shingle down

galvanized iron under the damaged shingle. This piece of metal should be wider than the damaged shingle, and it should be tapped or forced upward so that it extends well up under the next row of shingles above the damaged one.

In some cases, it may be necessary to pry up the shingle above and remove nails which are in the way. If so, do this chore carefully, lifting the shingle gently so as not to crack it. A warm day when shingles are most pliable is best for this job. When replacing the nails after the metal piece is in position, drive them firmly into place, then cover the exposed nailheads with a dab of cement.

In many cases an examination of the shingles over the leaking area will show no defects which could possibly have caused the trouble. Nine times out of ten the trouble will then be due to defective flashing in a roof valley, around a vent pipe or chimney, or alongside a dormer which is located nearby. This flashing is usually made of a rustproof metal such as copper or galvanized iron. In either case, cracks or punctures may have developed, or part of the metal may have pulled away from under the shingles at either side so that a small leak occurs each time water runs down.

If the flashing is cracked, badly bent or rusted through in many places, complete replacement is usually advisable. This is a job which calls for

Metal patch can be used under damaged shingle

the services of an experienced roofing contractor. However, if only one or two small defects are noticed, or if the homeowner wishes to make semipermanent repairs himself, most leaks of this kind can usually be repaired quite simply. The homeowner simply brushes or trowels on a heavy layer of roofing cement, after first brushing the old surface clean of all dust and grit. For maximum durability, this patch should then be covered with a piece of heavy tar paper or roofing felt, after which a second layer of roofing cement is spread on over the top of this.

Flat roofs, or roofs which have only a slight slope, are usually covered with built-up roll roofing, rather than with shingles. This type of roof consists of several layers of asphalt-impregnated felt with a coat of roofing compound applied between each layer.

Leaks may occur in this type of roof after several years because blisters and cracks have developed in the top layer of felt, because nails have worked loose around the edges or along the seams or because the roofing material has begun to dry out. Leaks of this kind are often simple to repair unless the condition is so widespread that a complete new roof covering is required.

To locate the source of trouble, the homeowner should climb up on the roof on the first nice day and examine it carefully. He should look for defects such as loose nails, blistered sections, dried-out or cracked

Leaks often develop around vent pipes

areas or openings where seams overlap or where the roof meets the flashing around the edges. If the entire roof seems dry and has many small checks or crazed areas, the best thing to do is to recoat the entire surface with an asphalt-type roof coating. Better yet, the handyman can apply an aluminum-fibered coating which is specifically designed for this purpose. These can be applied with a large paintbrush or with a long-handled roofing brush.

Repairs should be made first wherever defects are noticed. Loose or missing nails should be hammered down, but not so snug that the heads cut into the surface of the roofing material. The nailhead should then be covered with a liberal application of roof cement to prevent leaks from developing.

Blistered sections can most easily be repaired by following the technique shown. The blister is first sliced lengthwise with a sharp knife. A putty knife is then used to work roof compound under both sides of the blistered area, after first brushing out loose dirt or gravel and after making certain that the inside of the blister is perfectly dry.

The roof covering is then pressed down flat against the surface and nailed along both edges as indicated. Additional compound is then smeared over the resultant seam, as well as over all the exposed nailheads. For a more permanent job an extra patch of roofing felt can be laid on over the entire area, after first coating the area liberally with roofing compound.

If the blistered area is torn or badly dried out so that a simple patching job of this kind is impractical, the best solution lies in replacing the entire section, as shown in the second drawing. To simplify replacement, the patch should be cut out in square or rectangular sections, cutting through only one layer at a time. The knife blade can be dipped in turpentine at frequent intervals to simplify cutting. After cutting out a square from the top layer, cut out a smaller square from the second layer of roofing underneath.

To replace these squares of defective material, matching squares of new roofing felt should be cut to fit. A layer of compound should be spread under each square, then the patch pressed down to fit inside the opening previously cut. The small square on the bottom is installed first and an additional layer of compound is spread on before the second

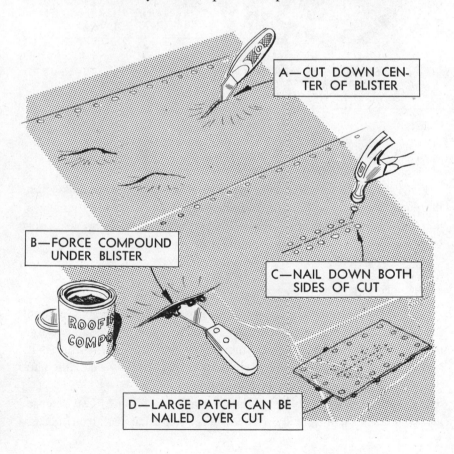

A—CUT DOWN CENTER OF BLISTER

B—FORCE COMPOUND UNDER BLISTER

C—NAIL DOWN BOTH SIDES OF CUT

D—LARGE PATCH CAN BE NAILED OVER CUT

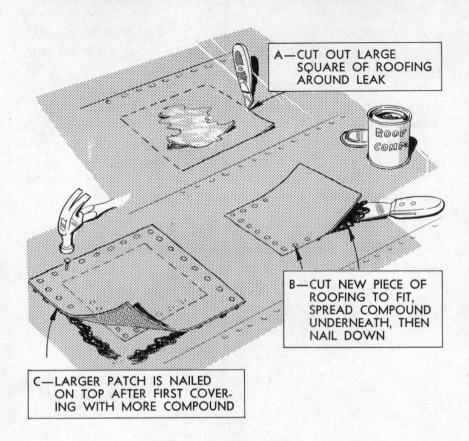

A—CUT OUT LARGE SQUARE OF ROOFING AROUND LEAK

B—CUT NEW PIECE OF ROOFING TO FIT, SPREAD COMPOUND UNDERNEATH, THEN NAIL DOWN

C—LARGER PATCH IS NAILED ON TOP AFTER FIRST COVERING WITH MORE COMPOUND

square is applied on top. Each piece should be tapped down with a block of wood to assure uniform contact.

Nails should be driven around the edge of the last piece to make sure the patch stays down. It is then finished off at the surface by nailing a larger square over the entire area. A final layer of cement is applied over these nails and along the edges to finish it off neatly.

Rust Prevention

Rust is the ever-present enemy of all exposed ferrous metals around the house (iron, steel, galvanized metal, etc.). It not only is an eyesore in itself, it also causes unsightly staining of nearby painted surfaces. If allowed to develop, rust will eventually cause severe weakening and complete breakdown of the metal structure.

As with most other types of home maintenance, the best defense against rust is to prevent corrosion before it can happen. Iron fences, railings, grills and other metalwork around the outside of the house should always be protected against the elements by coating it with at least two coats of exterior paint. The first coat should be a good quality, rust-inhibitive metal primer, such as red lead or zinc chromate. This primer should be applied to all surfaces, visible or not, if complete protection is to be assured. Failure to coat the back or underside of the metal is a common fault in many homes.

Though many homeowners are aware of the need for coating all sides of the metal whenever possible, few realize that even a small scratch or skip which leaves the bare metal exposed will give rust a chance to start. Once this happens, it is not only the exposed portion which rusts. The corrosion continues to spread under the painted areas and eventually causes the paint to crack and peel off around it.

Before painting any metal, make certain it is as clean as possible with no grease or oil on the surface. Since new metal frequently has a light film of oil applied at the shop to prevent rusting in transit, it is a wise precaution to wipe new metal down with a solvent, such as benzine or turpentine, before painting. Brush the primer on liberally and allow this to dry completely. When hard, brush on one or two coats of exterior enamel or trim paint, working the finish well into all crevices and joints.

On older, previously painted surfaces where rust has already begun to form, extra preparation is required. Contrary to popular opinion, ordinary metal primers will not stick over the rust, so there is no sense in just painting right over it. All of the rust must first be thoroughly removed with steel wool, aluminum oxide paper, emery cloth or a wire brush. Rub till the metal is shiny and new-looking once more, then apply the metal primer and finish coat as described above.

To eliminate the job of having to polish rusty metal clean before priming it, special rust-inhibitive primers are available. These are formulated with special oils which enable them to adhere satisfactorily over sound rust without having to first scrape or sand it all off. To use them, simply knock off the loose, flaking particles of rust with a wire brush, then apply the primer right over the corroded areas. The paint is designed to eat its way into and through the rust and to bond firmly to the sound metal underneath.

Top coats of the same type of paint are also available in several different colors. These provide added protection against rust when applied over the primer specified, though they can also be used over conventional paints if desired.

Screens, Window

When window screens develop loose, wobbly joints, they can be reinforced by screwing metal angle irons or mending plates across the inside corners. Be sure you force the corners tightly together before screws are inserted. If a gap is still visible on the other side, hammer in corrugated metal fasteners to draw the individual frame members together more tightly. These will be scarcely visible from the outside when painted over. For corner joints that are really weak, or where wood is cracked so that screws will not hold, triangular-shaped wooden reinforcing blocks can be screwed and glued to the edges against the inside corner of the weakened frame.

If one side of the screen frame has begun to rot away completely, the entire length should be replaced with a new piece of wood of matching dimensions. Saw out the old piece by cutting straight across at one corner; then attach a new piece with wood dowels and glue. Assemble the joint with glue, then bore holes for the reinforcing dowels. Tap these into position after coating each one with glue. If more than one of the screen frame members is rotted, chances are that repairs are hardly worthwhile and a new screen should be purchased.

Screen wire made of copper, bronze or galvanized metal needs periodic painting or varnishing to protect it against corrosion and stain-

Brackets are used to reinforce corners

Corrugated fastener will close open joints

Applicator is used for coating wire mesh

ing. One of the simplest ways to accomplish this is to lay each screen horizontally across two sawhorses and then paint the wire with a special screen-painting applicator. This consists of a piece of carpet fastened to the bottom of a wooden, metal or plastic holder. Specially formulated screen wire enamel (in dark green or black) or thinned-down spar varnish is usually used.

To apply, pour the paint or varnish into a shallow pan, then dip the carpet applicator into the liquid. Wipe off the excess, then rub briskly over the surface of the mesh on each side. For best results, the molding should be pried off so that the wire underneath can also be painted. When the job is done, nail the molding back into position, countersink the nails, then fill the remaining holes with putty.

To patch small holes in metal mesh, ready-made screen patches or scrap pieces of matching wire mesh can be used. Be sure not to use dissimilar metals, since patches should be of the same material if electrolytic action is to be avoided and uniform appearance preserved. The patch should be larger than the damaged area and should have a few wires unraveled around all the edges so that about ½ inch of wire is exposed on all sides. Bend these wires at right angles to the surface and press the patch on over the damaged area so that the individual wires go through the mesh and stick out on the inside. Folding these ends in tightly will then hold the patch in place, much the way a staple holds two sheets of paper.

To patch holes in plastic wire, which will not hold a "crease" when folded, clear plastic cement can be used. If preferred, the patch can also be held in place by "darning." To accomplish this, the screen should be taken off and laid flat and the patch placed in position over the hole. Unravel a long strand of the plastic wire and carefully feed this back and forth through the holes in the screening till the patch has been "sewn" in position.

If the screen wire is badly torn in many places, or if corrosion is so far advanced that cleaning and painting seem hopeless, the only solution lies in re-covering with new wire. The task is a comparatively simple one which requires no special tools, regardless of whether the screen frames are made of wood or aluminum.

Though there are many different kinds of metal and plastic screening material from which he can choose, the handyman will find that fiber glass insect screening will probably be easiest of all to install. It has a soft, lightweight body which cannot crease or dent, and it is easy to stretch tight by hand. The plastic cuts easily with ordinary household scissors, and once installed it will never corrode, stretch or shrink. It will never need painting, and comes in various colors. Fiber glass screening also has excellent see-through visibility and an exceptionally high resistance to impact.

To cover a wooden frame, begin by first prying off the old moldings, working as carefully as possible so that the moldings can be saved for re-use. Next, remove the old screen wire and pull out all old tacks or staples. Though the mesh can be pulled tight by hand, the job will be faster and neater if the following method is used: Place 1-inch wooden blocks under each short side of the screen frame after laying it flat on a

*Staple gun is used to fasten
wire down*

Mesh can be cut to fit with scissors

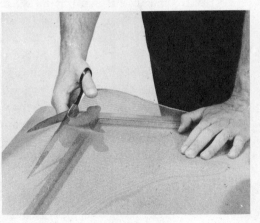

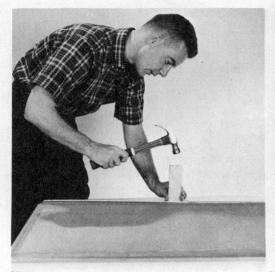

Spline is tapped into groove with wood block

Sharp knife is used to trim
off excess

workbench or table. Then use C-clamps or bar clamps at the mid-point of each long side, clamping the screen frame down to the worktable at its center, so that the entire frame is bowed slightly downward in the middle. If the screening is installed while frames are bowed in this manner, it will be stretched even tighter after the clamps are released.

When cutting the screen mesh to size, allow an extra ½ inch of material on all sides beyond the outside of the molding. This allows for a "hem" which is folded over under the molding. This double thickness assures a better grip when staples or nails are driven in. Though carpet tacks or small nails can be used, a staple gun will speed the job up considerably. It also makes stretching easier since only one hand is required for fastening.

After the screening has been cut to size (including the ½-inch excess around the edges), you can proceed as follows:

(1) Starting on one of the long sides, tack or staple the mesh into each corner, allowing the excess ½ inch to extend out beyond the molding. Then fasten it in the center, midway between the corners.

(2) Fold over the ½ inch of excess, then drive tacks or staples through the doubled thickness at 1-inch intervals. Make sure screening is kept tightly stretched to avoid bunching at any point.

(3) Do the opposite long side of the screen next, making certain that the screen wire is pulled tight across the frame. Follow the same procedure as just completed on the first side.

(4) Fasten the screening to one of the short sides, then to the other short side, again making certain that the mesh is pulled tight in all directions. If the frame has been clamped in a bowed position as described earlier, remove clamps and wood-block supports. Then replace moldings, using small nails or wire brads.

On aluminum frames, the wire mesh is held in place with a plastic spline or strip. This fits into a groove around the edge of the screen frame and is pressed down on top of the screening so that the mesh is clamped tightly into the spline groove. It grips firmly without need for tacks or staples.

To install plastic screening on an aluminum frame, begin by first prying out the plastic spline. Pull out the old screen wire and lay the frame flat on a worktable or bench. Then proceed as follows:

(1) Cut the screening to size, making it at least as large as the *outside* size of the screen frame. Lay screening over the top of the frame and trim off corners at a 45-degree angle. Make certain that the line of cut leaves enough material in each corner to reach into the spline groove.

(2) With screening in place on top of the frame, lay the spline for one of the long sides on top of the screening. Then use a tapered block of wood or a thick-bladed screwdriver to tap the spline into its groove, beginning at one end and working your way along its length.

(3) Install the spline on the opposite long side of the frame, pulling the mesh tight as the spline is forced into its groove. Be careful that the screening is not pulled so tight that the frame is bowed or twisted.

(4) Tap the splines into place on each of the short sides, then use a sharp knife or razor blade to trim off excess screening material on the outside of the spline.

Shingles, Wood and Asbestos

Homes which have wood or asbestos shingles on the outside walls should be inspected at least once a year to make certain that none of the shingles are split or missing and to check for those which may be so badly damaged that complete replacement is required.

In many cases, shingles start to sag or bulge simply because the nails have worked loose. When this condition is first noticed, the old nails should be hammered back in to secure the shingle in its original position. If the nails fail to hold, an extra nail should be driven in an inch or two away from the old one. Only rustproof nails of the serrated or "threaded" type should be used. These grip better and are much less likely to work loose in the future.

Before driving nails through asbestos shingles, drill a small pilot hole to avoid splitting the shingle. Wood shingles generally do not require predrilling, but in many cases a pilot hole is still advisable, especially if shingles are old and dry or if nails must be driven close to the edge. With either type of shingle, care should be exercised not to hammer the nails in too far since heavy blows near the surface may damage or split the shingle.

When shingles are split (with both halves still in place), replacement is seldom required. A simple repair can usually be effected by first sliding a sheet of waterproof paper (tar paper or roofing felt will do) under the split, then driving nails in on both sides near the butt (lower) end of the shingle.

If a shingle is cracked in more than two places, or if a shingle has been badly smashed by some sort of accident, complete replacement is advisable. Since all shingles are installed with the lower half of one shingle overlapping the upper part of the shingle below it, replacement is more than a matter of simply prying off the defective member and nailing up a new one.

As indicated in the drawings, the nails which hold the shingle on top of the defective one will have to be removed in order to free the upper edge of the broken shingle. After this is done, the shingle can simply be pulled forward at the bottom to pry out the nails along the lower edge. The shingle can then be slid out from the bottom so that a new one can be inserted in its place.

Though the techniques involved in replacing either a wood or asbestos shingle are basically the same, there are differences in the methods that are normally used to cut off the nails which hold it in place. Asbestos shingles are usually installed with each shingle flat against the one below it, while wood shingles often have an extra wood strip to separate the shingles. They may also be installed in a double layer to create the "shadow" effect usually preferred for wood shingle houses.

Since asbestos shingles are brittle, one of the simplest methods that can be used is to smash what's left of the shingle with a hammer, then pull out the nails which originally held it in place. However, this requires considerable care in order to avoid damaging the shingles directly below or alongside the broken one. For this reason, the preferred method is first to cut off the nails by using one of the four methods illustrated. Once the nails have been removed from the shingle above, the damaged shingle can be pried out and pulled free from the bottom.

Like the asbestos shingle nails, wood shingle nails can also be cut off by sliding a hacksaw blade underneath the shingle and then cutting from

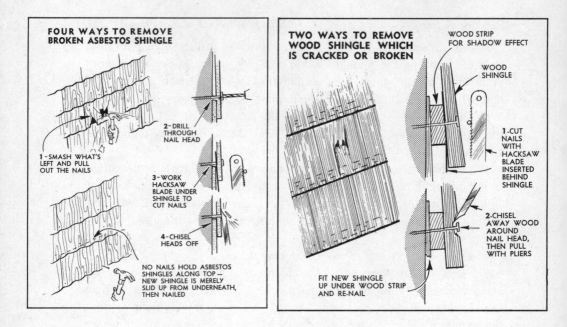

FOUR WAYS TO REMOVE
BROKEN ASBESTOS SHINGLE

1 - SMASH WHAT'S
LEFT AND PULL
OUT THE NAILS

2 - DRILL
THROUGH
NAIL HEAD

3 - WORK
HACKSAW
BLADE UNDER
SHINGLE TO
CUT NAILS

4 - CHISEL
HEADS OFF

NO NAILS HOLD ASBESTOS
SHINGLES ALONG TOP —
NEW SHINGLE IS MERELY
SLID UP FROM UNDERNEATH,
THEN NAILED

TWO WAYS TO REMOVE
WOOD SHINGLE WHICH
IS CRACKED OR BROKEN

WOOD STRIP
FOR SHADOW EFFECT

WOOD
SHINGLE

1 - CUT
NAILS
WITH
HACKSAW
BLADE
INSERTED
BEHIND
SHINGLE

2 - CHISEL
AWAY WOOD
AROUND
NAIL HEAD,
THEN PULL
WITH PLIERS

FIT NEW SHINGLE
UP UNDER WOOD STRIP
AND RE-NAIL

behind. The alternate method shown is to pull the nail out from the front after first chiseling away enough wood to expose the nailhead. This is more tedious, but it may be simpler in those situations where difficulty is encountered in reaching underneath with a hacksaw blade.

In either case, after the defective shingle has been cut free and removed, the new shingle should be slid up from underneath and then renailed top and bottom, following the techniques described above.

Siding, Clapboard

Homeowners who have clapboard siding on the outside of their houses should periodically inspect all boards for cracks or other defects. Small cracks, warped boards or open joints may be scarcely noticeable when they first develop, but if not attended to promptly, they will permit damaging moisture to work its way in behind the siding. This not only causes paint to peel, but may cause rotting out of complete sections so that extensive re-siding may be required.

While cracks are still small (and not too widespread), repairs can be made by filling with a good grade of calking compound or white lead putty. This should be packed in tightly and the board nailed down along the edges if it has begun to work loose. To prevent splitting of old, dried wood when nails must be hammered in close to the ends, small pilot holes should be drilled first. Nails are then countersunk so that the heads are below the surface, and the holes which remain filled with putty. Putty and calking should then be allowed to dry for a day or two before touching up with exterior house paint.

When a length of clapboard is badly cracked, severely checked or rotted, the only sure cure lies in replacing the entire section. For the neatest repair, a full length should be removed and replaced with a new board. However, if this is impractical, the defective section can be cut out and replaced with a new piece as illustrated. Since clapboards overlap each other, the board that must be replaced will be held along its top edge by nails driven through the lower edge of the board above it. These make it difficult to pry off the defective board, since part will always be caught underneath the piece above.

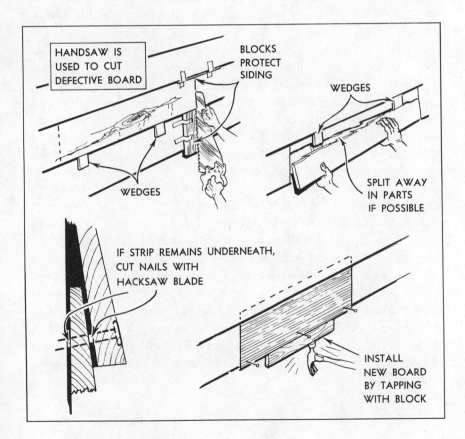

HANDSAW IS USED TO CUT DEFECTIVE BOARD

BLOCKS PROTECT SIDING

WEDGES

WEDGES

SPLIT AWAY IN PARTS IF POSSIBLE

IF STRIP REMAINS UNDERNEATH, CUT NAILS WITH HACKSAW BLADE

INSTALL NEW BOARD BY TAPPING WITH BLOCK

To facilitate removal, wedges are first driven under the damaged board to pry it out slightly from the board below. A handsaw is then used to cut through the damaged board as shown. Though an ordinary crosscut saw can be used for this job, a square-pointed hacksaw will simplify the job of cutting right up to the edge of the board above. To protect the boards below and above the damaged one, blocks of wood can be taped into position as indicated.

After making cuts on both sides, move the wedges to pry up the boards above. The old cracked board can then be split away in sections by simply pulling upward with the hands or by prying and chopping with a chisel. Care should be exercised to avoid driving the chisel through the board into the tar paper covering underneath.

In some cases a narrow strip will remain under the edge of the board directly above. When this happens, the simplest way to remove the strip is to cut the nails which hold it in place. To do this without damaging the other board, a hacksaw blade can be forced up under the board to cut the nails off in back. The strip can then be pried out with a narrow chisel or a screwdriver.

After the old piece has been removed, the tar paper or building paper behind the siding should be inspected to see whether there are any tears or cuts visible. If so, roofing compound or asphalt cement should be smeared over the damaged areas to seal them. If large gaps are noticeable, a new sheet of tar paper should be nailed over the entire area and the edges covered with cement.

A new length of matching clapboard (beveled siding) is now cut for a snug fit to replace the damaged section just removed. This is installed by tapping upward from the bottom, using a block of wood along the edge to avoid damaging or denting the new section. After the lower edge lines up exactly with the boards at each end, it is fastened in place by driving nails along the bottom edge about 1 inch up from the bottom. A second row of nails is then driven through the lower edge of the board above it to catch the top edge of the new board at the same time.

Nailheads should be countersunk below the surface and the entire board painted with exterior primer as soon as possible. After this first coat is dry, the end joints where the new board meets the old should be sealed with calking compound and nail holes filled with putty. A final coat of paint can then be applied to blend the patch in with the surrounding wall area.

Siding, Shingles. SEE SHINGLES, WOOD AND ASBESTOS

Storm Windows

To make certain that storm windows will provide the protection expected of them and to help prolong the life and appearance of each unit, you must make certain that each one fits properly; and each one should be inspected annually to see whether repairs are needed or repainting is necessary. Self-storing aluminum combination units (these have interchangeable screen panels and storm sash) are supposedly maintenance-free, but they also will benefit from an annual checkup to see whether cleaning, lubrication or other minor adjustments are required.

Since wooden storm windows which have been stored in basements or garages will undoubtedly need washing before they are hung, you can

Old putty is removed before replacing with fresh compound   *Putty should be neatly beveled with knife*

inspect each one as it is cleaned. If a pane of glass is cracked, it should be replaced promptly. A broken pane not only permits heat to escape but can be a decided hazard, since it may fall out completely later on.

While checking the glass, also inspect the condition of the putty around the outside of each pane. If the old putty is cracked or missing entirely, the rabbet should be scraped clean, primed with linseed oil or exterior oil paint and new glazing compound applied. If this is neglected, wind-driven rain or snow will work its way inside the storm window, partially nullifying the protection that the sash is supposed to provide. In addition, water soaking into the exposed wood around the edges of

Metal braces will reinforce corners

Loose joints can be tightened with hammer-in fasteners

the glass will cause rotting and swelling of the wood frame, shortening its life considerably.

If the frames are loose and wobbly, or if corner joints have sprung open, metal braces or corner irons can be screwed against the outside to reinforce the corners. Open joints should be tapped shut with a hammer and wood block and braces installed. An effective repair can sometimes be made simply by hammering in one or two corrugated fasteners or multipronged fasteners. These not only brace the corner, they also help draw the wood parts back together again.

Because wood swells when moisture is absorbed, it is important that wooden storm sash be kept well protected with paint on both sides and around all edges. This is particularly true of exposed end grain along the top and bottom edges, so the handyman should touch these up whenever bare wood is visible. Apply only thin coats to avoid building up a thick film which might interfere with the proper fit of the storm sash inside the window frame.

To be fully effective, a storm window should fit quite snugly inside its opening in the window frame. However, it should never be so tight that hammering is required to force it into position. When swelling or paint build-up causes a storm window to stick in this manner, you should plane or sand the edges as much as necessary to make it fit in smoothly.

If a sizable amount of wood must be removed, an equal amount should be planed from each side—instead of trimming all the excess off one side only. If a storm window drags at the bottom, the screws which hold the hangers in place at the top should be checked first to make certain that they have not worked loose.

If a storm window fits loosely even when hooked shut, it may be that the screw eyes which engage the hooks need to be moved slightly, so that the window will be pulled in more tightly. Better yet, there are adjustable arms or brackets which can be installed on each side. These permit regulating the closing tension, while at the same time enabling the homeowner to prop the storm window partly open when fresh air is desired.

The principal value of a storm window is as a barrier which traps dead air between it and the regular house window. However, if the storm window fits so loosely that air flows freely in around the edges, the major part of its insulating effectiveness is lost. To correct a condition of this kind (that is, where a storm window does not fit tightly around the edges), a felt or foam-type insulation can be installed around all sides. This material is sold in roll form in practically all hardware stores, and it is nailed on so that its soft outer edge presses against the inside face of the storm window when the window is pulled tightly shut. This weatherstripping can be left up from year to year since it will not interfere with installation of screens in the summertime.

Though aluminum storm windows do not have to be painted to protect them from the elements, the metal will benefit from a periodic cleaning and polishing. Aluminum does not rust or corrode in the sense that iron or steel does, but it does oxidize and form tiny pits which accumulate dirt and roughen the finish. This pitting can be minimized by washing periodically with one of the special aluminum cleaning and polishing agents which are sold for just this purpose.

Since aluminum windows have sliding panels or frames which move up and down, it is important that the guide tracks be kept clean. A stiff brush or vacuum cleaner nozzle is excellent for this job, while a rag moistened with solvent (mineral spirits or benzine) can be used to wipe out accumulated grease and grit which may have caked into the channels. To keep all parts moving freely, they should also be lubricated periodically (after cleaning) with a dry powdered or stick-type lubricant,

Metal windows can be lubricated with silicone spray

or with one of the new silicone-containing lubricants which dry to a nonsticky film. Regardless of the type of lubricant used, it should be brushed or sprayed inside all the tracks and along the edges of each sash frame if possible.

Stucco Patching

Cement plaster, stucco and mortar all consist of the same standard formulation: 1 part portland cement to 3 parts clean, coarse sand or other aggregate, such as perlite or vermiculite. To simplify matters, most hardware and building supply stores sell ready-mixed sand and cement in various-sized bags. All these require is the addition of enough water to make an easily workable mix of exactly the right consistency. Properly prepared stucco or mortar should be stiff enough to hold its shape, yet pliable enough to be easily molded without crumbling under the action of the trowel.

To repair minor cracks and to replace small sections which have broken off on corners or along the bottom of a wall, here is the procedure to be followed:

(1) Remove all loose or broken pieces of old stucco and cement. If necessary, use a hammer and a cold chisel to chip off stubborn sections and cut back to where the old material is still adhering firmly.

(2) Undercut the sides or edges of each crack so that the opening is wider at the bottom than it is at the surface. This assures a good mechanical bond or "key" when the new mortar is applied.

Large cracks in stucco must be cleaned and patched

Waterproof paper and lath are covered with three coats of mortar

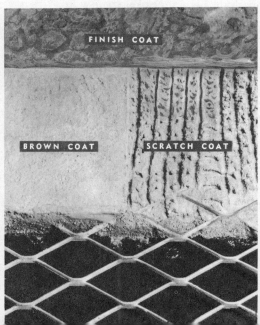

(3) Use a stiff brush to dust out all loose crumbling material and wet the edges of the patch or crack thoroughly with clean water. Fill the opening with freshly mixed mortar, packing it in tightly with a pointed trowel.

(4) Deeper cracks or openings which go all the way through the masonry and down to the lath should be filled in two applications. The first coat should be built up to within ¼ inch from the top, and it should be allowed to set for about two days. Wet it down again before applying the second coat.

Larger patches (more than about 12 inches across) usually require that whole sections be ripped out completely and replaced from the lath out. This calls for a bit more work, though the same basic procedure is followed. Rip off all of the old defective masonry and examine the exposed wood or metal lath for signs of rotting or rusting. If it looks bad, rip the lath off down to the bare siding. Nail on new building paper with large-headed galvanized nails, and then cover with rustproof wire lath. This metal lath should be nailed on with special double-headed furring nails which are designed to hold the mesh away from the wall a fraction of an inch.

Stucco is generally applied in three coats. The first and second coats are known as the "scratch" and "brown" coats respectively. Both consist of a standard mortar mix as described above. Use a square plasterer's trowel and scrub the first coat on so that it goes completely through the metal mesh and bonds securely behind it. Work from the bottom up, spreading the mortar on until the lath is completely covered.

Dash stucco on with brush for rough finish

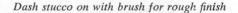

Allow this scratch coat to stiffen slightly, then cross-scratch the surface with a scrap piece of wire mesh or a serrated tool. Let this harden for about two days, keeping it damp for at least 24 hours by sprinkling occasionally with a fine mist.

The second, or brown, coat is troweled on after first thoroughly wetting down the surface of the scratch coat. This application should be thick enough to even out all irregularities in the scratch coat and it should bring the surface up to within ⅛ of an inch of the surrounding wall surface. It must be pressed on firmly to insure a good bond.

Allow this coat to harden for another seven days, and again wet it down thoroughly before applying the final coat. The finish coat can consist of the same mixture, but it usually has some lime added to make it more workable. One common formula consists of 1 part cement, 1 part lime and 4 parts sand. If color is required, add lime-proof powdered colors which are available at most hardware stores and lumberyards.

Trowel this finish coat to a smooth even finish which is flush with the surrounding surface. To achieve a uniform, sand-finished texture, allow the mortar to stiffen slightly, then rub, in a circular motion, with a wooden float. To match a rough, spattered type of finish, thin out the stucco slightly with additional water and extra sand. Then spatter the wet material on with a whisk broom or a stiff brush while the final coat is still soft. Other textures are achieved by working the final coat with a trowel, by dashing on pebbles or other granular material or by roughing up the surface with a sponge, a stiff brush or a wad of burlap.

Termites, Prevention and Cure

Though there are actually many different species of termites, the kind that does practically all of the damage to dwellings is the subterranean termite. As its name implies, this type lives underground, building colonies in damp locations wherever a source of wood (its principal food) is available in the soil. The colony multiplies rapidly; then, as its population increases, worker termites are sent out in search of additional sources of food. They avoid exposure to both daylight and open air and, whenever possible, will work their way into the wooden structure of nearby houses without disclosing their supply lines.

Since these insects cannot survive except under controlled conditions of moisture and temperature, they will never expose themselves to the drying effect of open air, except during swarming time in the spring. Termites will tunnel through the soft parts of an entire wood beam without ever breaking through to the outside. As a result, the destructive

Termites chew tunnels through the earth in their search for wood   *Termites eat through lumber and rarely break through surface*   *Termites build mud tubes to travel from ground across foundation*

effects can sometimes go completely unnoticed until the damage is so severe that complete collapse takes place. However, this type of damage will take many years, so even when an infestation is finally detected, there is no need to panic or to act hastily.

Wherever possible, subterranean termites will work beneath the surface of the ground to bore into those wooden members which come in direct contact with the soil. However, these ingenious insects will also build mud tubes or tunnels through cracks in masonry foundations, through the hollow cores of cement blocks and even along the surfaces of metal pipes, foundation walls and similar surfaces. In extreme cases termites have even been known to build tubes straight up—unsupported —to reach from the ground in a damp crawl space to wooden beams overhead.

The mudlike tubes or tunnels described above vary in size from ¼ to ½ inch in width, and they are half-round in cross section. They enable the termites to travel back and forth from the underground colony to the wooden structure without exposing themselves to sunlight or open air. The termites must return to the ground at least once a day to replenish their supply of moisture and to bring food to the other members of the colony.

When a colony gets large enough, warm weather is the signal for the younger kings and queens, the reproductive members of the colony, to fly out in their annual attempt to establish new colonies. During this period they fly about in the open air on mating flights, then shed their wings before settling permanently into their new underground homes.

It is the appearance of a swarm of these flying insects or of a large number of discarded termite wings near a wall that often gives the homeowner his first warning that one or more established termite colonies are located nearby. In some cases these swarms may be mistaken for flying ants, since both insects look similar to the uninitiated eye. Actually, the difference in appearance is quite pronounced. The termite has a comparatively straight, oblong body of equal thickness along its entire length. The ant has an hour-glass-shaped, segmented body which is joined in the center by a thin, wiry stem. Termites are usually less than half an inch in length, and their wings will be opaque and whitish in color. An ant's wings are transparent, with dark veins visible.

Since termites must return to the soil at least once a day, the most effective method of attack is to poison the soil around the house by treating it with special insecticides made for this purpose. One of the safest and most effective is the type containing chlordane. Another, equally effective compound is heptachlor. Both of these chemicals come in concentrated form, and both are diluted with water according to the directions on the container.

To insure complete protection, a trench must be dug around the entire foundation to a depth of at least 30 inches. Part of the poison is then poured into this trench, while the balance is mixed with the soil as it is replaced. Applied in the proportions recommended by the manufacturer —and in the proper concentration—this will provide a long-lasting poison barrier which will kill termites on contact for as long as five years. Termites already in the building will die off in a short while as they attempt to return to their underground colony.

Many homes have concrete slab floors (porches, patios and garages) laid on the ground right next to the house wall. Termites often come up through the soil under these slabs and work their way into the house through cracks or open joints where the slab meets the house wall. The only way to poison the soil in this area is to chop holes through the concrete floor, then pour or pump the solution through.

Since these termite-proofing methods require a great deal of excavation, handling of potentially dangerous insecticides and careful measuring of ingredients, most homeowners will find it advisable to consult a professional exterminator if complete termite protection is desired—or if a termite infestation is suspected. If a reputable firm is hired, they will be fully equipped and trained to locate the potential danger points and to take the necessary precautionary measures. They also will be able to

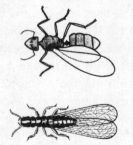

Winged termite (left) has a thicker waist than ant (right)

advise the homeowner about important structural changes that should be made to eliminate defects which permit termites to enter.

Though the best way to determine whether termites are present is to call in a reliable exterminator, alert homeowners can check for signs of activity themselves by making a careful examination of the premises at least once a year. Here are some of the more important places to look:

(1) During spring and early summer watch for swarms of flying insects or for clusters of discarded termite wings in or near the house.

(2) Inspect foundation walls—inside and outside—for signs of shelter tubes or tunnels. If any are seen scrape them away. This will cut off the termites from their source of moisture and those remaining in the wood will soon die.

(3) Keep wooden fences or trellises several inches away from the house so that termites cannot use them as a point of entry. Check all lumber which is in contact with the ground, as well as those parts which are less than 6 inches above the soil. Probe with an icepick or sharp knife to see whether the inside is hollow or whether the wood feels soft and spongy.

(4) Check unfinished crawl spaces for signs of termite tunnels and for places where soil may have banked up against the wall. Make certain these spaces are well ventilated so that moisture can escape, because termites love dampness.

(5) Patch all cracks in masonry foundations and calk openings around pipes which pass through these walls.

(6) Never pile firewood or scrap lumber against the house, and remove waste material of this kind which may be buried in the soil near the foundation. Also pay particular attention to cellar window wells where debris tends to accumulate, providing termites with access to basement window frames as well as to moist soil.

Walls, Exterior, Cleaning and Stain Removal

When an improvement-minded homeowner notices that the outside of his house looks dingy or dirty, he usually jumps to the conclusion that a new paint job is required. Yet in many cases the old paint film is still in perfect condition. It has merely been clouded over with accumulated dust and dirt.

A good exterior paint job will last about five years, so if the house has been painted within the past year or two, washing may be all that is required to restore its original, fresh-looking brilliance. Repainting is not only unnecessary, it may actually do more harm than good. Tests have proven that it is best not to repaint exterior surfaces until the last coat of paint has almost entirely worn through. This eliminates the danger of the paint film building up to an excessive thickness over a period of years, a condition which eventually causes cracking and peeling because of the sheer weight of the paint itself.

To prevent this, modern exterior house paints are designed to wear down gradually by chalking away at the surface when exposed to the elements. As this chalkiness is washed away by the rain, it carries the dirt and dust with it and should keep the paint looking fresh and clean for the life of the coating.

However, this system does not always work as it should. Many parts of the house are sheltered from the elements and do not get the same amount of exposure as others, with the result that air-borne dust and grime accumulate rapidly. In many cases all that is required is a thorough hosing down with a strong stream of water. But for a really new-looking job (especially on white houses) the entire house should be completely washed down. The whole job can be accomplished in less than one day with no specialized equipment or supplies. To simplify the task, start on the shady side of the house and follow the sun around so as to avoid working on hot surfaces.

Always wash one side of the house at a time. Begin by wetting down the entire wall with the hose turned on full force. Work from the bottom up to prevent streaking, and pay particular attention to sheltered areas under cornices and eaves. This simple hosing will flush away loose dirt, but it will not remove soot or other oily grime. Detergents will be needed to dissolve dirt of this kind.

The easiest way to apply this detergent is to squirt it on with a siphon-type garden sprayer of the kind generally sold for spraying insecticides on trees and tall shrubs. It screws onto the end of the hose so that when the water is turned on the liquid concentrate in the jar is siphoned out and is mixed in with the spray from the hose. Since the detergent will be highly diluted, mix as strong a solution as possible, and select one which gives little or no suds.

Squirt the detergent over one section at a time, then flush off with a strong stream of clean water. Work from the bottom up so that dirty water will be running down only over wet areas, and never allow the dirty solution to dry on the surface.

For a more thorough job, particularly on stubborn areas where simple flushing doesn't seem to do the trick, a hose brush of the type commonly sold for washing windows or automobiles should be used. These have hollow handles and screw onto the end of a garden hose so that water flows out through the center of the bristles. Some models also have a detergent dispenser built into the handle, and incorporate a valve which gives the user a choice of either detergent-laden water or clean rinse water.

When using one of these brushes, wet the dirty area first with clean water. Then scrub vigorously with the brush dipped into detergent, with the water turned off. As the dirt loosens up, turn the water back on and continue scrubbing while flushing away with clean water.

To simplify washing the high spots or other hard-to-reach areas, a temporary extension handle can be rigged up with a long wooden floor brush handle, a 1-inch aluminum tube or a lightweight pole. Splice this to the hose brush handle by overlapping about 16 inches and then wrapping with waterproof plastic tape.

For really difficult spots which do not succumb to this type of washing, the homeowner may have to resort to the old-fashioned scrub brush and bucket. Use a solution made by mixing 1 pound of trisodium phosphate (commonly sold in paint stores under the name of Beatsall) dissolved in a pailful of hot water. Wear rubber gloves to protect your hands and

Pole taped to hose brush extends reach

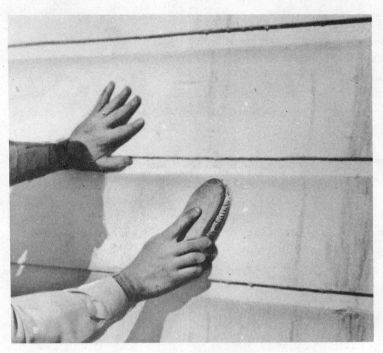

Scrub off dirt marks with stuff-bristle brush

scrub thoroughly till the surface is as clean as possible. Then flush off immediately with plenty of clean water.

Metal stains such as those caused by oxidation below copper screens are virtually impossible to remove once they have been allowed to remain on the surface for some time. In some cases bleaching is effective. For this, use oxalic acid crystals (available in all paint stores) dissolved in hot water. Mix ¾ of a pound of crystals in 1 gallon of hot water and apply to the stained areas with a sponge. Allow to dry for four or five minutes, then rub off with a cloth. Though two or three applications of this kind may not remove them entirely, the stains will be lightened considerably and will be much less noticeable.

For deeply imbedded rust stains which are quite old, or for rust stains on porous masonry surfaces, you can also try the following treatment: dissolve 1 part sodium citrate crystals in 6 parts water, then add 6 parts ordinary glycerine. Mix this with powdered whiting to form a thick paste, then trowel on over the stain and cover with plastic to retard drying. Soak overnight, then moisten the paste with fresh solution and reapply if necessary.

The greenish stains which are caused by copper or bronze oxidizing can often be removed by scrubbing with abrasive-type cleaning powder

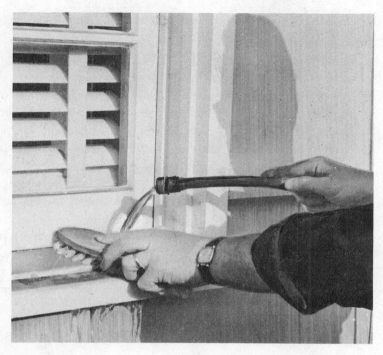

Periodic washing will prevent streaking

or very fine steel wool. Then scrub with ordinary household ammonia and water if the stain persists. To remove these stains from stucco or concrete, mix 1 part sal ammoniac with 4 parts whiting. Moisten this with enough household ammonia to make a thick paste, then trowel it on over the stain and cover with plastic to keep moist. Remove after several hours and rinse with clear water. If necessary, a second or even a third application may be applied.

Painted or varnished woodwork which is marred by the appearance of dirty or grayish-looking mildew stains must be scrubbed clean with a solution that will also kill the mildew that is present. To mix this solution, add 2 tablespoonsful of trisodium phosphate to a gallon of water. Then pour in 8 ounces of household bleach or disinfectant. Scrub this on over the surface and allow to soak for 10 or 15 minutes. Then rinse off with plenty of clear water. Where possible, repaint as soon as possible with a mildew-resistant coating.

When oil stains occur on a masonry wall, the best method is to apply a paste made of powdered whiting and a saturated solution of trisodium phosphate (about 1 pound of the cleanser to 1 gallon of water). Spread this over the stain at least ½-inch thick, then let dry and scrape off. Finish by washing with clear water, and reapply if necessary.

To clean unpainted brick or masonry walls, and to remove cement spots and similar stains from these surfaces, commercial muriatic acid (available in paint stores) is usually used. This liquid is mixed with 2 or 3 parts water, then scrubbed on with a stiff fiber brush. Allow it to soak for approximately 15 minutes, then wash the acid off completely by flooding with a hose. Because the solution is extremely caustic, wear rubber gloves and goggles, and avoid all contact with skin or clothing.

Smoke stains on concrete or brick are particularly difficult to remove. However, they often can be lightened considerably by scrubbing with a strong solution of trisodium phosphate and water. In this case, mix about ½ pound of the powder with each gallon of water, and try to soak the surface thoroughly with this solution before actually scrubbing. Scour stubborn spots by rubbing with a cloth which has been first dipped into this solution, then into powdered pumice or similar abrasive powder. On brickwork, try rubbing the stained bricks with a scrap piece of brick of the same color.

IV

Painting and Papering

Many homeowners feel that the only precaution required for a good paint job is to buy a top quality paint, then smear it on liberally with a brush or roller. Actually, a good quality paint is only one of several important ingredients needed for every good paint job. For long-lasting results and a professional-looking finish, there are many other factors that must be taken into consideration. For example, selecting the right kind of paint is just as important as selecting the best quality. Brushes and rollers both come in many different sizes and styles, and choosing the right one will not only make the work go faster, but will give a better-looking finish when the job is done.

There are also precautions that must be observed in preparing the surface in each case, as well as application techniques that should be mastered for each paint. These questions, as well as many other problems of painting and finishing, will be thoroughly discussed in this section. Charts contained in the articles on Exterior and Interior Painting will guide you in selecting the right type of paint to be used on each surface, and specific painting or finishing problems will be discussed under the appropriate headings throughout this section.

All too often, people who actually enjoy painting are reluctant to get started because they dread the job of cleaning up afterward. In most cases this is due either to poor planning (not having all the necessary tools and materials on hand) or to a lack of knowledge about the many time- and work-saving materials that are available.

Since most paint jobs are planned for weekends, when stores are closed, the home decorator should make certain that he has all supplies on hand before starting. Besides the necessary paints, brushes, rollers and solvents, he may need sandpaper, putty, patching compound, scrapers, mixing buckets, sticks, masking tape and ladders. In making up this list, the paint dealer can prove helpful by suggesting other supplies or equipment that may be needed.

One annoying problem that can easily be eliminated is the need for wiping up spatters or smears which accidentally splash onto furniture or floors. Professional painters always cover everything with large canvas drop cloths or tarpaulins, and do-it-yourselfers should follow this same practice. Though canvas cloths may be too expensive for occasional use, homeowners can purchase inexpensive drop cloths of plastic or specially treated paper. These are available in most paint and hardware stores for as little as a dollar or less.

Measuring 9 × 12 feet, these plastic or paper cloths are large enough to cover floors, furniture or shrubbery. They eliminate the need for removing the larger pieces of furniture when painting an entire room since the pieces can be shoved into the center of the room and covered. In most cases the ceiling can be painted by reaching in from the sides, though in others it may be advisable to use two ladders and a heavy plank to bridge the pile of furniture in the center. When these lightweight plastic or paper drop cloths are used outdoors, rocks or other weights can be used to hold down the corners.

Because every paint job involves a certain amount of mixing and pouring (the only sure way to make certain that the paint is properly mixed), extra mixing pails or buckets will usually be required. To eliminate the need for cleaning and storing these afterward, inexpensive cardboard pails are available. Made in three sizes—from 1½ to 5 quarts —these cardboard buckets cost only a few cents apiece, so they can simply be thrown away when the job is done. They are not only handy for mixing, they can be used for washing brushes or rollers when the day's work is done.

If the bottom of a roller tray is covered with a layer of brown wrapping paper before the paint is poured in, there will be no need for washing it later on. When this "liner" is peeled out afterward, all the paint will peel out with it, leaving only a slight oily film which can easily be wiped off with a dry rag. This trick also eliminates the need for a lot of washing and cleaning when switching from one color to another in the same tray.

To keep the unskilled home painter from smearing paint onto the glass or other nearby surfaces when painting windows, doors and woodwork, inexpensive metal or plastic shields can be used. Consisting of a sheet of metal or plastic, these guards can be moved along with the brush while the edge is being painted. Smears will then fall on the shield rather than the glass or other surface being protected. To protect wide surfaces while spraying or brushing, rolls of masking paper up to 9 inches in width can be purchased. Now available with adhesive strips along one edge (like masking tape), these rolls of masking paper enable the handyman to protect wide sections with a single strip without a great deal of intricate fitting and cutting.

Since even the most careful painter is bound to get some smears onto his hands or face, a cream-type waterless hand cleaner should be kept on hand to simplify the problem of cleaning your skin without using irritating solvents. These waterless cleaners remove even dried spots without difficulty and are widely used by professional painters instead of turpentine or similar solvents. All the user need do is massage vigorously over the skin, then wipe off with a clean dry cloth. Protective creams which are smeared on beforehand can also be used. These dry into the skin without leaving any visible film, yet they permit washing off all paint smears with soap and water when the job is done.

Brick and Concrete. SEE STUCCO AND MASONRY.

Brushes, Selection and Use

Paintbrushes are made in a wide variety of sizes and styles and in a great many different price ranges. To be sure of achieving the best possible results with any type of finish, always buy the best quality available. A good paintbrush will not only do a better job, it will last longer and will require less effort to use.

At one time, all good quality paintbrushes were made of imported Chinese hog bristle. However, in recent years, nylon bristles have become increasingly popular. This has been due principally to two factors: natural hog bristles have become increasingly scarce due to the virtual elimination of overseas sources, and nylon bristles have been greatly improved by new manufacturing processes which create artificially "flagged" or "exploded tip" bristles that rival natural bristles in paint-spreading qualities.

When comparing brushes of equivalent size and style for quality, examine the bristles carefully. Good brushes should have a high percentage of bristles with split or flagged ends, since these split ends are important to the paint-holding capacity of a brush, as well as to its ability to spread paint smoothly. The bristles should vary in length so that the brush will wear evenly, and the shorter bristles should also have flagged tips or split ends.

Generally speaking, brushes with longer bristles cost more than those with shorter bristles (assuming the bristles are of equal quality). In addition, the more expensive brush will be thicker at the ferrule, indicating that more bristles have been used in forming it. However, the purchaser should make certain that the brush does not have an excessively thick filler block in the center. This makes the brush look thicker, but it leaves the brush virtually hollow on the inside. Bristles should also feel springy and elastic when pressure is applied, but they should not fan out excessively when the bristle tips are pressed against a flat surface.

In addition to selecting a good quality brush, the home painter should also make certain that he selects the best size and style for the job at hand. As a rule, a larger brush will require fewer strokes, and thus will make it easier to achieve a smooth, brush-free finish.

For painting cabinets, doors and trim, flat brushes 2½ to 3½ inches in width are just about right. A 4-inch brush is usually used for exterior siding, shingles or stucco, while a round or oval-shaped brush works

Latex paint permits washing brush in water

Bristles should be agitated with fingers

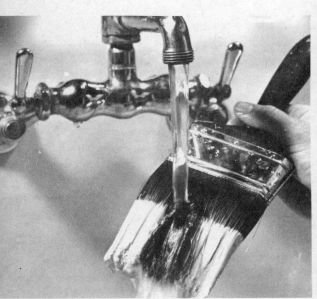

best on pipes and railings. For painting windows the handyman can select a 1½- or 2-inch angular sash brush (the bristle tips are cut off at an angle so the brush can be used edgewise).

Contrary to popular opinion, the job of cleaning a brush is actually a simple task which should take only a few minutes if attended to promptly. After wiping off excess paint, rub the bristles vigorously against sheets of old newspaper to remove as much paint as possible before washing. If a water-thinned paint was used, the brush should then be washed out in running water, taking care to flush all paint out of the center of the brush as well as off the outside. This is followed by a thorough shaking to remove excess water.

Brushes that have been used in a solvent-thinned paint should be washed out with several rinses of solvent (turpentine, benzine or mineral spirits) or with a commercially prepared liquid brush cleaner. If a solvent is used, the bristles should be worked vigorously underneath the surface of the liquid till the solvent has removed as much paint as possible. Two or three rinses will be needed to get bristles completely clean. If the brush is to be used again within a day or so, it can now be wrapped in heavy paper to preserve it. If the brush will be stored for a lengthy period of time, a final rinsing with detergent and warm water is advisable. Comb

Brushes should be suspended so tips do not touch bottom

Wrap brushes in heavy paper, as shown

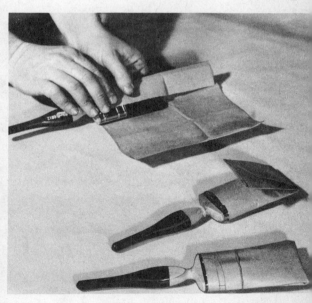

the bristles smooth and let them dry completely, then wrap in paper or foil to preserve the shape.

Commercially prepared brush cleaners are usually faster-working and more thorough than an ordinary solvent. Some types merely require that the brush be vigorously worked under the surface of the liquid till all pigment settles to the bottom. With other types, the bristles are worked in the liquid till the brush is thoroughly permeated with the cleaner. The brush can then be washed out in running water, since the cleaner makes the oil paint water-soluble.

Most of these commercially prepared brush cleaners can be used over and over again until the liquid is completely saturated with old paint. They not only do a thorough job of cleaning brushes after use, but are ideal for rapid cleaning of brushes when switching from one color to another.

Regardless of the type of cleaner and the cleaning method, brushes should be combed out with a metal brush comb or with an old coarse-toothed comb of any kind. Then wrap the brushes in heavy paper to help the bristles hold their shape. For best results, it is advisable to store brushes flat in a drawer or on a shelf rather than hanging them up on a wall rack.

Cabinets, Kitchen, Enameling

Though home painters often will not hesitate when faced with the job of repainting walls and ceilings, many are reluctant to tackle the job of repainting kitchen cabinets. Contrary to popular opinion, a smooth, professional-looking job can be achieved by the home decorator, provided the right materials are used and the proper techniques are followed.

Since the doors are the most prominent part of any kitchen cabinet, these obviously should get the most attention. Most professionals agree that the best way to get a smooth, uniform finish is to take the doors down and remove all hardware before refinishing them. If the paint is to be applied by brush, the doors can be laid flat so that the paint will flow out to a smooth, ripple-free coating. If the doors are to be sprayed, they can be propped up in the basement or garage, sprayed and allowed to dry before rehanging.

By removing all hardware first, the handyman will find it simpler to sand the surface smooth, and he will be able to apply the new paint more easily with full-length strokes. The extra time and effort required will be more than repaid in work saved when trying to "cut in" around hinges and knobs and in wiping off paint smears.

When painting kitchen cabinets, doors should be taken off

If the existing finish is in fairly good condition and the new paint is approximately the same color as the old, one coat of enamel often will be sufficient. However, if the old finish is badly worn or nicked, or if a considerable change of color is contemplated, two coats will probably be required. In this case, the handyman will find it best to apply a base coat of enamel undercoat (sometimes called underbody), followed by a top coat of quick-drying enamel. Though a high-gloss enamel finish is usually preferred, a semigloss enamel can also be used.

To apply the paint, a brush, a spray gun, a small mohair roller or a mohair-faced applicator can be used. Rollers work well with the undercoat and with the semigloss enamels. However, they will not give as smooth a finish when used with a high-gloss enamel. Spray guns which do not require excessive thinning of the paint will give excellent results with all finishes, but some practice may be required to get a really good finish.

A soft-bristled, fully stocked paintbrush (2½ or 3 inches wide is a good size) will give excellent results with all finishes if properly handled. The brush should be dipped into the paint no more than one-third its bristle length, then tapped lightly against the inside rim of the can to remove the excess (never wipe off the excess by drawing the brush across the rim). Flow the paint on with light, parallel strokes, avoiding any tendency to "scrub" it on. Brush across the width of the door while keeping the brush fully loaded at all times.

As each door is covered, the paint is cross-stroked without dipping the brush again. The bristle tips are dragged lightly along the length of the door at right angles to the original strokes. These cross-strokes should be made in one motion, from one end of the cabinet door to the other while holding the brush at a 45-degree angle to the surface. This tends to level out all brush marks left by the original strokes and helps to smooth out any irregularities in the finish.

Mohair-faced applicator pads also do a remarkably effective job of spreading on a smooth coat of enamel. If handled with reasonable care, they will spread the paint on in a smooth, uniform coating, and in less time than would normally be required with a conventional paintbrush. To use them effectively, the paint must be poured into a shallow tin or roller pan and then spread on with no more pressure than is required to apply the paint evenly.

Since no paint job can be any smoother than the surface beneath it, it is particularly important that the old surface be prepared properly before the first can of paint is opened. Paint cannot adhere satisfactorily over a surface which is dirty or greasy, so the first step is to scrub the cabinets thoroughly with a powerful detergent solution. Allow this to dry completely, then sand with fine-grit paper to smooth off scratches and nicks and to dull down any gloss which remains. If preferred, a "liquid sandpaper" or "surface preparer" solution can be used. This liquid is simply wiped on to remove old wax, grease and dirt and to dull down the gloss.

Bad nicks and deep scratches require more vigorous sanding with a coarser-grit (medium) sandpaper first. A finer grit is then used to remove scratches left by the coarser paper. In extreme cases, where the old finish is very rough or badly marred, complete removal of the old finish may be the best solution. Deep gouges, cracks or other depressions should be filled in with a water-mixed wood putty or a ready-mixed wood plastic compound.

After the doors have been taken down, the hardware removed and all surfaces prepared as described above, the first coat of underbody is applied. This is allowed to dry for at least 24 hours, then sanded lightly with fine-grit paper. Dust thoroughly to remove all grit left by the sanding, then apply the finish coat of enamel. If this finish coat is to be a definite color, the handyman will find it easier to tint the undercoat (which only comes in white) before it is applied. This will make it easier to cover with the colored enamel on the second coat.

In those cases where there is doubt as to whether one or two coats will be required, the handyman can safely go ahead with applying a first coat of the regular enamel, skipping the undercoat. If the job looks satisfactory with one coat, he can leave it as is. However, if a second coat is required, the first coat can be sanded lightly with fine-grit paper to dull down the gloss. After this, a second coat of enamel is applied to finish the job.

Exterior Painting

Besides adding immeasurably to the overall appearance of your house, a good outside paint job is essential to the proper maintenance of your home, particularly on trim and siding. Even the best quality paints will seldom last more than five or six years, and in many cases repainting of some areas will be required at much more frequent intervals.

For best results and maximum ease of application, outside paint should never be applied when temperatures are below 50 or above 90 degrees. You should also avoid working on days which are exceptionally windy, and solvent-thinned oil paints should never be applied when surfaces are damp after a rain. Latex-type paints thin with water, so they can be safely applied directly over a damp surface without difficulty.

The most important part of any exterior paint job is the preparatory work that must be done before the first can of paint is actually opened. Outside paints get severe wear, so there is almost always some cracking, peeling or blistering of the old film. These defective areas should be scraped clean before any new paint is applied. Applying fresh paint over an old finish which is blistered or cracked is not only a waste of time and money, it hastens the day when complete removal of the old finish may become necessary.

A hand scraper or a stiff putty knife can be used for most scraping operations. To "feather out" the rough edges which are left, sandpaper (or a sanding machine) can be used. Touch up the bare spots which remain with exterior primer, using one which is designed for the particular surface being painted. Ample drying time should be allowed before proceeding with additional coats.

When paint must be completely removed from exterior moldings, doors or window trim, a chemical paint remover will do the job faster than scraping. The thick, semipaste type should be used, flowing it on heavily with a single stroke of the brush. This softens up the old finish so that it can easily be scraped off with a putty knife or steel wool.

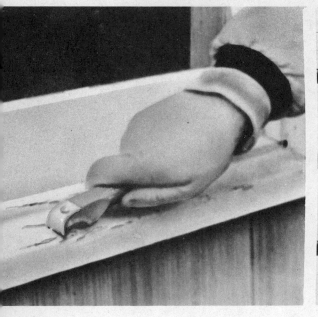 

Hand scraper is useful for small areas   *Bare spots are touched up first*

After sanding and scraping wherever necessary, all puttying, calking and patching of cracks should be completed. Window sash should be checked to make certain that the putty is sound around each pane of glass. Defective portions should be scraped out and replaced with fresh glazing compound after first brushing the rabbet clean and coating the exposed wood with linseed oil or primer.

Putty should also be used to fill nail holes or small cracks in wood trim and siding. Calking compound is used for larger cracks and for open joints where walls and trim are joined. On masonry surfaces, cracks can be filled with patching cement or with one of the new vinyl-concrete patching materials.

Door and window frames should be inspected around the outside to see that the calking is in good condition. Material which is cracked or dried out should be scraped out completely, then replaced with fresh compound. Use a calking gun to force the material into the joint. Dust and dirt should be cleaned out with a stiff brush before the compound is applied, and the surface must be dry if a good bond is to be insured.

Since paint will not adhere over a dirty or dusty surface, the handyman will find it advisable to wash some areas down with a strong detergent solution before painting. This is particularly true under overhanging eaves and in sheltered areas which are not exposed to the natural

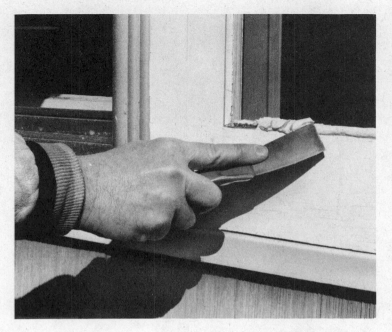

Putty should be replaced when necessary

action of wind and rain. In many cases, these overhangs will be coated with an oily scum that must be removed; otherwise peeling is certain to occur. If mildew stains are noticed, special treatment will be required. (See MILDEW STAINS.)

Rusty metalwork should also be scraped clean, then painted with a special rust-resistant primer which is designed for surfaces of this kind. The metal can then be painted with an ordinary trim paint to match the rest of the house.

Though two coats of paint are usually recommended for a lasting paint job, surfaces in relatively good condition may need only one coat. However, areas which are badly worn will require two coats: one primer or undercoat, and one finishing coat. For more specific information on this, the homeowner should read the manufacturer's instructions carefully before proceeding with the job.

As a rule, exterior paints should be applied liberally by flowing the paint on with a fully loaded brush. The brush should be dipped into the paint no more than one-third its bristle length, then tapped on the inside rim of the can to remove the excess. To mix the paint properly, first pour off some of the oil into a separate can. A stick is then used to mix up the contents on the bottom, after which the oil can be poured back into the original can and the paint stirred once more.

Paint outside by working from top down

Though the sequence may have to be varied in certain cases, it is generally best to work from the top down. Paint across each wall in horizontal laps, then proceed in successive laps down to the bottom. As a rule, it is best to do walls or siding first, cornices and fascia boards second and windows, doors and other trim last. Storm sash and screens can be stored in the garage to be completed on days when weather prohibits working outdoors. Since primers are available only in white, it may be best to tint them to approximately the same shade when a dark color will be used for the final coat. This will simplify the job of covering with one coat when the final color is applied.

To help select the right paint for each surface, remember that exterior paints can be loosely classified as falling into four general categories: house paints, shake and shingle paints, masonry paints and trim paints. Some of these are made only in conventional, oil-based form; others are available in latex-type, water-thinned formulations. Many of the newer outdoor paints are actually multipurpose coatings which can be used over many different surfaces; hence they may fit into more than one category.

House paints are intended mainly for use on clapboard and vertical wood siding, but they also can be used on trim and other wood surfaces. The most widely sold varieties are those which have a linseed oil base and thin with turpentine. These dry to a glossy finish and give good one-coat coverage when used on repaint work.

Where the old surface is badly weathered, two coats of oil-base house paint can be applied, though one coat of primer and one coat of finish will do a better job. Since these oil paints are slow drying, at least three or four days' drying time is required between coats. In addition, it is important that oil paints be applied only on a dry surface; otherwise blistering and peeling are almost certain to occur.

The water-thinned, latex-type house paints not only thin with water, they also simplify cleanup, since brushes and tools can be washed with water. Unlike the oil-base house paints, these latex paints dry to a dull finish, and they can be applied over a damp surface without difficulty.

When applied over the primer recommended by the manufacturer, these latex house paints are much more resistant to blistering and peeling which is caused by trapped moisture behind the film. However, this feature usually is lost when the paint is applied over an old surface that is already covered with several coats of a conventional oil paint. To get the full benefits of the blister-proof characteristics of this paint, all of the old paint would have to be removed first, then a special primer applied as recommended by the manufacturer.

As a general rule, latex paints will not cover as well as the oil paints. In addition, they call for more care in preparing the surface, since the paints do not have the penetration or the adhesive qualities of a good oil paint. It is for this reason that many brands recommend a special primer or a liquid additive which must be mixed in with the first coat.

Shingle paints are intended mainly for use on wood shingles or cedar shakes. They dry with a dull finish and form a permeable, "breathing" type of film which is less likely to blister and peel as moisture penetrates into the back of the shingle.

Most shingle paints have an oil or alkyd resin base which thins with turpentine or a similar solvent. On shingles which are in reasonably good shape, one coat often will be sufficient. However, where the old finish is chalking or badly eroded, a coat of special primer usually will be recommended for the first coat. When in doubt, it is best to apply one coat of the recommended primer before applying the finish.

Since the water-thinned latex house paints have all the characteristics desired in a shake and shingle paint, they also can be used on wood shingles. However, most brands call for a first coat of special primer as a base.

Masonry paints also dry to a flat finish and form a "breathing" type of film which will stand up well over damp surfaces. Since these characteristics are almost identical to those required in a shake and shingle paint, many shingle paints are also sold as masonry paints. Like the shingle paints, masonry paints are available in either the solvent-thinned (alkyd or linseed oil) types or the water-thinned latex types. The water-thinned types are currently more popular. They are easier to apply and have shown excellent resistance to attack by excess alkali, a condition often encountered in masonry walls.

Most latex masonry paints require a special bonding primer when they are to be applied over an old surface which is chalky or flaking. For extreme cases an oil-base bonding liquid may be required to help seal the old surface and to provide a firm foundation for the finish coat.

Powdered cement paints, which must be mixed with water before use, are one of the oldest types of masonry paint on the market. Still lower in cost than any type of ready-mixed paint, these masonry coatings can be applied only over a porous masonry surface—unpainted brick, stucco or concrete—or over surfaces which previously have been coated with this same kind of paint. For proper adhesion, the old surface must be wet down thoroughly beforehand and the cement paint applied while the surface is still damp.

Trim paints are hard drying, enamel-like finishes which dry to an exceptionally high gloss. They are made in very bright colors, as well as in black and white, and are designed for use on shutters, doors, windows and other surfaces which get hard wear. They also are used on screens, railings and outdoor furniture and are currently available only in the standard, turpentine-thinned varieties. Because they form a hard, brittle film which is not as flexible as that of a house paint, trim paints are not suitable for use on clapboard, siding or other large surfaces.

Natural or clear finishes are used on modern or contemporary homes to maintain the warm beauty of the natural wood. While most natural finishes are practically clear and have little or no color of their own, many are available with colored pigment added to give a tinted or stained effect to the finish. These usually are penetrating-type finishes which leave no surface film and which do not dry with a glossy or "built-up" finish. When a gloss is desired, an additional coat of clear glossy material can be applied over them.

The homeowner who chooses a natural-type exterior finish will avoid disappointment if the limitations inherent in this type of finish are first clearly understood. No natural finish, regardless of whether it is clear or partially pigmented, will stand up as long as a conventional opaque house paint. While a good house paint will last anywhere from four to eight years, even the best of natural finishes will last no more than two or three years. Under severe exposure conditions, varnish finishes may have to be renewed annually.

Paint stands up longer because the heavy percentage of pigment it contains shields the wood from the damaging rays of the sun. The pigment also helps mechanically to reinforce and strengthen the coating

EXTERIOR PAINT SELECTION

	OIL BASE HOUSE PAINT	LATEX HOUSE PAINT	TRIM	SHAKE & SHINGLE	LATEX MASONRY	POWDERED CEMENT PAINT	LATEX FLOOR	DECK ENAMEL	EXTERIOR ENAMEL
CLAPBOARD AND SIDING	A	A			B				
WOOD SHINGLES		A			A				
ASBESTOS SHINGLES		A			B	A			
BRICK, STUCCO						A	B*		
CEMENT BLOCK		B				A	A		
WINDOWS, DOORS AND TRIM	B		A						
STORM SASH AND SCREENS			A						
METAL RAILINGS AND WINDOWS	B		A						A
FENCES	A	B	A						
WOOD FLOORS								A	
CONCRETE FLOORS							A	B	
OUTDOOR FURNITURE				A					A

A—Most often recommended.

B—Also suitable.

*Can only be used on unpainted surface, or over same type of paint.

itself. That is why coatings which are even partially pigmented will always last longer than the completely clear ones. Not only will a colored finish give longer service, the wood itself will be protected more thoroughly from the sun; hence its color will be better preserved.

Exterior stains are usually referred to as shingle stains. They differ from ordinary tinted sealers or varnishes in that they usually have a much higher percentage of pigment, which gives them more hiding power. In some cases the grain of the wood is almost entirely obscured. A few are so heavy-bodied as to be more like a paint than a stain. Though sometimes referred to as natural finishes, shingle stains are not truly natural in appearance unless they are thin enough to permit the natural grain of the wood to show through clearly.

When a glossy finish is desired on siding or other large surfaces, resin-free, processed oils will provide a better finish than ordinary varnish. They are not as likely to turn brittle with age and are therefore less likely to crack. However, their inherently "soft" finish makes them less suitable for use on doors, porch trim and other frequently handled surfaces which must stand up under physical abuse as well as weathering. On these surfaces, as well as on natural-finish furniture, floors and other areas which get hard wear, a top quality spar varnish would still be the best choice.

Floor Paints

Though any good grade of enamel will stand up reasonably well when used on floors, it is best to use a paint which is specifically designed to resist the abrasion and exposure required of a good quality floor paint. Usually referred to as porch and deck enamels, paints designed specifically for this purpose come in three general types: oil- or alkyd-based floor enamels; solvent-thinned, rubber-base floor paints; and the newer water-thinned, latex floor paints.

The oil- and alkyd-based floor enamels are the most widely used types and dry with the highest gloss of all. They are suitable for use over wood as well as concrete, but most brands will not stand up as well as the rubber or latex varieties when applied to concrete slabs, such as patios and driveways, which are in direct contact with the ground. All oil-based paints are susceptible to attack by moisture which seeps up from underneath the slab. In addition, they generally do not stand up as well where excess alkali is present, a condition frequently encountered in concrete. However, their high gloss and exceptional adhesion make them preferable for use on wood floors, as well as on masonry floors where these conditions are not encountered.

When applying an oil-based floor enamel, always brush it out thoroughly and avoid excessively heavy applications. Two thin coats will stand up better than one thick coat, and there will be less likelihood of wrinkling, cracking or peeling. The paint can be applied with either brush or roller, but better penetration will be achieved if the first coat is thinned slightly with turpentine. The second coat generally should be used as it comes from the can.

These paints should never be applied over concrete which is the least bit damp or which has not aged for at least several months. In addition, floors which have a smooth, troweled finish should be etched first by washing with muriatic acid. This gives a "tooth" to the surface so that the paint can grip satisfactorily. Muriatic acid is available in liquid form at all paint stores. It should be diluted with 2 to 3 parts water in a bucket made of wood, enamelware, china or glass. Rubber gloves should be worn to protect the hands and the acid should be allowed to soak on the surface for several minutes. It is then flushed off with plenty of water and the floor allowed to dry thoroughly.

On many concrete floors, excess alkali will also have to be neutralized before an oil-based paint can be applied safely. To do this, wash the surface with a zinc sulphate solution, mopping it on over the surface and allowing it to dry without rinsing. Loose crystals which remain should then be brushed off before paint is applied.

The solvent-thinned, rubber-base floor paints are most widely used by commercial and industrial establishments, though several companies also make them available to homeowners. They are applied much like the oil-base floor paints, except that neutralizing with zinc sulphate is seldom required. These rubber-base paints have exceptional resistance to abrasion and hard wear, and they usually will stand up better than the oil-base paints on concrete floors which are in direct contact with the ground. However, their adhesion may not be as good over old surfaces, so it is essential that all smooth floors be etched with acid (as described above) before painting. In addition, it is extremely important that the floor be absolutely clean and as dust-free as possible before the first coat of paint is applied.

Though these rubber-base paints wear exceptionally well, they are subject to attack by gasoline and some greases, so they are not advisable for use on garage floors or other areas where these materials may be encountered. They can be applied over other floor paints, but maximum

To spread paint quickly on concrete floors use ordinary floor brush

adhesion will be assured if they are applied over previously unpainted concrete or over themselves. Generally speaking, they are not recommended for use on wood floors.

The water-thinned latex floor paints (latex does not mean rubber) have several popular features. They dry quickly (less than an hour in most cases) and they have little or no odor. In addition, no acid washes or other special rinses are required and cleanup is greatly simplified since brushes or other tools can be washed out with water. They dry to a dull finish rather than a high gloss, and they can be applied over a damp surface since the solvent is water. Though they can be walked upon within an hour, they should not be subject to dampness or rain for at least 24 hours. In addition, the second coat should not be applied till the following day. Though these paints can be used on previously painted wooden floors, they are generally not suitable for use over raw or unpainted wood floors.

One feature which has made latex floor paints popular for use on basement floors is that this is the only type of floor over which resilient floor tiles can be laid later on. This means that if a basement is painted with this type of floor paint, tiles can be laid later on without need for removing all of the old paint first.

Regardless of which floor paint is used, it is imperative that the floor be thoroughly cleaned first. Wash off all grease, wax or oil and sweep up all dust before any paint is applied. This is especially true of both the latex-emulsion and the rubber-base floor paints. Both of these wear well, but they have poor penetration and will not adhere properly if there is any dust or powdery residue left on the surface. As a rule, one of the best floor cleaners for removing oil or wax, as well as general dust and dirt, is a solution of trisodium phosphate, commonly sold in all paint stores under a brand name such as Beatsall. Use about a ¼ pound of the crystals to each gallon of hot water and scrub on with a stiff brush. Then rinse thoroughly with plenty of clean water.

In addition to cleaning the surface beforehand, you must remember that no paint can adhere satisfactorily if it is applied over old coats which are already peeling or flaking. Scrape off any of the old finish which is not adhering satisfactorily, using a wire brush or steel putty knife. In extreme cases it may be necessary to use a chemical paint remover to take off all of the old paint so that the new finish can bond directly with the concrete. When repainting, remember that two coats should always be applied, even if the first coat looks as though it has covered satisfactorily.

Gold-leafing

As the name implies, gold leaf actually consists of tissue-thin leaves of real gold which are applied over the surface. While not as simple to apply as many other types of finishes, the technique of applying gold leaf is one which can be mastered by anyone willing to devote a little time and patience to the task.

Gold leaf is sold in most art supply stores and in many well-stocked paint stores. It is available in various colors, the most popular being the XX 23-karat gold. Beginners will have less trouble with the type which is sold for gilding in the wind (outdoors). This leaf, which is variously called patent leaf, outdoor gold or transfer gold, is manufactured with each leaf lightly adhered to a square of thin white tissue paper. This makes it much easier for the amateur to handle and eliminates the need for a gilder's tip, a special soft brush which is used to pick up ordinary unbacked gold leaf.

Most gold leaf is made in one standard size, 3⅜ inches square. The smallest unit or package in which it is sold is a "book" which contains 25 leaves. Allowing for the normal amount of waste due to lapping, a book of 25 leaves will cover approximately 1½ square feet.

All successful applications of gold leaf require that the surface first be properly prepared. It must be as smooth as possible and absolutely free of all wax, grease and dirt. To avoid trouble, amateurs should limit their early efforts to comparatively small flat surfaces or to simple designs on larger surfaces. A picture frame is a popular project for the amateur gilder—but select a rather plain one which is not covered with ornate carvings.

If the frame is an old, previously finished one, begin by first washing it thoroughly with nonflammable cleaning fluid to remove all dust and grime. Then apply a thin coat of shellac which has been diluted with an equal part of denatured alcohol. If the frame is unfinished, the raw wood will have to be sealed by brushing on three or four thin coats of a good spar varnish, after diluting with about 25 per cent turpentine. Allow each coat to dry thoroughly, and rub lightly between coats with #00 steel wool for the smoothest possible results.

The liquid which actually binds the gold leaf to the surface is called gold size. It is sold in the same stores that sell the gold leaf and is available in two types: a quick-drying or synthetic size and a slow-drying or "fat" oil size. Unless time is short, the slow size should be used. It allows more time for the gilding operation and makes it easier to achieve a really brilliant job.

After the surface has been properly prepared and sealed, brush on a thin, uniform coat of the size. Make absolutely certain there are no skips

Gold size is applied with soft brush   *Lay leaf onto surface and smooth out all wrinkles*

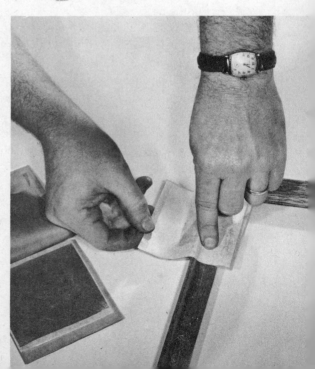

or misses as the gold will not adhere where no size is applied. When only part of the surface is to be gilded, or when only a design is to be covered, rather than a solid coating, apply the size in only the pattern desired. The gold will adhere over the sized areas only, and when the excess leaf is rubbed off afterward, the gold that remains will follow the exact pattern of the size.

Allow the size to dry for 12 to 18 hours—or until the proper "tack" is achieved. To make sure the size has just the right amount of tackiness, test it with a knuckle. The size should not stick to, or come off on, the finger, but a very slight pull should be felt when the finger is removed. The size will hold this tack for another 6 to 10 hours, so don't rush the work at this point.

When the size has dried sufficiently, the frame is ready for gilding. Carefully pick up each leaf, holding it by the corners of the thin backing paper. Lay the gold onto the surface smoothly and evenly, then rub the back of the protecting paper with your finger tips to make sure that the gold is thoroughly adhered at all points. For shallow grooves press the gold carefully into position with a fingernail or with a small cotton swab. Be careful to avoid tearing if at all possible.

After laying each leaf, peel off the tissue paper backing and continue with the next one, overlapping each leaf about ¼ inch. Continue laying the gold in this manner until the entire surface is covered. If the leaf tears in spots, or if some parts do not adhere evenly, patch them promptly by

Patch corners by pressing on pieces of leftover gold   *Finished job is burnished by rubbing with cotton*

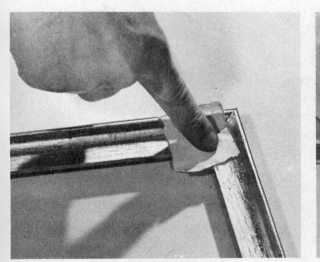
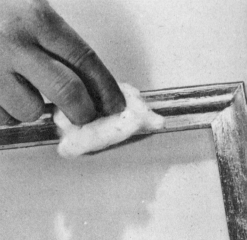

rubbing additional small pieces of the gold over the damaged areas.

Allow the gilded area to dry overnight, then burnish lightly by rubbing briskly over the entire surface with a wad of soft, clean, absorbent cotton. This brings up the final high luster and removes all overlapping edges and superfluous gold.

For maximum brilliance gold leaf should not be overcoated unless necessary to protect it against frequent handling. For objects such as lamps, cigarette boxes and the like, apply a thin protective coating of fresh white shellac diluted with 2 parts of denatured alcohol.

Graining Technique

Any home handyman can, with just a little practice, do a reasonably good job of creating a wood-grain effect over any paintable surface. The technique, once mastered, will enable you to refinish a metal radiator cover so that it blends in with a wood-paneled wall or to apply a wood-grain finish over previously painted wood or metal cabinets, doors and moldings.

Though exact duplication of a specific wood finish is a difficult task which calls for a great deal of skill, you can do a presentable job of painting on a finish which will closely resemble natural wood in color and appearance. Broadly speaking, there are three steps involved: application of a ground coat or base coat which supplies the needed background color; application of pigmented graining color or heavy stain over this and application of one or two coats of clear varnish to protect the finish.

The base coat should be a low-luster finish, such as a satin-sheen enamel or good quality enamel underbody. While most professionals prefer to tint this to their own color to get the exact shade required, home painters will find it easier to buy a ready-mixed ground coat or base coat. This comes in a neutral buff or beige color which is adequate as a background for most wood-grain effects. If a different shade is required, you can purchase white underbody and tint it yourself, using colors-in-oil or tinting colors which come in tubes.

The base coat should be applied as smoothly as possible with none of the original color showing through. One coat will suffice in most cases, but a second coat should be applied if the first coat does not cover uniformly. This is allowed to dry overnight before proceeding with application of the graining color on top.

For the graining color, a ready-mixed pigmented oil stain can be purchased. This eliminates the job of mixing your own. The pigmented

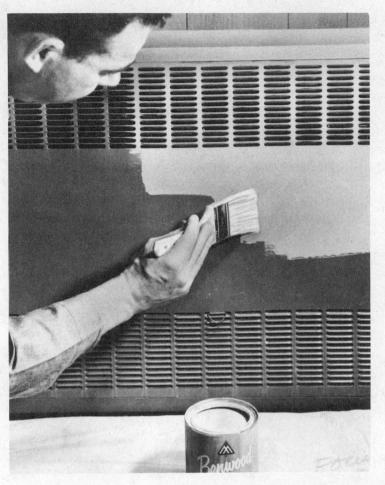

A suitable ground color is painted on first

stains differ from other oil stains in that they are partially opaque and contain sufficient pigment to "take hold" when applied over a ground coat. Penetrating oil stains and alcohol-based spirit stains will not work over a painted-on base coat since these stains can only be applied over a porous wood surface.

The stain or graining color required can be selected by consulting the manufacturer's color card. These sample cards are usually made up by applying the stain over a base coat or ground color, rather than by actual application over raw wood. When selecting a color, remember that the stain can be lightened or darkened during application simply by varying the amount which is brushed on. Intermediate colors also can be achieved by purchasing two or more stains and intermixing them to attain the exact shade required.

Stain is applied with coarse-bristle brush

If you wish, you can mix your own stain-type graining color. Buy some glazing liquid, dilute with a small amount of turpentine, then add the required tinting oil color till you achieve the graining color desired. Glazing liquid is a special oil which is sold for this purpose in many paint stores. Flatting oil also can be used, but it will not work as smoothly.

The graining color or stain is best applied with a cheap, coarse-bristled paintbrush. For a pronounced grain the bristles can be cut down with a razor blade till only 1 or 2 inches of hair remains. The brush is dipped into the stain, then wiped off till almost dry. Then spread the color on in long parallel strokes, covering one section at a time and with no attempt to eliminate brush marks. Instead of brushing in straight lines, the hand should be moved slightly from one side to the other, while slowly twisting the handle back and forth. This will create a series of wavy lines which will closely resemble wood grain in texture and appearance.

After several square feet have been covered, the handyman should allow the stain to set for about 10 or 15 minutes. Then with the same brush—or with a second dry brush—go over the surface once more to

Rubber tool is used to streak the stain

accentuate the grained effect and to brush in additional streaks. If the stain tends to sag or flow together, the brush should be wiped dry on a clean rag, then once more rubbed over the surface. Experimentation on scrap surfaces may be required to determine the amount of weaving required to achieve the desired grain pattern and to see whether the stain has to set a bit longer before the grain pattern will stay put.

Another method commonly used to achieve a grained effect is to use a rubber graining comb or graining tool (available in most paint stores) to streak the stain. Drag the graining tool over the surface in one direction only, slowly weaving and twisting it to create a realistic-looking wood-grain pattern. A small whisk broom or coarse pad of steel wool also can be used to comb out the graining color. Regardless of the tool selected, the idea is to wipe off the graining color in streaks so that the base coat shows through to create the contrast required.

After graining is complete, the surface should be allowed to dry for at least eight hours, then covered with one or two coats of clear varnish. Though a high-gloss varnish can be used, the effect will generally be more pleasing (and defects less noticeable) if a semigloss or low-luster varnish is used. One coat will be sufficient on most surfaces, but a second coat should be applied to table tops, chairs and other surfaces which will get hard wear.

Interior Painting, Ceilings, Walls and Woodwork

Before starting to paint one or more rooms in your house, make certain that you have all the necessary materials on hand, particularly if the job is to be done on a weekend, when stores will normally be closed. Besides the paint itself, you will need brushes, rollers, patching compound, sandpaper, putty knives and drop cloths. To stir the paint properly, you will also need one or more mixing pails (cardboard or metal), as well as a few mixing sticks. Turpentine or other solvents will also be required, unless a water-thinned, latex paint is being used.

To prepare the room for painting, all chairs, lamps, vases and other small items should be removed. Large pieces which are too bulky to be moved should be pushed into the center of the room and then covered

Furniture can be grouped in center of room for covering

with large plastic, paper or canvas drop cloths. Inexpensive covers of this kind are available in almost all paint stores.

Since paint will stick properly only on a clean surface, walls, ceilings and woodwork should be cleaned wherever necessary. In most cases dusting or vacuuming is all that will be required. However, badly soiled or greasy areas on kitchen walls and ceilings will have to be scrubbed with detergent before paint can be applied safely. Glossy areas should be dulled down by sanding or by wiping with a liquid surface preparer which is sold for just this purpose.

Cracks and holes in walls and ceilings should be filled next. For small openings a prepared spackling compound is used, while for larger openings patching plaster may be required. Cracks should be cut open with a pointed tool (a beer can opener works well) to insure a good bond when the patching material is applied.

After patches are dry and hard, they should be sanded smooth with a medium-grit paper, then dusted thoroughly. Depending on the brand and type of paint used, "touching up" these patches may or may not be necessary. If in doubt, it is best to apply a thin coat of the paint over the patched area, then allow this to dry before painting the entire wall or ceiling. With modern flat wall paints—particularly in the lighter colors—this preliminary step is not usually required. This is particularly true if a two-coat job is contemplated.

Since a roller can be used with practically any type of paint and is so much faster and easier than a brush on large areas, most home painters will prefer to use a roller instead of a brush on walls and ceilings. A room should always be painted by doing the ceilings first, the walls second and the woodwork, such as doors and windows, last.

To reach into corners where walls and ceilings meet and to coat areas adjacent to trim or cabinets, a brush will be needed. Generally speaking, it is best to paint these corners with the brush first, then follow up with the roller. When two people are working together, the work will usually go smoothly if one person uses a brush to paint around edges and in corners while the other follows behind with the roller.

When using a roller, the home painter should work with a slow, steady stroke with the cover uniformly loaded with paint at all times. On walls, the first stroke should always be in an upward direction. On ceilings, the first stroke should be away from the user, rather than toward him.

To avoid splattering and a streaky, uneven finish, only a moderate amount of pressure should be applied and the roller should never be moved with rapid strokes which make it spin unnecessarily. To minimize the

When painting with roller, a brush is still needed in corners

possibility of lap marks that may not show up till after the paint is dry, a wall or ceiling should always be completed from end to end before stopping.

When painting ceilings, it is generally best to start in one corner and then work across the shortest dimension in 3- or 4-foot-wide strips. When painting walls, start in one corner near the top. Paint from top to bottom, a strip at a time, without giving the edge of each succeeding section a chance to dry completely. If necessary to stop before a complete wall is finished, try to end up near a door frame or other natural break in the surface.

Though rollers can sometimes be used on large flush doors, a brush is usually required for windows and other trim. To keep paint smears off the glass when painting windows, masking tape can be used. If preferred, dried paint spatters can be scraped off later with a single-edged razor blade. The movable window sash should be painted first, then the window frame and sill.

When painting doors, the reverse procedure is usually followed. Door frames are painted first, after which the edges of the door itself are painted. If the door is paneled, the panels and moldings should be completed before the face of the door is coated. On paneled doors of this kind, a constant check must be made as work progresses to watch for "runs" or drips which may occur in the lower corners of each panel.

The baseboards around the bottom of the room are usually painted last. To protect carpeting or floors, a piece of stiff cardboard or sheet metal can be held against the bottom and moved along as painting progresses. This protective shield should be held flat against the floor with one edge pressing tight against the bottom of the baseboard. This not only protects the floor, but also keeps the brush from picking up dirt.

In most rooms a flat paint will be used on both walls and ceilings. Contrary to popular opinion, there is no important difference between a ceiling paint and a wall paint, except that a flat selected for ceilings usually has more hiding power (for one-coat coverage). It is also less washable, since this is seldom required on ceilings.

Flat paints are made either with an alkyd base that thins with turpentine or with a latex base that thins with water. The latex type may have either a vinyl or an acrylic base, or it may consist of a combination of both.

As a rule, alkyd flats give more hiding with one coat than comparable latex flats, but they require that brushes and other tools be washed with turpentine or a similar solvent. Though many brands have a typical solvent odor which irritates some people, special odorless varieties are also available. However, to keep these odorless, there are special thinners that must be used instead of turpentine.

Since latex flats thin with water, they also permit the homeowner to wash out his brush or roller with water, thus simplifying cleanup. They also spread easier—especially on porous surfaces—and seldom require a primer of any kind. In addition, there is never a painty odor, and they dry quickly so that a second coat can often be applied on the same day.

Semigloss and high-gloss enamels are usually used on doors, windows and other woodwork. Though flat paint also can be used on these surfaces, the glossier finishes are tougher and will make it easier to wash off finger marks or stains. Because of the increased washability afforded by these finishes, semigloss enamels are also frequently used on walls and ceilings in kitchens, bathrooms and laundry rooms. They vary in luster from a dull, satin finish (often referred to as an eggshell finish) to a high gloss. As a rule, the glossier finishes will withstand the most scrubbing and hard wear.

Up until a few years ago, all enamels and gloss paints were solvent-

	ALKYD FLAT	LATEX FLAT	LOW LUSTRE ENAMEL	HIGH GLOSS ENAMEL	LATEX SEMI-GLOSS	ALKYD FLOOR ENAMEL	LATEX FLOOR PAINT	HIGH GLOSS VARNISH	SEMI-GLOSS VARNISH	WOOD SEALER	CEMENT PAINT
WALLS AND CEILINGS	A	A	A†	B†	B†						
WOODWORK, DOORS, WINDOWS	B	B	A	A	A						
KITCHEN CABINETS				B	A	B			A	B	
METAL DOORS AND WINDOWS	B			A	A						
RADIATORS AND PIPES	A			B							
FURNITURE AND BUILT-INS				A	A	B			A	A	B*
CONCRETE WALLS		A						B			B*
CONCRETE FLOORS						A	A				
WOOD FLOORS								A	A	A*	
WOOD PANELING	B		A						A	A*	
METAL RAILINGS	B			A	A						
RESILIENT TILE FLOORS								A			

A — Most often used.
B — Also suitable.
* — Can only be applied over same type finish, or over unfinished surface.
† — Usually in kitchens, bathrooms and laundry rooms.

thinned; latex paints were only available with a flat finish. However, most companies now produce latex enamels in a semi-gloss finish, and some also make them with a comparatively high gloss finish. These are tougher and more washable than the latex flats, but most experts agree that they are still not quite as tough as the solvent-thinned alkyd or polyurethane enamels. Also, they do not cover quite as well in one coat where a considerable color change is called for, and they do not flow out to as smooth a finish as the solvent-based enamels do.

When a clear finish is desired for use on natural wood cabinets or woodwork, an interior varnish is usually used. These do not necessarily have to give a high-gloss finish. Most large manufacturers produce semigloss or satin-finish varnishes, as well as the more common high-gloss varieties. Though these are not quite as tough as the glossy varnishes, they will give excellent service on most interior applications.

In addition to the paints listed in the chart, there are a number of special primers or undercoats which may be required on some surfaces. When a dark-colored flat will be used on walls or ceilings, many manufacturers recommend that a primer and sealer be applied first. When a radical change of color makes it obvious that two coats of paint will be required on walls or ceilings, a primer and sealer should also be used for the first coat, particularly if the finish coat will be an alkyd flat. Latex flats usually serve as their own primer so that two coats of the same paint can be applied.

When a base coat or primer is required under an enamel finish, an undercoat or underbody is usually used. This may also be advisable when the old finish is badly worn, when painting over a high-gloss finish or when an extreme change of color indicates ahead of time that two coats of paint will be required. An undercoat or primer will also be required when painting over previously unpainted surfaces of any kind.

Regardless of the type of paint being used, the homeowner should read the label carefully before starting. Follow all recommendations as to mixing, thinning and application. Since no paint can adhere properly over a dirty or greasy surface, such areas should be scrubbed down thoroughly before the first coat of paint is applied. Peeling or flaking paint should always be scraped away till only a sound surface remains, and rough spots should be sanded smooth or patched if a professional-looking finish is to be achieved.

Metal Surfaces, How to Paint

When used around the outside of the house, most metals eventually rust, tarnish or oxidize unless they are adequately protected by paint or other weatherproof coating. Even where painting is not absolutely essential for the protection of the metal, homeowners may still prefer to paint them because a change in color is desired or because they want the metal trim or hardware to be less noticeable.

To achieve a lasting paint job on metal furniture, railings or other fixtures, careful attention must be given to proper preparation of the surfaces beforehand. It is also important that the right kind of paint be used, particularly for the first, or priming, coat. The prime coat required will vary with the type of metal being painted. It should provide a good adhesion to the surface, while at the same time providing the necessary protection from the elements.

All metal surfaces must be cleaned thoroughly before paint can adhere satisfactorily. Dirt, grease, rust and other foreign matter must be washed

PREPARATION REQUIRED BEFORE PAINTING

TYPE OF METAL	SURFACE PREPARATION	PAINTING REQUIREMENTS
GALVANIZED METAL	If possible allow to weather for at least six months. Otherwise, treat with special metal wash. Remove all grease, dirt and rust.	First coat should be special zinc dust or zinc oxide primer—or a pigmented, shellac base primer. Then finish with regular oil paint.
IRON AND STEEL (already rusted)	Use a wire brush to knock off loose scales of rust and peeling paint. Wash off grease and dirt with solvent, and sand down pitted areas.	Coat with special metal primer which is designed to stick over rust. Then apply second coat of same type paint in color desired.
IRON AND STEEL (little or no rust)	Use emery cloth or steel wool to polish off all mild corrosion. If painted, sand down old finish lightly. Wash off grease and dirt with solvent.	Apply first coat of red lead or zinc chromate metal primer. Then finish with enamel or metallic, aluminum paint.
COPPER AND BRASS	Best not to paint until it weathers sufficiently to become dull and tarnished. Wash down with grease solvent without scratching tarnish. Bright metal should be wiped down with lacquer thinners.	Give first coat of metal primer which contains only lead—no zinc. Then finish with enamel or house paint, preferably one which is zinc-free.
ALUMINUM	Allow to weather for at least two months, then scrub with strong detergent. Sand badly pitted areas smooth with fine sandpaper.	Apply first coat of zinc chromate metal primer. If not near seacoast, aluminum paint can also be used. Then finish with enamel or house paint.

or scraped off to permit paint to bond to the metal itself. However, when painting copper, brass or aluminum, abrasives should not be used. Copper and brass will take paint better if they are first permitted to become dull or tarnished, while aluminum accepts paint most readily after it has begun to oxidize. The oxides create a permanent bond and serve as an excellent foundation for the paint which is applied over it.

Unlike the nonferrous metals just mentioned, iron and steel do not merely tarnish or oxidize—they rust or corrode when unprotected. When this flaky coating forms, it interferes greatly with paint adhesion and usually has to be removed completely before paint can be applied. If another coat of paint is simply brushed on over the rust, chances are that the rust will continue spreading underneath the paint to cause premature peeling and flaking.

To eliminate the necessity for wire brushing and scraping on old rusty metal, there are now special paints available which are designed to adhere over rust. These metal primers can be applied directly over firm, solid rust without the necessity for scraping or sanding. Loose, flaking particles should be brushed off so that the surface underneath is firm and sound. The primer can then be brushed on directly over the rusted metal. It contains special oils which eat their way into and through the rust so as to bond securely to the metal underneath. Not only do these primers insure good adhesion for subsequent coats, they also prevent rust from spreading further after they have been applied.

Galvanized iron is iron which has been coated or plated with zinc. When comparatively fresh, it provides a poor foundation for paint and frequently causes extensive peeling. To prevent this, it is best to allow galvanized iron to weather for at least 6 to 12 months before painting. When this is impractical, special metal washes can be used to condition

Exposed metal surfaces are protected with anticorrosion paint

the galvanized surface before the prime coat is applied.

For years it was thought that washing with ordinary vinegar was sufficient. However, recent research by manufacturers in the industry has indicated that this offers little or no guarantee against future peeling. Prepared metal washes which work much better are available from many paint stores and sign supply shops, or they can be mixed at home by adding ½ pound of copper sulfate to 1 gallon of water. This is applied to the galvanized coating with a brush and allowed to dry, then rinsed off with clear water.

A far more satisfactory method for painting galvanized surfaces consists of first applying a prime coat of specially formulated zinc dust or zinc oxide metal primer. Make certain the brand selected specifically states on the label that it is suitable for use over galvanized surfaces without further treatment. If this type of primer is not locally available, one of the pigmented, shellac-based primers can be used. These alcohol-thinned primers are made by several companies and have excellent adhesion over practically any surface, including galvanized iron. They dry quickly to a flat white finish and provide an excellent foundation for subsequent coats of paint.

As in painting most other metals, it is essential that the galvanized surface be thoroughly clean before any paint is applied. To remove grease or oil (always present to some extent on new metal), wash down with a strong detergent solution. If preferred, benzine or a similar grease solvent can be used.

Bright new surfaces of copper or brass (or brass-plated steel) also have a light coating of grease or oil applied to them during the original manufacturing process. This is one reason why they should be allowed to weather or tarnish before being painted. If copper gutters are to be painted, allow them to become thoroughly dull and tarnished, remembering that the heavier the tarnish, the better the paint will hold.

When painting highly polished copper or brass hardware or lighting fixtures, it should be remembered that a thin coat of lacquer has usually been applied at the factory to retard tarnishing. When tarnished spots first become noticeable, they will usually be in an irregular pattern, since only part of the lacquer will wear off while some sections remain. Before painting fixtures or hardware of this kind, wipe off the remaining lacquer with paint remover or lacquer thinner.

While it is true that aluminum does not "rust" in the sense that iron does, it does react with the elements, and will eventually oxidize to a point where it becomes pitted and mottled-looking. For this reason, as well as because many simply want a change in color, homeowners in recent years have become increasingly interested in painting these aluminum surfaces. The oxide film which forms adheres very firmly and, unlike rust on iron, need not be removed before painting, since it makes an excellent foundation for paint. To paint aluminum successfully, here is the procedure to follow:

(1) Allow the surface to weather for at least two months before painting. If essential that it be painted sooner, it will be necessary first to scrub thoroughly with a strong grease solvent such as trisodium phosphate.

(2) Wipe off all surface dust and dirt with a stiff-bristled brush, then wash if necessary. Badly pitted rough spots should be sanded smooth with fine sandpaper.

(3) Apply a first coat of metal primer, using either aluminum paint or a zinc chromate primer (zinc chromate is best near the seacoast).

(4) Finish with one or two coats of good quality outdoor enamel or aluminum paint. Windows and doors on the outside of the house can also be finished with matching trim or house paints if preferred.

Mildew Stains

When a paint job begins to look dirty or stained, there is a better than even chance that it is not dirt at all but probably mildew. Though mildew can sometimes occur on interior surfaces (particularly on damp walls, or in bathrooms and laundry rooms), the condition most often occurs on outside surfaces. Under superficial examination with the naked eye, these mildew discolorations often look much like dirt, but it is important that the homeowner differentiate between the two if proper corrective measures are to be taken.

Unlike dirt, mildew stains cannot permanently be eliminated by simple washing. If the condition is not corrected in time, it may actually cause complete breakdown of the paint film itself. In addition, if fresh paint is applied directly over the mildew, discolorations will probably reappear on the new coating in a short while.

Mildew is caused by fungi which are found almost everywhere. These are actually live growths which feed on organic matter, such as wood, paper, leather, paint or plastics. They reproduce at an exceedingly rapid rate from microscopic spores which are carried through the air. When they land on the paint or other material, they begin growing and spreading almost immediately if conditions are right. In the process they actually feed on and decompose the paint film and will eventually destroy it entirely.

In order for mildew to grow, moisture and a reasonable amount of warmth must be present. For this reason, shaded or protected portions of the house, which remain damp longer after a rain, are usually attacked most severely. In addition, periods of hot, humid weather are particularly conducive to mildew growth, especially if this weather occurs while the paint is still very fresh and soft. Because mildew grows more easily on soft paint films than it does on hard, enamel-like finishes, it is more likely to be found on regular house paints than it is on the hard-drying sash and trim paints. However, hardness of the finish alone is not a guarantee that mildew cannot or will not occur.

To tell whether a paint discoloration is caused by mildew or dirt, there are two simple tests the homeowner can make. The first consists of examining the stains under a high-power magnifying glass. Dirt will look like particles of sand or like gritty specks on the surface. Mildew will have a weblike, filamentous appearance which spreads out from a central, more darkened area (something like a spider web). It usually will be darker and more uniform in color than ordinary dirt.

In their early stages, mildew spores which have not developed and spread fully may also look like tiny erupting "pimples" or miniature craters which pop open. These will eventually spread out with the cobweb-like growth described.

A second, more positive test which the inexperienced homeowner can easily make to differentiate between mildew and dirt is to apply a few drops of common household bleaching solution, such as Clorox, to the stain. If mildew is present, the stain will bleach out in a minute or so and will disappear completely, leaving the surface absolutely clean. Dirt stains will be affected very little, if at all. It is important that only fresh bleach be used for this test. Bleach which has been standing for six months or more may no longer be sufficiently potent to give an accurate test.

If it is determined that mildew is present, it is important to kill the growth as soon as possible and to repeat the process again before a fresh coat of paint is applied. To remove the stains and to kill the fungi which caused them, the mildewed surfaces should be scrubbed down with a solution consisting of 3 heaping tablespoons of trisodium phosphate (sold in paint stores under the common name of Beatsall), 1½ cups of a bleach-type disinfectant, such as Clorox, and 1 gallon of water.

Scrub this solution on with a soft brush, then rinse thoroughly with plenty of clean water, preferably by washing with a hose.

After the surface has been rinsed, it should be allowed to dry thoroughly for at least a day or two. Then repaint as soon as possible with a properly formulated mildew-resistant house paint. Top quality house paints which are recommended for this purpose will clearly state on the label that appropriate mildewcides have been added in the factory. If a house paint of this kind is not readily available or if the homeowner is in doubt as to the mildew resistant qualities of the particular brand he is using, special mildewcides can be purchased separately in small bottles at most paint stores. These can be added to any regular house paint so as to make it mildew resistant and thus prevent the possibility of growth recurring. If two coats of paint are required, both should be of the mildew-resistant variety.

Peeling and Blistering Problems, Exterior

When a homeowner notices paint peeling around the outside of his house, his first impulse is to blame the paint itself. In most cases this actually is not so. Nine times out of ten the trouble is caused either by a structural defect which permits moisture to seep in behind the paint film or by improper preparation of the surface.

Though all outside paints are designed to shed water, they will not adhere for very long to a surface which is continuously wet underneath. If defective calking, open seams, leaky gutters or corroded flashing permits moisture to seep into the wall and soak the wood or masonry behind the paint, blistering and peeling is almost certain to occur. The moisture in the wall is vaporized by the heat of the sun and drawn outward, pushing the paint off with it. This type of defect is most easily recognized by the fact that the paint usually peels right down to the bare wood, rather than merely flaking off on top.

To correct a situation of this kind, the homeowner must first fill in or repair all open seams and similar defects. He should then allow the wall to dry thoroughly before repainting. Thorough scraping and sanding is also necessary to remove the old, defective paint before the new material is applied. Painting directly over the peeling paint (even if partially removed) will only cause the new material to peel again in the near future.

On exterior walls of wood, peeling often can be caused by moisture vapor which penetrates the walls from inside the house during periods

Water that seeps behind siding is cause of most peeling

when interior humidity is exceptionally high. This often happens during the winter months when shower baths, clothes dryers and other water-using appliances give off large amounts of water vapor which is trapped indoors by windows and doors that are tightly closed. When this moisture vapor reaches the hollow space behind the siding, it condenses on the cold surfaces and soaks into the wood to cause peeling later on.

To keep this from happening, the homeowner should make every effort to eliminate all possible sources of excess humidity on the interior of the house. He should use ventilating fans in kitchens, bathrooms and laundries, and remember to open windows at least once or twice a day on each floor.

Since even these measures will not always prove adequate, many experts recommend the insertion of small ventilating louvers or miniature vents in the outside wall. Less than 1 inch in diameter, these vents are installed by simply drilling a hole in the siding, then pushing the vent into place in the opening. One vent is required in each closed-off area

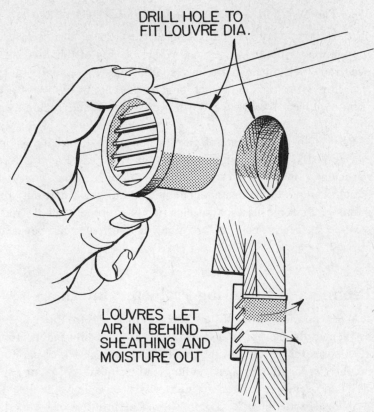

DRILL HOLE TO
FIT LOUVRE DIA.

LOUVRES LET
AIR IN BEHIND
SHEATHING AND
MOISTURE OUT

Installation of louvres will help to cure this condition

between studs to permit vapor to escape freely to the outside without causing damage.

When only the top layer of paint peels off, leaving the old paint underneath still intact, the trouble is most likely due to the paint having been applied while the surface was damp or coated with dust and dirt. This happens most often on the undersides of overhanging eaves, in sheltered areas under roof overhangs, and in other locations which are protected from the weather.

Dirt which accumulates on these surfaces is not washed off by wind or rain as quickly as it is on the exposed vertical walls of the house. Because of this, these surfaces should be wiped clean before paint is applied. If these areas are not wiped down with solvent or scrubbed with detergent solution, the fresh paint will adhere to the dirt, rather than to the old paint. As a result, adhesion is extremely poor, causing paint to peel within less than a year in most cases.

To prevent this happening on the next paint job, the homeowner should make every effort to clean all surfaces of dirt, grease or other foreign matter before repainting. Where peeling of this kind has already occurred, the homeowner's only solution lies in removing as much of the old paint as possible by scraping or sanding, or by use of a chemical paint remover. Then wipe down with solvent and repaint with fresh material.

Painting over old coats of paint which are badly chalking or dusting can be just as bad as painting over a dirty surface. For this reason it is particularly important (especially on masonry) that you follow the manufacturer's directions about removing old chalk and dust before re-painting. In some cases a special bonding primer will be required to seal the surface properly before a new coat of paint can be satisfactorily applied.

Peeling and Blistering Problems, Interior

When interior paints blister, peel or crack, the trouble can sometimes be blamed on the use of a defective or poor-quality paint. However, in most cases the problem will actually be due to a lack of careful surface preparation or to improper handling and techniques of paint application.

When peeling occurs on an interior wall or ceiling, the first thing you should suspect is some kind of moisture leak inside of or behind that wall. If it happens on an outside wall, there may be moisture seeping in through small cracks or other openings in the siding or exterior masonry, or the water may be coming in through open joints around window frames and other trim on the outside of your house.

Bear in mind that the leak may not be directly opposite the place where interior peeling is noticeable. Water can work its way into a wall, dripping down or traveling sideways along a beam for some distance before actually soaking into the plaster on the wall or ceiling of the house. In the same way, a roof leak at the top of the house can sometimes cause ceilings on stories below to blister and peel because water travels down through the wall till it hits a horizontal ceiling beam on the first floor. In most cases you will be able to tell whether or not water is the actual cause of the trouble because of the characteristic staining on the plaster.

Even after a leak has been repaired, blistering and peeling may some-times continue after the surface has been repainted. A probable cause is that the damage was not properly repaired before new paint was applied.

The old plaster may be crumbling or loose; unless it is properly patched, new paint applied over it will continue to peel.

Peeling sometimes occurs around the edges of metal casement windows because of condensation. As warm moist air from the inside condenses on the cold metal frame, the accumulated moisture tends to seep into open joints between the plaster and the metal, saturating the plaster and working its way out through the paint, causing the paint to blister and peel in the process. To prevent this, install storm windows when possible and apply caulking around both the inside and the outside of the frame.

In older houses, another common cause of peeling is the accumulation of many layers of paint over brittle old coats that no longer adhere properly. As each additional layer is applied the condition worsens, until finally whole sections start to crack and loosen. When this happens, all the old coats of paint must be taken off with paint remover before the new finish is applied.

Another common cause of paint peeling in kitchens, bathrooms and work areas is failure to clean the surface beforehand. Every paint can has instructions on the label which advise that the finish be applied only over a clean, dry surface, yet this warning is all too often ignored. Paint applied over a dirty or greasy surface will not dry or adhere properly; it will often crack and peel back to show the layer of dirty paint underneath.

This problem is particularly acute around fireplaces and radiators, since wall areas near these units are frequently much dirtier than walls elsewhere. Wash walls before painting; never apply paint when the wall or radiator is hot. Brushing paint on a heated surface causes premature drying, making it almost impossible to achieve a good bonding with the surface.

Removing Paint and Varnish

When faced with the job of removing old paint or varnish before a new finish is applied, there are several methods the handyman can use: he can scrape the paint off, he can sand the paint off or he can use a prepared chemical remover to soften up the old finish so that it can easily be scraped or wiped off. On outdoor surfaces professional painters often use a fourth method: they burn the paint off with a blowtorch. However, this is a hazardous procedure which is not recommended for the amateur, especially when working indoors.

Hand scraping is seldom practical when a sizable area must be stripped clean or when all of the old finish must be completely removed. However, it is often the simplest method to use when preparing a previously painted or varnished surface which has only scattered sections that need removing. This situation most frequently occurs when blistering, cracking or peeling paint must be removed on inside woodwork or exterior trim.

The most widely used scraper is the so-called hook-type scraper. This has a metal blade which is drawn over the surface by pulling or dragging the tool toward you. It is used by bearing down hard while keeping the handle almost parallel to the surface. The edge of the blade then scrapes the surface without cutting or gouging. For best results, blades should be replaced as soon as they start to dull, or they can be sharpened by filing or grinding.

Removing paint by sanding it off is often the preferred method when working on fine cabinets (such as those which are covered with thin veneer or delicate inlay work), as well as on those jobs where only part of the finish is to be removed. For example, when revarnishing furniture or cabinets, merely sanding off the top layer of varnish will often do the trick. Hand sanding is safer than power sanding or scraping for jobs of this kind since these latter methods are likely to remove too much of the old finish.

Portable power sanders of various types can greatly speed the job of removing old finishes from flat surfaces. Circular disc sanders, such as those frequently sold for use with electric drills, should be used only on rough, exterior surfaces or where appearances are secondary. They are seldom suitable for sanding off finishes on interior doors, woodwork or paneling, and they should never be used on furniture or other fine pieces. The circular discs often cause gouging and burning, but they do a fast job of removing scaling paint on outside clapboard, siding and trim.

For sanding off finishes on furniture, cabinets and the like, two types of machines can be used: belt sanders and orbital sanders. Both hold the abrasive paper in a flat pad which moves parallel to the surface so that there is little or no danger of gouging or digging in. Belt sanders are heavier-duty machines and they will generally work faster than the orbital sanders. With either machine, a coarser-grit paper should be used for preliminary removal of the old finish and a medium grit used for finishing off. To remove scratches which are left, the piece can then be gone over a third time with a fine-grit paper before you start to apply the new finish.

The use of a chemical paint and varnish remover is by far the most popular method for removing an old finish. On carved or intricately curved pieces it may be the only practical method available. These removers consist of specially formulated solvent mixtures which, when applied over the old finish, will soften it sufficiently so that it can be scraped off easily with a dull putty knife or coarse steel wool. Some removers come in liquid form, but the thicker, creamier mixtures (usually referred to as semipaste) are much more popular for use on furniture. On the vertical surfaces, running and dripping of the liquid type might otherwise become a problem. In addition, the semipaste removers are slower drying, so they give the user more time to work and permit covering larger areas in a single application.

Most conventional paint removers contain either wax or paraffin to help retard evaporation of the solvents and to slow up the drying time. This wax tends to remain on the surface as a light film after the remover

Sanding off paint on outside with disc sander

SANDING PAD

has been scraped off, and it must be completely washed off before a new coat of paint or varnish can safely be applied. If the wax were not cleaned off first, the new finish would not dry properly or adhere firmly. To remove the wax, the surface must be washed down with a rag saturated in denatured alcohol, turpentine, benzine or a similar solvent.

Removers are also available without a wax base. These contain other chemicals to retard drying and they are usually referred to as "no-wash" or "self-neutralizing" removers. They require no after-rinse before the new finish can be applied. Generally a bit more expensive than the wax-base types, these no-wash removers are also available in both liquid and semipaste forms.

All of the wax-base removers and many of the no-wash removers are extremely inflammable, so they must be used with extreme caution where any danger of spark or fire is present. However, the newer no-wash removers are also available in a nonflammable variety, and these are strongly recommended for use in basements, garages and other confined areas. Though they usually cost more than the other types, the non-flammable removers are well worth the difference when working indoors.

Some of the nonflammable removers are also available in the so-called

After remover is applied, old paint bubbles up

water-wash type. This is a wax-free remover which is soluble in water so that the residue can be washed off without scraping. When applied to the surface, it softens up the old finish just like any other remover, but then it can be washed off with water or a wet rag. This type can be used only on surfaces which will not be damaged by water, and it may require several rinses to leave the surface clean.

Regardless of the type of remover being used, there are certain techniques that must be followed if satisfactory results are to be assured. Always spread the remover on with a fully loaded brush, using the flat side to slap it on, and brush in one direction only. Pick up more remover after each stroke, and avoid trying to cover too large an area at one time. Leave the film undisturbed without additional brushing to give the chemicals time to work and to keep air away from the surface.

When the old finish is thoroughly softened and shows signs of heavy wrinkling, scrape it off with a dull knife or similar tool. Scraping should be done carefully to avoid gouging the surface, and additional coats of remover should be applied to stubborn spots. Ideally speaking, the remover should be applied heavily enough, and allowed to stand long enough, to remove all the paint down to the bare wood in a single operation. On carved or grooved surfaces, an old toothbrush or small, pointed stick will sometimes come in handy to reach into crevices where the putty knife or steel wool will not work.

Rollers, Selection and Use

Contrary to popular belief, paint rollers can be used with almost any type of paint—flat, gloss, latex or oil-base—and they can be used on most rough surfaces, as well as on smooth walls and ceilings.

Rollers can be purchased with many different types of covers, each varying as to the type of fiber used and as to the length (or depth) of the nap. The most popular is a medium-length nap (⅜ to ½ inch), lamb's wool type of fabric, usually made of a synthetic fiber rather than real lamb's wool. This is the cover most often used for painting walls and ceilings, regardless of whether a latex or alkyd-based flat is being used. Short-nap mohair covers are also available for use with glossy or semigloss enamels. These covers leave little or no stipple, so they give a smoother job when a glossy finish is desired.

Deep-pile rollers, which have a longer nap, are also available. These have fibers which may be either ¾ or 1¼ inches in length. They are specifically designed for use on rough surfaces, such as porous concrete,

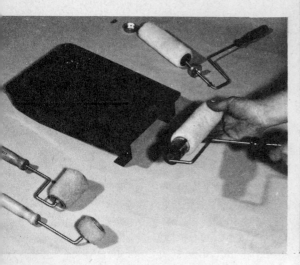

*Rollers come in various widths to
suit all purposes*

Long-nap rollers for painting brick

cinder block or stucco, and they can even be used for painting woven wire fences and coarse-textured ceilings. The extra-long fibers on this type of cover penetrate into all the crevices and indentations, and it will do the job much faster than a brush.

Regardless of the type of cover required, homeowners should never purchase a roller or roller cover on the basis of price alone. Cheap rollers are harder to take apart and clean. They also may not work as smoothly because they usually have inefficient bearings and poorly designed handles. A good quality cover will be made of fiber that will not mat, cake or shed. The core will be made of hard plastic so that the cover can stand repeated washing without falling apart.

When painting walls or ceilings with a roller, do corners first with a small paintbrush since it will be impossible to reach right into the corner with the roller. After corners and edges have been painted with a brush, start in one corner and coat the rest of the wall or ceiling with your roller, crisscrossing strokes lightly so as to leave no "holidays," or misses. Always make the first stroke in an *upward* direction when painting walls so that there will be less chance of excess paint oozing or dripping from the fully loaded roller. Work with a slow, steady motion, and never allow the roller to spin if you want to avoid getting spattered with paint.

For painting narrow areas, as well as for use on flat trim (both inside and out), there are inexpensive rollers available which measure only 3 inches in width. To reach all the way into corners when both surfaces will be painted the same color, there are doughnut-shaped rollers, called

Doughnut-shaped roller is designed for painting in corners

Roll out excess paint on old newspapers

corner rollers. These eliminate the need for a brush in the corners. When using one of these rollers, you still paint corners first, then finish the larger areas with the regular roller.

The one feature that seems to disturb home painters most is the task of cleaning a roller cover after the job is done. Yet if the job is tackled immediately, it should take no more than a few minutes. Start by first rolling out as much of the excess paint as possible, using old newspapers or scrap boards. Then remove the cover from its handle and wash immediately in the appropriate solvent for the type of paint you have been using. Washing should be thorough, not just a simple matter of swishing the cover around. The cover must be wrung out thoroughly under the surface of the liquid till all pigment has been flushed away.

If a water-thinned paint has been used, simply wash under running water as soon as the job is finished. Solvent-thinned paints require that

Cover is preserved by wrapping in foil

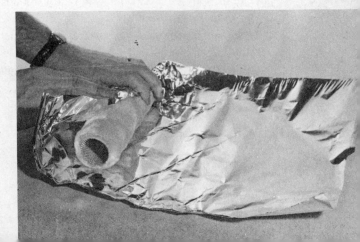

the cover be rinsed in turpentine, mineral spirits or a similar solvent. Better yet, one of the special liquid cleaners which are sold for just this purpose can be used. These liquids can be used over and over again, and they do a quicker and more thorough job of flushing pigment out of the fibers.

After cleaning, wring out the excess liquid by squeezing the fibers between your fingers. Wipe immediately with a clean cloth, then wrap in sheet plastic or aluminum foil to keep the cover soft and ready for use the next time it is needed.

Shingles, Asbestos

When asbestos-cement shingles were first introduced some years ago, a great deal of their appeal lay in the fact that they would never require painting. While paint is not required to protect them from the weather, most homeowners have found that painting is nevertheless desirable from a decorative standpoint. The original shingles may have become dirty-looking, or a simple change of color may be desired.

Early attempts to paint these materials frequently resulted in disappointment because the alkalies present in all these shingles combined with the oils in conventional house paints to make a soluble soap which caused an early breakdown in the paint film. A joint study made by the National Paint, Varnish and Lacquer Association and the Asbestos-Cement Products Association indicates that for a lasting paint job on asbestos shingles, two precautions must be observed: proper preparation of the surface and the use of the right kind of paint.

Preparation consists simply of making certain that the surface is clean and free of all dirt, loose paint and grease. If dirt is present, the shingles should be scrubbed thoroughly with a wax-free detergent and water, then brushed vigorously to remove loose dust, soot and other foreign matter. If a solvent-thinned paint will be used, the surface must be absolutely dry as well.

Two types of paint are recommended: solvent-thinned resin coatings and emulsion or latex-type water-thinned coatings. In either case two coats should be applied.

The solvent-thinned paints are usually derivatives or modifications of rubber, or they may be based on chlorinated rubber vehicles. Manufacturers who produce these paints label them as satisfactory for use over asbestos shingles, and they usually produce a special asbestos shingle primer which they recommend for the first coat. In some cases

*Asbestos-cement shingles can
be painted with special coatings*

the same material is used for both coats, but a special bonding liquid must be mixed in with the first coat to provide the necessary adhesion.

Exterior latex paints differ from the solvent-thinned coatings in that the latex is dispersed in water so that the paint can be thinned with water instead of with turpentine or other solvents. Generally speaking, they are easier to apply and will dry more quickly. In addition, they can be applied satisfactorily over a damp surface. Equipment, such as brushes or rollers, is easily cleaned by simply rinsing with water before the paint has a chance to dry. Many of these water-thinned latex paints also form "breathing" films which permit trapped moisture vapor to pass through harmlessly. This means that blistering, and subsequent peeling, is unlikely to occur because of moisture in the wall. As with the solvent-thinned resin paints, two coats must be applied for a satisfactory job.

Shingles, Wood

Wood shingles on the outside of a house can be finished with several different kinds of paint, as well as with various types of shingle stain. Since even the "experts" do not always agree as to which type is best under all circumstances, the homeowner is often confused when faced with the task of selecting the best paint or stain for use on his shingles.

At one time, wood shingles were almost always stained, seldom painted. Stains were usually a dark shade of brown, gray or green, and most stains had either a creosote or a linseed oil base. One reason for this was that conventional oil paints give a heavy gloss finish which generally is not desirable for use on shingles. In addition, these paints tended to crack and peel when applied over the rough, porous surface of typical hand-split shingles.

However, with the advent of the machine-cut, striated shingle (usually referred to as cedar shakes) and with the homeowner's increasing demand for the light colors, other types of heavier-bodied stains with increased hiding power have been introduced. There are also several different kinds of paints available. These opaque paints are formulated to dry to a flat or low-luster finish instead of a gloss, and—even more important—they form a "breathing" or semipermeable type of film which permits trapped moisture to escape safely without causing blistering or peeling.

The shingle paints currently available (usually referred to as shake and shingle paints) generally fall into one of two catergories: solvent-thinned, oil-base paints which have an alkyd or linseed oil base and

Shingle paints have oil or latex base

water-thinned latex house paints which are also recommended for use on shingles. Both of these paints are more resistant to blistering than the conventional glossy house paints. Since they are also opaque, they enable the homeowner to change the color of his shingle completely whenever he desires, though several coats may be required if an extreme color change is being made.

When a two-coat paint job is required, or when the old finish is badly eroded and chalking, a special primer often will be recommended for the first coat. To make certain he is using the proper primer, the homeowner should study the manufacturer's recommendations carefully before beginning. Some latex paints will require an oil-base primer, and some shake and shingle paints will recommend a special additive for the first coat instead of a separate primer. In any case, two coats of the same finish coat should never be applied unless this is the procedure recommended by the manufacturer of the particular brand of paint.

When trying to decide between a water-thinned latex type of paint and a solvent-thinned oil paint, the homeowner should keep these points in mind:

(1) Latex paints are usually more blister resistant than the oil paints, provided the right kind of primer is used underneath.

(2) Latex paints usually dry more quickly—a matter of hours in most cases. This means that in many instances two coats can be applied in the same day, and there is less likelihood of wind-blown dust or sand spoiling the job before it has had a chance to set up completely.

(3) Latex paints can be applied over a damp surface—even immediately after a rain or in the early morning hours while there is still dew on the surface.

(4) Oil paints usually have more hiding power than the latex paints, so where a change of color is involved, the homeowner is more likely to get away with one coat when an oil paint is used.

(5) Latex paints permit easy cleanup; brushes and hands can be washed in running water. But the same latex paints tend to rust unprotected metal. As a result, the user must be careful about applying them over exposed nailheads or other metal surfaces which have not previously been primed with an oil paint.

(6) In most cases the home handyman will find that latex paints are easier to brush out; but an oil paint has greater penetrating power and is more likely to hold if the old surface is chalky or badly worn.

Even before the homeowner is faced with the problem of trying to decide between a latex shingle paint and an oil-based shingle paint, he often receives conflicting advice as to whether a paint or a stain is best to use. Generally speaking, the choice will be limited by several factors. First, if paint has been used previously, only a paint can be used thereafter (unless the old paint is completely gone). If a stain has always been used, either a paint or stain can be used over it. The one danger to watch out for here is in those cases where a creosote stain has been used previously. This leaves a residue which will "bleed" through successive coats of paint which may be applied over it.

Another factor to be considered when trying to decide between a paint and a stain is the appearance or effect desired. Paint generally tends to build up and give a "painty" effect which some people find objectionable on wood shingles. Stain, on the other hand, soaks in and penetrates the wood, giving a more natural-looking effect which does not hide the grain and texture of the wood as much as a paint will. As a general rule, a paint job will stay fresh-looking longer than a stain job. However, since a stain leaves no appreciable surface coating, it cannot blister, peel or chalk. Instead, the color merely fades away as the shingles weather. This will be more easily understood if the homeowner remembers that a stain tends to dye the wood, while a paint serves to coat the wood. Thus a new coat of stain will cover effectively only if a similar—or darker— color is to be used, while paint can be used whenever a drastic change in color is desired.

Spray Painting

Properly handled, a good paint sprayer enables you to do a faster and neater job of painting furniture, cabinets, fences and other hard-to-paint objects. For those who do not actually own one, portable spray outfits can be rented from many paint stores, hardware stores and tool rental agencies. For small jobs where a special color is not required, there are also aerosol-type paint spray "bombs" which can be used.

Almost any type of paint or finish can be applied by spraying. Paints that are formulated for brushing will frequently require some thinning, but this will vary with the type of equipment and material to be used. For best results, check with your paint supplier and with the directions that come with the gun. Always experiment on scrap material first to make certain you have the best possible mixture before starting the finished project.

Spraying should always be done in a well-ventilated room or out of doors on a calm day. Remember that the overspray or drift can carry for quite some distance, so when spraying in an occupied area be sure to protect the surrounding floors, walls and furniture.

Most spray guns have two controls that you will have to adjust. One regulates the amount of air fed through the nozzle and the other controls the amount of paint supplied. Experiment with these until you have achieved a spray pattern which is not too misty, yet does not spit or sputter. The size of the pattern can be varied by increasing or decreasing the amount of paint or fluid fed through the nozzle. It is usually easiest to start with both controls wide open, then gradually shut down one or both till the best possible results are achieved.

The spray gun should always be held in as nearly vertical a position as possible, with the tip about 6 to 8 inches away from the surface. Move the gun with straight, parallel strokes, so that it remains equidistant from the surface at all times and never swing the gun in an arc. This would move it closer to the surface at the center of each stroke with the result that the paint would be piled on unevenly.

When spraying a flat surface, always press the trigger and start the stroke while aiming slightly off to one side of the object. Move all the way across if possible, and do not release the trigger till the gun has passed slightly beyond the surface on the opposite side. Strokes should be alternated from left to right and each one overlapped about 50 per cent to insure adequate coverage. To avoid piling the paint on so heavily

Picket fences can be covered quickly by spray painting

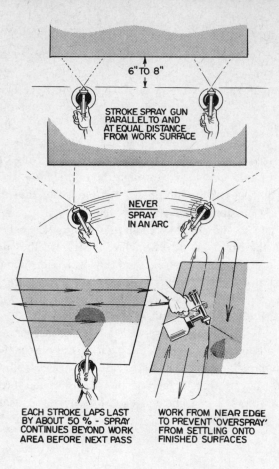

6" TO 8"

STROKE SPRAY GUN
PARALLEL TO AND
AT EQUAL DISTANCE
FROM WORK SURFACE

NEVER
SPRAY
IN AN ARC

EACH STROKE LAPS LAST
BY ABOUT 50 % - SPRAY
CONTINUES BEYOND WORK
AREA BEFORE NEXT PASS

WORK FROM NEAR EDGE
TO PREVENT 'OVERSPRAY'
FROM SETTLING ONTO
FINISHED SURFACES

that it sags or "curtains," remember to keep the gun moving while the trigger is being pressed. Never stop, not even for a moment, and always press or release the trigger while the gun is actually in motion.

When spraying table tops or other surfaces that angle away from you, spray the nearest parts first. Then, as the gun is directed at the more distant, uncoated portions, there will be no danger of the overspray settling as a fine sandy mist on the previously finished sections. For this same reason, always do the least important, hard-to-reach parts of any furniture first. Leave the tops and other prominent areas for last.

The biggest percentage of all spraying troubles comes from dirt or other foreign matter inside the gun or tip. To prevent this, always strain the paint through a double thickness of cheesecloth or through an old piece of nylon stocking. When the gun must be sharply tilted, keep the paint cup only half-filled so that paint will not flow into and clog the tiny air passages in the handle. Better yet, equip your gun with an angular nozzle if one is available. These permit spraying at a 45-degree angle without having to tip the gun. Unfortunately, however, they are not made for every type of gun.

Equally important to proper operation is that the gun be cleaned with the appropriate solvent immediately after each use. This is usually a simple operation taking no more than a few minutes. First, drain out all excess paint from the cup and fluid tube. Then wipe off with an old rag and pour some solvent into the cup. Spray this out through the tip with a series of short bursts, spraying into a carton or onto old newspapers. Next, unscrew the tip and rinse off the pieces with additional solvent.

Remember, the paint-soaked rags or papers which are kept can be a serious fire hazard if left indoors. Discard them outdoors, or store them in a covered metal can.

For many small jobs you may find it more convenient to use an aerosol-type paint spray "bomb." To be sure of good results, remember that these paints are comparatively thin, so figure on applying two thin coats rather than one heavy coat. By attempting to put on too much at one time in any spray operation, you run the risk of causing runs, drips and general sagging of the film.

Aerosol bomb speeds jobs of refinishing

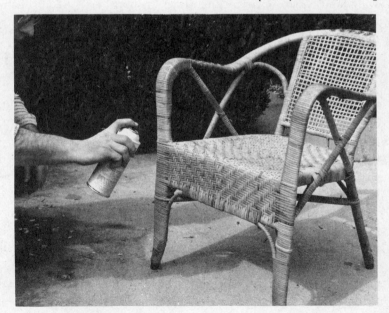

A requirement all too often ignored when working with aerosol-type spray paints is the need for thorough shaking, or agitation, before the aerosol button is depressed for the first time. Most spray paints contain an agitator ball which can be heard rattling around on the inside when the can is shaken. The purpose of this ball is to help agitate the contents of the can so as to insure a uniform mixture before spraying is begun. A few quick shakes are not enough: pigmented finishes require at least 30 seconds of agitation to insure uniform misting.

Spraying technique is similar to that employed when you are working with a conventional spray gun. The can should be moved back and forth by moving your arm so that the spray remains always at a constant distance from the surface. Care must be exercised to avoid "arcing" the stroke by swinging the can so that it is closer at the center of the stroke than it is at each end. With most paints, spray nozzles should be held 8 to 12 inches from the work surface.

Holding the spray can too close will not permit all the gas to escape from the paint before it dries so that pinholes and small craters will be left in the finish. Holding the can too far away will permit the spray to disperse too rapidly, resulting in partial drying of the paint before it strikes the surface. This gives a dusty, chalklike spray which will not look smooth or adhere properly.

When spraying intricately carved or molded surfaces, the home painter will find it easier to work with a series of short bursts, rather than in one continuous spray. This enables him to observe the progress of the work more closely and eliminates the danger of piling up too much paint on narrow crevices. Small objects are best mounted on some sort of turntable, or they can be placed on top of a carton which can then be turned at frequent intervals while spraying.

To insure proper atomization of the paint, it is important that the contents of the can be approximately at room temperature (60 to 90 degrees) before starting. Work surfaces should also be at approximately the same temperature level if proper adhesion is to be insured. When spraying outdoors, avoid spraying in windy or breezy locations, and indoors make certain there are no open flames present in the same room. Adequate ventilation should be provided, and nearby surfaces should be protected with drop cloths of some kind. Masking tape can be used to protect adjacent surfaces when only part of a surface is to be sprayed.

When putting the spray away between jobs, clean out the spray nozzle and the discharge tube by inverting the can and pressing the spray button four or five times. Repeat until no more paint (only gas) comes out to make certain that the nozzle and tube on the inside are completely clean. Then wipe the nozzle opening clean, using a piece of cloth wrapped around one finger.

Stucco and Masonry

Though ordinary outside house paints, designed mainly for use on wood, can be used with a reasonable amount of success on masonry and stucco, best results will be assured if a good quality masonry paint is used. These coatings will stand up better under the moisture and alkali conditions encountered in this type of wall, and they dry to a flat or low-luster finish which is much more desirable on surfaces of this kind.

The home painter who goes shopping for a masonry paint will find that his dealer probably carries several different types, so that it becomes difficult to determine which one is "best" for his particular house. Since experts in the industry do not yet agree among themselves on this question and since conditions on different surfaces and in different locations can vary greatly, it is difficult to make a flat prediction as to which type of masonry paint will stand up better on any particular job.

However, there are a number of features which are characteristic of each type of masonry paint. The homeowner should keep these characteristics in mind while shopping. In addition, he should carefully study the label and the technical literature accompanying each product, so that the manufacturer's recommendations can be used as a further guide.

In spite of variations in individual brands, most of the masonry paints sold today fall into one of these five categories:

Oil-based stucco paints. Containing linseed oil as a vehicle, these "old-style" cement and stucco paints are similar to regular gloss house paints except that they dry to a flat or low-luster finish. They give a solid, "non-breathing" type of film which stands up reasonably well over smooth, close-textured surfaces, but they should never be applied over masonry surfaces which are less than six months old. They will not wear well on open-textured cement or concrete block or on surfaces where moisture tends to seep into or behind the wall. Many brands also tend to chalk excessively as they age.

Alkyd exterior paints. These new-type, flat-drying masonry paints thin with turpentine like regular oil paints, and they can be used over wood shingles as well as on masonry. They form a permeable type of film which is less susceptible to moisture damage, and they have excellent hiding and brushing characteristics. However, when they are to be applied over

porous or badly eroded old finishes, or over surfaces which have begun
to chalk freely, a special primer must be applied first. With some brands
a bonding liquid is added to the finish coat so that it serves as its own
prime coat.

Solvent-thinned rubber-base paints. These thin with turpentine or a
similar solvent and are exceptionally easy to brush on. They hide well
with one coat and have exceptionally high resistance to moisture and the
excess alkali conditions frequently encountered in masonry. They also
stand up well on asbestos-cement shingles when an alkyd primer is applied first. They do not adhere satisfactorily when used over chalky
surfaces, particularly when applied over old whitewash or over powdered,
cold-water cement paints.

Latex or plastic emulsion paints. These are the newest addition to the
field of exterior masonry paints. They have become increasingly popular
in recent years because of their quick-drying characteristics (as little as
two hours) and because of the fact that they thin with water; hence no
turpentine or other solvent is needed. Recent experience has also
indicated that they stand up better than most other types on unpainted
brick and similar surfaces, and they are most resistant of all to accumulation of dirt and stains.

Latex emulsion paints also have better color retention than most other
masonry paints, and they can be used over fresh masonry surfaces, even

Rollers can be used on brick and masonry

while still damp or immediately after a rain. However, when they are applied over old paint which shows signs of chalking or dusting, a special bonding primer or masonry surface conditioner must be applied first—if extensive and premature peeling is to be avoided.

Powdered cement paints. Containing a high percentage of portland cement as one of their principal ingredients, these paints come in powder form and must be mixed with water immediately before use. They cost less than any other type of masonry paint, but they can be applied only over surfaces which have previously been painted with the same type of paint or over unpainted masonry surfaces. To assure good adhesion, the walls must be wet down before application and kept damp while the material is applied. For best results, the coating should be sprinkled lightly during the first 24 hours to keep the paint from drying out too rapidly.

Powdered cement paints tend to assume a translucent "wet" look when rained upon and colors will look darker. However, when the walls dry, the original opaque color is restored. These coatings will not stand up well over smooth or glazed bricks, and they also give poor results when used over old, secondhand bricks which are stained or dirty. Unlike the other types of masonry paint, powdered cement paints cannot be used on asbestos-cement shingles.

Regardless of the type of masonry paint selected, the homeowner

Dirt and flaking paint is removed with wire brush

must remember to prepare the surface carefully if he wants to avoid disappointment. Use a stiff wire brush and a scraper to remove old, flaking material and to rub off, as much as possible, old coatings which are chalking or dusting heavily. If the old paint is flaking and peeling so badly that there is no solid foundation left, over which new paint can be applied, the only sure cure lies in having the walls sandblasted clean to remove the old finish completely before the new paint is applied.

Varnishing Techniques

Preparation for a varnish finish must be more thorough than that required for an opaque painted finish because the transparent varnish will show up every flaw in the wood. Always sand the surface as smooth as possible and remove all stains or blemishes before you start. Then dust thoroughly. The fine grit left after sanding is a primary cause of rough-looking, "sandy" finishes.

A good quality bristle brush, perfectly clean, is a must for good varnishing. The brush should be soft and pliable with plenty of flagged bristles. Never dip it into the varnish more than one-third its length, and always flow the varnish on liberally with long strokes applied parallel to the grain. Most important of all, never wipe excess varnish off the brush by dragging the bristles across the rim of the can. Instead, tap the tips of the bristles lightly against the inside of the container above the surface of the liquid. Wiping across the rim causes tiny bubbles to form in the fluid and these will make it almost impossible to achieve a smooth finish.

Air bubbles on the surface also can be caused by pressing down too hard on the brush. Varnish should be brushed on with only light to moderate pressure. After covering the panel in one direction, cross-stroke immediately by brushing across the grain at right angles to the original strokes. Finish off by lightly stroking a third time with the grain, using an almost dry brush and touching the surface with the tips only. This crisscrossing method will virtually eliminate all brush strokes so that a uniform application is assured.

Varnishing should never be done in a dusty location, or in garages or basements which are damp or cold. When possible, lay pieces horizontally, and always remove all hardware and knobs before starting. Chests or cabinets that have drawers are best done with the drawers removed so that each one can be stood up with its front in a horizontal position.

When more than one coat of varnish is to be applied, the first coat

Varnish should be flowed on with long strokes

Remove excess by tapping against inside

should be thinned with about 10 per cent turpentine. Successive coats can then be applied as they come from the can. For a super-smooth finish, sand lightly between coats. Use #2/0 very fine sandpaper and rub with the grain. Remember to dust thoroughly before applying the next coat. The best way to pick up the dust is to use a tack rag, a specially treated sticky cloth which is available at many paint and hardware stores.

Just as important as the techniques involved is the handyman's choice of the right kind of varnish. Contrary to popular opinion, all varnishes are not alike and all are not suitable for every job. Most well-stocked paint stores carry many different types, each designed for one or more specific purposes. To make sure you are getting the right one for the job at hand, always read the label carefully.

Varnishes vary in many respects. Some are much clearer than others —an important point to consider when light finishes are involved. Varnishes also vary in their resistance to water and alcohol staining and in the glossiness of the final finish. Some dry with an extremely high gloss, while others dry to a completely flat finish. For most furniture and paneling a semigloss or satin-finish varnish is preferred. This eliminates the need for rubbing down or dulling the final coat.

As a general rule, the glossy varnishes give a tougher finish than the duller ones. For this reason professionals prefer to use hard-drying, glossy varnishes on table tops, counter tops and other surfaces which get hard wear. They allow the final coat to harden thoroughly, then rub it down to a smooth, satin finish which, while still lustrous, does not have an objectionable "wet" shine.

For this type of rubbed finish a special varnish is usually used. Called a cabinet rubbing varnish, it dries in one day to an exceptionally hard finish which takes rubbing beautifully. The handyman interested in trying his hand at this type of finishing operation will need some powdered pumice stone, powdered rottenstone and crude oil.

Allow the final varnish coat to dry till thoroughly hardened (check the label for this), then make a paste of the pumice stone and crude oil. Mix the two together right on the surface, then fold a heavy, lintless cloth into a small pad. Press this pad into the paste and rub over the surface with straight strokes, parallel to the grain. Use only a moderate amount of pressure and rub until the surface feels smooth and is free of all "pimples" or blemishes.

Next, use a clean, dry cloth to wipe all pumice off the surface. Use another cloth moistened with turpentine to clean off the residue, then wipe again with a clean cloth till the surface is dry. This will leave the surface slightly cloudy because of fine scratches which are left by the pumice stone.

To restore the luster, a second rubbing is required, this time with powdered rottenstone and crude oil. Mix a paste as described before, then rub with a pad of clean felt or similar material. Again rub in straight, parallel strokes which follow the grain. When the surface has been polished to the luster desired, wipe off all the paste with a clean cloth and polish with a soft dry cloth till the surface is so clean and dry that the polishing cloth causes a squeaking noise under your hand. Any good quality furniture polish can then be applied after a day or two.

Wallpaper, How to Hang

Modern wallpapers and fabric-type wall coverings are not only more durable and more stain resistant than ever before, they are also much easier to hang. Most are printed on special water-resistant backgrounds which are less likely to tear when wet; and a sizable percentage of them are now available with the edges (the selvage on each side) already trimmed off. There are also a great many patterns which can be purchased with paste already applied to the back, and for those that have to be pasted, there are nonstaining cellulose adhesives available.

The basic techniques involved in hanging all wall coverings are pretty much the same. However, the vinyl and canvas materials may require a special adhesive, and extra care must be taken to prevent blistering and curling along the edges. To avoid these troubles, the manufacturer's recommendations and instructions should be followed carefully.

New wallpaper can be applied directly over the old paper in most cases, but the old paper must be adhering tightly and all loose edges should be torn off first. If in doubt about whether or not to remove the old wall covering, consult your dealer or the manufacturer's instruction sheet. When hanging most fabric-type wall coverings (canvas or vinyl), you will find it is usually advisable to remove the old wallpaper first. Painted or bare plaster walls should be given a coat of wall size before hanging. This is a watery glue solution (sold in powdered form) which is simply wiped on with a sponge.

When measuring strips to length before cutting them off the roll, the handyman should always allow an extra 3 or 4 inches at each end (top and bottom). This excess is allowed to lap onto the ceiling at the top and onto the baseboard at the bottom. It is then trimmed off on the wall with a razor blade. This assures a neat fit at the top and bottom. Trying to cut pieces of exact length beforehand will almost certainly result in a poor fit along the ceiling and along the baseboard since floors and ceilings are seldom exactly straight.

Paste is applied to back of each strip   *Fold strips over after pasting*

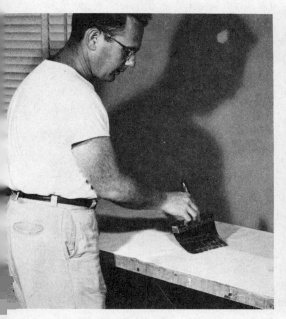

To facilitate pasting and handling of each strip before it is hung, a long, smooth table (at least 5 feet) will be required. Many dealers rent or lend folding tables of this kind. Each strip of paper is laid face down on the table so that paste can be applied to the back. Since the strip will be longer than the table, paste is first applied to a little more than half its length. The pasted portion is then folded over against itself, back-to-back with the pattern side out. In this way, the pasted side will be folded on the inside.

The strip is now slid lengthwise along the table so that the pasted portion hangs over the end while the unpasted section lies on the table. Paste is then applied to the rest of the sheet, after which this too is folded over back-to-back. If the selvage has not been removed at the factory, trimming is done now, using a long straightedge. The edges of the folded strip are lined up so that they are exactly over one another, then the straightedge is laid precisely along the indicated trim line. A razor blade is now used to slice off the selvage along this side with a single cut. The strip can then be turned around and the selvage removed from the opposite side in the same manner.

The first strip is usually hung in a corner of the room or against a door frame. Since strips will be hung in sequence all the way around the room, chances are that when the last strip is hung it will not exactly match this first strip. To make this mismatch least noticeable, the most inconspicuous corner of the room should be selected as the starting point.

If the first strip is in a corner, it should be positioned so that about 1 inch of the edge folds around the corner. Check with a plumb line to make certain the other edge of this first strip is absolutely plumb since corners are not always that accurate. This process should be repeated in each corner of the room: fold a strip no more than 1 inch around the corner (slicing it down the middle if necessary) and plumb the first strip on the next wall.

To hang each strip, leave the paper folded just as it was on the table. The upper half is unfolded first and smoothed onto the wall with a damp sponge or wide smoothing brush. After the top half has been smoothed out against the wall with its edge lined up properly, the bottom half is unfolded and smoothed down. When all bubbles and wrinkles have been smoothed out, the excess at the top and bottom should be trimmed off with a razor blade.

Succeeding strips are hung in the same manner as the first strip, butting the edge of each one carefully against the edge of the strip just installed. Before cutting each strip to length, hold the roll against the strip just hung to make certain that a proper match will be obtained after the

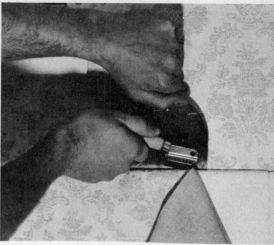

Air bubbles can be removed with sponge or brush

Excess is trimmed off with razor knife

strip has been cut to length. On some patterns it may be necessary to waste a section at the top in order to secure a proper match. Each strip is applied to the wall a slight fraction of an inch away from the preceding one and then slid over till a perfect match is achieved.

Seams should be rolled down after every two or three strips have been hung. For this job a wooden or plastic seam roller is used. However, these cannot be used on embossed papers and on some textured materials. Instead, seams will have to be pressed down by patting firmly with a sponge. Excess paste which oozes out, or paste which is accidentally smeared onto the face of the pattern, should be wiped off promptly as each strip is hung. On most water-resistant papers the safest procedure is to sponge each strip down completely after it is hung. At the same time, wipe off all paste which has been smeared onto ceilings, baseboards or other trim.

Wallpaper, How to Remove

Though new wallpaper can be hung safely over old wallpaper in a great many instances, sooner or later there comes a time when the old paper will have to be removed completely. This may be because there are already too many layers on the wall (three is the maximum recommended by most experts), or it may be because the old wallpaper has started to crack or peel and is no longer sticking tightly.

When faced with this problem, you can tackle it in one of two ways: you can rent a wallpaper-removing machine which literally "steams" the old paper off the wall or you can scrape it off by hand. A steaming machine will make the job a lot easier and it will enable you to finish in a fraction of the time required for scraping by hand.

These machines can be rented for from $4 to $6 per day from most paint and wallpaper stores and from practically all tool rental agencies. The smaller units are all-electric and need only be plugged into an ordinary outlet to operate. Larger capacity, kerosene-electric units are also available. These put out considerably more steam, hence they make any job go faster.

All wallpaper-removing machines work on the same basic principle. Water in a tank is heated to the boiling point so that steam is created. This steam flows through a hose into a hollow applicator pan or plate which is attached to the other end. This pan has a series of small holes on the working face through which the steam escapes. When this face is held against the wall, the steam soaks into and softens the paper so that it can easily be stripped off by scraping with a wide putty knife.

When using one of these machines, hold the pan flat against the wallpaper and keep it in one spot for about half a minute. Then start moving it along slowly, holding the pan in one hand while scraping the softened paper off with the other hand. Generally, it is best to work from the bottom up, since the rising steam will tend to soften the paper immediately above it. For the same reason it is best to do walls first and ceilings last if both have wallpaper to be removed.

Since the room in which the machine is being used will rapidly fill up with steam, it is important that doors leading to other parts of the house are closed and that windows in the room are opened at the top to insure adequate ventilation and to permit excess moisture to escape freely to the outside.

Though they speed the job up considerably, steamers cannot be used satisfactorily in rooms which have papered ceilings, when the paper on the ceiling is not to be removed. They may also cause water-spotting of painted ceilings which will not be recoated, and can actually remove part of the paint on ceilings that have been coated with water-soluble paints. In these cases—or in the event that a wallpaper steamer is not available—hand soaking and scraping will be required. Plain hot water can be used, but the job will go faster if a liquid wallpaper remover (available at paint stores) is added to the water. These liquids help the water soak through and soften up the paste underneath.

To apply the water to the wall, a large paintbrush can be used. An

Hose carries hot steam to applicator, which is held against the wall

even better method is to use a pump-type garden sprayer or a regular paint sprayer. A wool-type paint roller can also be used. Regardless of the method of application used, soak the paper thoroughly, a section at a time. If there are several layers of paper on the wall, two or three repeat applications may be required. Scrape off with a wide putty knife, re-wetting areas as necessary when they begin to dry out.

Many wallpapers have plastic coatings to make them more washable. This will prevent penetration of either water or steam. To soften these papers, it may be necessary to cut through the plastic coating so that the water or steam can penetrate to the back to soften them up. This is best done by rubbing vigorously with very coarse sandpaper till the surface is thoroughly scratched. Then steam or soak off as just described.

Canvas-backed, fabric-type wall coverings are easiest of all to remove. They require neither soaking nor steaming. To remove them, simply scrape one corner loose with a knife, then peel the rest off by pulling backwards at a close angle to the wall. Don't jerk or yank the material, just pull steadily. If some parts tear loose and stick to the wall, dampen them with water later on, then scrape off like ordinary wallpaper.

Windows and Doors, Painting Techniques

Though roller applicators have made the job of painting walls and ceilings easier than ever, weekend decorators often run into trouble when windows and paneled doors must be painted. These surfaces still call for use of an ordinary paintbrush. In order to do a neat job, you have to make certain that the right kind of brush is used and that the proper sequences are followed.

For painting windows, an angular sash brush is easiest for the amateur to handle. It has a long handle, which simplifies the job of holding it steady, and the bristle tips are trimmed at an angle so that when the brush is used edgewise there will be no need to press it out of shape. The 1½- or 2-inch size is best for most jobs, though smaller sizes are sometimes used on metal casement windows which have very narrow strips.

To avoid smearing paint onto the glass, there are a number of different painting "aids" that can be used. Probably the most popular is a metal or plastic paint shield formed into a thin, curved strip (like a venetian blind slat). This is held with its edge pressed against the molding and is slid along with the brush to protect the glass against accidental smearing. Shields of this kind can be purchased at most paint and hardware stores, or a simple one can be improvised from a scrap piece of tin or thin cardboard. To keep the shield itself from smearing paint onto the glass, wipe its edge off with a rag whenever paint accumulates.

Masking tape affords another popular method for protecting the glass. However, care must be exercised in applying the tape to make certain a neat job will result. Do not allow the tape to lap up onto the wood, as this will leave unpainted areas showing when the tape is peeled off afterward. By the same token, if the edge of the tape is not butted neatly against the wood, part of the glass may be left exposed, permitting paint smears to show when the tape is removed.

For the fastest job of painting windows, amateur painters would do well to imitate the professional; that is, learn how to "cut in" a window with only the paintbrush. The right technique calls for dipping the brush not more than one-third its length into the paint, then gently slapping off the excess by tapping against the inside rim of the can. Press the bristle tips lightly against the wood away from the glass and press down with a slight twisting motion. This causes the bristles to fan out so they form a sharp chisel edge. The brush is then moved steadily along the length of the molding while extra pressure is applied until the bristle tips just contact the glass. With practice, strokes can be made to coat the molding evenly and little or none of the paint will be smeared onto the glass.

Any paint that does get onto the glass can be removed easily by wiping while still wet, using a rag wrapped around one finger. If preferred,

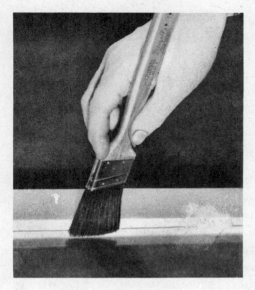

This type of brush is handy for painting sash

the paint can be left on the glass, then scraped off with a razor blade on the following day.

To permit reaching all parts of both the upper and lower sash and to prevent accidentally skipping some parts, the proper sequence must be followed. First raise the bottom sash as high as it will go and lower the top sash at least halfway down. Paint all the wooden divider strips between the panes on the lowered top sash first. Don't forget the exposed

Numbers indicate painting sequence to be followed

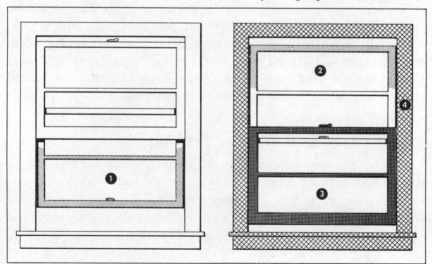

bottom rail of this top sash. Do horizontal members first, vertical pieces last.

Next, lower the bottom sash and raise the upper sash back up until it is within a few inches of the top. Paint the bottom sash next and complete all parts of the upper sash that you could not reach before. Keep checking for runs and sags in the corners where moldings meet.

Paint the window frame and surrounding trim after the sashes are completed. Do the head jamb across the top (this is the channel into which the upper sash fits) first. Then paint the channels on both sides where they are visible on the inside when the window is closed. Do the surrounding face trim and window frame next, leaving the window sill for last.

Make a final check of all corners and edges to see whether runs or sags have developed. If so, smooth them out by picking at them lightly with one corner of your almost dry brush. Be sure to leave the window slightly open top and bottom while the paint dries, to prevent sticking.

When painting paneled doors, the homeowner's job is easier since there is no problem of "cutting in" or protecting glass. Remove as much ornamental hardware as possible, then start by painting the molded edges around each panel. After the edges are done, paint the panel itself, smoothing out the paint by cross-stroking lightly with an almost dry brush. Avoid smearing paint onto the face of the crosspieces, or stiles, if at all possible, even though this will be painted with the same paint later on. Paint that overlaps the face will start to set up, and this will form a thick edge which will interfere with smooth application when the rest of the door is painted.

After the panels have been finished, the edges of the door should be painted. Horizontal crosspieces, or stiles, are done next, and vertical pieces last. Avoid heavy overlapping at the corners by stopping where members meet and prevent brush marks by finishing off with light, parallel strokes along the length of each piece. Paint the framework around the door last, after the door itself has been finished.

Wood Paneling, Finishing Techniques

To protect a wood panel wall against warping or swelling and to keep it clean and attractive-looking, the wood panels should be carefully finished as soon as possible after they are installed. A properly applied finish will not only bring out the beauty of the wood's natural color and grain, but can also improve the appearance of a less attractive wood.

Though there are literally dozens of different finishes which can be applied—and an even larger variety of finishing materials that can be used—the accompanying chart outlines the finishes that are most widely used and tells how to achieve each of them. There are undoubtedly other methods for obtaining each of these finishes, but the procedures outlined are those which have proved simplest for amateurs to follow.

All of these finishing methods are designed for use over new or unfinished wood only. To refinish old panels it is usually necessary to first remove all of the old finish down to the bare wood. This is most easily done with a prepared paint and varnish remover, or by rubbing down with steel wool and sandpaper. It must be remembered that this will remove the surface finish only—not the stain (if a stain had been applied). Stain penetrates into, and literally dyes, the fibers of the wood. It can only be lightened or removed by bleaching with a prepared wood bleach after all of the old varnish, wax or other finishing material has been removed.

TYPE FINISH	PRELIMINARY STEPS	FINAL FINISHING
Clear or Natural (using penetrating sealer to give waxed or oil-type finish).	Brush on first coat of penetrating sealer. Wipe off excess with clean rag after allowing to set for five or ten minutes.	Let first coat dry overnight, then brush on second coat and rub off as before. Allow to dry hard, then rub on thin coat of paste wax. Buff to luster desired.
Clear or Natural (using surface-type coating to give hard built-up finish).	Brush on first coat of varnish, shellac or lacquer—or use sealer coat recommended by manufacturer of finish that will be used.	Let first coat dry overnight, then sand lightly. Apply second coat. For tough finish apply third coat after second has dried.
Stained Finish (to tint wood darker before finishing).	For uniform effect on soft woods apply thin coat of clear resin sealer before staining. Allow to dry, then brush on oil stain or colored stain-sealer. Wipe off after five or ten minutes.	After stain has dried, brush on two coats of varnish in either a high-gloss or a semigloss finish. Two coats of shellac can also be used.
Blond Finish (light-colored modern finish).	On light woods brush on a coat of pigmented white (or pastel-colored) stain, then wipe off. Thinned-down paint can also be used. On dark woods bleaching with a prepared wood bleach is required first.	Allow stain to dry, then apply two coats of water-white, satin-finish varnish or clear plastic coating in satin finish. Let first coat dry hard before applying second one.

Wood stains should be tested for effects

Before installing new paneling, the homeowner should decide on the type of finish he intends to apply. If a stain is to be used, tests should be made first on sizable pieces of scrap material to make certain that the effect desired will be achieved. It must be remembered that no two woods absorb stain in exactly the same manner and that even a clear sealer or varnish will change the color of the wood to some extent. The exact extent of the color change can be determined only by application on a piece of the same kind of wood.

Once the type of finish has been selected, you can save yourself a lot of labor by applying the preliminary coats of stain or sealer before the panels are erected. This enables you to do the job quickly while boards are lying horizontally (across sawhorses) at a convenient working height. It also permits you to coat all the edges so that shrinkage which may occur later on will not expose a lighter-colored, unfinished strip between panel joints. With this method only the last coat will have to be applied after the panels have been put up.

Most wood finishes fall into one of two classes: the penetrating type, which soaks into the pores of the wood and leaves little or no surface film, or surface coatings which leave a hard "built-up" finish similar to that of a "piano" or furniture-type finish. It will be noted that the chart gives both methods for achieving a clear, or natural, finish.

If a stained or dark-colored effect is desired in a penetrating type of finish (rather than with a varnish or shellac), a colored sealer can be used instead of a clear one. For this, apply two coats of colored sealer, then follow with one coat of paste wax. This gives a waxed or oil-type finish in which the colored sealer stains the wood to the tint desired.

Regardless of the type of finish selected, a good wood finishing job can be accomplished only if the wood itself is first properly prepared and if a few basic rules are carefully followed. Here are some of the more important pointers that should be kept in mind:

(1) Sand the wood as smooth as possible before starting to apply any type of finish.

(2) Dust thoroughly before starting, and dust again between coats, particularly if additional sandpapering is done.

(3) Always test stains beforehand on a sample piece of the same kind of wood. Never be guided by a printed color card alone or by wood samples exhibited by the dealer.

(4) When applying more than one coat of varnish, lacquer or shellac, sand lightly between coats to insure a satiny smooth finish coat.

(5) When using a penetrating sealer, remember to follow the manufacturer's directions about wiping off the excess after each coat has been applied.

(6) When brushing on a clear finish of any kind, remember that two or three thin coats will always produce a better finish than one heavy coat.

(7) Regardless of the type of finish applied, its surface will stay fresh-looking longer if it is protected with a light coat of paste wax after the job is finished.

V

Plumbing and Heating

Most plumbers report that nearly two-thirds of their service calls are for minor repairs that could easily have been handled by the homeowner himself. Though the parts required may cost only a few cents, the high cost of labor, coupled with the economic necessity for making a minimum service charge on all calls, often results in a plumber submitting a bill which may run as high as $7 for installing a 5-cent washer (a job which may take only a few minutes).

To keep expenses of this kind from adding needlessly to the cost of running your house and to solve the problem of "what to do" when a plumber can't be located immediately (especially on weekends or holidays), you should familiarize yourself with the important parts of your home's plumbing system, and you should learn how to handle many simple repair jobs yourself.

The Home Plumbing System. Even though the job of repairing a leaky faucet or clearing a clogged drain does not require a complete knowledge of the home plumbing system, a basic understanding of how this system operates will enable you to handle all emergencies more intelligently.

One of the first things you should do is to learn the location of the main shutoff valve that controls the water supply for your house. In most cases this valve will be located somewhere near the water meter in the basement or utility room. It should be prominently tagged so that every member of the house can find it when necessary. When a sudden emergency threatens to flood part of the house, a quick turn of this valve can shut off everything till you have a chance to locate and repair the cause of the trouble.

Besides locating the main valve, you should also learn where all the other valves are located throughout the house. There should be separate hot and cold water valves for each sink, tub and other fixture throughout the home. Each of these should be clearly marked with a suitable tag so that the correct valve can be located quickly when a repair must be made. In addition to the water valves, there may also be gas valves, steam valves and hot water heating valves. Trying to find the right one in a hurry can lead to a great deal of confusion unless the location of each one is known and clearly marked.

Basically speaking, your home plumbing system consists of two different parts: the water supply piping which brings hot and cold water to each fixture and the drainpipes which carry waste water away from each of these same fixtures. The supply pipes are connected to a single main pipe which brings the water into the house. Branches are then run off wherever necessary to supply bathrooms, kitchens, etc. Sinks, tubs and other fixtures which require both hot and cold water supplies usually have two parallel lines running alongside each other, one for the hot and one for the cold water. The hot water heater is usually located near the furnace, but it may also be an integral part of the furnace itself.

Though fresh water is fed to the various fixtures by hydraulic pressure (the water comes into the main pipe under pressure from outside), the waste water is carried away by gravity alone. It is for this reason that all pipes in the drainage system must pitch downward till they eventually empty into the main drain line at the bottom of the house. This drain, in turn, connects with the municipal sewer or with a private waste disposal system, such as a septic tank or cesspool.

In addition to the drainpipes themselves, the drainage system includes one or more large-diameter vertical vent pipes. These extend up through the roof of the house, and they serve two important functions: they facilitate the rapid flow of waste down the waste pipes by permitting trapped air to escape, much as the second hole in a beverage can permits the fluid to flow out more easily, and they permit noxious gases which may drift up from the sewer lines to escape safely to the outside without seeping into the house itself.

Pipe and Fittings. Pipes used in the home plumbing system generally fall into one of three categories: iron or steel pipe which is joined with threaded fittings, copper pipe or tubing which is joined with soldered fittings and heavy, cast-iron soil pipe which is joined with special fittings that must be sealed with melted lead and calking.

Cast-iron soil pipe is very bulky and extremely difficult to work with. It is used mainly for the large waste lines which carry drainage away from toilets, bathtubs and similar fixtures. Steel and copper pipe, on the other hand, can be assembled by anyone who is reasonably adept with common hand tools. The steel pipe can be purchased cut to size and already threaded at each end, while the copper pipe is easily cut with an ordinary hacksaw. A small propane torch is the only special tool needed for "sweat-soldering" these fittings in place.

The Home Heating System. Most modern heating systems fall into one of four principal categories: hot water, steam, hot air or electric heating. Hot water and steam systems both use pipes to carry the hot water or steam to radiators throughout the house. Heat is generated in a centrally located boiler, and the cooled water or condensed steam returns to this boiler after it has dissipated its heat in radiators throughout the house.

In a hot air system, the boiler is replaced by a central heating chamber in the furnace. Ducts are then used to carry the heated air to registers located in each room throughout the house. A secondary system of ducts then carries the cold air back to the furnace so that it can be reheated and recirculated once more.

Electric heating is still relatively new and not yet widely used in northern climates because of its higher operating cost. Unlike the other systems, with electric heat there is no central furnace since each "radiator" is actually its own "furnace." This system provides exceptional flexibility because each room can have its own thermostatic control. Individual units can also be turned quickly on or off as required.

Regardless of the type of fuel used, all modern heating systems have a thermostat centrally located in the living quarters. This automatically calls for heat when the temperature falls below a preset level. Additional thermostatic controls are built into the boiler or heating chamber in the furnace so that the hot water, steam or hot air on the inside is kept at a fairly constant temperature. Thus it is instantly ready to supply heat when the thermostat upstairs starts the circulator going.

Cesspools and Septic Tanks, Care of

Homes which are built away from city sewage lines (this includes all rural homes and a great many suburban homes) must depend on a private sewage system to handle waste disposal from the household plumbing system. One of two types of disposal systems will be installed: a cesspool or a septic tank. A basic knowledge of how each of these operates, as well as some pointers on their care and maintenance, will help the homeowner avoid annoying and expensive breakdowns and will assure him of a system which is always safe and sanitary.

A cesspool consists of a simple covered pit that has its sides lined with masonry blocks that have been laid up without mortar. The household sewer line discharges raw sewage directly into this so that the liquid portion can be disposed of by seeping, or leaching, into the surrounding soil. Solids settle to the bottom and are retained inside the pit.

Because they allow raw sewage to seep directly into the surrounding soil, cesspools can be used only in porous or sandy soils, never in swampy areas or in heavy clay soils. They must be located at least 150 feet away from wells and 15 or 20 feet away from building foundations. Some communities forbid cesspools entirely, while others limit their depth and location. The local Health Department or Building Department will usually supply complete information on any restrictions that must be observed.

A cesspool begins to fill up and overflow when the openings in its masonry wall clog up with grease or other insoluble material. Pumping out or emptying the cesspool may then give only temporary relief, since this does not always eliminate the clogging condition. As a result, the cesspool often refills rapidly. To eliminate this, an entirely new cesspool may have to be built, or a second one can be connected to the old one to dispose of the overflow.

Septic tanks provide a more satisfactory method of home sewage disposal. They are designed to decompose solids and treat sewage by bacterial action before it seeps away into the earth. The tank itself is usually built of masonry or steel and it is watertight in construction. As sewage from the house line enters the tank, solids separate from the liquid and settle to the bottom. Bacterial action then works to decompose this accumulated matter. The insoluble portion remains on the bottom of the tank, while liquids overflow into a series of disposal lines which are buried beneath the soil and radiate outward from a central distribution point in various directions.

Called the drainage field, this network of disposal lines consists of large-diameter clay pipe which is laid out so that seepage takes place through the joints between each section. The layout of this drainage field and the size of the septic tank required depend on the number of occupants in the house and on local soil conditions.

Since septic tanks are designed to retain a layer of sludge (decomposed solids) at the bottom, they must be cleaned out periodically to prevent this solid layer from building up sufficiently to cause clogging of the disposal lines or of the household sewer line. Under ordinary use the tank may need cleaning at 2- to 4-year intervals, but most experts recommend that the sludge level be inspected every 12 to 18 months. This is accomplished by opening a special manhole cover or trapdoor located at or near ground level. This inspection, as well as cleaning when necessary, is best accomplished by a specially equipped septic tank serviceman.

Since grease tends to clog both cesspools and septic tanks and since it slows up bacterial action in even the best designed tanks, homeowners should avoid pouring fats or oils down the household drain whenever possible. These should be disposed of by storing in cans, then throwing them out with the kitchen garbage. In large, multiple-family homes, special grease traps are usually installed to catch waste grease before it enters the sewer line.

Since some fats and oils obviously will find their way into the waste line from dishwashing or bathing, you should take steps to dissolve this grease at periodic intervals by using a prepared household drain cleaner. Most of these compounds contain caustic soda, so they must be used with extreme caution according to the directions on the label. Contrary to popular belief, these drain cleaners will not harm septic tanks or slow up the bacterial action when used in normal amounts. However, their action is such that they do dissolve the trapped grease in the line, thus preventing a buildup of heavy accumulations.

To further extend the life of the home sewage system, insoluble solid material, such as heavy paper, rags, coffee grounds and other foreign matter, should never be flushed down the drain. Kitchen sink garbage disposal units greatly increase the load on the home sewage system, so check carefully before installing an appliance of this kind. In addition,

Chemical cleaners rid pipes of grease and will not affect septic tank

roof gutters, storm drains and other large-volume water wastes should never be connected to a septic tank or cesspool.

Chimney Repairs

Chimneys are an essential part of the home heating plant and they need to be inspected and maintained periodically if a major breakdown is to be avoided. One of the most important precautions is a periodic cleaning, or "sweeping," to remove draft-killing dirt and soot. Excess accumulations cut down on burner efficiency and can waste considerable amounts of fuel. In addition, they constitute a serious fire hazard if allowed to build up over a period of years. Chimney cleaning is best accomplished by professionals who use large vacuum cleaners and other specialized equipment. It should be done about once every four or five years, and is usually part of the service rendered by the man who supplies your fuel. If he doesn't do this kind of work himself, ask him to recommend someone who does.

For those homeowners who do not mind a bit of climbing, the job of cleaning the chimney is not a difficult one, provided it has not been neglected for too long a time. Begin by shutting off the main furnace switch so that the burner cannot go on accidentally while you are working. Then fill a burlap bag with rags, straw or sawdust and add one or two large stones to furnish the necessary weight. Tie this to a long rope,

To sweep down chimney drag a burlap bag up and down on the inside

Removing ashes and soot through clean-out door in basement

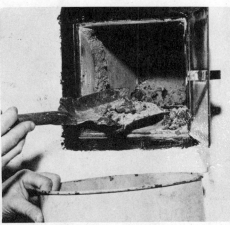

then lower it into your chimney while standing on the roof and drag it up and down on the inside as shown. Accumulated soot and dirt will be knocked to the bottom where it can be removed later on through the cleanout door in the basement.

This cleanout door should be tightly closed afterward so that no air leaks are possible after the job is complete. Most experts advise sealing around the edges of the door with asbestos cement to be assured of a truly airtight joint. The cement is easily broken away the next time the door must be opened.

Aside from periodic cleaning, the chimney structure itself should be regularly inspected for defects in the mortar joints, chimney cap or flashing. Most repairs will be simple, and can easily be taken care of by the home handyman who is willing to do his own climbing and tuck-pointing (replacing of defective mortar joints). For those who cannot do their own, a mason or bricklayer will have to be called in.

Beginning at the very top, look over the cement chimney cap. This protects the bricks against the weather by keeping out water, so its effectiveness is lost if the cement is cracked. If cracks are discovered, or if pieces are missing, fill in with mortar cement. Ready-mixed mortar can be purchased in dry form at most hardware stores, or the homeowner can mix his own with 3 parts fine sand and 1 part cement. Add just enough water to make a stiff, plastic mixture; then, after wetting the crack down with water, fill the opening with the cement.

If the chimney cap is so badly cracked that it is loose in many sections,

Mortar cement is used to fill in cracks in chimney caps

Mortar is also used to repair defective joints in brickwork

the entire slab should be removed. A new cap can then be built up by troweling on several thick layers of cement and sloping the top layer so water will run off.

Now inspect all exposed brickwork for signs of loose, crumbling mortar and open joints. These should be repaired promptly by tuck-pointing. Begin by raking out the joints with an old screwdriver or cold chisel to a depth of at least ½ inch, or till all defective mortar has been scraped out. Dust out with a whisk broom or other stiff brush, then soak with water. Fill with freshly mixed mortar, using a small triangular pointing trowel.

As each joint is filled, scrape off the surplus and rake out lightly by undercutting with the point of the trowel so that the joint is slightly recessed. This makes a neater-looking job and helps the joint shed water.

If extensive loosening of bricks is noticed, or if whole sections seem to need replacing, a professional mason should be called in to rebuild the chimney. Extensive cracking of the chimney inside the house (below the roof line) is another indication that professional help probably will be required.

Drains, Clogged

Clearing a clogged sink or toilet drain is usually a simple job which calls for use of a force cup or plunger (often referred to as a "plumber's helper"), a spring steel plumber's "snake" or auger, a large wrench and some drainpipe cleaner. Needless to say, all of these tools will not be required for every job, but the wise homeowner will keep everything handy for immediate use should an emergency arise (particularly on weekends or evenings, when stores are closed).

To simplify the job, a clogged drain should be attended to as soon as the homeowner notices that water is not running out of a fixture as quickly as it should. A partially clogged drain is easier to clear than one which has become totally blocked. In kitchen sinks blockages are often caused by accumulations of grease, coffee grounds, small pieces of food and other foreign matter in the drainpipe or in the trap under the sink. In bathroom sinks, hair, lint and greasy cosmetics can have much the same effect.

The first place to look when trouble occurs is in the drain outlet inside the sink itself. Most modern sinks and tubs have a lint trap built in as part of this discharge outlet. This can become clogged with hair, paper or pieces of undissolved soap. Built-in drain stoppers can easily be taken out to remove accumulations of this kind. If water still does not flow out freely when the stopper or lint trap is removed, the trouble is in the drainpipe or trap below the sink.

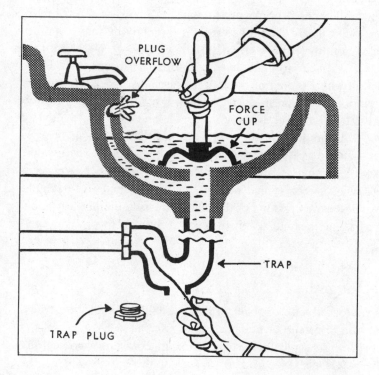

Most mild stoppages can be cleared by proper use of the rubber force cup. This is a bell-shaped rubber cup about 5 or 6 inches in diameter connected to the end of a wooden handle. For this tool to work properly there must be at least 3 or 4 inches of water in the bottom of the sink, tub or toilet bowl. The rubber cup is positioned over the drain opening with the wooden handle held in both hands. The handle is then pressed down suddenly to create pressure in the line, after which it is jerked upward to create a suction action which is even more effective. This alternate push-pull action should be repeated vigorously at least 10 or 12 times to dislodge foreign matter and to break up stoppages.

To make certain that the full force of the pressure created will be confined inside the clogged drain, a damp rag should be used to plug the overflow openings in bathtubs and bathroom sinks. In addition, the drain stopper or sink strainer should be removed before the force cup is used. When the clogged pipe is finally cleared, the water will rush out of the sink or bowl with a quick, sudden gurgle.

If repeated use of the rubber force cup does not clear the drain, a chemical drainpipe cleaner will sometimes do the trick. These cleaners are extremely caustic and highly poisonous, so they must be handled with a great deal of care. Rubber gloves should be worn to protect the hands, and the chemical should not be allowed to contact skin or clothing.

Before using a drainpipe cleaner in a fixture which is already filled with water, most of the water should be dipped out first. The compound is then poured directly into the drain opening without allowing the chemical to come in contact with the porcelain or enamel if possible. The amount of cleaner to use and the time required for the chemical to do its job will vary with the extent of the stoppage. In some cases several hours may be required or more than one application may be needed. Once the drain has been opened, it should be flushed thoroughly with plenty of water to rid the pipe of all remaining caustic solution.

If both of these methods fail to do the trick, the trouble is probably due to a more seriously clogged trap or drainpipe underneath the fixture. In this event, a steel auger or snake will have to be used. On sinks the job is best done from below after removing the special cleanout plug from the bottom of the U-shaped trap which is located directly beneath all sinks. A large pan should be placed under the trap to catch waste water when the plug is removed. This plug is actually a shallow nut which must be carefully unscrewed with a large wrench to avoid stripping the threads. If the trap does not have a cleanout plug of this kind at the bot-

To open a clogged sink drain loosen the two trap fittings with a wrench

Remove trap by pulling downward without break-gaskets

tom, the entire U-shaped piece will have to be removed by loosening the slip nuts at either end. If these nuts are of chrome or polished brass, they can be wrapped with tape to protect the finish against scratching before placing the wrench over them.

After the cleanout plug or the entire trap has been removed, the wire drain auger should be forced into the pipe to remove the obstruction. The auger should first be worked downward through the sink opening at the top to make sure that the vertical pipe is clear all the way down to the trap. The next step is to insert the snake through the trap opening at the bottom and force it upward into the horizontal drainpipe where it disappears through the wall behind the fixture. Twisting the handle of the auger or wiggling the end of the wire snake will cause the hook or coiled spring at the tip of the tool to bite into the obstruction inside the pipe. This will either push it out of the way by breaking it up or permit the item blocking the pipe to be drawn back through the cleanout opening.

The drain auger or plumber's snake can also be used to free clogged toilet bowls. Since these fixtures all have a built-in "reverse action" or U-shaped trap of their own, considerable pressure may have to be applied to the end of the snake in order to force it up and over the drain-pipe opening. For stoppages of this kind, an auger at least 6 to 8 feet in length will usually be required. The wire should be worked vigorously back and forth as soon as an obstruction is felt to break up the blockage so that it can be easily flushed away with water.

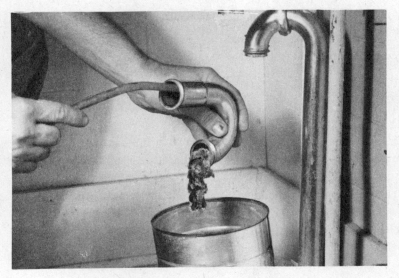

Clean out the trap and upper drain with rubber-covered wire

When all of these cleanout methods fail to do the job, or when several fixtures seem clogged at the same time, the trouble is probably in one of the main household waste lines. If so, a professional plumbing con-

tractor should be called in as soon as possible. He will have the specialized equipment and knowledge required for a large-scale job of this kind.

Faucets, Leaking

A leaky faucet or valve is not only annoying, but can also add dollars to the homeowner's annual water bill. If the leak occurs in a hot water line, fuel is also being wasted.

If water seems to be leaking out around the stem (just below the handle), it usually means that the faucet or valve needs new packing under the cap-nut (this is the bonnet-shaped nut or threaded cover through which the stem protrudes).

If, on the other hand, the faucet or valve drips or leaks even when turned completely off, the trouble is probably due to a worn washer on the inside. If replacing the washer doesn't stop the drip or if washers seem to wear out at frequent intervals, chances are that the metal seat against which the washer presses (to shut off the water) is rough and worn and needs resurfacing or replacing.

To repair a leak around the stem of the valve, first try tightening the cap-nut or packing nut with a large wrench. In many cases a small

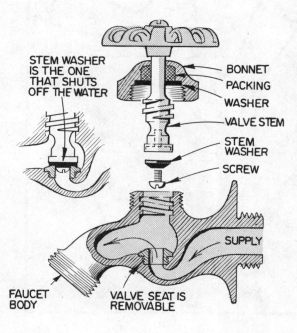

Loosen nut to remove housing. The cap nut is under this housing.

After loosening cap nut, new packing material is wound around stem

fraction of a turn is all that will be needed to stop the leak. If tightening this nut doesn't stop the drip or if the nut has to be tightened so much that the handle can no longer be turned easily, the packing on the inside will have to be replaced.

To replace this packing, first shut off the water supply to the fixture. Then remove the faucet or valve handle so that the cap-nut can be unscrewed and slid off over the stem. The faucet handle is often held on by a screw at the top. On some faucets this screw may be covered by a decorative cap or plate which either snaps out or screws out of a recess in the center of the handle. In other cases the handle may be held on by a small set screw or nut on the underside. When this screw or nut is loosened, the bottom of the handle can be tapped upward while rocking gently, until the handle can be pulled off.

Once the handle is off, the cap-nut or bonnet can be unscrewed and slid upward to expose the packing underneath it. The old packing material is dug out with a screwdriver blade, then new packing material is installed. This is purchased in the form of a graphite-impregnated, string-like material which is wrapped around the stem of the valve under the cap-nut.

Some of the newer faucets have a specially shaped plastic ring instead of this packing. In this case a matching ring should be purchased from the supply house. If in doubt as to the size required or if difficulty is encountered in matching the existing packing material, unscrew the entire stem and packing assembly and bring this to your dealer to be sure you get matching replacement parts.

To cure a faucet which drips or a valve which will not shut off completely, the entire stem assembly must be unscrewed from the faucet body so that the washer at the lower end can be replaced. To do this, first remove the faucet handle as previously described, then unscrew and lift off the packing nut or bonnet which holds the stem in place.

On modern, decorative faucets, there will often be a chrome housing or decorative escutcheon plate which must be removed first to expose the packing nut underneath. These bell-shaped housings are usually held down by a large flat nut directly on top, so this will have to be unscrewed first. After this nut is removed, the housing can be slid up over the end of the stem to expose the large packing nut underneath. After this packing nut has been completely loosened, the faucet stem, or spindle, can be unscrewed by simply turning it in the same direction as though the water were being turned on.

The washer at the bottom end of the stem is held in place by a brass screw that goes through the center. The screw is removed first, after

Select new washer of right size to replace old one

which the old washer can be pried out with the point of a knife or the tip of a screwdriver. The new washer should match the old one in size, thickness and shape. For best results, a new brass screw should also be used to hold the washer in place.

The faucet can now be reassembled by replacing the stem in the faucet body, then tightening down the packing nut or bonnet. The faucet should be opened or closed tightly a few times to help set the new washer, after which the water can be turned on once more.

If the faucet continues to drip even after a new washer has been inserted, the valve seat is probably nicked or scratched and needs regrinding. Most hardware stores sell low-cost seat-dressing tools which are made for just this purpose. These are inserted in the faucet body, after the stem has been removed, so that the end of the tool presses down against the faucet seat. A matching bonnet nut on this tool will hold the shaft straight and true and will help the user exert the downward pressure required while it is rotated. In most cases only one or two turns of the tool is all that will be necessary to remove nicks and scratches on the surface of the seat.

After the job is done, the seat-dressing tool is removed and the inside of the faucet flushed out by turning the water on for a moment before reinserting the faucet stem.

Faucet Sprays

One of the many little conveniences which modern plumbing affords is the automatic thumb-control dishwasher spray on kitchen sinks. When these need repair or replacing, they can easily be serviced by the home handyman because the industry has standardized all replacement equipment and parts, regardless of the brand of sink and faucet involved. These prepackaged parts are sold, complete with instructions for installation, at most hardware stores and at practically all plumbing supply houses.

To service a faucet spray unit, the handyman must first understand the principle on which it operates. The heart of the system is a little mechanism called a diverter valve. This is located inside the faucet in a special chamber just below the base of the swing spout as indicated in the accompanying drawing. This valve normally permits water to flow freely through the spout when the spray attachment is not in use. However, when the thumb-control valve on the spray is open, an imbalance of water pressure is created to operate the valve. A piston-like unit snaps down, shutting off most of the water supply through the spout and diverting it through the hose which leads to the spray head.

This valve cannot be put into any faucet which was not originally made with a chamber for the valve. Three different styles are currently being manufactured, but all use the same principle of operation. When a replacement unit is required, the homeowner can bring his old one to the dealer for comparison with an illustrated replacement chart which will indicate the correct new shape he should buy.

When an automatic spray is not operating properly, the water will not divert to the spray head when the thumb control is depressed. In most cases the trouble is located in one of four places: the spout nozzle or the aerator attached to the end of it is partially clogged, the spray head itself is partially clogged, the connecting hose is defective or leaking or the diverter valve is not operating properly.

To locate the source of trouble, always check the aerator first. This is a strainer-like gadget which screws onto the end of the spout nozzle to minimize splashing. Unscrew this aerator and try the spray head without it. If water now diverts satisfactorily, the aerator screen is partially clogged. Clean carefully with a toothpick or brush, then flush thoroughly with clean water before replacing.

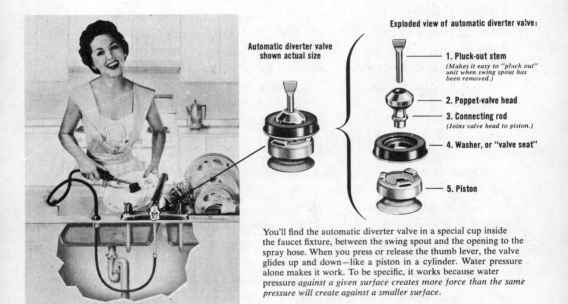

Automatic diverter valve shown actual size

Exploded view of automatic diverter valve:

1. Pluck-out stem
(Makes it easy to "pluck out" unit when swing spout has been removed.)

2. Poppet-valve head

3. Connecting rod
(Joins valve head to piston.)

4. Washer, or "valve seat"

5. Piston

You'll find the automatic diverter valve in a special cup inside the faucet fixture, between the swing spout and the opening to the spray hose. When you press or release the thumb lever, the valve glides up and down—like a piston in a cylinder. Water pressure alone makes it work. To be specific, it works because water pressure *against a given surface creates more force than the same pressure will create against a smaller surface.*

If the aerator nozzle is not clogged, it may be that the spray head is. Remove its nozzle, or head, and run water through in reverse to flush out sediment and to make certain there is no dirt on the inside.

If the spray head is broken, cracked, hopelessly clogged or otherwise defective, or if a more modern version is desired, one of the new replacement heads may be purchased and installed. These come in two models: a standard spray (called Rinse-Quik) or a deluxe dishwashing spray which dispenses either suds or clear water. This deluxe model also has a replaceable brush on the end. Either model can be used to replace any existing thumb-control spray, regardless of the shape of the original attachment.

The next most likely source of trouble is the hose which connects the spray head to the faucet itself. This attaches to the bottom of the faucet body under the sink and loops down under the sink, coming up through the extra hole provided on the deck of the sink. Kinks or leaks in this hose will cause trouble, so make certain it hangs free and does not bind around pipes, cleaning supplies or other materials which may be stored in the space below. It is usually a good idea to have someone pull the spray head up and down a few times while you watch the action from underneath to make sure the hose always has freedom of movement.

If the hose appears defective, a new one should be purchased and installed. These are standardized in 30- and 48-inch lengths. The shorter hose is for faucets which are mounted on the wall, while the longer one is for the more popular, deck-mounted types. Both hoses come with universal couplings which can be adapted to fit any kind of faucet connection.

If the aerator, the spray head and the hose all seem satisfactory, yet the water still fails to divert properly, chances are that the diverter valve on the inside needs replacing. Unscrew the collar or coupling nut around the base of the swing spout, then lift the entire spout off to expose the valve. Lift the valve out by grasping the "pluck-out" stem on the top, then put the spout back on temporarily without the valve and flush hot water through. Replace the diverter and try again. If it is damaged and still fails to operate properly, replace with a new one, making certain that the new one is installed with the "pluck-out" stem pointing up.

If an old faucet is being replaced and a new one is desired with an automatic spray attachment, the homeowner should remember to buy one which has a built-in automatic diverter valve. When replacing an existing double-control faucet with a new one which will have a spray attachment, an additional (fourth) hole will be required in the sink top.

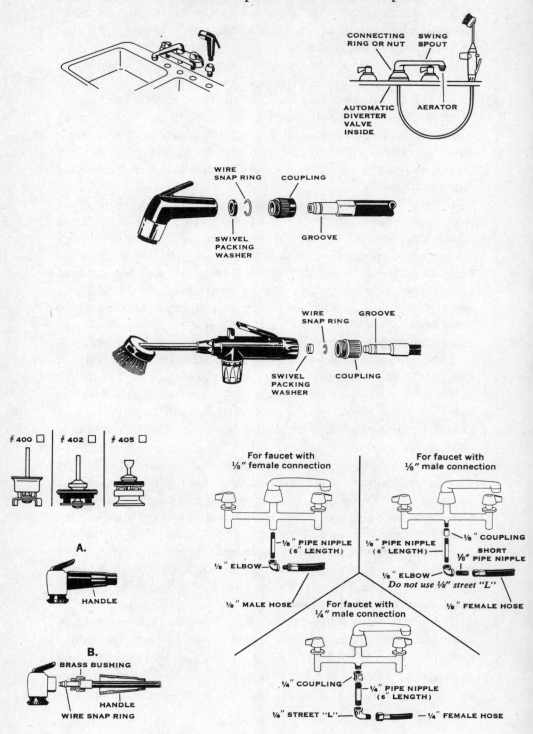

Since boring this hole through the enameled porcelain finish is a tricky job which only an expert should attempt, a simpler solution lies in purchasing one of the new single-control faucets of the type which does not need a fourth hole for the spray attachment.

Fireplace Troubles, How to Cure

A properly designed fireplace should burn its fuel efficiently without smoking excessively and without need for continual tending or relighting. Assuming that the fireplace has been properly constructed and that it is structurally sound, most smoking troubles can be traced to improper fire-building techniques, improper fuel or improper maintenance of the fireplace and chimney.

Since every fire needs a plentiful supply of air and an adequate draft (flow of air up the chimney) to burn properly, the first thing the homeowner should do is make certain that the damper is fully opened before a fire is lit. On most home fireplaces, the damper should be all the way open to provide adequate draft, particularly when the fire is being lit.

To supply the large amounts of air needed, the homeowner should also make certain that a window or door in the room is open slightly to permit an adequate supply of fresh air to enter. Modern homes are built so tightly (calking, weatherstripping, etc.) that there are no natural air leaks to feed the fire, hence the need to open at least one window or door. Otherwise there will be insufficient oxygen to feed the flames, thus causing inefficient burning and excessive smoking.

One of the most common reasons for a smoky fireplace is a downdraft in the chimney. This results when cold air flows downward so that smoke is blown out into the room instead of flowing up through the chimney. A properly designed fireplace will have a smoke shelf built in at the base of the chimney to deflect down-drafts by turning them back upward so that they join the normal upward draft, rather than puffing out into the room. This effect is heightened by the open damper which also tends to deflect the air upward before it can reach the fireplace opening.

Down-drafts can also be caused by insufficient ventilation inside the room. Failure to open a window or door may keep the fire from burning properly, and this in turn will keep the inside of the chimney from heating up as it should. A cold chimney is far more susceptible to downdrafts than a hot chimney because the heated lining helps speed the upward flow of air, thus increasing the draft so that the fire burns with less smoke.

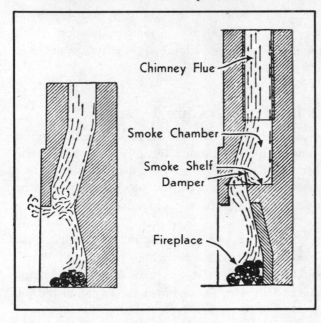

For maximum efficiency when building a fire, lay the logs across andirons, grates or similar supports so that air flows freely in under the fire to force flames upward. When starting the fire, most experts recommend that one or two sheets of newspaper be burned first by holding them up in the throat of the chimney or by laying them across the tops of the logs and igniting them before lighting the rest of the fire. The paper burns rapidly and preheats the chimney air to simplify the problem of getting the fire started.

Though "experts" differ as to the best technique to follow when building a fire, one generally accepted method consists of first laying a generous amount of crumpled newspaper on the hearth between the andirons. Kindling wood is then spread generously over this layer of newspaper and one of the thickest logs is placed across the back of the andirons. This should be as close to the back of the fireplace as possible, but not quite touching it. A second log is then placed an inch or so in front of this, and a few additional sticks of kindling are laid across these two. A third log is then placed on top to form a sort of pyramid with air space between all logs so that flames can lick freely up between them.

A mistake frequently made is in building the fire too far forward so that the rear wall of the fireplace does not get properly heated. A heated back wall helps increase the draft and tends to suck smoke and flames rearward with less chance of sparks or smoke spurting out into the room.

Another common mistake often made by the inexperienced fire-tender is to try to build a fire with only one or two logs, instead of using at least three. A single log is difficult to ignite properly, and even two logs do not provide an efficient bed with adequate fuel-burning capacity.

Use of too many logs, on the other hand, is also a common fault and can prove hazardous. Building too big a fire can create more smoke and draft than the chimney can safely handle, increasing the possibility of sparks or smoke being thrown out into the room. For best results, the homeowner should start with three medium-size logs as described above, then add additional logs as needed if the fire is to be kept burning.

If a fireplace continues to smoke steadily, even though proper fire-building practices have been observed, the homeowner should check the condition of his chimney to see that the flue is clean. The smoke shelf should also be inspected to see whether it is caked with soot or other debris which may have fallen down through the flue. The handyman can inspect his chimney pipe and flue by looking upward through the opening on a bright day, using a mirror if necessary to enable him to see past the damper.

The condition of the damper itself should also be checked to make certain that it actually opens fully when the damper handle is pushed to the open position. In some cases soot may have built up around the damper opening so that the draft is seriously cut down even when the damper is all the way open.

If a thorough cleaning of the chimney, smoke shelf and damper opening still fails to provide adequate draft (assuming there is proper interior ventilation as previously mentioned), the homeowner should check his chimney on the outside to see whether overhanging tree branches or other structures are interfering with proper draft or creating artificial down-drafts. The chimney should be at least 2 to 3 feet higher than any part of the roof or other nearby structure.

If, in spite of everything, the fireplace still continues to smoke when a fire is lit, the trouble probably lies with some basic fault in its original design or construction. The most common defect is a flue opening which is too small in proportion to the size of the fireplace opening. If this is suspected, the homeowner should measure the area of the flue opening (this may have to be done at the top of the chimney on the roof) and then measure the area of the fireplace opening. Good design calls for a flue area which is at least one-twelfth the area of the fireplace opening.

If the flue is smaller than this, the fireplace opening on the inside should be reduced. There are several ways this can be done. The easiest method is to build (or have built) a metal hood across the top of the fireplace opening.

To determine how effective a hood of this sort will be, there is a simple test that can be made. Build a small fire in the fireplace, then hold a wide board or sheet of metal across the top of the opening. Keep lowering this shield to increase the draft until a point is reached where the fire draws properly without smoking. This will indicate the size of metal hood or masonry fill-in that will be required to properly close down the fireplace opening.

In extreme cases where a sizable reduction in the size of the opening is called for, there are two additional methods that can be used. The first calls for raising the hearth by having a bricklayer put down one or two additional layers of brick so as to close the opening from the bottom up. The other method is to close in the sides of the fireplace by installing one or more vertical rows of fire brick against the wall on either side.

Another structural defect which will cause a fireplace to smoke unnecessarily is a damper which is located too low. For efficient operation, the damper should be near the front of the fireplace, and it should be at least 4 to 6 inches above the top of the fireplace opening. The sloping back wall of the fireplace should come up to meet it and act as a reflector to throw heat out into the room while guiding smoke up through the damper opening. If the damper is too low, some of this smoke will be deflected out into the room instead. To correct this, a metal hood or masonry fill-in can be installed as described above.

In order for the chimney to draw off smoke effectively, there should be no more than one fireplace connected to each chimney flue or chimney opening. When additional fireplaces or heating units are installed, a separate flue or chimney should be provided for each one.

Heating System Maintenance

Though many homeowners think only of their furnaces when the heating system is mentioned, modern systems actually consist of many interconnected parts that must all function in unison. In addition to the furnace itself (which includes a central boiler or heating chamber) there are also the connecting pipes or ducts, as well as the various radiators or registers in each room. These are all designed to disperse heat uniformly throughout the house so that occupants will be comfortable all through the winter with little or no attention on the homeowner's part. This is accomplished by means of a series of automatic controls which must

Motors on circulators and blowers need oiling about three times a year

be adjusted and regulated periodically if maximum efficiency is to be assured.

If all parts of your system are not functioning properly, you may be wasting a substantial part of your heating dollar. Since automatic heating plants are intricate mechanical affairs, major adjustments and repairs should be left to the services of a professional heating serviceman. However, there are a number of things that you can and should do for yourself, regardless of the type of heating system you may have.

Oil burner motors must be lubricated with #10- or #20-weight oil at least two or three times a year, as should blowers and blower motors on hot air systems. Circulating hot water systems also have a circulator motor and pump, both of which will probably need regular oiling.

Thermostats can be one common source of trouble, causing uneven heating with alternate spells of either too much or too little heat. For maximum efficiency thermostats should always be located on an inside wall, away from drafts and sources of heat, and about 5 feet up from the floor. If possible, it should be in a spot which is in the path of natural air circulation for the house, but it should never be located near an outside door or window. Neither should it be installed behind doors, furniture or drapes—and never where it is subject to cold drafts or any source of heat. Even the heat from a nearby lamp or television set will throw

Filters should be changed as soon as they become clogged

it off. It may then fail to call for heat, though the rest of the house is chilly.

If a thermostat is much more than six or seven years old, it should be viewed with suspicion and inspected by a serviceman to make certain that it is still operating efficiently. Modern thermostatic controls can be regulated so that heat is fed to the house in a series of short "dribbles" (at frequent intervals) rather than in a series of widely separated, long bursts of heat. Shorter intervals between burner operations help keep the temperature on a more even keel and they will not allow it to cool off to the point where radiators get completely cold.

Forced air heating systems usually have special filters located in or near the furnace to trap unwanted dust and lint. These filters should be checked at least two or three times a year and replaced when they become partially clogged. Generally speaking, a filter should be renewed if light cannot be seen through it when it is held up to a window or other source of light.

Hot water heating systems have radiators that have air vents near the top. These should be bled at the beginning of each heating season to release trapped air so that the heated water may flow through more freely. Starting with the highest radiator in the house, each vent should be opened for a moment until water begins to flow. It is then closed immediately to prevent losing any more water than necessary. To make

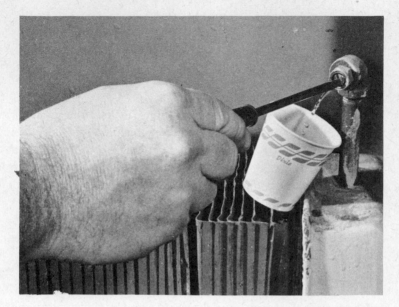

Radiator is bled by opening vent till water flows

certain that the radiators are putting out all their heat, a vacuum cleaner should be used to remove dust and lint from between the fins and from openings in radiator covers and grills.

In steam-heated homes, faulty vent valves often prevent the radiators from heating up properly and are probably the greatest single cause of uneven heating. These valves are supposed to allow trapped air to escape automatically, but if they fail to function properly they will keep the steam from filling up the inside of the radiator. Clogged vents often can be cleaned out by boiling, but since they are relatively inexpensive, the best solution lies in replacing the valve entirely.

A vacuum should be used to draw accumulated dust from between fins of radiators

Adjustable vent valves are also available to permit regulating the speed with which various radiators heat up. These permit you to slow down the radiators which are nearest to the furnace, so those which are farther away can heat up more quickly.

In some homes an inadequate heating plant, or a design problem inherent in the structure of the house, makes it difficult to maintain uniform room-to-room temperatures under all outdoor weather conditions. This may be because one part of the house is sheltered from the elements much more than another, or it may be because one side of the house receives a great deal more sunshine than the others.

To correct a condition of this kind, a heating expert should be called in to see whether present radiators can be relocated or whether the system can be balanced to provide more heat in some rooms than in others. For the best solution, the home should be divided into separate heating zones, each controlled by its own thermostat. Though this involves a sizable expense, the increased comfort and fuel savings which will eventually result more than compensate the homeowner for the cost involved.

Insulation, Selection and Use

By keeping the heat where it belongs (inside during the winter and outside during the summer), insulation performs two important functions in any modern home: it helps make the house a more comfortable place in which to live all year round, and it cuts down substantially on the annual cost of heating or cooling the home. For a house located in the northern half of the country, good insulation can actually pay for itself in fuel savings in as little as three years.

For a really complete job, the insulation should have been installed while the house was under construction. However, even if your home is already finished, there is still a great deal you can do to cut down on heat loss. You can put up your own insulation in an unfinished attic, under the floor of unheated crawl spaces, on walls which adjoin an unheated garage and in the walls and ceilings of new additions which may be built on later.

Most of the insulation currently being used in homes will fall into one of four categories: loose fill, blankets or batts, foam and rigid panels. Loose fill comes in large bags and is either poured into the spaces between the beams on an attic floor, or into the hollow wall cavities when this can be done from above. It is also used by pro-

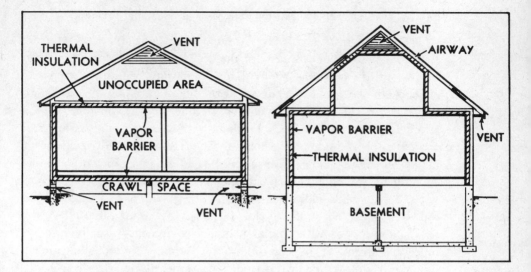

fessionals with special equipment who blow it into the wall cavities of existing homes that have no insulation in their outside walls.

Most of the loose fill insulation used in recent years is either a fibrous material such as mineral wool, or a cellulosic material which is made out of reprocessed paper or cardboard that is chemically treated to make it fire resistant. The cellulose material is almost always blown in, regardless of whether it is being spread over an attic floor, or blown into the walls.

The simplest insulating material for unoccupied attic is loose fill

Blankets or batts (basically the same, except that blankets come in long rolls and are not as easy for the do-it-yourselfer to handle) come in two or three widths to fit different spacings between beams or studs, and in various thicknesses with different ratings or insulating values. Most have a vapor barrier on one side (aluminum foil or specially impregnated paper), but batts without vapor barriers are also available for adding more insulation where there is already some down on an attic floor and more is needed (and assuming the original insulation has a vapor barrier underneath). You do not want a second vapor barrier when additional material is put down.

Foam insulation is strictly for existing walls, and it must be professionally applied with special pumping equipment—usually through holes bored in the outside siding. It has one big advantage over blown-in cellulose or mineral wool: It is generally less likely to settle as the years go by, and thus less likely to leave voids where heat can be lost. As a rule it costs more than blown-in insulation, and more expertise is required to install it properly, so selection of a reputable contractor who is experienced in working with this material is essential.

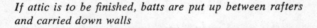

If attic is to be finished, batts are put up between rafters and carried down walls

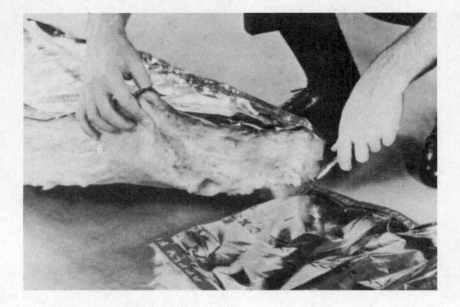

Combination batts have reflective foil on one side

Rigid boards or panels of insulation have limited use on existing houses—they are most often used in new construction as a form of sheathing under the exterior siding. However, homeowners can also use them in existing homes to insulate basement walls and crawl space enclosures, but since most of these panels are made of a plastic that is inflammable, local building codes usually require that they then be covered on the inside with ½-inch thick gypsum board.

The insulating value of any of these materials is determined by its R-value—a rating that is required on all insulation sold. The higher the R-value for a given material or given thickness of that material (for example loose fill which can vary in thickness when applied over an attic floor), the more insulation value that material has. This means that when shopping for insulating batts, blankets or boards you don't buy according to thickness; you go by the R-value which should be marked on that product. For those who live in cold climates, attic insulation should have a value of at least R-22—still higher if you have all-electric heat. Walls are probably limited as to how much insulation they will hold, but where possible they should have insulation rated at least R-11 or R-13. The same rating is recommended for floors over unheated crawl spaces.

Noisy Plumbing, How to Cure

A home plumbing system which hammers, bangs, squeals or creaks every time the water is turned on or off is not only hard on the homeowner's nerves, it is also hard on the plumbing system itself. These noises usually indicate exceptional vibration at some point, and if not corrected in time, the conditions responsible may shake mountings and connections loose and may even cause pipes to burst.

One of the most common noises is a hammering or banging sound which is heard every time a faucet is suddenly closed. This is caused by the momentum of the fast-moving water when it is slammed to a sudden stop by the closing of a valve. The hammering sound which results is due to the fact that water cannot be compressed, so it bangs around inside the pipe, vibrating back and forth till its forward motion ceases.

In some cases, this condition would not occur if the pipe were rigidly supported along its entire length so that the pipe itself could not vibrate or "give." This is particularly true at elbows and other joints where the pipe makes a sharp bend or sudden turn. To check for a potential trouble spot of this kind, inspect all the exposed lengths of pipe. Look for signs of sagging and for straps or mounting brackets which may have worked loose. Copper water ·pipes in the ¾- and 1-inch sizes should be supported by straps which are spaced no more than 8 feet apart. Half-inch pipe should be supported at 6-foot intervals.

*Pipe straps should be
tight to prevent
vibration*

Metal strapping will hold pipes against beams

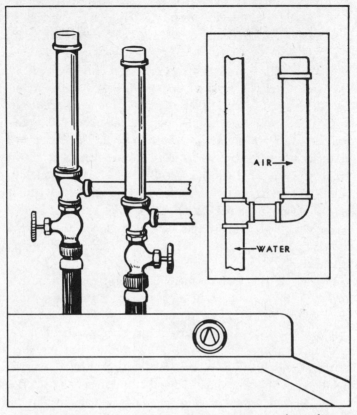

Anti-hammer chambers consist of vertical lengths of pipe capped at the top

When checking these supports, pay particular attention to elbows and tees. If possible, there should be a clamp or strap on each side of the elbow, or a wooden block can be installed so that it presses against the side of the pipe just past the turn. For maximum effectiveness, this brace or supporting block should be installed against the piece of pipe on the far side of the turn—in other words against the side which the water will be hitting as it makes its turn.

When additional braces or supporting straps are not enough to cure the problem, anti-hammer air chambers are usually required to absorb the shock. There are specially designed diaphragm- or globe-type air chambers available for this purpose, though the simplest kind consists simply of a vertical, 2-foot-length of pipe which is cut into the water line just before the fixture. This piece of pipe is tightly capped at the upper end so that a column of air is sealed inside. When water flowing through the pipe is brought to a sudden stop, the impact causes some of it to back up into this air chamber. The trapped air on the inside compresses under the impact, creating a "cushion" which absorbs the shock harmlessly and keeps the water from banging around inside the piping. Anti-hammer chambers can be the same diameter as the supply pipe, but they are much more effective if a larger-size pipe is used.

Air chambers of this kind are best installed in the water line just before the highest faucet. When this is impractical because it would mean ripping open walls, the installation of a chamber close to the water meter will usually work almost as well. Air chambers can also be placed in other locations if necessary—in fact, anywhere that the exposed water pipe can be reached so that a suitable tee can be cut into the line. In many homes a frequent cause of hammering is the automatic washing machine with its quick-acting valves that turn the water on and off repeatedly. To eliminate this condition, shock-absorbing air chambers should be installed immediately over each faucet that supplies the washing machine.

For an air chamber to maintain its efficiency, it must be completely airtight at the top. Once the air leaks out, water will gradually enter the pipe, filling the chamber to the point where its cushioning effect is completely lost. To make certain this does not happen, the threads on the cap or plug should be liberally coated with plumber's compound before screwing it into place, and the cap must be screwed down very tightly. If at any time the air chamber does become waterlogged because a slow leak develops around the threads, the plug at the top can be removed and the chamber drained. Then the plug or cap is replaced with an additional application of compound on the threads.

A chattering or squealing noise that occurs when a faucet is opened, or when a faucet is left partly open, is usually due to trouble in the faucet itself. The washer on the inside may be loose or badly worn, or the screw which holds the washer in place may have worked loose. Remove the faucet stem to check the condition of the washer and its retaining screw. If these parts seem all right, check the threads on the faucet spindle itself. If they are badly worn or if there is excessive play when the spindle is in place, chances are that a new faucet will be required to permanently eliminate the noise.

A creaking sound coming from a hot water line is usually caused by rapid expansion of the pipe when hot water is drawn into what was previously a cold pipe. The noise may be caused by the pipe rubbing against a beam or other structural member as it expands. If this occurs in an accessible location, a cure can be effected by wedging pieces of asbestos or other heat-resistant fabric between the pipe and the beam. Where this is impractical, the noise can usually be minimized by installation of a spiral expansion coil in the hot water line near the water heater in the basement or utility room. This coil consists of a long length of copper tubing wound into a fairly tight spiral and sealed off at one end. The other end is connected into the water line close to the heater by means of a suitable connecting tee. The operating principle is much like that of the anti-hammer air chamber just described.

Steam and hot water heating systems also may develop hammering or knocking noises under certain conditions. If this occurs in or near a radiator (particularly in a steam heating system), the trouble may be due to improper pitch of the radiator. If the radiator slopes the wrong way, accumulated condensation in the form of water will settle at the bottom instead of draining back down through the pipes. To correct this condition, the far end of the radiator (the end away from the inlet valve) should be shimmed up slightly so that the radiator tilts toward the valve. This will expedite drainage of condensed water at the bottom.

Another possible cause of trouble in hot water or steam heating systems is the valve on each radiator. These valves are designed for only one purpose: to turn the radiator off and on. They should never be partly open or partly closed; they should be turned on or off all the way. A partly open valve restricts flow of water or steam into the radiator and is a frequent cause of hammering or knocking noises in the system.

Pipes, Copper, Soldering and Joining

Copper pipe or tubing is used in many home water supply systems. This type of pipe is assembled with special fittings which are joined to the pipe with soldering techniques that are not difficult for the handyman to master.

Unlike threaded pipe, copper pipe requires no expensive tools or special equipment. This makes it much easier for amateurs to complete simple plumbing installations and to make needed repairs themselves. The only tools required are a propane gas torch, a fine-toothed hacksaw or tubing cutter, wire solder and flux, and some fine steel wool or emery cloth. Working techniques are comparatively simple, but there are a few simple precautions which must be observed if the soldered joints are to be leakproof and adequately strong.

To install a length of copper tubing, the handyman begins by first cutting the pipe to size, using either a fine-toothed hacksaw or one of

Steel wool can be used to clean surfaces to be soldered

A thin layer of soldering flux is spread on outside of pipe

the special tubing cutters which are sold for just this purpose. A small, half-round file is used to remove all burrs and ragged edges from the end of the tubing. A piece of fine steel wool or a strip of emery cloth is then used to polish the end of this tubing until the part that goes inside the fitting is bright and shining.

This polishing or cleaning operation is extremely important because cleanliness is absolutely essential for any properly soldered joint. In addition to cleaning the outside of the pipe, the inside of the fitting must be cleaned and polished in the same way. A thin layer of soldering flux is then smeared over the outside of the tubing and on the inside of the fitting to which it will be joined. The two parts should be pressed together and the pieces twisted slightly to make certain that the flux is evenly distributed around the inside of the joint.

While the pipe and fitting are supported in the position required, the flame is moved over and concentrated on the fitting exclusively. It should be aimed away from the point where the pipe enters the fitting, concentrating the heat on the heaviest part of the fitting itself. After a minute or two the pipe should be hot enough so that the solder will melt on contact with the hot metal, without the flame being aimed directly at the solder. When hot enough, capillary action will draw the molten solder into the joint so that little or none remains on the ouside.

Experienced plumbers usually find it more convenient to bend the last inch or two of their solder at right angles to form a sort of hook in the end. This makes it easier to move the end of the solder around the entire circumference of the opening, so that solder will be drawn uniformly in on all sides. The bent end also provides a simple method of gauging the amount of solder which has gone into the joint. Only an inch or so is required for a tight fit. Too much solder may build up on the inside and create an obstruction which will cut down on the flow of water.

If the solder does not melt instantly on contact with the metal, the joint has not been heated enough. If it melts, but is not drawn into the joint quickly, the center of the fitting is not hot enough, or the metal has not been properly cleaned on the inside. As soon as solder has been sucked in around all sides, the flame should be removed and excess metal wiped away from the outside with a piece of steel wool or heavy cloth.

When a second joint must be soldered close to a previously finished one, difficulty may be encountered with transmitted heat which will tend to loosen up the solder in the first joint. To avoid this, fittings can be wrapped with a wet rag to keep them cool while heat is applied nearby. Keep the flame aimed away from the finished section and keep it moving steadily around the circumference of the tube so as to heat the new joint as quickly as possible.

When assembling T-joints or elbows, the handyman will find it easier to fit all pieces of pipe in place at one time, then solder the two or three connections simultaneously. In other words, heat need only be applied

Joint is heated by pointing the flame at the fitting

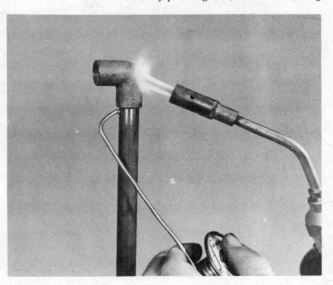

to the fitting once, then solder is flowed rapidly into each side of the elbow or tee so that all connections are made at once.

Pipes, Leaking, How to Repair

When leaks develop in a water pipe, prompt action is usually required to prevent extensive damage. Obviously, the first step that should be taken is to stop the flow of water by closing the appropriate supply valve. If in doubt about which valve to close, the homeowner can shut off the main valve which is located next to the water meter—usually in the basement or utility room.

Since it is impractical and inconvenient to leave the water turned off any longer than absolutely necessary, it is imperative that repairs of this kind be made as quickly as possible. If a plumber can be located (and induced to come over immediately), the situation can, of course, be cleared up quickly. However, when leaks occur on weekends or holidays, or when every plumber in the neighborhood seems to be busy, then the homeowner may find it necessary to make temporary repairs himself.

In most cases, only a few simple tools and materials will be required, and in many instances the repair can be a permanent affair which will last indefinitely. If the leak is in a pipe located inside the wall, floor or

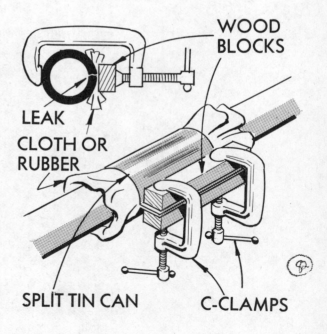

WOOD
BLOCKS

LEAK

CLOTH OR
RUBBER

SPLIT TIN CAN   C-CLAMPS

ceiling, the enclosure will have to be ripped open first to enable the handyman to locate the source of trouble. (A plumber would have to do this anyway, so there is no need to hesitate about this part of the job.)

For a really quick, emergency repair, an ordinary C-clamp can be used (as shown in the drawing). Pressure can be applied to the leak by using a small block of wood and a rubber gasket. A pipe clamp can also be improvised from sheet metal and held in place with the clamp as shown. This may not stop the leak completely, but it will allow use of the pipe till a more permanent repair can be made.

In many cases a temporary repair can also be made with ordinary plastic tape wrapped around the outside of the pipe. This will work on simple pinhole leaks, but the outside of the pipe should be dried off completely to give the tape a chance to stick before the water is turned back on. For best results, wrap the tape spirally so that each turn overlaps the adjoining one, and apply at last two or three layers over the leaky section.

Homeowners who are reasonably handy can usually make a permanent repair by replacing the defective length of pipe completely. The usual method for doing this is to cut through the center to break the pipe in two. Both halves are then unscrewed and replaced with two shorter sections. These can then be joined with a union in the center.

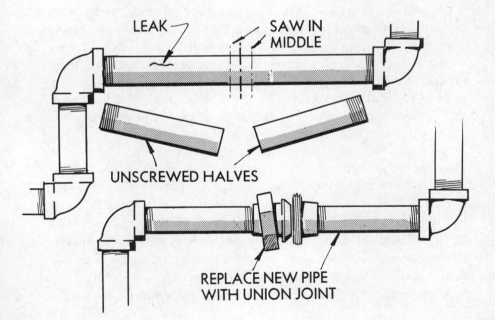

LEAK

SAW IN MIDDLE

UNSCREWED HALVES

REPLACE NEW PIPE WITH UNION JOINT

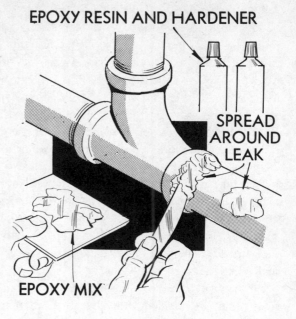

EPOXY RESIN AND HARDENER

SPREAD AROUND LEAK

EPOXY MIX

This type of fitting permits the handyman to screw the two pipe lengths in place first, then connect them together in the center. In most communities, lengths of pipe can be purchased already threaded at both ends so that no cutting or threading by the home handyman will be required.

Another simple method for making permanent repairs on leaky joints and fittings is to use an epoxy patching compound. These two-part plastic resins will adhere to copper, steel, brass and other metals, and they harden overnight to form a permanent repair which will easily withstand normal household water pressures. Directions on the container give mixing and application instructions, but for a secure bond it is imperative that the surface of the pipe be absolutely clean and dry before the patching material is applied.

Epoxy patching materials also can be used to repair leaks which occur along the length of the pipe. For a pinhole leak, simply drain the pipe dry, rub the metal clean with steel wool, then smear on a liberal application of the compound. For larger patches or cracks, the hole can be covered with fiber-glass patching material with the epoxy applied under and over it to form a laminated patch which will last indefinitely. Kits containing the fiber glass and the necessary resins are available in most hardware and auto and marine supply stores.

Another relatively permanent repair can be made with a commercial

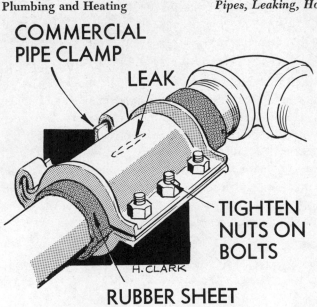

COMMERCIAL
PIPE CLAMP

LEAK

TIGHTEN
NUTS ON
BOLTS

H. CLARK

RUBBER SHEET

pipe clamp similar to the one illustrated. The hole is covered with sheet rubber (a piece of old inner tube or rubber matting works well), after which the clamp is applied and tightened securely. If a clamp of this kind is not readily available, a similar repair can be made by slitting a length of larger-diameter pipe so as to form two halves which will fit over the outside of the leaking pipe. This can be held in place with hose clamps or tightly wrapped wire after first wrapping the leaky pipe with rubber as described above.

One of the most common leaks is the type which occurs at a threaded joint. In many cases this can be corrected simply by tightening the fitting slightly, using two wrenches. One should be applied to the fitting to hold it stationary while the other one is used to turn the pipe. Though by turning the pipe you will be unscrewing the opposite end from another fitting, a slight turn will often stop the leak without loosening the other end sufficiently to cause additional trouble.

Leaks of this kind can be cured permanently by unscrewing the fitting entirely. The threads can then be coated with pipe-joint compound and wrapped with fine twine or heavy thread before reassembling. Sometimes compound alone will do the trick, but the string or thread provides an added filler which will swell when wet and help to stop leaks that might otherwise develop.

When leaks develop in soldered connections in copper tubing or pipe, this usually means that the solder on the inside has cracked or loosened. This type of leak can be repaired by heating the joint with a torch to melt the old solder and then applying new solder to the fitting.

Before tackling a repair of this kind, the handyman should make certain that all water is drained out of the pipe; otherwise, dangerous steam pressures could be built up. In addition, a slight amount of water on the inside will keep the fitting from heating up properly and will interfere with effective soldering. Heat should be directed at the center of the fitting until it is hot enough to melt the solder when it is touched against the outside of the pipe. The molten solder is drawn into the fitting by capillary action when the joint is hot enough.

Pipes, Noisy. SEE NOISY PLUMBING, HOW TO CURE.

Pipes, Plastic

Using flexible plastic pipe which is sold in coils up to 100 feet in length, any homeowner can now bring the convenience of running water to his outdoor patio or terrace or to any other part of his yard or garden. Frequently used for underground lawn sprinkling systems and suitable for any outdoor use where cold water is needed, this pipe is ideal for do-it-your-selfers who would like to install a backyard shower, drinking fountain, lawn sprinkling system or additional faucet.

Though there are many different types and sizes of plastic pipe available, the most popular variety for home use is flexible polyethylene pipe which has an inside diameter of ½, ¾ or 1 inch. This pipe is extremely light in weight, and it can be cut with an ordinary sharp knife or a fine-toothed hacksaw blade. To connect the pipe, a wide variety of elbows, tees, connectors and other fittings of rigid polyethylene are available. These have serrated nipples that form a press fit inside the pipe. The connection is made watertight and permanent by stainless steel clamps which are wrapped around the outside of the pipe. The clamps are easily tightened with an ordinary screwdriver or wrench and they make a tight joint which can be buried directly underground without loosening.

When ordinary metal pipe is buried underground, care must be taken in the wintertime to drain the water out before temperatures drop below freezing. Otherwise, pipe and fittings would rupture as freezing water on the inside expanded. However, with plastic pipe no such precautions

Plastic pipe is light
in weight and comes
in coils

*Full selection of plastic fittings is
available*

*Serrated fitting
hooks pipes together
when fastened with
metal clamps*

are necessary. Since the pipe is flexible and not damaged by freezing, it does not have to be drained in the winter. This means that plastic pipe need only be buried a few inches below the surface—or just deep enough to protect the pipe against accidental damage by digging or cultivation at some time in the future.

To connect plastic pipe to the existing household water lines, there are a number of special adapter fittings available. These are threaded at one end to fit connections on standard threaded pipe, while the other end has a serrated fitting to accept the plastic pipe. Adapters are available in straight or elbow form, and they come in sizes to fit all standard pipes. There are also adapters available to fit on the outside of a standard hose faucet (these have a female garden hose thread) when connection is to be made directly to an existing outdoor faucet.

For a more permanent connection, the existing hose faucet should be removed entirely and replaced with a matching metal (threaded) tee and the old faucet then screwed back into one end of the tee. The plastic pipe adapter is then screwed into the other leg of the tee. This will enable the homeowner to use his old garden hose faucet in the normal way, while giving him a permanent connection for his plastic pipe. To permit him to shut off the water supply to the plastic pipe, a valve can be installed at some point just below the new metal tee.

Since polyethylene pipe is currently made for cold water use only, it cannot be used where hot water must be carried. If the pipe is to be used to carry water for drinking or cooking, the homeowner should make certain he purchases a brand which bears the seal of approval of the National Sanitation Foundation. Pipes which do not bear this seal have not been approved for drinking water, so they may impart impurities to the water which would make it unfit for human consumption.

Pipes, Sweating

Cold water pipes which "sweat" and drip on hot, humid days can be a nuisance in basements and other indoor areas where piping is exposed. This condition is not only messy, but can cause pipes and fittings to corrode and can cause damage to household articles which are stored nearby.

While adequate ventilation will help alleviate a condition of this kind, the only sure cure lies in covering the pipes with a moistureproof insulating material of some kind. This covering will keep the warm, humid air from coming in contact with the cold metal pipes, thus preventing condensation and subsequent dripping.

To provide complete protection, the wrapping or covering used should not only be a good insulator, it should also incorporate a vaporproof covering which will keep the material from becoming saturated with moisture. There are a number of materials which can be used, and practically all of them can easily be applied by any homeowner without special tools or equipment.

Pipe covers for use in the home generally fall into one of three classifi-

Paper tape is wrapped over fiberglass insulation

cations: a ribbon- or tapelike material which is wrapped spirally around the pipe; a flexible, foamed plastic tube which fits over the outside of the pipe and a thick mastic compound which is simply spread on over the surface of the pipe.

The most widely sold type, and the one most often used by do-it-yourselfers, is the wrap-on insulating tape. Two varieties are currently available. One is made of fiber glass, while the other consists of several ribbons of a sticky plastic-cork compound in roll form. The fiber-glass insulation comes with a separate vapor-sealing tape which must be wrapped on afterward to provide the needed vapor barrier. The plastic-cork wrapping needs no separate vapor seal since it will not absorb moisture and is waterproof by itself.

When applying these wrap-on types of insulating materials, you start at one end of each length of pipe and wrap the material loosely around the outside for several feet. The coils are then pushed tightly together before proceeding. In the case of the plastic-cork type, the material can simply be pressed against itself with your hands in order to make it stick. The fiber glass is held in place by a vapor-barrier tape which is wrapped around the outside. In both cases additional short pieces should be installed around the outside of valves, elbows and other fittings to keep the covering continuous.

Both of these wrap-on pipe covers are sold through hardware stores, lumberyards and plumbing supply dealers. Though costs vary for different-sized pipes, you can figure on spending somewhere between $1.25 and $1.75 for each 10-foot length of ½-inch-diameter pipe that must be covered.

Foamed plastic tubing for covering pipes costs more than the wrap-on

Insulated covering of foamed plastic is slit open on one side

*Insulating mastic can be brushed on
over pipes and tank*

tapes. However, the finished job is generally neater-looking, and the material is somewhat quicker to install. Available in sizes to fit either galvanized pipe or copper tubing, this material can be purchased in some hardware stores and from many plumbing and heating supply dealers. Average cost will run somewhere between 30 and 40 cents per running foot for the most commonly used sizes.

To install this material over an existing pipe line, the foamed plastic tube must be slit lengthwise so it can be slid into place over the pipe. (On new installations the foam covering is pulled on over the pipe like a sleeve.) After the plastic tube is in place, the slit, or open seam is permanently sealed by use of a special adhesive or by strips of ordinary masking tape. The plastic is flexible enough to permit bending around corners. However, mitered joints should be cut where the covering has to fit over elbows or similar fittings. Short pieces can be cut to size and taped or cemented together to form separate covers for valves and similar fittings.

For covering the outside of large-diameter pipes, cold water tanks and similar surfaces which may be subject to condensation, there is also a mastic compound that can be applied. A brush or trowel can be used, or it can be smeared on with the bare hands. Available in 1-gallon cans (which will cover approximately 6 square feet), this thick mastic coating is applied like plaster in layers at least ¼-inch thick.

An ordinary whisk broom is the most satisfactory kind of brush to use on tanks and large pipes. Small-diameter pipes can be most easily coated by spreading the material on with the bare hands. While still damp, the material can be easily washed off (or thinned if necessary) with water. Like the mastic tape, this coating requires no separate vapor seal since it will not absorb moisture.

Radiators. SEE HEATING SYSTEM MAINTENANCE.

Septic Tanks. SEE CESSPOOLS AND SEPTIC TANKS.
Care of.

Toilet Tank Repairs

Though the flush tank which is mounted on the wall behind most home toilets seems quite complicated at first glance when the mechanism on the inside is examined, it is actually a fairly simply contraption which is no more difficult to repair than an ordinary faucet.

Basically, every flush tank mechanism consists of two control valves. The levers and other parts merely serve to open or close these valves at the proper time. At the bottom of the tank there is the flush valve seat. This is kept closed by a rubber flush ball. When the handle on the outside of the tank is pressed down, it raises a trip lever. This in turn pulls the lift wire and ball stem upward, lifting the rubber flush ball off its seat. The water inside the tank then pours out through this large opening to flush out the toilet bowl.

The rubber flush ball was originally held in place against its seat by water pressure which was pressing down on it. However, once lifted upward by the lift wire it floats to the top of the water and remains there as the water level sinks. As the tank empties, the flush ball gradually settles back onto its seat to seal up the opening tightly once more so that the tank can refill with water.

The refilling operation is controlled by a second valve mechanism called the inlet valve or ballcock. As the water level inside the tank was dropping, the hollow metal or plastic float ball was also dropping, pulling the float arm down with it. This arm opens the inlet valve inside the ballcock and permits water from the supply line to pour into the tank through the refill tube.

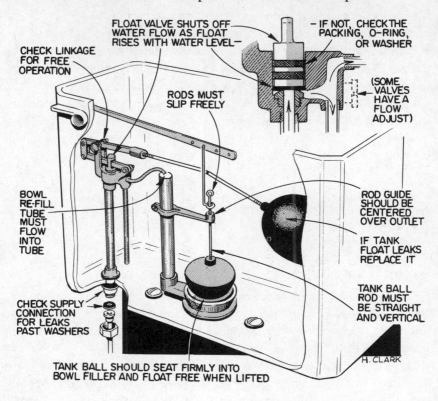

CHECK LINKAGE FOR FREE OPERATION

FLOAT VALVE SHUTS OFF WATER FLOW AS FLOAT RISES WITH WATER LEVEL—

– IF NOT, CHECK THE PACKING, O-RING, OR WASHER

RODS MUST SLIP FREELY

(SOME VALVES HAVE A FLOW ADJUST)

BOWL RE-FILL TUBE MUST FLOW INTO TUBE

ROD GUIDE SHOULD BE CENTERED OVER OUTLET

IF TANK FLOAT LEAKS REPLACE IT

CHECK SUPPLY CONNECTION FOR LEAKS PAST WASHERS

TANK BALL ROD MUST BE STRAIGHT AND VERTICAL

H. CLARK

TANK BALL SHOULD SEAT FIRMLY INTO BOWL FILLER AND FLOAT FREE WHEN LIFTED

As the rising water forces the float ball upward, it gradually shuts off the inlet valve until the flow of water is stopped entirely when the tank is full. If this valve fails to operate properly, the water does not shut off at the right time. The excess water then flows out through the overflow pipe which sticks up vertically on the inside. A refill tube which replaces water in the toilet bowl after it has been flushed also squirts a small stream of water through this overflow pipe while the bowl is flushing. This refills the trap built into the waste pipe to keep sewer gases from escaping into the house.

If, after flushing, water continues running from the tank into the bowl, yet the tank does not refill properly, the trouble is in the rubber flush ball valve. In most cases the flush ball will be worn so that it does not seat properly against the flush valve seat. Since it is made of rubber, it eventually becomes spongy or ragged and replacement becomes necessary.

To replace this ball, first shut off the water supply to the toilet tank.

If this is inconvenient, the same effect can be achieved by tying the float ball arm as high as it will go, using a piece of string tied to an overhead object. This will keep the inlet valve closed so that it will not refill when the tank is emptied. Empty the tank by flushing, then hold the ball stem in one hand and unscrew the ball from its lower end with your hand. Before replacing with a new one, clean off the exposed metal valve seat by rubbing lightly with a piece of fine steel wool. If the threaded stem rod on which the ball fits is corroded or bent, it may be a good idea also to install a new ball stem at the same time.

The water can now be turned back on so that the entire flushing operation can be checked. If the new ball does not seat properly after the tank has emptied, it may not be centered properly over its opening at the bottom. This can be caused by a bent ball stem rod or by a stem guide which is slightly out of alignment. If the stem is bent, it's best to replace it. If the stem guide is out of alignment, it can easily be adjusted. Loosen the set screw which holds it in place, then jiggle the guide back and forth until it causes the ball to drop directly onto the center of the seat. Then tighten it permanently in this position.

When a tank fills properly after it is flushed, yet water continues to pour in until it runs out through the overflow pipe, the trouble is in the float mechanism or in the inlet valve which it controls. Try lifting up on the float arm slightly with one finger. If this stops the hissing noise and shuts off the flow of water, the float ball is leaking and needs replacing or the float arm needs adjusting.

Unscrew the float ball from the end of its arm and shake it to see whether there is any water on the inside. If there is, the ball is defective and must be replaced. If the ball is not leaky, the trouble is probably due to improper float arm adjustment. To correct this, bend the wire arm slightly downward in the middle so that the ball is about ½-inch lower inside the tank. Then turn the water on and try flushing again. This time the water should shut off when its level reaches to within about 1 inch from the top of the overflow pipe. If it still continues to rise, try bending the float arm a little lower.

If the previous test of pulling up on the float arm fails to shut off the flow of water, adjusting the float arm or replacing the ball will be of no avail. The trouble is then in the ballcock itself. The washer on the inside may be worn or the plunger may be clogged with rust and dirt. To dis-assemble most models, there are two thumbscrews or pins which must be pulled out first. These release the entire float arm mechanism, includ-ing the attached linkage at the top of the ballcock. The stem and plunger can then be lifted out to expose a leather washer at the bottom of the plunger. This washer may be a force fit in its recess, or it may be held in place by a single screw in the center. Most models also have an additional washer or O-ring which fits into a groove around the body of the plunger. To play safe, this ring-shaped washer should be replaced at the same time.

If the entire ballcock mechanism is so badly corroded that parts of it break while being handled or if the valve seat on the inside seems badly worn, the best bet is to replace the entire unit. Ballcocks cost only a few dollars, and a new one will assure trouble-free operation for many years to come. Hardware stores now sell improved modern versions which are completely silent in operation and which come complete with all necessary connecting fittings, as well as complete installation instructions.

VI

Electrical Repairs

MAJOR ELECTRICAL REPAIRS, such as those which involve working on house wiring inside the walls, should always be left to the services of a licensed electrician—unless you are exceptionally experienced in this field. However, minor repairs, such as replacing frayed cords, broken plugs or defective switches, can safely be tackled by any home mechanic, provided elementary precautions are observed and you are at least moderately familiar with how your household electrical system functions.

When a fuse blows, the trouble may be due to one of two causes: a short has developed or the circuit has been overloaded. When a short develops because of a defect in an appliance or because of frayed insulation on one of the wires, current flows directly from one leg of the circuit to the other without the resistance normally encountered in the light or appliance. This overloads the wires and causes the fuse to blow. (See FUSES AND CIRCUIT BREAKERS.)

An overload occurs when too many appliances or lights are plugged into a single circuit. This draws more current than the wires can safely carry, so the fuse blows to prevent damage to the wiring. This problem (overloading) is particularly prevalent in older homes where homeowners keep adding appliances to antiquated wiring systems that are already overworked. Experts have estimated that three out of five houses are inadequately wired, either because of an insufficient number of circuits or because the main service entrance is not large enough to supply the amount of power required. This condition also may be encountered in newer homes where a house has been wired with circuits that are barely adequate to handle today's needs, without allowing for the additional equipment that probably will be installed later on.

To understand the problems that may be encountered, you can liken the electrical wires to a series of pipe lines in the plumbing system. Just as each pipe is large enough to carry only a certain amount of water under a given amount of pressure, so too is an electrical wire only adequate to carry a given amount of current (amperes) under a given amount of voltage (pressure). The number of watts used by any appliance is the product of the amperes it draws multiplied by the voltage under which this amperage is supplied. For example, a household appliance which draws 5 amperes at 110 volts would be drawing a total of 550 watts.

Since a given wire can carry only a certain number of watts safely without overheating, it is easy to understand why house circuits must be divided up to distribute the load so that no one circuit carries more than its maximum safe capacity.

Lighting and general-purpose circuits throughout the house are usually designed to carry 15 or 20 amperes and are intended only for use with lights and small portable appliances. Major appliances which draw considerable amounts of power (especially motor-driven appliances which have a high starting load) are best supplied by separate circuits. This includes furnaces, large air conditioners, refrigerators and similar pieces of equipment. Since the fuse or circuit breaker in each circuit is designed to "blow" when the wires are overloaded, it is easy to understand how dangerous the practice of installing a larger fuse can be. Instead of the fuse blowing, the wires can melt or overheat—a common cause of fire.

The addition of more circuits is practical only if an adequate service entrance has already been installed. Thus, a 60-ampere fuse box and main switch can provide only a total of 60 amperes of current. If more current is needed, the addition of more circuits inside the house will in no way alleviate this condition. Instead, the homeowner must plan on having a larger service entrance installed. A larger box may also be required when an existing fuse box does not have enough room for additional circuits.

When new wiring is contemplated, or when planning wiring for a new addition to the house, the homeowner should see to it that plenty of outlets are installed so that long extension cords will not be required and so that multiple use of a single outlet will not become necessary. In addition, the outlets in each room should be divided up wherever practical so that all the outlets are not on one fuse. Then if one fuse blows, the entire room will not be plunged into darkness. This is particularly advisable in upstairs bedrooms, as well as in basement playrooms and other areas where sudden darkness may pose a serious safety hazard.

In addition to providing for adequate outlets, the homeowner should plan his wiring so that there will be adequate switches installed in all passageways. These should permit turning lights on and off throughout the house without need for walking through darkened rooms or hallways. Three- or four-way switches will be required in most cases at either end of a hallway, as well as at the top and bottom of each flight of stairs.

Appliance Care and Repair

Manufacturers of home appliances usually recommend that their products be returned to an authorized service center when repairs become necessary or when replacement parts are needed, and this is generally a good rule for the homeowner to follow. However, in many cases the trouble is not caused by an actual breakdown in the appliance itself. It may be caused by a defective cord, plug or switch or by a simple lack of proper cleaning or lubrication.

When an appliance fails to operate after it has been plugged into a wall outlet, the first thing that should be checked is to make certain that the outlet itself is actually "hot." A blown fuse or defective receptacle may be at fault, so this should be checked by trying the appliance in more than one outlet or by testing with a lamp which is known to be in operating condition.

Assuming that the current supply or wall outlet is not at fault, the next most likely source of trouble might be the appliance plug or cord or any switches that may be built into the unit. Examine the plug first. If its prongs are badly bent, corroded or loose, chances are that a new plug will be required. Wiggle the wires around while pushing them in and out at the point where they enter the plug body. See whether the insulation is cracked or worn, and make certain the wires are still firmly connected on the inside. Bear in mind that a loose connection will cause arcing or sparking each time the wire is jiggled. This will not only interfere with proper operation of the appliance, but may create a dangerous fire hazard.

When a new cord or plug is required, the cord should be connected to the plug by tying an Underwriters' knot on the inside as shown. This relieves strain on the cord to keep it from being pulled off the terminal screws when the cord is yanked or when someone accidentally trips over it. Make certain you wrap the bared ends of the wire around the terminal screws in a clockwise direction so that the wires will get tighter as the screw is tightened. Also make certain no bared ends protrude where an accidental short could occur.

Some appliances, such as electric irons and frying pans, have a female appliance plug at the other end of the cord to connect the cord with the appliance. These flat appliance plugs are subject to considerable abuse and they can cause shorts or breakdowns which may be blamed on the appliance itself. The drawing shows the danger points to check and illustrates how the wires are connected to the terminal screws on each female prong. It is important when reassembling this plug that the spring guard be properly replaced where the cord leaves the plug body. This keeps the cord from kinking or wearing out prematurely.

Once cords and plugs have been eliminated, the next most common source of trouble is the switch. Since the switch, if there is one, is usually built into the casing or housing in some way, it probably will be necessary to remove the outer covering or housing of the appliance in order to expose the switch. Do this before you plug in the appliance. When the switch has been exposed, you can try shorting it out by temporarily connecting wires across the terminals so that the switch is no longer in the circuit. Then try plugging the appliance in to see whether it works. If so, the old switch is defective and a new one should be purchased and installed. Small switches of various kinds are available from many

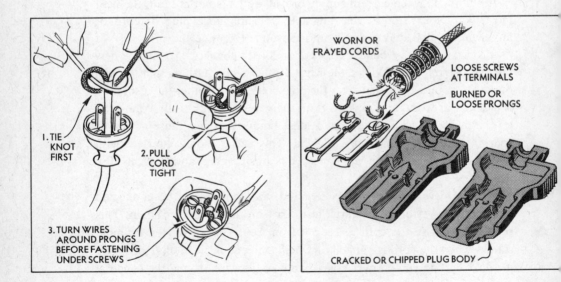

hardware dealers and electrical supply stores, or an identical unit can be ordered from the original manufacturer.

In addition to the switch—or perhaps instead of it—many appliances have contact points of various types located in the terminal box or terminal section where the wires enter the appliance. These contact points may be the two parts of the thermal control which turns the appliance on and off automatically (such as the thermostat in an electric frying pan) or they may simply be the points of contact where a manual switching lever turns the unit on or off. In any event, when these contact points become loose or dirty, they arc each time the circuit is closed. This arcing eventually builds up a heavy oxidized coating which interferes with the flow of current. In most cases the points can be restored by cleaning with very fine emery cloth or steel wool, or with a small, thin file.

Motor-driven appliances are susceptible to troubles caused by accumulation of dirt on rotating parts, as well as by lack of proper lubrication. The original instruction manuals should be studied (and filed for future reference) to determine what lubrication and other maintenance is required. (See MOTORS, CARE AND REPAIR.) Remember that most electrical appliances give off heat, and this means that they need adequate ventilation. Vents should never be allowed to remain clogged with dirt or food particles, and water should never be allowed on the

To keep sewing machine in top working order, periodic oiling is
necessary

inside unless specifically mentioned in the manufacturer's instructions.

In heating-type appliances, a frequent cause of trouble is a break in the heating element or coil. If the handyman is reasonably capable, he will find that in most cases it is not at all difficult to disassemble the appliance and install a new heating element himself, but he should make certain that the replacement unit is the one recommended by the original manufacturer. Before assuming that the entire heating element is at fault, the handyman should check the terminal points where the wire ends connect up with the regular appliance cord. A loose connection or broken wire at this point may be the cause of the trouble, instead of the heating element.

Doorbell, Installing Extra

Many homeowners have discovered that the original, centrally located doorbell or chimes cannot be heard in some parts of the house. To solve this problem, an additional bell or buzzer can easily be installed. The wiring job can safely be tackled by any home handyman because of the low voltages involved.

Wires for the additional doorbell or chime can be spliced into the circuit right at the terminals on the existing bell. Take the cover off the bell or buzzer and loosen up each of the exposed terminal screws without removing the original wires. New lengths of wire, to operate the additional bell, can then be attached to these same terminals without disturbing any of the original wiring.

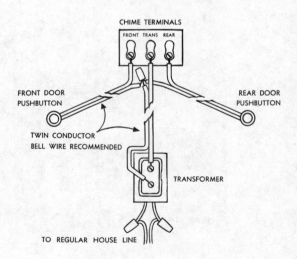

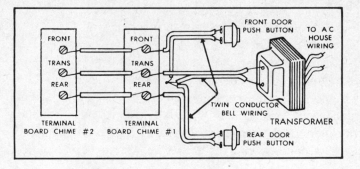

These wires must now be extended to the part of the house where the new bell is to be located. If it is to be installed in the basement, the wire can be run down to the floor along the edge of a nearby door frame or in a corner of the room. If there is a closet on the wall behind the bell, the wires can be concealed by drilling a hole through the wall and then bringing the wires down on the inside of the closet. A small hole is then drilled through the floor as close to the baseboard molding as possible. Feed the wire down through this opening and extend it along the joists below to the place where the new bell or buzzer is to be installed.

When the wires must be extended to the upper floors of the house, a hole will have to be drilled through some part of the ceiling. In most cases a nearby closet or stairway can be used to conceal the wires. Once brought to the floor upstairs, the wire can be stapled along the baseboards till it reaches the desired location.

Homes which have push buttons at both the front and the rear doors usually have a combination bell-buzzer (bell rings for the front door, buzzer for the back door) or a two-signal chime (two notes for the front door, one note for the back door). To add an extension to one of these units, three-conductor bell wire (or three single strands of one-conductor bell wire) must be used.

On removing the cover plate, you will notice that the combination bell-buzzer, or the two-tone chime, has three terminals instead of two. Loosen the three screws and insert one end of each of the three new wires under them. Then extend these wires in the manner previously described to the location where the new bell-buzzer or chime will be installed.

When you are hooking up these wires, care must be exercised to attach each wire correctly. The wire that is attached to the terminal marked "Rear" on the old unit must be attached to the same terminal on the new unit. In the same way, the other two wires must be attached to matching terminals on both sets of chimes or bell-buzzers.

If three-conductor bell wire (available at electrical supply houses only) is used, this job is comparatively simple. Each of the three wires has a different-colored insulation, so that all the homeowner has to do is attach the same colors to each matching terminal. If three-conductor bell wire is unobtainable and three strands of similarly colored single-conductor wire must be used, the homeowner will have to code each one ahead of time by coloring opposite ends of each wire with dabs of colored paint, tape or crayon.

The addition of an extra set of chimes usually means that a larger capacity transformer will be required. Check the voltage capacity of your present transformer (this is marked on the name plate) and give this figure to your dealer when purchasing a new set of chimes. He will be able to tell you whether a larger transformer will be required. In most cases, a 16- or 20-volt transformer is the minimum necessary to operate two sets of chimes satisfactorily.

These transformers are usually mounted on one side of the main fuse box or onto a board or panel nearby. However, they may also be mounted on the outside of any convenient junction box somewhere in the unfinished part of the basement. Either way, before attempting to disconnect this transformer, remember to *first shut off the power* by pulling the appropriate fuse or by shutting off all current at the main control panel.

The job of installing a new transformer is not a difficult one for the handyman experienced in doing electrical work around the house. Carefully observe the method by which the original transformer was mounted and, after disconnecting the old one, put the new one on in exactly the same manner. The two heavy wire leads on one side are spliced to the "live" wires (which supply the power) in the junction box or fuse box. The threaded terminals on the other side will be plainly marked, indicating that they are the low-voltage connections to which the bell wire will be fastened.

Since installation of this transformer involves working with 115-volt house wiring, inexperienced handymen who are not fully familiar with this type of electrical work would be better off calling in a licensed electrical contractor for this part of the job.

Doorbell Repairs

A basic knowledge of how the doorbell, or chime, circuit works will be helpful to the homeowner interested in servicing his own. The accompanying diagrams illustrate in simplified form the two most common circuits. One shows a single bell, or buzzer, controlled by a front button only; the other shows a two-way chime, or combination bell-buzzer, which can be rung from either a front or back door button and which gives a different signal for each.

If the bell or chime refuses to ring at all when the button is pushed, there are several things that could be wrong. The most frequent cause

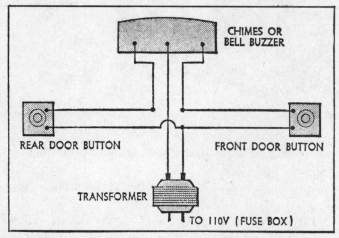

TWO-WAY—Circuit above gives signal from either button.

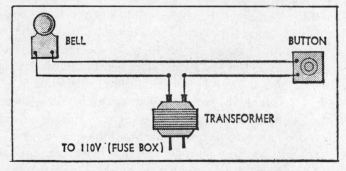

BELL—Circuit above gives signal from front door only.

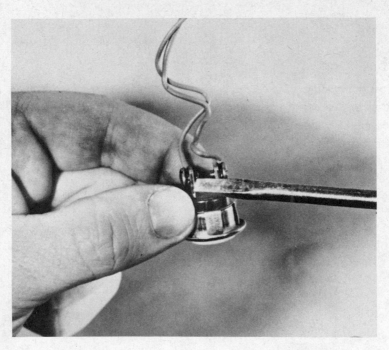

Testing doorbell push button by shorting terminals with screwdriver

of trouble is a faulty push button or loose connection, so start by checking this first. Remove the push button by unscrewing the mounting screws which hold it in place. Then check the wire connections in back to make certain they are tight.

If the terminal screws are tight but the bell still fails to ring, try shorting out the button by bridging the terminal screws with a scrap piece of wire or a bent paper clip. Or the wires can be disconnected entirely and the bared ends touched together instead. If the bell now rings, the trouble is in the button and a new one should be purchased and installed.

If shorting the wires fails to make the bell ring, the power supply should be checked next. Some older houses still use dry cells or batteries, but in most modern homes a transformer is wired into the household circuit to supply the necessary power. This is usually located in the basement alongside or on the main fuse box. Check the house fuses and the particular one which controls the transformer circuit first.

If the fuses seem all right, test the transformer to make certain that power is being delivered on its secondary side (this is the side which has the two small-diameter wires coming out to feed the bell or chime circuit). *Never* touch the heavy primary wires which connect the transformer with the fuse box or outlet box on which it is mounted. These large wires carry the 110-volt current from the house line and can give a serious shock if improperly handled.

To test the transformer, press a clean screwdriver or shiny nail briefly across the secondary terminals so that both terminals are touched at the same time. Small sparks indicate that the transformer is active and delivering power. An alternate and more positive method of checking the transformer consists of connecting a small 6-volt lamp across the terminals to see whether the lamp lights.

If the transformer seems to be operating and delivering current satisfactorily and if the push button test has indicated no trouble at that point, the next most likely source of trouble is at the doorbell or chime itself. Check for loose connections first by seeing whether all wires are connected and all terminal screws tight. Then try the push button again.

If the bell still fails to ring, check for dirt in the mechanism or for sticking parts. In the case of a bell or buzzer, the contact points may be dirty or pitted and a light brushing with fine sandpaper is all that will be needed. In the case of chimes, check the small steel rods which are supposed to move freely up and down to strike the chime bar. These may be stuck or clogged with dust, thus preventing their operating properly.

On some rare occasions, when the push button, power supply and doorbell or chime are all in good order, the trouble may be caused by a break in the wiring itself. Assuming there is power coming from the transformer (tested previously as described above), inspect as much of the wiring as is visible to check for breaks or broken connections. In most modern homes, all wires from the two buttons, the transformer and the chimes will meet at one central junction point where all splices can be examined simultaneously. Broken connections may sometimes be discovered at this point.

If the break in the wiring cannot be discovered by visual inspection, rig up a 6-volt test lamp with short wires attached to check the wiring in sections. At intervals, starting at the transformer and working up toward the bell or chimes, scrape a small bare spot in the wire or use a pin to puncture the insulation. Touch exposed spots with the two short leads from the test lamp to see whether the light goes on. When it fails to light, you will know that the broken wire has just been passed and that the length just tested needs to be replaced. When in doubt, or when the defective wire is hidden in the wall, the safest procedure is to install a completely new length of bell wire (of the same size and capacity as the old) from the transformer to the bell or chimes. The job of fishing this new wire through walls or floors can be simplified by attaching the new wire to the end of the old wire and then drawing the new one through as you pull the old one out.

When a bell rings continuously, or when a chime keeps on humming, a short circuit is indicated in the push button or in the push button leg of the circuit. First check to make certain the button itself isn't stuck, then disconnect the power source and check the wiring to find the place where insulation has been rubbed off or where wires are improperly contacting each other. If the trouble is due to faulty wiring inside the wall, replace with new wire as previously described.

Extension Cords, Selection and Use

When a lamp, power tool or portable household appliance must be used at some distance from the nearest electrical outlet, a flexible extension cord is usually used to extend the reach of the existing cord. If the wrong kind of cord is used—or if the right kind of cord is improperly used—a potential hazard is created.

Extension cords not only vary according to length and capacity (capacity is determined by the size wire they contain), they may also vary as to the conveniences they offer and the jobs which they will perform. Basically speaking, all cords are flexible connectors which contain two or three rubber-coated conduction wires. To make them fully flexible, the conductor wires usually consist of a series of fine strands of wire twisted together, rather than of solid metal.

Practically all of the homeowner's extension cord needs will be filled by one of three general types of cord: a heavy-duty rubber-coated cord (often referred to as type S) which is used for outdoor work or wherever heavy wear is expected; a thin, flat, rubber-coated lamp cord (usually called rip cord) which is used for small appliances and lamps and the special heating unit cords which usually have an asbestos covering.

To make certain that an extension cord has been approved for dependability and safety, the homeowner should look for the Underwriters' Laboratories inspection tag (UL) on all parts—that is, on plug, connector and cord. In addition, there is a special flag label which bears the initals S.E.C.C. This indicates that the entire cord set as assembled has been inspected and approved by the Safe Electrical Cord Committee.

Just as adequate wiring is required in household branch circuits to avoid overloading these circuits and to prevent burning out of fuses, so too is it essential that the homeowner remember to use an extension cord which is adequate for the power load it must carry. This is particularly true of extension cords which have double or triple outlets at one end.

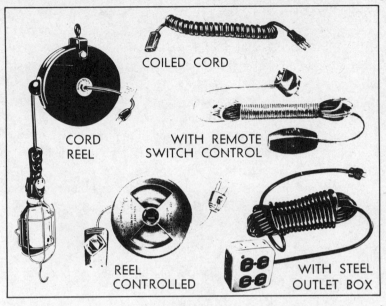

COILED CORD

CORD REEL

WITH REMOTE SWITCH CONTROL

REEL CONTROLLED

WITH STEEL OUTLET BOX

Some of the more popular types of extension cord

Remember that if several appliances or lights are plugged in at one time, and all are in use simultaneously, there is a good chance that the cord is being overloaded. This not only creates a fire hazard, but can cause breakdown of motor-driven appliances. The voltage drop which occurs can prevent the motor from getting sufficient power to operate properly.

Two factors affect the carrying capacity of any extension cord: the size wire it contains and the length of the cord. Ordinary light-duty lamp cord usually contains #18 wire, and it should never be used to carry power to heavy-duty power tools or appliances which draw more than 7 amperes. The ampere load of any appliance can usually be determined by studying the name plate which is attached to the appliance or tool.

If the ampere load is not indicated, remember that volts multiplied by amperes equal watts. Therefore, if the wattage is known, the ampere load can be determined. Simply divide by 110 (the household voltage). For example, a 750-watt appliance will be drawing just under 7 amperes.

Since long lengths of cord cause current-carrying capacity to drop, 18-gauge lamp cord wire will carry its full load of 7 amperes only for distances up to about 25 feet. If a longer cord is necessary, the wire must be thicker, meaning that at least #16 or #14 wire should be used. As a general rule, most experts recommend that #18 wire be used only for lamps and very small appliances, and then only for distances up to about 25 feet.

Heavier-duty (#16 or #14) wire should be used for motor-driven tools, electric hedge trimmers, shop motors and similar appliances. When cords 50 to 100 feet in length are required for powering tools around the outside of the house, make certain they are made of heavy-duty, 14-gauge wire. This will permit powering tools which draw up to 7 or 8 amperes (about ½ horsepower) without danger of overloading or of causing a damaging drop in voltage.

In addition to selecting the right type of approved cord for the job on hand, here are a number of other safety rules that should be observed whenever electrical extension cords are used:

(1) Never run cords over radiators, pipes or other ground metal. If heat or abrasion causes insulation to dry out and crack, a dangerous short circuit can occur.

Surface extension wiring is installed where permanent extensions are needed

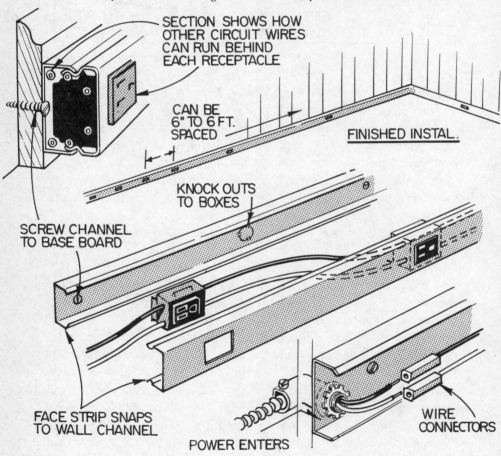

(2) Never allow cords to run under or over a door or under rugs. Continual opening and closing of the door or frequent stepping on the cord can cause damage to the insulation, often where it cannot easily be seen.

(3) Never yank a plug out of its socket by pulling on the cord. Instead, reach down and grab hold of the plug itself to remove it.

(4) Do not plug extension cords into a lamp socket. Always plug the extension directly into a convenient wall outlet. Lamp cords and sockets are not designed to carry much of a load.

(5) Repair or replace cords promptly when insulation becomes frayed or cracked. Also get into the habit of inspecting the cord carefully at frequent intervals to check for defects.

(6) Never use flexible extension cords to create additional "permanent" outlets by tacking or stapling them in place. This practice is extremely hazardous since insulation is easily damaged or cracked so that short circuits can occur.

When permanent extensions are required, use one of the new types of surface extension wiring instead. These contain heavy-duty, plastic-covered cables, receptacles, switches and other fixtures which are specifically designed for permanent mounting along walls or baseboards.

Fluorescent Lamps

Unlike an incandescent lamp, a fluorescent lamp has no filament which glows continuously to give light. Instead, the inside of the tube is filled with mercury vapor which is heated by special filaments at the tube end. This gas then transmits its energy to the phosphor coating inside the tube, and this is what glows to give visible light.

Because little or no energy is wasted in heat, fluorescent lamps give much more light per watt than incandescent lamps; therefore they are much more economical to use wherever a lot of light is needed for work or play. Under normal use a fluorescent lamp can be expected to give trouble-free illumination for anywhere from 2,000 to 3,000 hours of use.

Basically speaking, every fluorescent lighting fixture has only four important parts with which the homeowner need concern himself. There is the lamp itself, the two sockets which hold it (one at either end), the starter and the ballast. This last item (the ballast) is one which very seldom gives trouble. It is a transformer-like device which regulates the amount of current fed to the lamp and is usually concealed somewhere inside the fixture.

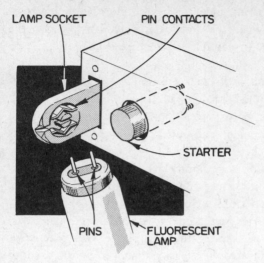

The life of a fluorescent lamp is greatly shortened by frequent turning on and off. A fluorescent tube wears out when the active material inside is used up. This is consumed at a much faster rate during the initial starting and blinking operation than it is during continuous use.

Since steady blinking wears tubes out much more quickly, it is important that the troubles which cause this defect be remedied promptly. Normally the tube should only blink once or twice after it is switched on and then burn steadily. (The exception to this would be some of the newer instant-start or rapid-start tubes.)

If the lamp continues to blink repeatedly before it stays lit, the first thing to check is to make certain that the pins at the end of the tube are firmly seated in their sockets. Loose or improper connections at this point will not only cause blinking, but may also cause complete failure. The pins are inserted in the socket by aligning them vertically, then pushing in and turning the tube a quarter of a turn to lock it in place.

The tube socket at either end also may be loose, thus causing poor contact with the pins. If so, tighten the mounting screw which holds this socket in place on the metal housing.

If connections are firm and the lamp still blinks excessively before starting, chances are that the trouble is in the starter. This device is usually located under the fluorescent tube near one end but it may also be located in back or on the outside of the fixture. Its function is simply to heat up the filaments until the tube lights. Once the tube is lit the starter cuts off the filament circuit and the lamp then glows without it.

Starters are removed or inserted by first pressing down and then giving them a half-turn to lift them out. They are made in various watt ratings which must match that of the lamp with which it will be used. A starter will usually outwear several bulbs, but its life will be shortened considerably if the light is turned on and off at frequent intervals. In most cases the lamp will have to be removed in order to get at the starter. The only way to be sure whether the starter is causing the trouble is to try a new one of the same capacity in its place.

If a lamp has to be turned on and off several times before it will stay lit, or if the ends of the lamp tend to glow brighter than the rest of the tube, once again the trouble can be blamed on a defective starter. Replace with a new one promptly since failure to do so will greatly shorten the life span of the tube.

If tests indicate that the starter is not defective yet the lamp still blinks, it may be that the tube itself is finally beginning to go. This can only be determined by replacing with a new one to see whether blinking continues.

One other reason that lamps may blink, even though both starter and tube are in good condition, is low temperature. Ordinary fluorescent lights are designed to work at temperatures above 50 degrees. In cold, unheated rooms, such as basements, garages or attics, special low-

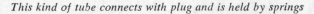

This kind of tube connects with plug and is held by springs

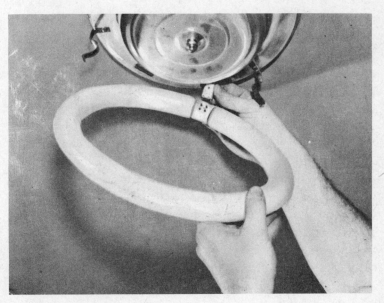

temperature lamps and thermal-type starters should be used.

Two other seldom encountered causes of blinking tubes are: low line voltage (caused by overloaded circuits) and loose connections at terminals, sockets, plug or internal wiring. The first can be corrected only by assuring a proper power supply and the second by checking over all connections till the loose or defective one is found.

When fluorescent tubes start to darken or turn black at the ends, this is normally no cause for worry. In most cases this merely indicates that the tube is nearing the end of its normal life, though it may continue to burn satisfactorily for some time yet. However, if blackening occurs while the tube is still comparatively new, chances are that the starter is defective.

In those rare cases where the lamp does not light at all and where everything else checks out all right, failure may be due to the ballast. The only way to check this is to replace with a new one. Make sure you buy one which matches the old one in capacity and type, since these are not interchangeable. The ballast also may be the troublemaker if a great deal of objectionable hum is noticed. The mounting screws may have worked loose so that it vibrates excessively, or improper assembly may cause it to transmit its vibration to the metal housing of the fixture. To cure this, tighten the mounting bolts which hold the ballast in place, or remount it entirely with small pieces of rubber underneath.

Fuses and Circuit Breakers

Every household electrical system has a number of built-in "safety valves"—the fuses or circuit breakers which are installed at the main control panel. When a short circuit or a dangerous overload causes more current to flow than the wires can safely handle, a fuse will blow or a circuit breaker will open. This shuts off the flow of current immediately and prevents dangerous overheating which could start a fire or melt the wires.

Fuses vary considerably in size, shape and capacity, but all work on the same general principle. A metal strip inside the fuse has a lower melting point than the copper wire used in that particular circuit. Each fuse is rated according to the amount of current it can handle. Thus, a 15-ampere fuse will "blow," or melt, when the current exceeds this amount. Inserting a larger fuse or, worse yet, replacing it with a penny or a piece of tinfoil is a dangerous trick which eliminates this safety factor.

Three types of fuse commonly used in home wiring

House fuses come in two basic styles: the screw-in, or plug-type fuse, and the cartridge fuse. Plug fuses screw into threaded sockets in the fuse block much like an ordinary light bulb. They have transparent windows at the top to enable the homeowner to see when they are blown. Cartridge fuses are used for large-capacity circuits, such as those required for the main service entrance or for an electric range. Those rated below 60 amperes have a plain metal cap at each end and are mounted between curved, spring-metal clips on the fuse block. Larger cartridge fuses (above 60 amperes) have flat metal blades at each end to snap into the holders.

The first thing any homeowner should do to minimize the inconvenience that can be caused by a blown fuse is to familiarize himself with the location of all fuse boxes and main shutoff switches. Also make certain all fuses are of the correct capacity so that replacements can be quickly made without worrying about what size to use. This information can be procured from the builder of the house, from the local lighting company or from a local electrician who can be called in to check the size of the wires in each circuit.

Besides knowing where all fuses and switches are located, the homeowner should also have a list posted to indicate which lights or outlets each fuse controls. Most fuse boxes have each fuse numbered on a chart pasted to the inside of the door. Corresponding numbered spaces on this chart should be filled in to indicate which circuit each fuse controls. To determine this, unscrew one fuse at a time with all lights and appliances turned on. As each fuse is removed check to see which lights go out and which outlets are dead. All these are on the same branch circuit and should be listed in the appropriate space. Then the next time a circuit fails, a quick glance at the control panel will indicate which fuse needs changing.

There are several common reasons why household fuses blow. One of the most frequent is that a branch circuit has been overloaded by plugging in too many lamps or appliances at one time. Another is a short circuit somewhere in the house wiring or in a defective lamp or appliance which was plugged in when the fuse blew. Sometimes a jammed motor will also cause enough of a temporary overload to burn out the branch fuse.

Whatever the cause, it is futile to replace the burned-out fuse with a new one until the source of trouble has been found and corrected. If uncertain as to exactly where the trouble lies, the homeowner should unplug all lamps and appliances and turn off all lights on that circuit before inserting a new fuse. Then, turn on the lights and plug in the appliances one at a time to see which one causes the fuse to blow. If the new fuse blows while all cords are still unplugged, the trouble is in some part of the house wiring and a licensed electrician should be called in. If all lights and appliances come back on satisfactorily but after a minute or two the fuse blows again, chances are that the circuit is merely overloaded and one or more appliances should be left unplugged.

When all the lights in the house go out at one time, it is usually an indication that one of the main fuses has blown, unless, of course, the whole neighborhood is without power. Changing a large main cartridge fuse is a job which is often left for an electrician, but when necessary the careful homeowner can easily change his own.

The first thing to do is to try to locate the cause of the short circuit or the source of the overload which caused the main fuse to blow. Unplug all suspected lamps and appliances, and before opening the fuse box, pull the main service entrance switch if there is one. Some modern installations do not have such a switch. Instead, the main fuses are hidden on the back of a removable insulated section of the box which is plainly labeled with the word "Main." Rings are provided for pulling this section out completely to get at the fuses mounted on the back. Pulling this out automatically shuts off all power so that the fuses can be changed without danger of shock.

Many boxes have main fuses behind removable panel

To pull cartridge fuses out of their spring-metal holders in older-type boxes, grasp them in the center with a pair of slip-joint pliers while wearing a dry glove. Use only one hand, and stand on a dry board or mat if the floor is damp. Most house wiring circuits have two main fuses, so replace both at the same time since with cartridge fuses it is difficult to tell which one has blown.

Circuit breakers are a newer and more convenient method for protecting house wiring. Instead of fuses, they have a series of switches with built-in thermal or magnetic controls which open automatically when the circuit is overloaded. To turn them back on, the switch is merely flipped to the closed position again after the overload has been corrected. Not only do circuit breakers eliminate the need for worrying about having replacement fuses on hand at all times, but they prevent anyone from accidentally (or purposely) inserting the wrong size fuse. The breaker switch is a permanent part of the original wiring, and its capacity cannot be changed without changing the entire unit.

Grounding Devices to Prevent Shocks

Most of the electric power tools and motor-driven appliances that you will buy nowadays have an electric plug with three prongs—the only exceptions being those tools (or in a few cases some appliances) that are described as being "shock resistant" or double insulated. On those with three-prong plugs the electric cord also has three wires; two are current-carrying wires and the third is a special ground wire. This ground wire is solidly attached to the metal frame of the appliance or power tool at one end, and to the third or offset prong on the plug at the end of the power cord.

Unlike the other two wires in the cord, this third wire carries no current under normal circumstances. It is purely a safety device that serves to "ground" the metal frame of the appliance so that, if an internal short should develop between the metal frame and one of the "hot" (current-carrying) wires, the third ground wire would cause the fuse to blow—thus preventing the possibility of a dangerous shock if a person should touch the "hot" frame while standing on damp ground, or while touching a grounded metal pipe or similar object which would provide a path for the current through the person's body.

To understand more fully how this third wire protects you against an internal electrical "short" in a tool or appliance, you must know something about how your house is wired. In 110-volt systems that meet today's standards there are two "hot" or current-carrying wires. One is black (it can also be red) and one is white. The black wire is called the "hot" wire, and the white wire is called the neutral. This white wire is not supposed to be broken by fuses or switches, and back at the main supply panel it is grounded—that is, it is connected to a water pipe or similar object that makes good electrical contact with the earth or ground.

In addition to the black and white wires there is also a third wire in modern wiring systems (usually green, though it may also be bare) which is the ground wire. This wire carries no current—it is designed only to act as an unbroken ground so that if a short should develop in a tool or appliance as described above—and if in addition there is a break in the white (neutral) wire, there would still be a continuous and unbroken ground wire that will cause the fuse to blow and thus protect against a dangerous shock when someone comes in contact with the "hot" framework of the defective appliance. This third ground wire is connected to the third hole in all wall receptacles so that three-

 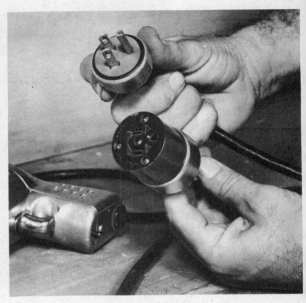

Plugs on many motor-driven appliances and tools have three prongs

To have the protection of a ground at a distance, a three-wire extension is used

prong plugs can be used to maintain the continuity of the ground. In houses with metal conduit or BX (metal sheathed) cable, the metal boxes and cable or conduit are all connected to this same ground. In older homes, wired before the Code was changed, these often serve as the ground because only two wires were used at that time.

The main purpose of grounding the white or neutral wire in the system originally was to provide a low-resistance path through which lightning charges could escape when the wires that carry current to the house are struck.

In the older style two-wire systems, with only the neutral wire grounded, everything is fine as long as the wiring and insulation is all in good condition. However, should the insulation become frayed where the wire passes through the frame, or should moisture get inside and provide an electrical path between the white or black wire and the frame, then a dangerous condition exists. The metal housing of the appliance or tool is now also "hot," yet the fuse will not blow. A person standing on damp ground or touching a pipe, sink or bathtub, while touching the housing then serves as a low resistance path for the current and could receive a lethal shock.

The third wire prevents this from happening because it connects the frame or housing directly to a ground in the house wiring system. When

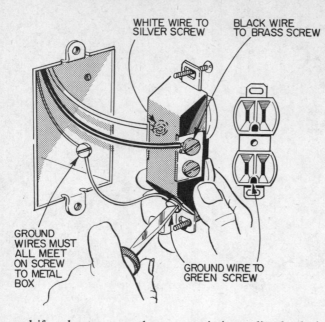

WHITE WIRE TO
SILVER SCREW

BLACK WIRE
TO BRASS SCREW

GROUND
WIRES MUST
ALL MEET
ON SCREW
TO METAL
BOX

GROUND WIRE TO
GREEN SCREW

and if a short occurs the current is immediately drained off and a fuse will blow—warning the owner that something is wrong. This grounding system is particularly important when working outside where damp ground is likely to be encountered.

(Double insulated tools and appliances get around the need for the third wire by means of their internal structure. The design is such that there is no chance of one of the hot wires coming in contact with the framework or housing, and the housing on these tools or appliances is often made of non-conductive plastic instead of metal.)

Because many older houses are still wired with the old system, and have outlets with only two prongs, it is important that the receptacles be changed to three-hole receptacles wherever a tool or appliance is likely to be plugged in. The electrician who does this will make certain the receptacle's third terminal (usually painted green) is connected to a ground. Adapters which convert from two-prong to three-prong, once widely used, are no longer approved for this purpose because all too often the extra "pigtail" on these adapters is not properly connected to a good ground. They have a terminal or threaded screw that is supposed to go under the screw that holds the wall plate in place, but in many cases people ignored connecting these. Even when they did, there was no assurance that the screw or the plate was properly grounded.

Lamp Repairs

Aside from the inconvenience it may cause, a defective floor or table lamp can also be a serious fire hazard and should be repaired promptly as soon as trouble is noticed.

Electrically speaking, all lamp circuits consist of three essential parts: the plug, the connecting cord and the lamp socket itself (usually with a built-in switch). Assuming that a fuse has not blown and that the bulb has been tested, all lamp troubles can be traced to one of these three components.

The most frequent cause of failure is a plug which does not make good contact in the wall outlet. To remedy this, try bending the prongs apart slightly to assure a firmer grip. Do not bend them toward each other. Also check the terminal screws to make certain that the wires have not worked loose or broken off at this point. If the prongs are loose, or if the plug looks doubtful, cut it off and replace it with a new one.

Begin by cutting off the end of the cord an inch or two from the old plug. Remove about 2 inches of the outer insulation without disturbing the rubber covering on the individual wires. If the cord is the flat, rubber-covered kind having two individual wires joined at the center, pull them apart for a distance of about 2 inches. With a sharp knife strip off about ½ inch of insulation from each wire. Be careful not to cut into the wire itself. Push both parts of the cord through the plug, and then tie the two ends in an Underwriters' knot as shown. Pull this knot back into the recess in the plug between the prongs. Then loop each wire around one of the prongs and wrap the exposed strands clockwise around the appropriate terminal screw. Make certain that at no point do either of the bared wires touch each other and that no loose strands stick out from under the screwheads.

Lamp sockets seldom give trouble, but when they do it is best to replace them rather than try to repair them. They are inexpensive and they most frequently break down because the switch mechanism has worn out. The most common type consists of a two-part brass shell with a built-in switch. The wire comes in through a cap at the bottom end and it is fastened to terminal screws inside the outer shell.

Before dismantling the socket, make certain the plug has been pulled

*Underwriters' knot should be tied in the cord before
connecting wires to plug terminals*

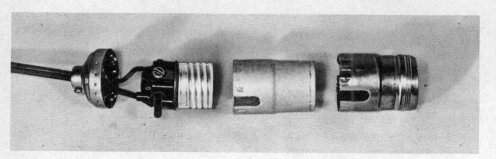

An exploded view of a typical lamp socket. The cardboard liner fits inside the shell.

out of the wall so that there is no danger of shock. Take off the shade and unscrew the bulb. Then look for a spot on the brass shell of the socket near the bottom cap where the word "Press" is engraved. With your thumb, press hard at this point while squeezing the opposite side of the shell with your other fingers. The body will then snap apart from the cap so it can be lifted off. Check the connections where the wires are wrapped around the terminals. The screws may have loosened, or a wire may have broken off. If so, make the necessary repairs and reassemble the socket.

If the connections seem all right, the trouble is probably in the socket mechanism itself. Discard it and replace with a new one. In most cases the original cap can be left in place and only a new body shell installed (the parts are usually interchangeable). If the old cap is damaged and must be replaced also, study the construction of the lamp carefully before removing it. The cap is usually threaded onto the end of a narrow piece of brass pipe which comes up through the center of the lamp mounting, or up from the back.

Since unscrewing this cap may sometimes loosen the whole assembly, it is best to do this job while the lamp is lying flat. Keep track of all parts that come loose so that they can be replaced in the same order when the new socket is installed.

When connecting the new socket, remember to wrap the wires around the terminal screws in a clockwise direction. Press the outer shell back into the cap, and do not forget the special insulated cardboard lining on the inside. This must be in position when the socket is reassembled to avoid dangerous short circuits.

A lamp cord should be replaced whenever signs of damaged insulation are noticed. If the lamp flickers when the cord is wiggled, there is probably a hidden break inside the wire. Rather than repairing the defective cord by splicing in a new section, it is far safer to replace it entirely.

To feed the wire through the lamp body, first disassemble the lamp socket. Disconnect the old cord from the body of the socket, then pull out from the bottom. If the wire runs up through the center of the lamp, tie a string onto the end of the old wire before pulling it through. When the string has come through at the bottom, it can be tied onto the new wire and used to pull it back up through the center of the lamp. Strip the insulation from the ends of the new wire and connect to the original socket, then reassemble.

Motors, Care and Repair

Though few people realize it, statistics indicate that the average home will have anywhere from 15 to 20 electric motors located throughout the house. Some are husky motors, such as those used to power oil burners, shop tools and other major appliances, while others are inconspicuous midgets that may be hidden away in phonograph tables, electric razors, clocks, fans and other small appliances. These electric motors will all last longer and perform better if they are regularly inspected and properly maintained. Many require periodic lubrication, while all will benefit from frequent cleaning and prompt attention to minor adjustments, such as tightening of drive belts or mounting bolts.

When a belt-driven power tool or appliance shows signs of overheating or not operating efficiently, the first thing the handyman should check is the condition of the belt. If the belt is frayed, worn or badly stretched out of shape, it should be replaced promptly. All belt-driven appliances and tools have adjustable mounts which permit regulating the tension on the fan belt and this too should be checked to see whether adjustments have worn or slipped so that excessive slack has developed.

While checking the fan belt, the mounting bolts which hold the motor in place should also be inspected to see whether vibration has caused them to loosen. If the motor fails to turn freely or if fuses blow as soon as the switch is turned on, check for an obstruction which may be causing binding or jamming of the pulleys or fan belt. A bent pulley, or a lack of proper alignment between pulleys, will also cause binding, jamming and overheating. To check for conditions of this kind, pull out the plug or disconnect the power supply, then try rotating the motor by hand to see whether it turns freely and easily.

Since accumulated dust and dirt can cause a motor to slow down or stall, it is also important that the motor be kept clean. Fluff or lint which accumulates inside the housing can actually create a fire hazard, and abrasive dirt can cause excessive wear of moving parts. Use a vacuum cleaner to remove dust from around the outside and to blow

Oil cups on motors should be checked regularly

out accumulated lint from the inside. A dry paintbrush is handy for cleaning out crevices and clogged ventilating ducts.

If the outside of the motor is coated with oil or grease, wipe clean with a rag dipped in carbon tetrachloride. Oil or grease is not only a fire hazard (should the motor spark), it tends to attract dust which will eventually be drawn into the motor.

Though some electric motors have sealed bearings which are lubricated for life, many have oil cups or oil holes which must be regularly filled. Oil holes will usually be marked, while oil cups have small hinged lids which can be lifted up to permit the tip of the oil can to fit inside. Most motors require lubrication only once or twice a year. Use lightweight household oil on very small motors and #20 oil on larger motors.

Excessive oiling probably causes more harm to electric motors than any other form of abuse. When filling oil cups, never allow them to overflow. When filling oil holes, apply only two or three drops at a time and make sure the oil does not spread over surrounding mechanisms. If excess oil is allowed to work its way into commutators, brushes or other working parts, it will interfere with proper electrical contact and will cut down greatly on the efficiency of the motor.

Very small motors in electric razors, kitchen mixers and other small appliances should be oiled with a hypodermic-type miniature oiler or with a medicine dropper, rather than by squirting directly from a can.

This permits more accurate control and enables you to measure out the few drops required without danger of overoiling.

Many small motors have carbon brushes which must be regularly inspected for wear. For specific information as to where these are located and how they can be reached for inspection, the manufacturer's instruction sheet should be consulted. In most cases, brushes will be located on opposite sides of the motor casing so they can be removed easily by unscrewing a plastic or metal cap which is accessible from the outside. Under this cap there will be a spring which serves to keep the carbon brush pressed against the rotating commutator inside the motor.

When brushes are badly worn, they should be replaced with a matching set of the type specified by the manufacturer. New brushes can usually be purchased from motor repair shops or from the authorized service station for the particular appliance involved. In most cases brushes will come complete with springs, but if they don't, replace the springs also—particularly if the old ones seem weak or stretched out of shape.

If a motor sparks excessively or if a distinctive odor of burnt insulation seems prevalent when the motor is running, chances are that either the brushes need replacing or the commutator needs cleaning (the commutator is the rotating part inside the motor against which the brushes make contact). The commutator can be examined by lifting off an inspection plate on many of the larger, brush-type motors. On electric drills and similar small appliances, commutators can usually be exposed by removing one-half the motor housing or case. This is usually held in place with several screws. Disassemble carefully, making certain you

Brushes should be replaced periodically

Motor with housing removed to show commutator

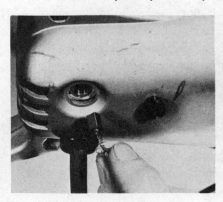
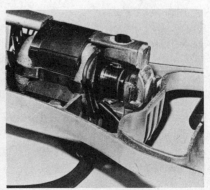

watch out for loose parts and making pencil marks to indicate how the housing goes back together again.

Commutator segments are made of copper and they should be smooth and polished-looking. If they are discolored by oil or grease, clean carefully by wiping with a rag saturated with carbon tetrachloride. If the metal is pitted or scratched, or if the solvent does not remove the discoloration, clean by rubbing lightly with very fine sandpaper (not emery cloth). This is best done by holding the abrasive against the face of the commutator while rotating the shaft steadily with the other hand. Bad pitting or deep scratching means that the motor must be sent in for complete overhaul.

When motors fail to start, the trouble is most often due to defects in the cord, the plug or the switch. Before assuming that the motor is defective, the handyman should check his power supply, his cord and plug (try substituting a temporary new one if in doubt) and the switch on the motor. To see whether the switch is the troublemaker, try shorting it out completely by connecting a temporary wire across its terminals. If the motor still fails to work, check connections under the terminal screws and look inside the motor housing for connections which may have vibrated loose or wires which seem to have broken.

Switches, Replacing

When wall switches fail to operate properly, or when a dangerous arcing, or sparking, condition is noticed, the homeowner can replace the switches quite easily, using modern types which can be installed in the original wall box in place of the old switch. In addition to simply turning the lights on and off, these new switches offer many refinements and conveniences.

Among the many variations available are: switches which turn lights on and off noiselessly, switches which glow in the dark, switches which can be set to go off or on at predetermined intervals, switches which have rotary knobs instead of toggles and switches which can be operated by lightly tapping with an elbow when the hands are full. In addition, there are special dimmer switches which can be used to control the brightness of the lights as well as to turn them on and off.

To install most of these switches, no rewiring or other alterations are required. The steps involved are simple. First—*and most important of all*—turn off the power by pulling the main switch or by unscrewing the appropriate branch fuse. Then unscrew the cover plate and remove

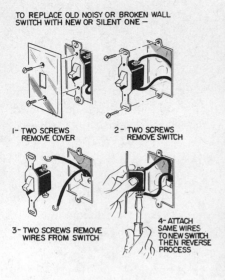

TO REPLACE OLD NOISY OR BROKEN WALL
SWITCH WITH NEW OR SILENT ONE —

1- TWO SCREWS
REMOVE COVER

2- TWO SCREWS
REMOVE SWITCH

3- TWO SCREWS REMOVE
WIRES FROM SWITCH

4- ATTACH
SAME WIRES
TO NEW SWITCH
THEN REVERSE
PROCESS

*Button switch has transparent cover
plate*

the two screws (one at the top and one at the bottom) which hold the switch in place against the front of the outlet box.

Pull the switch out of its recess and unhook the wires connected to it by loosening the terminal screws to which they are attached. Then hook these wires up to the terminals on the new switch, being careful to connect the black wire to the dark (brass-colored) terminal and the white wire to the light (silver-colored) terminal. Fold the wires back into the box and press the new switch into position against the front of the box. Tighten the screws which hold it in place, then screw the cover plate back in place to cover the opening. With most switches the same cover plate can be used, but with some, special matching plates will be supplied.

Switches which are silent in operation are probably the most popular of all. These are mercury switches, which resemble conventional toggle switches in appearance, and they are widely available in hardware stores and electrical supply houses.

Noiseless switches that feature a tap action, rather than a toggle action, are also available. These have a large single button that turns the lights on or off each time it is tapped. This means the button can be tapped with an elbow—or with almost any other part of the body—when hands are full. Screwless, spring-action terminals make it possible to connect many of these switches simply by pushing the bared wires into the openings in the back of the switch case. They are instantly locked firmly and permanently in position without any chance of working loose.

To save groping in the dark when climbing into bed or when leaving the house at night, switches with a built-in time delay can be installed. They operate like ordinary toggle switches when the lights are turned on. However, when flicked to the "off" position, a built-in timing mechanism keeps the light on for an extra minute or two, giving the homeowner time to find his way before the light goes out.

To carry this timing action still further, special switches also are available to turn lights or appliances off or on at predetermined intervals. Some of these units will fit into a standard switch box so that they can easily be installed in place of the standard wall switch. They have a special cover plate with a numbered dial and a rotary knob which can be set to the interval desired.

Probably the ultimate in wall switch luxury is a variable dimmer switch which permits controlling the brightness of the lights by regulating the voltage. These new devices have knobs or handles which can be dialed to the brightness level desired.

Actually, there are two different types from which the homeowner can choose: the inexpensive two-stage switches which have just three

Simple dimmer switch has only two settings

As knob on this switch is turned lights are gradually dimmed

settings (high, low and off) and the rotary, or continuous, dimmers which permit dialing to any point from full brightness to completely off.

The two-stage switches usually have a toggle which can be flicked to one of three settings. At the "high" setting lights are fully on. At the "low" setting lights operate at about 30 per cent of full brightness. The "off" position is usually in the center so that lights can be turned off or on without flicking through successive steps. Dimmer switches of this kind can be used only with incandescent lights. They come in different sizes to handle loads of from 300 to 500 watts, and they all fit into a standard wall outlet box.

Rotary dimmers, which permit continuous light control by simply turning a knob, cost considerably more, depending on capacity and design. To regulate the current, they use newly developed, solid-state, silicon-controlled rectifiers. The knob is rotated clockwise for full brightness and counterclockwise to dim the lights. When rotated to its dimmest position, the unit turns the lights completely off. (Some models have a positive on-off switch so that a definite click is heard when the knob is turned all the way to the left.)

Like the two-stage switches mentioned previously, these newly designed rotary dimmers also are designed to fit in any standard outlet box, hence they can easily be installed in lieu of existing switches. Models come in various sizes, or capacities, though the most popular ones for home use are usually designed to handle loads of from 400 to 600 watts. Where necessary, larger-capacity units also are available to handle loads of as much as 2500 watts.

Though most dimmer switches are designed for use only with incandescent lights, models are also available to control fluorescent lights. In addition to using a dimmer switch which is specially designed for this purpose, the fluorescent lights have to be rewired to include special dimming ballasts. Many manufacturers also recommend that, where a fluorescent dimmer is used, the bulb will have to burn for at least 100 hours before completely flicker-free lighting control can be assured.

Wires, Splicing and Joining

When two electric wires are joined together, the joint formed is normally called a splice. A good splice should not only be mechanically secure, it must also form an electrical connection which is just as efficient a conductor as the wire itself.

Depending on the techniques used in twisting or tying the wires together, there are three types of splices commonly used in household wiring and repair jobs: the pigtail splice, the Western Union splice and the tap splice (also called a branch splice).

The pigtail splice is most often used when wires are joined together inside an electrical outlet box or inside a junction box where wires come together in an electrical appliance. It is the quickest and easiest of all splices to make, but it is never used where there may be stress or strain put on the connection later on.

The Western Union splice is used wherever two lengths of wire are to be joined end-to-end, and it is particularly designed for those jobs where there is a likelihood of strain or pull being applied to the wires after the joint has been made. It is also the correct splice to use when lengthening extension cords, lamp cords and other appliance cords by adding a piece to one end.

The tap, or branch, splice is used whenever a second wire must be connected at right angles or when a wire must be tapped into a continuous main wire. This type of splice is not to be used where a considerable amount of stress or strain will be applied to the tapped wire, though its strength will be considerably increased if the splice is soldered when complete.

To make good electrical contact at the splice, wires must first be stripped of insulation to expose the bare metal on the inside. For most splices, anywhere from 1 to 3 inches of wire will have to be bared. An

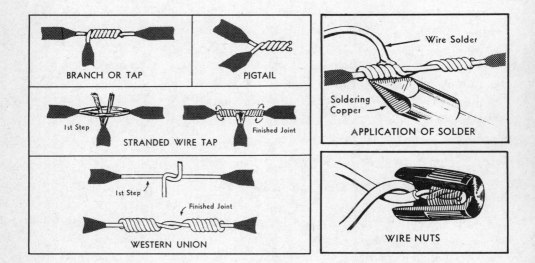

ordinary sharp pocketknife is the handiest tool for this job, but care should be exercised to avoid nicking or cutting into the metal wire when stripping off the insulation. The best way to avoid this danger is to remove the insulation by cutting at an angle—much as a pencil is sharpened. Cutting into the insulation at right angles to the wire increases the danger of nicking and may eventually result in causing a break at this point.

After the insulation has been stripped off, the bare metal should be scraped or sanded until it is bright and clean. Dirt or oxidation will interfere with a good electrical connection, and even a slight film will make it extremely difficult to solder the joint later on.

After the bared wires have been scraped clean, the appropriate splice is completed by wrapping the wires together as indicated in the drawing. On small-diameter wires, the splice can be made simply by wrapping tight with the fingers but the splice will then have to be completed by twisting tightly with a pair of pliers. Note that two methods are illustrated for making the branch, or tap, splice: one which is to be used when working with solid wire and the other when working with stranded wire.

When splicing lamp cords, extension cords and other two-conductor wires, cut them so that the individual splices will not fall directly opposite each other. Making two spliced joints so that they are directly alongside each other increases the danger of an accidental short later on. In addition, when the completed joint is wrapped with insulating tape, there will be an unsightly bulge or lump in the cord at this point. By cutting each pair of wires so that one wire is a few inches longer than the other splices can be arranged so they overlap, rather than lining up directly opposite each other.

For a really permanent splice which will be just as strong and efficient as the original wire—and for every permanent splice where there is a good chance of stress being applied later on—the completed joint should be soldered before it is wrapped with tape. Soldering can be accomplished with a small electric soldering iron or with a soldering copper which is heated separately with a blowtorch.

To prevent future corrosion, a rosin-core solder, or a solder in combination with a nonacid flux, should be used. Apply the iron to the joint so that the joint itself becomes hot enough to melt the solder. A poor joint results if the soldering iron is touched directly to the solder to melt it. When this happens the solder will form a weak crystalline coating which will not form the permanent bond required.

After soldering, wrap joints with insulating tape to cover the bared wires and prevent accidental shorts. There are two taping methods currently recommended. The older method calls for the use of a first layer of rubber tape, covered by a second layer of friction tape. The newer method uses only a single layer of plastic electrical tape. This has a very high insulating value, so only a single layer is required to protect adequately against shorting.

In either case the tape should be wrapped on spirally from one end of the joint to the other with succeeding turns overlapping each other. The usual procedure is to start on the tapered end of the insulation at one side, then work across the joint and end up on the tapered end of the insulation on the other side.

For rapid joining and covering of the pigtail splices which are so often used in household wiring, most electricians prefer to use plastic solderless connectors. These resemble oversized thimbles and are often called wire nuts. They have a funnel-shaped spiral spring insert on the inside. The wires to be joined are pushed into this, after which the connector is twisted tight to form the connection. Since all exposed wires are enclosed inside the plastic shell, no additional taping or wrapping is required. Another advantage of this type of solderless connector is that, should rewiring be required later on, the joint can easily be opened and closed again without need for cutting or soldering.

VII

Furniture Repairs
and Refinishing

Dᴇᴠᴏᴛᴇᴅ to simple repairs of the type often required on various types of furniture—indoor and outdoor—this section includes information on how to refinish furniture, as well as on touching up damaged finishes. For additional information on finishing techniques, on the selection and use of brushes and other equipment, the reader should refer to specific articles on each subject in Section V (Painting and Papering). For additional information on gluing and mending techniques, or on the tools and materials required for working on wood and metal furniture, refer to the appropriate articles in Section I (Tools and Materials).

Antique Finish

Homeowners interested in refinishing an old chest, table or similar piece of furniture can most easily solve their problem by giving the piece an "antique" finish. This popular finish blends with almost any decorative scheme, and it has three definite advantages:

First, it does not require that the old finish be removed. Second, it can be applied over any type of paintable surface, regardless of whether it now has a "natural" or painted finish and regardless of whether it is wood or metal. Third, this type of finish requires no unusual skills, so it can be easily applied by any home handyman or handywoman.

Though there are many variations in shading, and many different methods of achieving it, basically all antique finishes consist of a white or colored ground coat which has one or more "glaze" colors rubbed over it to give a translucent, two-tone color effect. The top color is often

403

a dark brown, muddy-colored glaze which when rubbed over white will make it look yellowed and aged (hence the term "antique white"). However, variations on this effect can be achieved by wiping on other colors, including tints such as pink, pale blue or gold.

Before starting the refinishing job, remove as much ornamental hardware as possible and make all necessary repairs by tightening loose joints, gluing down loose veneer, filling in open cracks and holes, and sanding down all rough spots. Remove wax, polish and dirt and dull the shine on the old finish (if any remains) by wiping the entire piece down with a prepared surface conditioner or "liquid sandpaper" of the type which is sold in most paint stores. If one of these is not available, the surface can be conditioned by washing with a strong detergent, then rubbing with fine sandpaper.

After the piece has been repaired, cleaned and dulled down where necessary, it is ready for its base coat of paint. Use a satin-finish enamel, and brush on smoothly with a clean brush. Allow this to dry for at least 24 hours, then brush on a second coat of the same material. It is a good idea to brush the paint onto several scrap pieces of wood so that tests can be made on these to determine the effect desired before working on the actual piece.

The last coat should be allowed to harden for at least two or three days before the antique glaze is applied over it. To mix the glaze, a

Ground color is brushed on first

thick, creamy liquid called glazing liquid should be purchased. Into this is added some raw umber or burnt umber (these are painters' tinting colors). A little turpentine is also added to bring the liquid to a thinner brushing consistency. Raw umber will give a muddy, grayish effect; burnt umber will give a warmer, more brownish effect.

The exact proportions to be used in mixing this glaze will vary with the effect desired and can be determined only by experimentation beforehand on scrap pieces. As a starting point, try adding about 1 teaspoonful of the paste colorant to ½ pint of the glaze coat. Thin this with about 10% turpentine, adding more if necessary to achieve easier spreading.

If the glaze coat, or glazing liquid, cannot be purchased locally, an oil called flatting oil can be used. This is thinner in consistency and a little more difficult to handle since it may show a tendency to run together and will not "stay put" as readily. Very little or no turpentine should be added if flatting oil is used.

The antique glaze is applied over the white paint by brushing it on sparingly. A wad of cheesecloth (bunched up, not folded) is then used to wipe most of it off. The depth of color can be varied by rubbing off more or less of the glaze and by rubbing in straight lines as well as with a circular motion. Experiment first on the scrap pieces to help decide on the method to be used. Rub with more pressure in the center of each

*The tinted glaze coat is brushed on over the white
and then wiped with cheesecloth*

panel and less pressure around the edges. This gives a lighter effect in the center while permitting the edges to gradually blend in with a darker shading. Pat lightly with the cheesecloth to eliminate sharp lines and distinct variations in shading.

Once the desired color and effect have been achieved, the entire piece is then antiqued or glazed (complete one side, or panel, at a time). Brush on the glaze coat, wait a minute or two, then wipe off with the cheesecloth. To achieve the most realistic effect, allow the dark glaze to remain almost full strength in the bottom of carvings or grooves, and wipe off down to the original color on all high spots.

Allow the finished piece to dry for at least 24 hours, then brush on a coat of clear, dull varnish to protect the finish. On dresser tops, table tops and other surfaces that will receive hard wear, a second coat of varnish is advisable after the first coat has thoroughly dried.

Chairs and Tables

When a chair or table has loose or wobbly joints, it is not only a nuisance, but can also prove dangerous. Loose joints are usually weak joints, and if neglected for long they may eventually permit the piece to collapse completely—with possible injury to the person using it.

Chairs are probably the most common offenders. Trouble develops when rungs no longer fit snugly into the holes in the chair leg or when legs work loose from their holes on the bottom of the chair seat. When this happens, squirting in a little additional glue is seldom enough. No wood glue will hold properly if the joint is no longer snug, and no glue can be expected to do a satisfactory job unless all of the old glue is scraped out first.

Bearing these points in mind, the handyman should always try to remove the rung completely before attempting to reglue it—if he can do so without damaging the piece. Old glue should be scraped off and the hole in which the rung fits scraped clean. This job should be done carefully to avoid enlarging the hole, since this would only tend to make for a looser fit which will be still more difficult to glue properly. After cleaning down to the bare wood, apply glue liberally to both surfaces. The joint is then reassembled by forcing the rung back into place. If the fit is slightly loose, the glue can be thickened with fine sawdust to make it act as a filler as well as an adhesive.

Another way to take up the slack on rungs which are loose inside their holes is to wrap the end of the rung with a layer of fine silk thread,

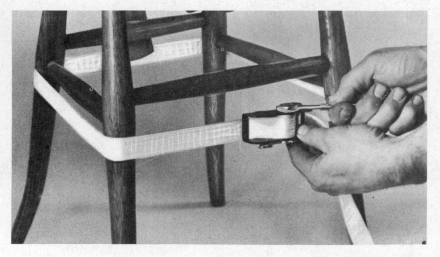

Web clamp has a lock which can be tightened with a wrench

after first coating heavily with glue. Additional glue is then smeared on over the outside of the thread wrapping before pushing the end back into place inside its hole.

To apply pressure to the joints after regluing, long bar clamps or cabinetmaker's clamps can be used. Belt-type webbing clamps are also ideal for jobs of this kind. However, in lieu of these specialized tools, an ordinary rope tourniquet can be improvised, as shown in the accompanying drawings. Tie the rope loosely around the outside of the legs, cushioning it at all points of contact with pieces of cardboard or wads of paper. A stick is then used to twist the rope tight and is tied in place after sufficient tension has been applied.

Instead of trying to enlarge the outside of a loose rung by wrapping

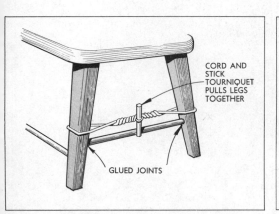

CORD AND STICK TOURNIQUET PULLS LEGS TOGETHER

GLUED JOINTS

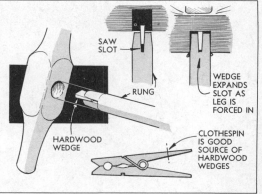

SAW SLOT

RUNG

HARDWOOD WEDGE

WEDGE EXPANDS SLOT AS LEG IS FORCED IN

CLOTHESPIN IS GOOD SOURCE OF HARDWOOD WEDGES

with thread, the handyman can make a more permanent repair by installing a wedge in the end of the rung as shown. A slot is cut across the end of the rung first, after which the wedge is pushed in. When the rung is reinserted in its hole (after being coated with glue), the pressure will force the wedge in still deeper, expanding the end and locking it securely in place. A rope tourniquet or bar clamp can then be used to hold the rung in place while the glue hardens.

When joints are fairly snug, so that complete removal of a rung is difficult or impractical, a simple repair can often be made by drilling a hole into the joint through one side of the leg. The drill bit should be allowed to penetrate only as far as the rung, without boring into the rung itself. Glue can then be forced into the joint through this hole with a special glue injector which is sold for this purpose. A hypodermic-type oiler which has been loaded with thin glue rather than oil can also be used. The hole which remains in the chair legs can be camouflaged afterward by filling with a matching color wood putty.

In addition to loose chair rungs, wobble can be caused by frames or rails working loose around the bottom of the chair seat. This usually happens on chairs with upholstered or padded seats when the chair legs are attached to the corner of the frame, rather than to the bottom of a solid wood seat. The easiest way to repair loose joints of this kind is to install corner braces on the underside.

If corner braces are already in place as part of the original frame, remove the existing screws and replace with larger screws before re-gluing. The combination of fresh glue and larger screws will greatly increase the strength of these braces and will usually add the necessary stiffening to the framework. If necessary, metal corner irons also can

Triangular wood block reinforces leg

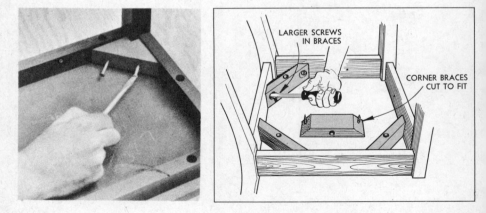

LARGER SCREWS
IN BRACES

CORNER BRACES
CUT TO FIT

be used to strengthen the joint where the chair frame meets the chair legs.

Another neat method for taking the wobble out of a loose chair frame or rail assembly is to use screw eyes and heavy wire to take up the play. Put one screw eye into the leg in each corner, then thread two lengths of heavy picture wire through them as shown. A turnbuckle in the center is then used to draw the wires taut and to serve as a permanent brace for the entire framework. Before tightening the turnbuckle, smear glue liberally over each of the corner joints to prevent future loosening.

When chair backs, legs or other framing members split, a successful repair can usually be made by regluing the pieces, particularly if the break is parallel to the grain. Line the broken parts up carefully, then spread glue liberally over both surfaces. If the piece is merely split, not completely broken in two, wedge the split open sufficiently to permit working glue into the crevice. Next, press the broken parts together and clamp securely, using C-clamps, cabinetmaker's clamps or bar clamps. In many cases clamping pressure can also be applied by wrapping securely with heavy tape or strong cord. Regardless of the type of clamp being used, care should be taken to protect finished surfaces by padding with cardboard before pressure is applied.

For bad splits and breaks on chair seats or table leaves, additional reinforcement often can be provided by installing wooden cleats on one side with glue and screws. The cleats can be of any suitable size, and they should be fastened in place against the bottom of the chair seat or table leaf so they will not be noticeable. An even better method is to reinforce the broken seat or table leaf with a sheet of plywood, cutting it only slightly smaller than the overall size of the broken member. Coat

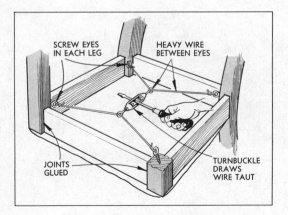

the face of the cleat with glue, then screw it in place against the bottom, using wood screws which are short enough so that they will not penetrate through the finish on top.

Drawers, Sticking

There are few things more annoying than a stubborn drawer which just won't open or close properly. If this happens only in damp weather, the trouble may be due to temporary swelling of the wood and it often can be corrected by simple lubrication. Use a block of paraffin, an ordinary wax candle or one of the special silicone lubricants which are sold for this purpose in all hardware stores. Remove the drawer completely and wipe off all dust from the edges. Also clean the guide strips on which it rides, then apply lubricant to these guides, as well as to the edges of the drawer itself.

One trick that frequently works when a drawer will open only a few inches, yet will not budge beyond this point, is first to open it as far as it will go, then slip a light bulb, plugged into the end of an extension cord, into the drawer. To prevent scorching, the bulb should be inside a wire cage of the type used on most trouble lights. If left on for several hours, the heat of the bulb will dry out the wood, shrinking the drawer sufficiently to permit pulling it open the rest of the way.

In those cases where lubrication alone does not seem to do the trick, sanding or planing may be required to shave down the sides or edges.

Lubricant is applied to drawer edges
with brush

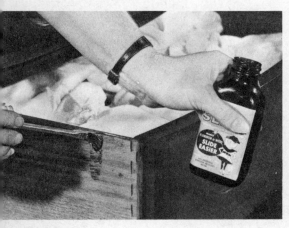
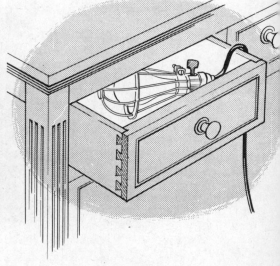

Examine the drawer and its guides inside the chest carefully to locate the place where rubbing occurs. The points of contact usually will show up as dark, polished areas along the edges or sides.

Use medium-grade sandpaper wrapped around a block of wood or a sharp plane to trim down these high spots. Try the drawer frequently to make certain no more wood is removed than absolutely necessary. If the sides of the drawer seem to be too high, do your planing on the top edge rather than on the bottom edge.

If the drawer seems to slide in smoothly until about the last inch or so, but then won't close the rest of the way until the front is lifted slightly, the trouble is probably due to the fact that the bottom edges of each side have worn down excessively, though the front panel on the drawer has not. This usually can be corrected by driving a few smooth-headed thumbtacks into the wooden tracks inside the chest so that the bottom edges of the drawer will ride on top of them. The tacks will not only raise the drawer slightly (so that the front panel will clear more easily), but will make a heavily loaded drawer slide better.

One fairly uncommon cause of improperly working drawers on large chests and double dressers is that the whole framework of the chest may be out of plumb, usually due to the fact that it is standing on an uneven or wavy floor. You can check for this with a carpenter's spirit level. The top of the chest should be level and the sides absolutely plumb if drawers are to work smoothly. If the chest is not standing level, shim up the legs by wedging thin strips of wood or folded cardboard under the low side. Continue wedging in this manner until the chest sits perfectly level—from front to back as well as from side to side.

Finishes, How to Repair

Wood furniture which is accidentally scratched, burned or otherwise marred often can be satisfactorily repaired without need for having the entire piece refinished. In many cases common household materials are the only supplies required.

Shallow scratches which are in the finish, but which do not go down into the wood itself, are probably the easiest of all defects to hide. In most cases they do not need to be filled in, but merely stained or colored to match the original finish. On a walnut finish, light-colored scratches can often be camouflaged by simply rubbing with the meat of a walnut or brazil nut. The finish is then restored by rubbing on a coat of paste wax and polishing to restore the original luster.

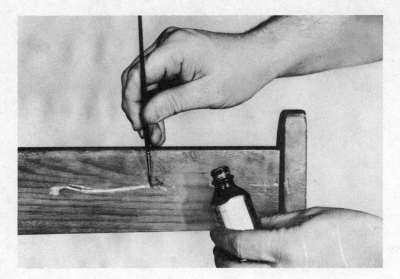

Iodine hides scratch on mahogany finish

Light-colored scratches on mahogany furniture can be repaired by touching up with a little ordinary iodine. Apply the iodine carefully with a very fine, pointed brush or with a toothpick which has a small piece of cotton wrapped around the tip. Try to avoid getting the iodine anywhere but inside the scratch itself, and wipe off excess promptly. Then allow to dry thoroughly and finish by waxing and polishing. If the iodine is too dark, try thinning with 50 per cent rubbing alcohol to lighten it.

Light scratches on dark furniture also can be touched up with ordinary shoe polish, colored stain wax—or even with children's wax crayons. There are also special touch-up materials available in most paint and hardware stores. These come in various shades to match all common woods. They come in small bottles or in handy applicators which resemble an ordinary fountain pen, except that the dispenser has a tiny brush at the tip instead of a point. In either case, try to apply the touch-up material inside the scratch only. Keep a rag handy to wipe off excess material promptly when it smears over adjoining surfaces.

Deeper scratches which need filling can be repaired in several different ways. The best repair (and the method used by most professionals) is to use stick shellac. This is made in a very wide selection of colors so that a shade can be found to match every furniture finish. To use, first heat a knife blade or spatula in the flame of an alcohol lamp or small torch. This is then used to melt the end of the shellac stick so the liquefied material can be "buttered" into the crevice. The shellac should be built up slightly higher than the surrounding surface, then shaved down

Burn marks should be scraped clean with knife

level by holding a razor blade flat against the surface. The repair is then polished smooth with powdered rottenstone and crude oil.

If the homeowner has difficulty in buying colored stick shellac locally (it is sold by paint stores and by suppliers of wood finishing materials), he can use specially colored wax repair sticks which are also sold for this purpose. These are much more widely available, but they do not make as permanent a repair as the shellac sticks. However, they are considerably easier to use, since no heating is required. Instead, a stick of the appropriate color is rubbed back and forth over the scratch mark like an ordinary crayon until the crevice is filled in. The patch is smoothed off by scraping level, then finished by rubbing with an oil-type furniture polish.

Cigarette burns and other bad scars usually call for removal of the finish over the damaged area. To do this, the handyman first scrapes the scarred surface away by holding a knife blade at right angles to the surface, then scraping back and forth carefully. The scar should then be rubbed smooth with a small piece of #0000 steel wool or ultrafine sandpaper wrapped around one finger tip.

To fill in this scarred area, a colored wood plastic or wood filler of the right shade is used. If the scrape mark is shallow, it may be easier to build up the scar by applying several coats of colored varnish or varnish stain in the right shade. Allow each coat to dry hard, then apply additional layers till the scar is filled in.

After the filler or varnish stain has dried hard, the patch should be

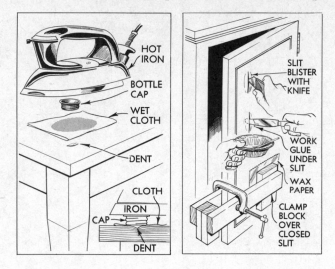

refinished by brushing on a thin coat of clear varnish or shellac. Let this dry, then polish with powdered rottenstone and crude oil. Finish with the type of furniture wax or polish normally used on that piece.

Small dents in the surface of a piece of wood furniture can be removed by steaming the compressed wood fibers so as to swell them back up to their original shape. In many cases this can be done without damaging the finish. To do this, first wipe the dented area lightly with turpentine to remove wax or polish. Then cover the dent with several thicknesses of damp cheesecloth and place a metal bottle cap (metal side down) directly over the dent. Now press a hot iron on top of this. The steam created will swell the wood to its original shape in many cases, though several applications may be required. If this method doesn't show results the first time, it may be necessary to scrape away the finish (so the steam can penetrate better) before repeating.

A common problem on finely finished table tops is the white ring sometimes left by wet glasses or hot dishes. Depending on the nature of the finish, these blemishes often can be removed by wiping lightly with a rag dampened with one of the following solvents: denatured alcohol, turpentine or lacquer thinner. They should be tested in an inconspicuous corner of the furniture first, and tried in that order. Use sparingly in each case. If the blemish still remains, try rubbing with a rag dipped into a paste of powdered rottenstone mixed with camphorated oil or linseed oil. Rub till the ring or mark disappears, then restore the finish by waxing and polishing. If the blemish is so deep that the rubbing wears partially through the finish, it may be necessary to apply a thin coat of varnish or shellac to build up the surface before waxing and polishing.

Veneer which has begun to buckle or blister can be repaired by first slitting the raised part with a sharp knife or razor blade. Then force a nonstaining glue underneath the bubble by depressing one side of the blister at a time. Work glue under the raised edge which remains, using a thin-bladed knife or spatula. Cover with a sheet of waxed paper to prevent sticking, then apply a heavy weight to hold the veneer down until the glue sets. Glue which oozes out should be wiped off promptly.

When small pieces of veneer are completely missing, repairs can be made by filling the cavities with water putty (made specifically for wood) or wood plastic of some kind. These materials can sometimes be colored to match, but in most cases complete refinishing of the entire surface will be necessary to hide the patch.

Frames, Picture, Repairing and Refinishing

The first rule to keep in mind when working on old picture frames is to handle them carefully. Avoid vigorous scrubbing or harsh treatments with strong solvents. The finish on many of these old frames is quite delicate and can easily be damaged beyond repair. If in doubt as to the effect of any cleaning material, test it carefully beforehand on an inconspicuous corner or along one of the top or bottom edges where damage is not as likely to show.

Since most old frames are covered with layers of dust or dirt, restoration should start by first giving the molding a thorough cleaning. Dust carefully with a clean bristle brush (a small paintbrush will do), making every effort to loosen dirt in crevices and corners. Follow with a gentle washing, using a generous wad of clean cotton which has been saturated with benzine or naphtha. Remember, these solvents are highly inflammable and must be used with caution and in a room with adequate ventilation.

If the frame is finished with genuine gold leaf, use a dilute solution of ammonia and water rather than a solvent. Apply this with a soft, camel's-hair brush, and do not rub, since gold leaf is easily damaged by even a slight amount of abrasion. Shake off excess liquid, then allow it to dry naturally or blot carefully with dry cotton or absorbent cloths.

After the frame has been thoroughly cleaned, stand it up and examine it while standing two or three feet away. If the moldings, joints and

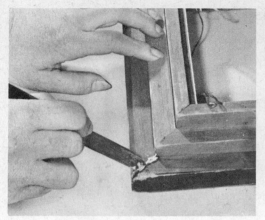 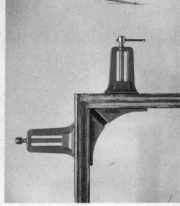

White glue can be forced into joint from back *Corner clamp makes sure
miter ends are joined
accurately*

finish look relatively sound, but the frame is merely dull and faded-looking, chances are that all you need do is apply a coat or two of clear varnish, using either the high-gloss or semigloss type. This should be put on in thin coats with a very soft brush, preferably one made of camel's hair, sable or ox hair.

Scratches or worn spots on dark finishes can be touched up successfully with a little pigmented oil stain in a matching shade before the varnish is applied. Spread the stain on carefully with a small piece of cloth or with a cotton swab. Blend in by "feathering" out the edges, and apply more than one coat if necessary to achieve a depth of color which is approximately equal to the rest of the molding. Allow this to dry overnight, then varnish the entire frame as described above.

If corner joints have worked loose, glue them back together again by forcing some nonstaining white glue into the crack. Use an artist's pallet knife, a thin putty knife or similar tool for this job. Scrape away as much of the old glue as possible, then work fresh glue in from the back side where practical. Frames which have all joints open are best disassembled completely and then reglued. Be sure to scrape away all old glue before reassembling, and clamp joints tightly with corner clamps. In an emergency, adequate clamping pressure can be applied by wrapping tightly with heavy string tied in both directions. Keep joints from slipping by driving small wire brads into each corner.

If carved frames have pieces chipped off, or if small sections of the molding are missing in some areas, a satisfactory repair can usually be made by using a powdered water putty, wood plastic or prepared spackling paste to build up the missing sections. All of these materials are sold in paint and hardware stores for filling holes and cracks in woodwork,

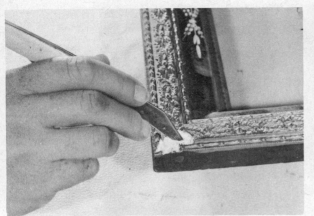 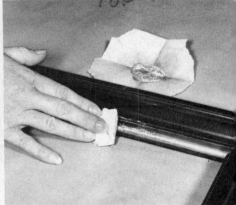

Broken moldings can be repaired by modeling new piece with water putty

Gilt powder is dusted on over varnish which has been allowed to dry until tacky

and all have excellent adhesive characteristics when applied to chipped or broken moldings on a picture frame. Use a knife blade or small spatula to press the compound into the opening or crevice, then try to shape it so as to match the original carving as closely as possible. If necessary, sandpaper, steel wool or a small scraper can be used to smooth the compound down after it has hardened. Artists' oil colors or tinting oil colors (sold for tinting paints) can then be used to color the patching material so that it matches the rest of the frame.

Gilt frames that have been damaged often can be touched up successfully with a good quality, ready-mixed gold paint. However, if the right shade of gold paint cannot be found—or if a brighter luster which more nearly approximates that of real gold leaf is desired—a different method can be used. Purchase some gilt powder (available at paint or artists' supply stores) instead of a ready-mixed gold paint. These powders are sold in a wide range of colors so there is a better chance of getting the shade needed.

Buff the damaged area lightly with fine steel wool, then brush on a thin coat of quick-drying glossy varnish and allow to dry until the finish is tacky. To test for the right amount of tackiness, touch lightly with a knuckle. If the varnish is dry enough, it will not smudge or come off on your finger, yet a slight tackiness will be felt as you pull away. Now dip a piece of clean felt or heavy cloth into the gilt powder and pat on over the tacky varnish. Apply liberally, and continue patting over the surface of the varnish until the entire area is evenly covered. Then allow to dry overnight. On the following day, burnish lightly with a wad of clean, dry cotton to remove excess powder.

If a gilt frame which has been touched up in this manner has an uneven appearance with some parts shinier than others, or if a newly applied gilt finish is to be toned down and softened, the gilt can be glazed over with white paint. This mellows the finish and blends irregularities. Use an off-white shade of flat paint, and thin with approximately 20 per cent turpentine. Brush on lightly with an almost dry brush and wipe off immediately with cheesecloth. The white will remain in the bottoms of grooves or carvings and will permit the gold to show through on all the high spots. If a duller, antique effect is preferred, use thinned-down raw umber (a dark brown tinting color which is sold in all paint stores) instead of the off-white flat.

Marble, Care and Cleaning

Ideally speaking, marble should be kept clean at all times so that it never really becomes dirty or soiled. Under these conditions, all that would be required would be an occasional washing with nothing but clean water and clean rags.

However, this obviously will not suffice if the marble has become badly soiled and stained through long neglect. In this case a more thorough cleaning will be required to restore its natural color and luster. Start by wetting the surface thoroughly, then scrub with a mild, nonabrasive detergent, using a clean fiber brush. Rinse by flooding with plenty of clean, hot water and repeat the washing if necessary. The final rinse should remove all traces of the detergent, after which the surface should be wiped dry with a clean, lintless cloth to avoid streaking.

Stains on marble are a frequent problem, since they will seldom come out with a simple washing. Most stains occur because spilled liquids are not wiped up promptly. This allows them to eat their way into the surface. The longer the stain is left, the harder it will be to remove, so for best results tackle it as quickly as possible.

These stains usually fall into one of three categories: organic stains, rust stains or oil stains. Each requires its own separate treatment.

Organic Stains. These usually vary in color and frequently spread out in an irregular shape similar to that of the staining object. This type of stain is most frequently caused by such agents as tea, coffee, soft drinks, fruit juices, iodine, ink and tobacco.

They can usually be removed by bleaching out with 17- to 20-volume hydrogen peroxide hair bleach (available at all drugstores). This should be mixed with powdered whiting (available at all paint stores) so as to form a thick paste. Spread this liberally over the stained area, then

Organic stains can be removed by applying thick paste of whiting and peroxide

add a few drops of household ammonia to start the reaction. Keep the paste damp by covering with a sheet of lightweight plastic and allow this to stand for several hours. Then remove the poultice by wetting. If necessary, apply a second or even a third application until the stain is gone. Then rinse the surface thoroughly with plenty of clean, hot water and dry immediately.

Rust Stains. This type of stain is caused by metallic objects, such as lamp bases, ash trays or bolts, that are left in contact with the marble for some time while moisture is present. It will be orange to brown in color and will take the shape of the staining object. If noticed immediately, it can usually be removed by rubbing vigorously with a clean, dry cloth. Otherwise, rust stains must be treated with a special reducing agent which is sold at most hardware stores specifically for this purpose. Reducing agents of this type also can be purchased from most chemical supply houses, and they should be applied according to the manufacturer's directions.

Oil Stains. These are usually darker in the center and they spread out in a circular shape. They can be caused by all kinds of greasy household substances and are probably the toughest of all marble stains to remove.

Start by first washing the surface with ammonia and then rinsing with plenty of clean, hot water. The stain must then be treated with a special solvent that can be purchased from hardware stores, department stores and marble dealers. You can also make your own by mixing amyl acetate (available at all chemical supply houses) with an equal part of acetone (available at most drugstores). This solvent is applied over the stain as a poultice which is mixed with whiting in much the same manner as previously described for the bleach. Allow it to dry thoroughly, then rinse off with plenty of hot water and repeat if necessary. If the discoloration remains even after several applications, you can try bleaching with hydrogen peroxide as described above.

After a piece of marble has been thoroughly cleaned and all stains have been removed, polishing will frequently be required to restore its original high luster. If the surface feels rough because of small scratches or other imperfections, it should be sanded smooth with #400-A, wet-or-dry sandpaper. When the area feels absolutely smooth, wipe off with a damp cloth, then wet the marble with clean water. Fold a piece of clean, lintless cloth into a small tight pad and, after dampening it slightly, dip the pad into a dish of tin oxide powder. This powder is available from chemical supply houses and at many large drugstores. Rub briskly over the wet spot until a shine appears, then wipe off immediately with a clean, damp cloth. Do not allow the powder to dry on the surface as it may leave a ring. If this should happen, rub again with a little more of the damp powder.

Once the luster has been restored, the marble should be maintained by waxing with a top quality colorless paste wax. Buff to a high shine, using a lamb's wool applicator or soft cloth. Renew this occasionally to help protect the surface against future staining or dulling.

Outdoor Furniture, Care and Repair

As each piece of outdoor furniture is removed from its winter storage place, it should be dusted thoroughly and washed down if necessary. Wood or plastic furniture can be scrubbed with a mild detergent solution and a stiff brush. However, aluminum furniture which is badly pitted may require rubbing with fine steel wool to remove the imbedded dirt.

While scrubbing and cleaning, check each piece for signs of looseness or wobble in the joints, and tighten any bolts or screws which may have worked loose. If these fasteners are rusted or if the threads are stripped so that they can no longer be tightened satisfactorily, replace them completely with bolts or screws of aluminum or similar corrosion-resistant metal. If difficulty is encountered in tightening or loosening a badly rusted bolt, apply a few drops of penetrating oil and tap lightly. Then try the wrench once more.

The handyman should also check pivoting joints on folding furniture to see that all parts work smoothly. A light coating of oil or silicone spray may be required to eliminate binding or stiffness, but caked-on dirt or grime should be cleaned off first. Chairs which have canvas or plastic

seats should also be inspected to see that the fastenings which hold the fabric in place are still holding firmly.

If the fabric itself is torn and beyond repair, replacement kits of plastic material are available for most chairs. In some instances you may be able to purchase a ready-made seat or back of exactly the right size. Otherwise the material will have to be purchased by the yard and then cut to fit, using the old fabric as a template or pattern.

Instead of the solid or one-piece plastic materials, chairs can be re-covered with plastic webbing in strip form. This material comes in rolls of various colors and it can be fastened to the framework of a wooden chair by stapling or tacking. It is fastened to metal chair frames with sheet metal screws.

Fabric cushions and seats of plastic or canvas that have faded or dis-colored can often be quickly rejuvenated by coating with a special spray which is sold for just this purpose. These sprays come in a wide range of colors and they help to waterproof and preserve the fabric, as well as to restore or change its color. Canvas paints can be applied with an or-dinary paintbrush, while others are packaged in aerosol spray cans. The plastic and leatherette finishes also are available in both aerosol and brush-on types.

Before refinishing wood or metal pieces that are coated with paint, clean and sand the surface thoroughly. Rusty spots on metal should be rubbed with steel wool till the metal is bright, then primed with a rust inhibitive metal primer before final painting. Painted wood pieces should be primed with a suitable undercoat wherever the bare wood is exposed, then all pieces finished with two coats of outdoor enamel.

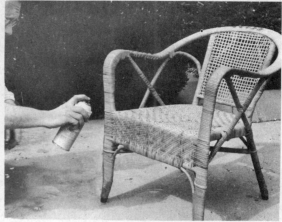

*Special sealer should be
applied to redwood*

Aerosol paints simplify finishing of woven furniture

Though redwood theoretically needs no finish, furniture made from this material will look better and last longer if coated annually with a pigmented redwood sealer. The sealer helps the wood shed water and keeps food and other stains from soaking in. The pigment in it restores the original redwood color, since the natural color is not permanent when the wood is left as is. These sealers should not be applied until the surface has been scrubbed clean and sanded off wherever necessary.

When coating redwood furniture with one of these penetrating finishes, the homeowner should make certain he turns the piece over and coats the bottom surfaces as well as the top. To keep wooden legs from soaking up moisture from the ground, the bottom ends should be protected with several coats of sealer at least once or twice a year.

Furniture made of woven peel or rattan also is supposed to be immune to damage by the weather. However, like the redwood pieces, this type of furniture also will look better and last longer if it is coated regularly with a protective finish of some sort. Since this material is not particularly porous, a spar varnish or weatherproof plastic coating should be used instead of a penetrating sealer. Though the varnish can be applied by brush, time and effort will be saved by spraying instead. A compact portable sprayer can be rented from a local tool rental agency, or the finish can be purchased in aerosol-type spray cans. For full protection, the underside should be coated, as well as the top and front of each piece.

Tubular aluminum furniture generally needs no painting or finishing. However, to prevent pitting and to make it easier to keep clean, a light coat of paste wax at least once or twice a year will prove beneficial.

Before rubbing the wax on, clean the metal down by rubbing with fine steel wool. Then wipe with a clean cloth that has been saturated in a solvent-type cleaner. Soap-impregnated steel wool pads, or a paste-type aluminum cleaner can also be used to clean the metal before waxing.

Refinishing Furniture

Though most furniture refinishing jobs must be preceded by complete removal of all the old finish, there are some occasions when this step is not required—as, for example, when a piece of old furniture is to be covered with an opaque paint or enamel. As long as the original finish is still adhering tightly and is in reasonably good condition, it will not have to be scraped off or removed.

However, to insure good adhesion there are two precautions that must be observed before the paint is applied. First, the old surface must be dulled down so that none of the original gloss remains; and second, all wax, polish and dirt must be washed off completely. The easiest way to accomplish both of these objectives in one operation is to use a prepared liquid surface conditioner that is available at most paint stores.

These liquids are wiped on with a clean rag immediately before painting. Also called liquid sandpaper, these liquids will remove all foreign matter and they will effectively dull down any gloss that remains. In the absence of one of these liquids, turpentine or denatured alcohol can be used to remove the wax or polish, and the gloss can be dulled by rubbing with fine sandpaper or steel wool.

In addition to cleaning and dulling down the old finish, sand all rough spots smooth and fill all nicks, cracks or holes with a plastic wood-patching compound. Let these patches dry hard, then sand smooth with fine sandpaper. At the same time tighten up all loose screws, reglue all loose joints and make any other structural repairs that may be necessary.

Another type of furniture finish which does not require complete removal of the old finish is one where mere brightening up of the old finish is desired without any appreciable change in color. Assuming that the old surface is only slightly marred, begin by treating the surface with a liquid conditioner as just described. Touch up nicks or scratches that go through to the raw wood by first rubbing with #00 steel wool till the spots feel absolutely smooth. Then touch these spots with a little matching oil stain, or with any of the furniture touch-up materials which are sold in all paint stores. For cracks or holes that require filling, use a colored plastic wood filler of the proper shade.

When a transparent or natural finish (stain, varnish or lacquer) is to be applied over an old piece of furniture which is badly scratched and discolored, complete removal of the old surface becomes a necessity. Though the job can be done by scraping and sanding alone, the work will go much faster if a chemical paint remover is used. For safety's sake, select one of the nonflammable varieties. A thick liquid or semipaste type will give you more time to work, and it will not be as likely to run or drip when used on vertical surfaces.

Paint remover should be applied in heavy layers with the flat side of an ordinary paintbrush. Stroke in one direction only, and do not brush back over the surface after the remover has been applied. Let this stand for 10 or 15 minutes, then scrape off the softened goo with a dull putty knife. On curved surfaces use coarse steel wool. On narrow moldings and in deep carvings try scrubbing out the softened finish with an old toothbrush or similar stiff-bristled brush.

Since many paint removers contain strong solvents which irritate the skin, rubber gloves should be worn and extreme care exercised to avoid spattering into face or eyes. In some cases, where many layers of varnish must be removed, more than one application of remover may be required.

While the paint remover will strip off all of the old surface finish, it will not remove the stain (which has penetrated into the wood) and will, therefore, do very little to change the color, except perhaps to lighten it slightly. For this reason if a lighter or entirely different colored stain is desired, the wood will first have to be lightened by bleaching.

The procedure is comparatively simple, requiring no special tools and only a moderate amount of time and patience. The ease of bleaching

Chemical remover softens finish for easy removal

varies with the type of wood involved. Light-colored woods are easiest, while darker-colored woods may require two, or even three, applications.

The first important prerequisite for a good bleaching job is that all of the old finish must have been completely removed. A really thorough job is essential, since even the slightest patch of old varnish will prevent the bleach from penetrating and may result in a dark stain in that spot. All metal hardware should also be removed, as the metal may be attacked by the bleaching chemicals.

Where only a slight amount of lightening is required, oxalic acid is usually used. Available at most paint and hardware stores, it is sold as crystals which are dissolved in hot water to make a bleaching solution. Spread this on over the surface while still hot, using a sponge or brush. Let it stand until completely dry, then brush off any crystals which form and rinse with plenty of clear water.

For a really thorough job of bleaching out a dark wood, such as mahogany, a commercially prepared, two-solution bleach works best. Rubber gloves should be worn to protect your hands, and care is required to avoid splashing it onto your clothing or onto exposed portions of your skin.

Start by pouring the first solution into a glass, enameled or wooden bowl. Scrub this onto the surface with a fiber brush, a rubber sponge or a folded pad of cotton waste. If you are working on old wood, dip a pad of fine steel wool into this solution and rub it vigorously into the wood, working parallel to the grain. The directions on the bottle will tell you how long to let this dry before applying the second solution.

Pour out what is left of this first solution (do *not* pour it back into the

A two-solution bleach will convert dark woods to a lighter finish.
Rubber gloves are required for protection.

FIVE POPULAR WOOD FINISHING TECHNIQUES

TYPE FINISH	PRELIMINARY STEPS	FINISHING COATS
Stained	Oil or penetrating type stain is applied in shade desired. On soft, porous wood, coat of resin sealer may be needed first to prevent blotching.	Thin coat of shellac may be applied first, followed by two or three coats of high gloss or semi-gloss varnish.
Clear or Natural	On soft wood apply first coat of clear shellac or penetrating sealer. Sand lightly.	Apply two or three coats of clear varnish or lacquer in gloss or semi-gloss lustre.
"Oiled" or Waxed	Apply two or three coats of penetrating sealer, wiping each one off after 10 minutes. Allow to dry thoroughly between coats.	Allow last coat to dry for 48 hours, then rub on a thin coat of paste wax. Buff to lustre desired.
Glazed or Antique	Paint on one or two base coats of satin finish white or light ivory enamel. Other colors can be used for different effects.	Allow to dry for 48 hours, then brush on glaze made by adding oil color to glazing liquid. Wipe off partially while still wet, varying pattern to achieve desired effect.
Blond	Dark woods must be bleached first by using prepared wood bleach, then coated with pigmented white stain or thinned-down white paint. Wipe off to achieve desired tone.	Finish with two coats of very clear semi-gloss or dull varnish. If wax is used over this, use a white wax.

bottle), then pour your second solution into the bowl and proceed to apply it in the same manner. Allow this to dry for at least six hours. If the wood is still not light enough, repeat the whole operation a second time.

When the wood has been bleached to the color you want, rinse with water to remove all traces of the acid, then sand smooth with fine sandpaper. This is necessary because the bleaching operation usually results in raising the grain slightly, causing a slight fuzziness which should be sanded off before the new finish is applied.

Since it would be hopeless to try to list all the finishes that can be applied and to describe all the techniques used to achieve them, the accompanying chart lists five of the most popular furniture finishes and briefly outlines the simplest method for achieving each of them. To help clarify the names used for each of these finishes (no two "experts" will agree on this), here is a description of each:

Stained. This refers to a finish where the natural wood is treated with a translucent, colored stain which actually dyes the wood to a different shade. Stains are usually darker than the original wood color, and they are used to accent the grain or to make the wood look like a different species. Most stains are applied with a brush, rag or spray, and all should be wiped off with a dry cloth as each panel or section is completed. Since a stain is not a finish in itself, a final varnish or similar clear finish is applied over it.

Clear or Natural. This type of finish is applied when the original color and grain of the wood is to be preserved as is, with as little color change as possible. It consists of a clear protective coating which merely protects and preserves the wood without changing its appearance to any appreciable extent. In addition to the conventional varnishes and lacquers, there are many types of clear plastic finish which can be applied to give the same effect.

"Oiled" or Waxed. Application of a true oiled finish is a classic technique which was often employed by old-time craftsmen and cabinetmakers. However, this type of finish requires coat after coat of linseed oil laboriously rubbed in with loving care. A much quicker and simpler way to achieve much the same effect is to use a modern penetrating sealer instead of linseed oil. This builds up to a dull but lustrous finish which is then protected with a final coat of paste wax. If properly applied according to directions on the can, these sealers give a durable, low-luster finish which will closely resemble an old-time hand-rubbed oil finish in appearance and durability.

Glazed or Antique. As indicated in the chart, this is actually a painted finish which is softened down by having a second translucent coat rubbed over it after the base coat is dry. It can be applied directly over an old finish without need for removal. In its most popular form this technique is used to achieve an antique white finish (a muddy brown or grayish glaze is rubbed over a white or off-white base). Glazing is also the method used to achieve an artificial grained effect. A suitably tinted glaze coat is spread on over a base coat and then wiped to give the appearance of a wood grain. The glaze is brushed on over one panel at a time, then immediately wiped off with wads of cheesecloth or steel wool, depending upon the effect desired.

Blond. This modern light finish can be achieved in one of two ways: by bleaching or by treating with pigmented light-colored stains or thinned-down paint. Bleach is used on the dark woods to lighten them first, after which a white- or blond-colored stain can be applied to lighten them further. This clouds the grain to some extent, giving the wood a light ivory or creamy effect, depending on the color of the stain and the original color of the wood.

Before applying any of these finishes, the handyman should remember that a certain amount of experimentation will always be required to achieve a specific effect. Wood stains, for example, will "take" differently on different types of wood—and even on two different pieces of the same type. To determine the final effect, the home finisher should apply the stain first on the back or on an inconspicuous edge before going ahead with the entire project.

In the same way, before applying a glazed or antique finish, the handyman should experiment on scrap surfaces. He can try varying the amount of color added to the glazing liquid, and he can experiment with different wiping techniques, using steel wool on one sample, cheesecloth on another and crumpled tissue paper or a dry brush on a third sample.

Table Tops, Recovering

Small tables which have tops that are badly marred or otherwise damaged can be given a new lease on life by resurfacing with a sheet of tough plastic laminate of the type commonly used on kitchen counters. No special skill is required, and the only tools needed are a coping saw or hacksaw and a flat metal file.

Start by first stripping off all of the old finish, using a heavy liquid or semipaste paint and varnish remover. After all varnish or lacquer is removed, the top is sanded smooth and holes filled where necessary. To preserve the existing finish around the edges and base of the table, mask-

Old top should be sanded down prior to covering

Sheet of plastic is cut to fit

Cement is then applied on both table top and back of plastic

ing tape can be used. This will keep the paint remover from dripping down onto the parts that are to be left as is.

A sheet of the plastic laminate can be purchased from local lumberyards or cabinet shops in most areas. This is cut to fit and applied in the following manner:

(1) Make a paper pattern of the table top, or lay the plastic on the floor, then turn the table upside down on top of this to trace its outline onto the face of the plastic sheet. Cut the plastic to the size and shape required, cutting on the outside of the line so the plastic is slightly larger (about $\frac{1}{16}$ of an inch) than the overall outline of the table top.

(2) Spread contact cement over the top of the table and onto the back of the plastic sheet, using the notched spreader supplied and following the manufacturer's directions as to drying time required.

(3) After the cement has dried sufficiently, the plastic sheet is carefully positioned on top of the table. One edge is lined up first, then the sheet is lowered slowly into place. Since the cement will "grab" instantly on contact, the sheet must be positioned properly the first time.

(4) After contact has been made, press down firmly over the entire area with the palms of your hands. Finish by rolling with an ordinary rolling pin or by tapping with a block of padded wood and a hammer.

(5) Trim off the edges of the plastic to make it flush with the edge of the table by filing with a large, flat metal file. For a neat edge, tilt the file backward so as to create a slight bevel. If desired, the edge of the table can be finished off with a decorative wood or metal molding. In this case, the plastic should be filed square rather than beveled.

Tables, Wobbly. SEE CHAIRS AND TABLES.

Plastic is carefully positioned on table top before pressing down

Rolling pin is used to ensure a good bond

Edges are then filed till sheets fits flush on all sides

Conclusion

J UST AS each journey—no matter how long—must start with a single step, so too should the reader begin his home maintenance chores by tackling and completing one simple project at a time.

In order to really master the many techniques that are described within the pages of this encyclopedia, the reader should study each of the applicable sections thoroughly before he starts to work. He should also make liberal use of the Table of Contents and the Index to make certain that other material which is closely connected to the same subject is also fully read and understood. He is then less likely to be confused when a shelf that he has recently erected comes crashing down. He will at least know *why* it came down—and how he can keep it from happening the next time.

Sources for Equipment
and Materials

PRACTICALLY all the materials and tools described in the pages of *The New York Times Complete Manual of Home Repair* can be purchased in local paint, hardware and department stores—or from lumber yards and building materials dealers. There are very few products that are of the so-called hard-to-find category. But for those who do run into difficulty in trying to locate some items, here are a number of retail outlets that will service mail-order requests for many different types of tools and equipment.

Silvo Hardware Co.
107 Walnut Street
Philadelphia, Pa. 19106

Albert Constantine & Sons, Inc.
2050 Eastchester Road
Bronx, New York 10461

Paul Silken & Co.
21 West 46th Street
New York, N.Y. 10036

Craftsman Wood Service
2729 S. Mary Street
Chicago, Illinois

Sears Roebuck & Co.
(branches in most cities)

Montgomery Ward & Co.
(branches in most cities)

TO FURTHER assist the reader in locating tools or other materials that may not be readily available through some retail outlets in local areas, here is an additional list of manufacturers who put out some of the more *specialized* products.

Adjustable Clamp Co. 406 N. Ashland Ave. Chicago, Ill. 60622	**Woodworking clamps of all types, including web clamp**
Stanley Tool Div. Stanley Works New Britain, Conn.	**Woodworking clamps, web clamp, hand tools and power tools. Also a full line of home and workshop hardware.**
United Shoe Machinery Corp. 221 Oley Street Reading, Pa. 19601	**Fasteners and anchors for plaster and masonry walls, hammer-in stud drivers, riveting tools, etc.**
Winchester Western Div. Olin Corp. 275 Winchester Ave. New Haven, Conn.	**Stud drivers and hammer-in masonry fasteners and tools**
Devcon Corp. Endicott St. Danvers, Mass. 01923	**Epoxy adhesives and epoxy waterproof coatings for basement walls**
Woodhill Chemical Corp. 18731 Cranwood Parkway Cleveland, Ohio 44128	**Same as above**

431

Boyle-Midway Div. of American Home Products 685 Third Avenue New York, N.Y. 10017	**Epoxy waterproofing for basements**
Thermwell Products Co. 150 East 7th St. Paterson, N.J. 07524	**Complete line of weatherstripping**
Macklanburg-Duncan Co. Oklahoma City, Okla. 73101	**Same as above**
Philip Carey Mfg. Co. 320 S. Wayne Ave. Cincinnati, Ohio 45215	**Sealer for blacktop driveways**
Borden Chemical Co. 350 Madison Avenue New York, N.Y. 10017	**Sealer for blacktop driveways and full line of glues**
Reardon Co. 7501 Page Ave., St. Louis, Mo.	**Latex patching cement and concrete patching and painting materials**
Commercial Chemical Co. 1021 Summer St. Cincinnati, Ohio 45204	**Patching cement for concrete**
Silcoa Products, Inc. 50 East 42nd St., New York, N.Y.	**Vinyl concrete patching cement**
Synkoloid Co. 3345 Medford Ave. Los Angeles, Calif. 90063	**Same as above**
Sicilian Asphalt Paving Co. 99 Paidge Ave. Brooklyn, New York 11222	**Blacktop patching materials**
Woodhill Chemical Co. 18731 Cranwood Parkway Cleveland, Ohio 44128	**Fiberglas and plastic patching kits for repairing gutters, downspouts, etc.**
Warner Mfg. Co. 801 16th Ave. S.E. Minneapolis, Minn. 55414	**Paperhanging tools and equipment, also graining tools**
Hyde Mfg. Co. Southbridge, Mass. 01550	**Same as above**
Red Devil, Inc. 2400 Vauxhall Rd. Union, N.J. 07083	**Same as above and Louvers for venting siding**
Mortell Co. 508 Burch St. Kankakee, Ill. 60901	**Plastic calking and insulation to wrap around pipes (to prevent sweating)**
Johns-Manville Co. 22 East 40th St. New York, N.Y. 10016	**Pipe insulation (to prevent sweating), also tapes and insulation**
Midget Louver Co. 6 Wall Street Norwalk, Conn. 06852	**Louvers for venting attics and siding**

Index